D1488521

Economics and National Security

Economics and National Security

A History of Their Interaction

Annual Supplement to Volume 23,

History of Political Economy

Edited by Craufurd D. Goodwin

Duke University Press

Durham and London 1991

Contents

vi   Contents

Economics and National Security

Introduction

Craufurd D. Goodwin

The collaborative project that yielded this volume was a response to a seeming paradox. While national security has been a dominant concern of the nation-state virtually from its beginning, and international conflict is with us today as much as ever, economists seem to have turned their attention very little to this area of policy. Even though defense and wartime expenditures have regularly consumed large portions of government income and national treasure, the economics profession has not created a true subdiscipline of defense or national security economics, as they have a health economics or an economics of education. There are few courses at universities on defense economics, few seminars at professional meetings, and until recently not a single specialized periodical. This volume attempts to answer the question, "Why?"

It was from a sense that the field of security studies would benefit from an infusion of economists and the economists' way of thinking that the Pew Charitable Trusts initiated a series of grants under its Economics and National Security Program. The Program assisted our project through a grant to Duke University, and we are most grateful to the Pew Charitable Trusts for making the inquiry possible.

The research team assembled to conduct an exploration into the history of the interaction between economics and national security began with the broad questions of whether the general perception of the neglect of national security by the economics discipline is an accurate one, and if so, for what reason. To focus our collaborative inquiry we began from a set of tentative hypotheses that might help to explain a surprising degree of disengagement by professional economists from an important collection of policy-relevant topics:

1. Economists have found the subject matter of security studies antithetical to their training and mindset and therefore have avoided this range of questions. Conflict and imposition of destruction on others seem rooted in irrational behavior and cannot be dealt with effectively in a market framework. This is not true for game theory, but game theorists have been among the relatively few economists who have been attracted to the area.

1

2. The state is the dominant player in the security field, and most economists have always been uneasy about applying analysis to a large public sector. The theory of public expenditures has been a neglected part of the discipline for much of its history. The American Institutionalists, on the other hand, have felt relatively comfortable explaining the public sector, and this may help to explain their prominence in early discussions of security and defense.

3. Public interest (including funding and student attention) in security questions is peculiarly mercurial, reflecting the course of conflict. In choosing careers and research agendas economists have recognized and avoided this hazard. Some economists who have moved to the area during wartime have found themselves high and dry with the return of peace, and this lesson has not been lost on others.

4. In addition to the difficulty of applying market analysis to security issues, there are other social and professional costs associated with research in the area. Data are hard to come by and may require security clearance. Unlike health, education, or agriculture, the "subject" of the defense sector seems not to respond directly to economists' overriding concern for human welfare, and the military have distinctly low status in the scholarly culture. These external circumstances have kept the discipline at arm's length.

5. Analysts outside the mainstream of established economics have tended to coopt this policy field, either as peace researchers on the left or as members of the military establishment on the right. Middle-of-the-roaders and agnostics have been reluctant to become tarred with either brush.

6. Early efforts by economists to cast light on problems of peace, war, and related issues did not bear fruit. Economists like to be useful, so they moved where their productivity seemed higher.

It must be left to the reader to decide whether evidence in the papers collected here tends to confirm or disprove these hypotheses.

These essays do not constitute a thorough or systematic coverage of all of the history of economic thought relevant to national security. Indeed it is doubtful that such a project would have been either possible or desirable. They do, however, hit many of the high spots, and together they constitute the first overall survey of this kind ever undertaken. The overwhelming impression one must gain from reading this collection is that the history is far richer and more fascinating than might have been suspected, even though modern professors may be disengaged substantially from a field in which their forebears had much to say.

The authors of these chapters went where their trained noses suggested that pay dirt might lie in their subjects, and they found a great deal of it. They also took whatever approach seemed most appropriate to each inquiry. Several of the essays examine the positions on security taken by schools of thought (classical, neoclassical, Marxist); others deal with individual thinkers (Pareto, Pigou, Veblen, Hitler, Rostow) who had a great deal to say on the subject. The first essay finds early economic thinkers' views of national security quite closely entangled with their views on philosophical and other issues. The same was found for economists in the twentieth century who, exposed to the terrible trauma of two world wars, nevertheless looked to the notion of global systems for answers to questions about how to achieve security, or who ventured into such novel theoretical approaches as the theory of games. Finally, we have a fascinating essay on the evolution of distinctive institutional structures in and around the United States government that forced a marriage of economics and national security, at least for several decades.

Drafts of these papers were presented at a conference at Duke University 10–12 August 1990. The spirited discussion there contributed much to the perfected versions which are published here.

Preclassical Perceptions of
Economy and Security

S. Todd Lowry

A rewarding survey of perspectives on economics and security from antiquity to the Enlightenment requires us to step back from modern definitions of economics and from contemporary political entities. Modern formulations of the economic problem and the political subject matter to which they are applied did not exist in premodern times. This does not mean, however, that many of the elements that make up modern analytic thought were not clearly developed. What is even more intriguing about the potentially instructive character of the study of earlier thought is the number of instances where clearly articulated analytic patterns carry their appeal as clarion formulations into other situations that not only did not, but could not have, reasonably supported their genesis. This problem of genesis and transfer of analytic perceptions suggests not only the allure but the tyranny of intellectual images and the viability of G. L. S. Shackle's caveat that "in natural science, what is thought is built upon what is seen; but in economics, what is seen is built upon what is thought" (1972, 66). Of course, any overarching ideological framework or expandable analytic system provides the substance for unified perspectives and a reference line from which to deviate in order to accommodate exceptions, inconsistencies, and contradictions.

Both generalizing concepts such as astronomical and astrological systems and expandable analytic systems such as subjective rationality and numerical consistency have had their place in the generation of economic theory and in perceptions of military security. Their appeal is frequently their traditional availability and public acceptability, so that the history of discussion of vital issues is, as often as not, the history of rhetorical formulations that are partially validated because people act in response to the comfort and cogency of persisting clichés.

In ancient Greece, which provides the beginnings of our continuous cumulative European intellectual heritage, we find two well-defined themes that have nourished the literature of economics and security. On the one hand there is an emphasis upon security through self-sufficiency

5

and isolation with overtones of a romanticized pristine agrarian tradition. On the other hand we have a concern for the standards of behavior of the individual leader or head of the functioning politicoeconomic unit with both practical and moral overtones.

From Hesiod to Shangri-la

Among the earliest Greek writings that have come down to us are the works of Hesiod from the eighth century B.C. In his *Works and Days* Hesiod portrayed the advantages of a self-sufficient agrarian existence, free from the need to go out across the dangerous waters of the Aegean in search of support by trade or raiding. This idealization of the basic agrarian economy which permitted a peaceful and virtuous life was extended in Homer's *Odyssey* to the concept of a prosperous city maintaining peace and prosperity through isolation. After years of wandering, Odysseus' (Ulysses') last stop before returning home to Ithaca was the island of Scheria, where King Alcinoös befriended him, receiving him in the city of Phaiacia. The populace of this prosperous city was apparently very uneasy about strangers. The city recognized that its security was based upon its remoteness, and it maintained contact with the outside world with fast ships that could cover great distances in a short time. This image of an economy based primarily upon agriculture and the possibility of building a prosperous community dependent upon isolation or remoteness for protection from raiders was not without empirical support. Theoretically, it was quite sound. Agriculture was the basis of the well-being of the vast majority of ancient populations, and with freedom from tribute or the marauding bands of freebooters that wandered along the coasts of Greece, small communities could accumulate reserves and infrastructure to provide a prosperous and pleasant life. This agrarian premise became romanticized in antiquity and was perpetuated through the Middle Ages and the Enlightenment. We find its economic echo in French physiocracy and Jeffersonian agrarian egalitarianism. Plato's dialogue *Critias* promulgated the tradition of the ideal state, "Atlantis," at some unknown location in the Atlantic Ocean, a long distance away, where civic and individual perfection blended to make a utopian society. Sir Thomas More's *Utopia* in the middle sixteenth century, with Francis Bacon's *New Atlantis* following shortly afterward, perpetuated this romantic tradition. After four centuries we could still observe the progeny of this genre of literature with the vehement assertion of U.S. isolationism in the late 1930s and in James Hilton's famous novel about Shangri-la. The more realistic versions of this tradition have their roots in antiquity.

An interest in historical and predictive analysis became an essential part of Greek social thought in classical antiquity. In Thucydides' analysis of the Peloponnesian Wars in late fifth-century B.C. Greece, we have the beginnings of what has been called "scientific history." It is this intertwining of economic and military analysis in realistic terms that requires our primary attention despite the unquestionable influence throughout history of the romantic agrarian isolationist tradition.

The Coincidence of the Economic and the Military Agenda

One of the most intriguing and puzzling variables throughout the history of the correlation between economic perspectives and policies on the one hand and military perspectives, policies, and technology on the other is the degree of coincidence of organizational and technological structures. Where ideology and economic vision support a system of order that in turn reinforces the sense of justice and propriety of the economic structure and, simultaneously, offers a foundation for the organizational and technological state of the military arts of the day, a society finds itself in an internally rational optimum state. This is something we find in the hoplite military system in the traditional polis of the golden age of Greece.

The "hoplite method of fighting" became recognizable as an emerging system of military organization and equipment around the beginning of the seventh century B.C. It was marked by the evolution of a heavy, full-body shield carried by a helmeted warrior armed with a heavy lance or thrusting spear. The essence and effectiveness of this equipment lay in its socioeconomic context. It grew out of the polis, which was the traditional agrarian village that had prospered as an aggregation of small freeholders living in subsistence agriculture. As the survival of these growing agricultural communities became increasingly dependent upon the courage and commitment of the heads of its constituent families, a new concept of citizenship emerged. This citizenship grew out of the communal tribalism of the past and stifled the presumptions of a traditional aristocracy associated with a more elite system of warfare in which the mounted leader or charioteer played a dominant role. It was not the hoplite that emerged as a significant military factor, but the *body of* hoplites. A relatively small corps of hoplites, friends and relatives operating in close formation, presenting a wall of overlapping body shields bristling with lances, functioned with a spirit of camaraderie and commitment that made it a novel military phenomenon in its day. As the hoplite contingents learned that holding their formation was the primary source of their power and survival, their training and organization emerged as the key to their military prowess. Such groups, able to wheel and bend their lines, even charge at a run without breaking the phalanx formation, became veritable modern tanks when operating against disorganized infantry. They were relatively immune to archery, and a match for cavalry. The mutual reinforcement that gave strength to the small Greek city-state consisted of the tradition of democratic citizenship and organization plus the military equipment that each hoplite freeholder supplied from his agricultural base. This provided the springboard for a growing military status and politicoeconomic tradition in Greece (Lowry 1987, 28 and n. 50).

The theoretical analysis of this Greek tradition is found in the introductory lines of Thucydides' *History of the Peloponnesian War.* Thucydides provided an explanation of the economic and cultural strength of the Attic Peninsula, which includes the city of Athens. The explanation was that the region was poor enough agriculturally that people had to develop habits of hard work and cooperation in order to survive and prosper. This created an equilibrium in that the area was not rich enough to tempt outside invaders, and its vigorous population was a significant deterrent to such depredations. The stability of this economy encouraged the immigration of similarly industrious people that added to the region's security. This early formulation of the challenge-and-response thesis in Thucydides (1.2), which dominated Arnold Toynbee's analysis of world history, has a special significance in early Greek thought. Thucydides continually emphasized the importance of training in the military successes in the wars. Emphasis on this component is also found in Xenophon's generalizations, in his *Oeconomicus,* on harmonization and coordination in matters ranging from estate management to military leadership and the organization of crews and equipment on galleys.

Thucydides' analysis probably characterized the economic life of the majority of the Greek city-states during the seventh and sixth centuries and into the fifth century B.C. Athens, however, lost the Peloponnesian War at the end of the fifth century partly because her economy, the group identity of her population, and her military strength ceased to coincide. As an outgrowth of the Persian invasions Athens built up a fleet and emerged as a major trading entrepôt and tribute-gathering power supporting a large navy. She was no longer able to field land forces that could meet the Spartan challenge on the mainland, and her economic interests led her to colonial adventurism in Sicily and the disastrous siege of Syracuse. Among traditional theorists, however, the old formulation persisted.

Plato, in his more practical blueprint for an ideal city, *The Laws,* recommended that a city be limited to 5,040 citizens, that is, heads of households (5.737c ff., 6.771a ff.). This dimension, influenced by a bit of Pythagorean numerology, has the bureaucratic virtue of being divisible into whole-number quotients by all of the first twelve numbers except eleven. Plato envisioned a small agrarian community, insulated from foreign trade, but with a more centralized administrative tradition that no longer coincided with the democratic aspect of the hoplite tradition. Aristotle, in his *Politics*, also envisioned a relatively small city-state as the ideal of political cohesion and defensibility, but his views, in the fourth century B.C., were already out of touch with the scale of warfare being introduced by Alexander the Great.

A footnote on the hoplite system of warfare in its heyday in the sixth century B.C. is suggestive of some modern comparison. Young men, seeking outside employment from constricted agricultural communities, found that they could export their military surplus. Bands of hoplite mercenaries were in great demand around the Mediterranean as bodyguards for authoritarian rulers and as elite troops in combat.

My generalization, to this point, has emphasized the significance and importance of the type of situation where the economy was congenial to the organizational and technological bases for security and, vice versa, the system of security coincided with the economy. This was apparently true in the early Greek polis with the technology of hoplite weaponry and organization. It was also true, to a certain extent, in the Athenian empire with its naval power and tribute system supporting the administrative and cultural center of the defense league against the Persian threat. These are facets of economic policy that resurface in mercantilist times, a period when Thucydides had a continuing influence marked by Thomas Hobbes's English translation of his work.

In Greek times political and economic theory defined and supported the policies that led to the strength of early Greek society, but the economic importance of trade and tribute combined with naval technology to make both Plato's and Aristotle's theoretical formulations obsolete. This sense of the importance of the coinciding of economic and military activities, so that they are mutually reinforcing, has a subliminal role in later periods. The manorial economy, the fortified castle, and the high cost of a knight's panoply provided a level of coincidence in feudal times. Seventeenth-century mercantilist thought that rationalized wealth through foreign trade, the expansion of sea power, and the accumulation of bullion that provided reserves for shipbuilding and the hiring of mercenaries expressed this pattern of mutually reinforcing coincidence. One might even analyze the near-ideological push for the development of a nuclear power base for domestic energy supplies as a subconscious commitment to the integration of nuclear arms and a domestic nuclear economy into a mutually supportive economic and military system. In this particular case, however, the technology appears to be flawed, carrying unacceptable externalities. But the ideological commitment to economic and military coincidence survives.

The Premise of Rationality and Individualism

We can pursue the concern over coincidence of economic and security systems into a discussion of the traditional belief in human rationality. This requires us to treat some of the historic concepts of leadership and of the individual negotiative process that have evolved into a modern commitment to game theory. In his *Merit and Responsibility* (1960) A. W. H. Adkins has provided us with an extensive analysis of the early Greek view of the moral and intellectual burden of the head of the extended family household. In both the pastoral and the agrarian economies of the eastern Mediterranean basin, the traditional family unit, in earliest times, stayed together, aggregating three and four generations, under the leadership and authority of a patriarchal head. This was the *paterfamilias* of classical Roman law, who had life-and-death judicial power over his family. The tradition persists to the present in the presumptive authority structure of traditional cultures in the Near East.

What is important is that the role of the head of the family was that of economic administrator, military leader, judge and jury, and high priest, dealing with the family gods. The family unit thus constituted the microeconomy of the ancient world. This was not only the operative unit of a "shame culture," where inefficiency would cause the family head to lose honor, status, and respect. The military stakes for which these economic units were forced to play were great. During the first half of the first millennium B.C. the eastern Mediterranean was a world where trade and raiding were considered equally acceptable entrepreneurial projects and the failure of the village or aggregation of extended family households at self-protection, one way or another, meant death for the adult males and enslavement for the women and children. By classical times, it is true, adult males were sufficiently valuable as galley slaves, field hands, miners, and laborers in other manageable labor-intensive projects that captives were sold rather than killed. Nevertheless the ethic of masculine virtue in traditional Greek society was one of winning in a zero-sum game. This can be characterized as a "success ethic" with no particular interest in the nobility of a losing effort. In military situations you fought if you could win, you fled or paid tribute if you could not. The shame was to miscalculate. Even in the Olympic Games there were only first prizes—no credit for coming in second. A loser was a loser. This survival or success ethic, deeply embedded in the microcosm of the politicoeconomic system, tended to be transferred to the broader perspectives on leadership at the level of city-state, alliance, and empire. Successful deception, trickery, fraud were, above all, successful; and as Adkins explains regarding the evolution of Greek morality, it was very difficult to establish the female virtues of trust, sympathy, and consideration that were necessary for democratic urban life.

From the point of view of modern economic theory and of security analysis this background is very important, because it is the intellectual ferment from which our traditions of rational calculation of social values and calculated dealings with others have descended. In Plato's dialogue *Protagoras* the hedonic calculus is worked out in precise detail, using pleasure and pain, discounted by time and intensity, to compare moral choices (Lowry 1987, ch. 2). This tradition of quantification was reinforced by the materialism of atomist philosophy and by Pythagorean mystic numerology. In this setting it should be no surprise that we find the use of subjective rationality in explaining both economic and security relations.

At the beginning of book 2 of Plato's *Republic* we find the social-compact thesis precisely elaborated in a form that has persisted in Western thought to the present (357a ff.). Plato, of course, being hostile to the principles of subjective rationality and relativism, has rhetorically, in the dialogue, poisoned the wells by portraying the spokesman for relativism as a blustering, pompous, obnoxious, greedy buffoon.

Glaucon, one of Plato's older brothers and a member of the discussion group, points out that what the discredited sophist, Thrasymachus, has been arguing is consistent with what most men believe, namely, that unjust conduct is preferable insofar as it is more personally advantageous and that men deviate from the optimization of their advantage reluctantly. This is no more nor less than the modern doctrine in international policy formation of eschewing ideology and ethics and asking the simple question, "Is it in the national interest?" Glaucon believes that this widely held doctrine deserves a fuller and fairer presentation. Despite this gesture toward academic balance and fairness Plato's rhetoric and staging set the argument up for ridicule and rejection. Nevertheless its lucid presentation has provided a clear statement of this analytic principle that has been part of the educational experience of every cultured person in the European tradition up to the early part of this century.

Glaucon's presentation deserves to be quoted in full so that the rationality and candor of the position can be fully appreciated.

> By nature, they say, that to commit injustice is a good and to suffer it is an evil, but that the excess of evil in being wronged is greater than the excess of good in doing wrong, so that when men do wrong and are wronged by one another and taste of both, those who lack the power to avoid the one and take the other determine that it is to their profit to make a compact with one another neither to commit nor to suffer injustice, and that this is the beginning of legislation and covenants between men, . . . and that this is the genesis and essential nature of justice—a compromise between the best, which

is to do wrong with impunity, and the worst, which is to be wronged and be impotent to get one's revenge. Justice, they tell us, being midway between the two, is accepted and approved, not as a real good, but as a thing honored in the lack of vigor to do injustice, since anyone who had the power to do it and was in reality "a man" would never make a compact with anybody. (*Rep.* 2.358e–359b, Hamilton and Cairnes, 606–7)

This passage contains a negative formulation of the social-contract thesis, conditioning justice (peace and respect for property rights) on the aggregate rational self-interest of the weaker majority. It takes the clear position that voluntary limits upon their self-interest by the powerful are irrational or even "mad." An equilibrium theory of profit and loss is presented as the basis for socioeconomic stability that can be extended to international stability and security among aggregations of smaller nations. The weak point in the argument is its emphasis upon the economics of the short run, in which the losses from wanton injustice by others—not only the loss of property but the resultant destruction, disruption, and insecurity—far exceed the benefits of injustice, the mere acquisition of property. This weighs the scales on the side of a rationalistic basis for natural society where the weaker parties can control the stronger. The longer-run concept, not developed here, is that the affirmative benefits from peace and security are so extensive that the powerful would not risk the slightest possibility of instability and insecurity that might impair the benefits of the division of labor and specialization. Plato goes to considerable lengths in the ensuing argument in book 2 of the *Republic* to demonstrate that the exceptionally gifted and powerful can always mislead and manipulate the majority and that where democratic self-interest governs, there is no equilibrium or stability but merely the selfish exercise of raw power and self-interest. Plato's antidote for this truer view of nature is the moral training of the elite, who can and will provide order and security in society if they come to understand that it is in the interest of their own personal ethical well-being to maintain a temperate and balanced life. Promoting social stability and order and optimizing natural specialization and division of labor are social standards that parallel personal ethical standards. This position promoted a long tradition of ethical elitism, characterized in feudal times as *noblesse oblige* and later influencing the entrepreneurial tradition that emerged in the eighteenth century (Lowry 1991).

The international aspect of this elitist formulation as a source of economic prosperity and military security is best illustrated by a discussion found in Xenophon's *Cyropaedia* (3.2.17–33). In this romanticized account of the education and performance of Cyrus the Great, Xenophon offers his contribution to the genre of "mirror for princes" literature, in which political and economic wisdom is presented as vital to the training of the elite, particularly of the absolute ruler, king, or emperor. Xenophon presents a situation where Cyrus conquered two hitherto independent and warring peoples. The Armenians were a herding people living in the mountains. The Chaldeans were an agricultural people living primarily on the plains. Their mutual distrust made peace between them impossible, and the conflict was obviously mutually destructive. Cyrus pointed out that by coming under his rule both could enjoy peace and security and economic prosperity. He further pointed out that the pastoral Armenians controlled some good agricultural land of which they made no good use, while the agricultural Chaldeans controlled some mountain pastures which were useless to them. Cyrus's offer to provide a garrison to guarantee peace and order in support of the mutual leasing of their improperly exploited resources was met with enthusiasm. It is obvious that administrative authority could provide the benefits of security that would increase economic well-being sufficiently to justify the tribute required by Cyrus to support his benevolent rule. There are other examples of this thesis of administrative elitism and individual rationality imposed upon a populace for its own good, but what is most important about this early Greek formulation is that it was embodied in literature that was part of the Roman and later European educational tradition that influenced political and economic thinking up to the nineteenth century. The hope of society and the world was stability and order imposed by authority, a Pax Romana, or Britannica, at the international level, with a Hobbesian sovereign providing an intelligent and well-trained brain in the head of the Leviathan. Hobbes, of course, was prepared to characterize life in a state of natural, unsupervised rational self-interest as "solitary, poor, nasty, brutish and short."

Despite the strong Platonic tradition emphasizing the primacy of unique intelligence and leadership, the opposing tradition sketched in book 2 of Plato's *Republic* persisted. Looking carefully at Plato's formulation of the social compact, one sees a theory of a mutually beneficial, rationally self-interested compromise with the actors settling for the second best. This is treated as a natural, rational reference base for predicting human behavior and dependable social relationships. Stated in these terms, the "prisoner's dilemma" formulation is a simple replication of a broader social theory that postulates a rational naturalism as the basis of predictable behavior upon which one can build a scientific pattern of prediction and planning.

It is even more interesting to note that this generalization of presumptive rational behavior achieved a place in the rhetoric manuals of the fifth century B.C. Corax and his pupil, Tisias, "attached great importance to . . . [probability] as a means of convincing a jury" (Dobson 1967, 12). Further, the more famous author of legal arguments, Antiphon, is said to have preferred probabilistic arguments even when evidence was available. To carry this institutionalization of rational predictability a step farther, we have the development of "sets" or fact situations where deductions from rational premises bind the players to an outcome. The one associated with Corax and Tisias is Corax's contract for instructing Tisias whereby he was to be paid when Tisias won his first case. Corax then sued Tisias, pointing out that he would either win by the verdict, or, if Tisias won the case, he would recover under the contract. This type of verbal game, where the parties are tied to a scheme of outcomes based on the precise terms of the agreement, borrows from emerging commercial law, but it also records the assembling of some of the elements of the fabric of game theory.

A later account from the Roman period is the story of the Soothsayer's Daughter. The daughter was taken by pirates, who notified the soothsayer that if he could correctly predict whether they planned to release her or hold her for ransom, they would release her. The soothsayer guessed that they planned to hold her for ransom. Of course, the pirates had to release the daughter to prove his prediction wrong, or alternatively, release her if he was right. This type of matching of two pairs of choices in a setting of rational commitment has similar elements to the prisoner's-dilemma game, replete with the strained assumption that relatives of prisoners can trust pirates, or that detained suspects can trust the authorities who are making promises to extort confessions. The lengths to which the police will go and their record of perfidy have led modern courts to refuse to admit most confessions in criminal trials. However, practical reality is no bar to the development of anecdotal formulations to aid in the search for a rationalistic naturalism as a base for predicting behavior through game theory.

The "Mirror for Princes" Literature

The formal theory put forward by Plato was simply that the optimum efficiency of the state could be achieved by assigning individuals to specialized tasks in conformity with their natural capacities. This concept of specialization and the division of labor was logically extended to the presumption that the most intelligent and competent administrator should be in charge of the state to optimize its efficiency. This natural leader would have no peer, and his capacity to lead would be recognized by all those with the rational capacities appropriate to the participating citizenry. However, such outstanding unique individuals, natural philosopher-kings, would have the capacity to manipulate and mislead the populace as demagogues if they were so inclined. Thus the only real hope for good government was the fact that men are rational, and that no one injures himself except out of ignorance. By the same token, no ruler would injure or weaken his state except out of ignorance. An intelligent man is as concerned with the balance and integrity of his own inner psyche and personality as he is with the prosperity and stability of the state he rules. Thus instruction, convincing argument, and a developed sense of ethical commitment to his own moral well-being are the avenues toward a prosperous and stable state.

This formulation of the theoretical basis for a strong authoritarian state, and the process by which it can be secured and advanced, coincided with a long and rich tradition of "wisdom literature" or literary tracts formulated as advice to young rulers just coming to power. Examples of this type of tract date back to around 2500 B.C. in ancient Egypt. The picture of the authoritarian individual as the vehicle for rational efficiency supported by wise counselors and teachers persisted through medieval times. To a significant extent it is recognizable up to the eighteenth century.

One of the most important of these instructional documents in medieval times was the *Secretum Secretorum* (Manzalaoui 1977), a pseudo-Aristotelian communication to Alexander the Great on how to run his empire effectively. This document apparently derives from an Arabic original in the eighth century A.D. It appeared in Latin translations as early as the twelfth century, and some five hundred manuscript copies survive. It was available in English by the late fourteenth century. In Arabic it was called the *Kitāb Sirr al-Asrār,* from which the Latin title was derived, but this was in fact the subtitle. The actual title was *The Book of the Science of Government, on the Good Ordering of Statescraft.* This Arabic work was in a tradition of Persian and Arabic tracts called "mirrors for princes," many of which contained considerably more economic theory than the *Secretum Secretorum.* Nevertheless the widespread influence of this manuscript suffices to clarify this deeply rooted individualistic elitism and the way in which rational processes were presumed to be implemented in political and economic decision making.

The importance of generating economic prosperity in the kingdom is presented in the *Secretum Secretorum* using the ruler of India as an example.

> That tyme he vsed also to reles part of his tributis, and dispense with marchantis of theire customes, and other rentes in parcell relesse, and tham truly kepe and defende. And this [is] a speciall cause why that Inde is so full of peple and richesse, for theder rynne all merchauntes fro euery side of the world. . . . Thereof groweth

the kynges tributes and rentes so grete, for there is none that dare offende by wronge a merchaunt. . . . And that stuffeth and kepeth their citees, multiplieth their rentes, and asscreseth thereby the kynges honoure and glory, wherfor quaken the enemyes and dare not stere. So lyveth the kyng surely and pesibly, and hath the desires of his wille. (37)

This passage, set in a discussion of the importance of internal security and of extending prosperity to rich and poor alike, amply demonstrates the practical wisdom of this instructional document. Its importance, however, lies elsewhere. The heavy emphasis of this tract is on the human component in the kingdom, emphasizing first and foremost the health and vigor of the king himself. For that reason it received its early attention from Roger Bacon as a medical treatise. Second, the ability of the king properly to choose and manage personnel is presented as a primary concern. Much of this material was possibly appended to the original treatise in the course of its medieval Muslim evolution. Nevertheless it achieved much status because of its detailed analyses of various indices of personal character. From the shifty-eyed to the dark-headed as well as every conceivable facet of facial features, appearances are credited with some revelatory value in predicting character. Mixed with this exaggerated emphasis upon physiognomy are some very shrewd observations on managerial policy, such as advice to recognize that trusted secretaries are vital and should be well paid since they are the keepers of secrets.

The ultimate emphasis is on the skill and charisma of the king and his ability to promote not only prosperity, stability, and justice at home but honor and military respect abroad. These are essentially personal qualities, and it should be remarked how much we still rely on this tradition of personal aplomb and charisma in international relations. Any modern observer of the preparation for and the press reporting of international summit meetings should be aware that we are still functioning, to a surprising degree, within the confines of the *Kitāb,* where rationality must be funneled through the personality of a selected leader. It is his or her particular level of acumen, health, vigor, and charisma that will ultimately tip the balance toward or away from economic and military stability. The aggregation of potential advisers and astrologers is still with us.

Erasmus and the Moral Prince

In the second decade of the sixteenth century Desiderius Erasmus, a leading Renaissance scholar, wrote a book addressed to the young prince who was later to become Charles V of Spain and ruler of the remnant of The Holy Roman Empire. This tract, the *Institutio Principis*

Christiani or *Education of a Christian Prince,* is a conspicuous example of the "mirror for princes" genre of academic instructional literature. Its religious and moralizing rhetoric are only thin veils for its Platonistic elite individualism, rationalism, and practical economic considerations.

The extended advice on protection of oneself from degrading influences, debauchery, flatterers, and self-serving advisors is practical politics in the setting of absolute monarchy. However, our interest in this widely circulated document can be satisfied with a few excerpts from chapter 11, "On Beginning War," toward the end of the book. The continuity in Erasmus' thought of the Platonic theme is quite specific in his summing up of the problems of war.

> Lastly, when the prince has put away all personal feelings, let him take a rational estimate long enough to reckon what the war will cost and whether the final end to be gained is worth that much—even if victory is certain, . . . Weigh the worries, the expenditures, the trials, the long wearisome preparation, . . . in addition to paying out money you must coax and humor the mercenary soldiers, who are absolutely the most abject and execrable type of human being. . . .
>
> The wisdom of princes will be too costly for the world if they persist in learning from experience how dreadful war is, so that when they are old men, they may say: "I did not believe that war was so utterly destructive!" . . . These things should better be learned from books. ([1515] 1936, 249–50)

This concern with the external politicoeconomic costs of war did not limit Erasmus' appreciation of the relationship between domestic economic interests and foreign wars. Granted, he was dealing with an essentially subsistence-agrarian economy that suffered disruptive famine from time to time. Such disturbances of the nascent eruptions of urbanized technology in some of the commercial centers of Europe repeatedly frustrated promises of cumulative growth. Erasmus nevertheless recognized the threat of the Renaissance equivalent of our military-industrial complex. The feudal nobility constituted a power center with vested economic prerogatives and a conspicuous military role in the state. Erasmus warned, "It too often happens that nobles, who are more lavish than their private means allow, when the opportunity is presented stir up war in order to replenish their resources even at home by the plunder of their peoples" (252). He even suggested that some leaders, that is, princes, were not above using warfare as a device to reduce or subdue their subjects.

Given the nature of the economy and the economic understanding of the times, it is important to recognize that the primary source of economic well-being for the agricultural populace was peace and order. The vicissitudes of climate were bad enough without the problems associated with marching armies, whether pillaging invaders or pilfering mercenaries. The same can be said for the commercial world, which profited more from the secure movement of goods than from wartime shortages. The dependence of the monarch on the internal condition of his realm was well understood in the "mirror for princes" literature from antiquity. Erasmus pointed out that "a good prince measures everything by the advantage of his people, otherwise he is not even a prince. . . . A large part of the ruling authority is in the consent of the people, which is the factor that first created kings" (252).

This extension of elite rationalism to embrace natural genesis is Aristotelian and provides the bridge between rational authority and a concern for the natural rights of the populace, including the condition of the domestic economy. The idea that the security of the monarchy itself required some compromise with the interests of the people is implicit in Aristotle's *Politics* and occurs in Plutarch's contribution to the "mirror for princes" tradition in his "To an Uneducated Ruler." The statement is made that "one might more truly say that rulers serve god for the care and preservation of men, in order that of the glorious gifts that the gods give to men they may distribute some and safeguard others" (section 3, 780, pp. 57–59). Plutarch goes on to present a ruler's justification when his wife chided him for eroding his children's inheritance by giving democratic concessions to his subjects. The ruler replied that by sacrificing quantity, he was securing the stability of his children's patrimony. Erasmus cites this tract, paraphrasing the statement of Theopompus, "that he was not interested in knowing how great a kingdom he should leave to his children but only how much better and more secure he should leave it" ([1515] 1936, 247). This discussion occurs in Erasmus's chapter "On the Occupation of the Prince in Peace," in which the opportunities for public works, aiding agricultural productivity, and extension of cultivation are reviewed. The consistency with physiocracy of the accumulated perceptions in the "mirror for princes" tradition is deserving of more attention, but intervening concerns with the apparently discontinuous phase in economic thought designated as "mercantilism" have distracted scholars from this continuity.

Interpreting Mercantilism

In order to discuss any facet of the politicoeconomic and commercial literature of the sixteenth to the eighteenth century, scholars must wend their way between the Scylla of a hopeless quantity of specific policy- and problem-oriented literature on the one hand and the Charybdis of trying to abstract from, or generalize, this array of disparate material on the other. The period can be viewed as the seedbed of classical economic theory or as the graveyard of Scholasticism. One can follow Eli Heckscher and generalize mercantilist literature as expressions of concern for national power, or Joyce Appleby and analyze the emergence of a faith in natural regulatory processes. One can also emphasize the philosophical character of the Enlightenment, the emergence of Protestantism, the significance of the psychology of the age of discovery, the influx of American bullion, and the import of vast amounts of cheap produce from colonies. In addition the ideological and bureaucratic florescence associated with the emerging nation-states, vernacular education, and the printing press all can support major analytic themes. The clear-cut theoretical revolution came at the end of this period with the struggle to analyze the emerging phenomenon of industrial capitalism and, for our purposes, a new industrial understanding of internal and external security and military power. At the beginning of this period the character of the theoretical revolution, if any, was much more diffuse and blurred—despite Thomas Kuhn's use of the Copernican system as the prototype of his theory of scientific revolutions.

There is considerable support for the thesis that the extension of the perspectives in the "mirror for princes" tradition sheds more light on practical attitudes toward economic policy and security during this period than anachronistic perspectives that developed in later times. The rhetoric of scholarship may have changed from the fawning dedication to the ruler by the ambitious intellectual, "clutching at the hem of power." Nevertheless, theoretical advice was written for the person in authority, the administrator, the statesman, or the ruler. This focus of formal thought, theory and history, on the rational improvement of an administrative elite is illustrated by the widely circulated and reprinted *Mirror for Magistrates* of 1559, which was a group project to bring the lessons of medieval English history to the aid and edification of men of affairs. It is also worthy of note that as late as the eighteenth century Sir James Steuart's contribution to economics, as well as Adam Smith's *Wealth of Nations,* was formulated as advice to decision makers. Of course, as the ideological commitment came to emphasize the viability of self-regulating market processes, the advice became secondary and the economics literature became nominally analytical, explaining natural processes and advising laissez faire. In addition, as David McNally points out in his recent book, the laissez-faire formulation in French physiocracy did not mitigate a primary commitment to administrative promulgation of rational policy. This is an extremely important point because it helps explain the divergence between the ideological rhetoric of laissez-faire naturalism and the continuity of the tradition of a belief in and primary reliance on a decision-making rational elite.

Summary and Conclusions

The unifying character of preclassical economic thought was rooted in the primary importance of agriculture as the dominant occupation and immediate foundation upon which the superstructure of urban life, imperial power, emerging nationalism, and even nascent capitalism were based. The earliest economic thought was framed in terms of the patriarchal head of the household, the head of the *latifundium*, the manor lord, and the emperor or king. The focus of decision-making power on a single authority was consistent with the dual role of the military and civilian head of the political economy, whose rational efficiency was augmented by training and advice from scholars and sage advisors. This has been the legacy of the preclassical milieu. Despite a rhetorically dominant naturalistic ideology and legitimate concern for the industrial productivity of the macroeconomic system, the substantial reality of the contribution of economic thought to modern concerns for international security has been in the form of programs for reinforcing and augmenting individual information and rationality. The premise that other competing interests function at the same level leads to the projection of individual, rational decision-making into a study of the anticipatable rationality of the other side. This has become "game theory" and is part of the wider problem of anticipating outcomes by projecting substantive and rational inputs. In antiquity and early modern times there was a greater emphasis upon the possibility of capriciousness rather than the rationality of the individual. The body of pseudoscientific literature using physiognomy and numerology to predict individual behavior from the *Secretum Secretorum* was even then recognized as a subject for systematic analysis, and it is this variable and its cultivation that still dominates economics and international security theory at the broadest level.

References

Adkins, A. W. H. 1960. *Merit and Responsibility: A Study in Greek Values*. Oxford: Clarendon Press.

Appleby, Joyce Oldham. 1978. *Economic Thought and Ideology in Seventeenth-Century England*. Princeton: Princeton University Press.

Campbell, Lilly B., ed. [1559] 1938. *The Mirror for Magistrates*. Cambridge: Cambridge University Press.

Dobson, J. F. 1967. *The Greek Orators*. Freeport, N.Y.: Books for Libraries Press.

Erasmus, Desiderius. [1515] 1936. *The Education of a Christian Prince*. Translated with an introduction by Lester K. Born. New York: Columbia University Press.

Heckscher, Eli F. 1935. *Mercantilism*. Translated by M. Shapiro. London: George Allen & Unwin.

Lowry, S. Todd. 1987. *The Archaeology of Economic Ideas: The Classical Greek Tradition*. Durham: Duke University Press.

————. 1991. Understanding Ethical Individualism. In *Perspectives in the History of Economic Thought,* vol. 5. Edited by William J. Barber. London: Edward Elgar.

McNally, David. 1988. *Political Economy and the Rise of Capitalism: A Reinterpretation*. Berkeley and Los Angeles: University of California Press.

Manzalaoui, M. A., ed. 1977. *Secretum Secretorum: Nine English Versions*. Vol. 1, *Texts*. Oxford: Oxford University Press.

Plato. 1961. *The Collected Dialogues of Plato*. Edited by Edith Hamilton and Huntington Cairnes. Bollingen Series 71. Princeton: Princeton University Press.

Plutarch. 1949. To an Uneducated Ruler. In *Plutarch's Moralia,* 10: 53–71. Loeb Classical Library. Cambridge: Harvard University Press; London: Heinemann.

Shackle, G. L. S. 1972. *Epistemics and Economics*. Cambridge: Cambridge University Press.

National Security in
Classical Political Economy

Craufurd D. Goodwin

> The art of War . . . the noblest of all arts.
> —ADAM SMITH ([1776] 1976, 697)

> War is always a game of hazard.
> —JOHN RAE ([1834] 1965, 132)

> Security . . . the most important of all services.
> —NASSAU SENIOR ([1836] 1938, 75)

Classical political economy was forged on the anvil of war. The Seven Years' War had barely ended when Smith published *The Wealth of Nations,* and the Napoleonic Wars were the backdrop of discussion in Malthus's *Essay* and Ricardo's *Principles*. Only John Stuart Mill and the later classicals had the luxury of reflecting on international conflict with the detachment born of the nineteenth-century Pax Britannica.

It might be expected that the classical economists would have eschewed the study of conflict. After all, theirs was a concern with "order" directed by predominantly rational actors toward the satisfaction of human wants. On the surface, at least, war was quintessentially a process of disorder, the destruction of goods and services for no evident want-satisfying purpose, and governed by human "passions" rather than "the interests," to use Albert Hirschman's familiar juxtaposition. To cap it all, war was a process that required public action rather than private market behavior; it involved threats, alarums, stratagems, imposition of costs to achieve an objective, and all the other tactics of an activist state that classical economists sought to avoid—and that their nemesis, their mercantilist predecessors, had attended to above all. War was a process of disequilibrium, and it was hard to see how equilibrium market analysis could cast much light upon it. Finally, as individuals the classical economists were not warlike types or apt to dwell on the study of conflict. There was among them a colonel of marines (Torrens), but their leading lights were an absentminded professor, a clergyman, a retiring stockbroker, and a polymath raised by his father to read Latin

23

while practically an infant. The classical economists were not exactly a bunch of sissies, but they came close.

So did the classical economists have nothing to say about national security? Was it a subject that they avoided, as we shall see that later economists have tended to do? Not quite! Issues of national security were, in fact, taken up frequently by the classicals, and a number of their observations and speculations stand up well to the test of time. What follows is not a systematic survey of their attention to this subject, but rather some reflections on several security-related topics that interested these economists the most.

Why Is There War?

A basic question for all economists regarding society has to be "Why is destructive conflict so prevalent among nations?" Rational behavior would seem to point toward the formation of some sort of global social compact that will conserve productive capacity for the creation of goods and services that respond to human wants. But no such compact exists! Conflict is virtually an unremitting feature of the human condition. Wars and preparations for war, indeed, do exactly the opposite of the economic growth process. They create pain rather than pleasure. Several of the classical economists addressed this question of why men fight and answered it in a fashion that was consistent with their method of inquiry overall.

Adam Smith approached this question both logically and historically (mainly in book 5, chapter 1, "Of the Expences of the Sovereign or Commonwealth"), and he was led to an optimistic conclusion. His thoughts on the subject are contained in widely distributed comments on particular historical examples of conflict. Wars, he believed, arose when nations estimated that the potential returns from conflict exceeded their costs. These calculations changed as economies moved through the familiar development stages, and after a point the likelihood of war having a positive payoff grew less as growth progressed. For a while, however, the situation grew worse rather than better. Shepherds and husbandmen were more effective at warfare than the more primitive hunter-gatherers because they had some working capital with which to pursue conflict. Hunters made major sacrifices when they left their prey to pursue an enemy; herdsmen on the other hand could bring their flocks with them. Settled farmers found the opportunity costs of war reduced to a minimum because up to one-fifth of the agricultural population could be released for warfare during the off season. But with the advent of manufactures the costs of war increased, both because of the complexity of weapons and because as few as one one-hundredth of the manufacturing population could be spared without loss of production. When manufacturing succeeded settled agriculture as the dominant

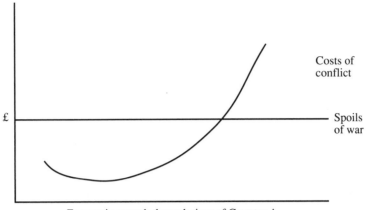

Economic growth through time of Country A
Stages of national growth:
hunting→pastoral→agricultural→manufacturing

Figure 1. Adam Smith's understanding of the changing desirability of offensive warfare to an advanced nation (Country A) facing less developed neighbors

economic activity, the provisioning of a standing army had to be added to production forgone in estimating the costs of national defense.

Smith concluded from all this that as nations grew richer, their proclivity to engage in offensive conflict declined; but ironically, because of their prosperity their attractiveness to less affluent aggressors also increased, and therefore their need for defense grew steadily. Smith's explanation of how to calculate the likelihood that one nation will attack a neighbor may be portrayed in figure 1, wherein two functions, reflecting costs and benefits of offensive warfare for a nation, at their intersection determine two ranges along the *x* axis (economic growth through time). In the left-hand range, to the left of the intersection, so long as a nation is confident it can win, it may find it beneficial to attack another nation. As a nation grows economically, however, the gains to be received from defeating a neighbor in war decline while at the same time the opportunity cost of the conflict grows. In the right-hand range, reached in the manufacturing stage of development, even if a nation wins a war militarily it will lose economically. Happily therefore, no rational, welfare-maximizing nation can be expected to engage in offensive warfare in this advanced state.

It is striking that despite the century and more of bloody conflict based on religious intolerance and issues of dynastic succession that Europe had just been through at the time Smith wrote, he was able to present an explanation for the likelihood of peace or war rooted in the consequences of economic growth alone. The implications of his interpretation were both ominous and hopeful. On the dark side, he showed that economic growth increased the rewards of aggression by the poor against the rich, while the rising costs might cause defense to be neglected by the rich. On the bright side, modern technology in the hands of an efficient defense force should be able to deter all aggression that poorer nations might have in prospect. Clearly Smith discerned a parallel between the problem of domestic security within a state and the problem of security among nations. Just as persons with property were always at risk from those without property, so rich nations faced a similar hazard from the poor nations. And just as internal police could bring domestic tranquility, so an efficient military establishment could be expected to yield a satisfactory level of national security by tilting the cost-benefit calculations of any aggressor into the negative.

Whereas Smith found the cause of war in human cupidity and the conditions of economic growth—subjects that he explored throughout *The Wealth of Nations*—Malthus found the answer to the question "Why war?" in his own obsession: population pressure. Human history, he explained, was punctuated by periodic outmigrations of excess population from nations in search of mere subsistence or a better life. "Want was the goad that drove the Scythian shepherds from their native haunts, like so many famished wolves in search of prey" (Malthus [1798] 1986, 20). While wars were a result of population pressure, however, they were also its corrective, one of those positive checks which "shorten the natural duration of human life" ([1798] 1986, 47; [1826] 1986, 16). The effect of conflict in curtailing population pressure was greater in wars among nations in a savage state. There "the predominant principle of self-preservation . . . prevents the admission of any of those ideas of honour and gallantry in war, which prevail among more civilized nations" ([1826] 1986, 37). In a word, casualties were very high. Indeed in parts of Africa and Asia war seemed to be the most effective restraint on the principle of population increase: "we can only be astonished at the force of that principle . . . which could furnish fresh harvests of human beings for the scythe of each successive conqueror" ([1826] 1986, 77). In modern Europe, Malthus noted, the interactive, cause-and-effect relationship between population pressure and war no longer applied: "War, the predominant check to the population of savage nations, has certainly abated, even including the late unhappy revolutionary contests" ([1826] 1986, 315). But Malthus did not follow Smith and explore the remaining causes of war under these "civilized" conditions.

As warfare and the prospect of it decreased during the nineteenth century the classical economists seemed to dwell less and less on its causes. John Stuart Mill was even able to report in his *Principles* (1848) that by that date conflict had come to be associated mainly with colonies: "wars, and the destruction they cause, are now usually confined, in almost every country, to those distant and outlying possessions at which it comes into contact with savages" ([1848] 1965, 707).

Costs and Benefits of Conflict

The classical economists were concerned to understand not only the causes of war but also how to calculate the full economic import of war, including the costs of preparation for it. Smith took pains to scold his mercantilist predecessors who had, characteristically, stressed the money cost. The real costs of war to a nation, he asserted, were the "produce of its domestic industry" used directly in the conflict or sent abroad to purchase those "consumable goods" in "distant countries." Money was only a measure of the real cost, not the cost itself. Increased taxes and changes in the balance of international payments were the visible manifestations of the costs of war and defense to the citizenry. Because war was preferably fought abroad, foreign exchange was critical to the war effort. Typically in wartime, domestically produced commodities were required for use at home and could not be shipped abroad to pay for expeditions. Thus countries with exports of "finer and more improved manufactures" were best situated to sustain a war effort. In general, whereas "treasure" had been needed to conduct war effectively in more primitive times, now it was necessary instead to have a vibrant and robust economy reflected in the capacity to "draw from their subjects extraordinary aids upon extraordinary occasions" (Smith [1776] 1976, 440, 441, 444, 446).

At various points in *The Wealth of Nations* Smith made shrewd observations about aspects of defense costs. For example, he noted that soldiers receive pay "less than that of common labourers, and in actual service their fatigues are much greater." This was because their "youthful fancies" and "romantic lapses" led them to overestimate the likelihood of "acquiring honour and distinction." If the costs of war were sufficiently modest, he observed, taxpayers were willing to pay for them, because "to them this amusement compensates the small difference between the taxes which they pay on account of the war, and those which they had been accustomed to pay in time of peace. They are commonly dissatisfied with the return of peace, which puts an end to their amusement, and to a thousand visionary hopes of conquest and national glory, from a longer continuance of the war" ([1776] 1976, 920). On the other hand, when taxes were already extremely onerous, taxpayers resisted further levies until the crisis became extreme. In such a condition there was no alternative but to issue public debt: "When a nation is already over burdened with taxes, nothing but the necessities of a new war, nothing but either the animosity of national vengeance, or the anxiety for national security, can induce the people to submit, with tolerable patience, to a new tax. Hence the usual misapplication of the sinking fund" (921). Many politicians today would agree.

In an important passage in *The Wealth of Nations* Smith observed that in most cases the costs of modern war were mainly in forgone current consumption: "a certain portion of the revenue of private people is only turned away from maintaining one species of unproductive labour, towards maintaining another" (925). The productive capacity of the economy was seldom damaged through conflict: "War would not necessarily have occasioned the destruction of any old capitals, and peace would have occasioned the accumulation of many more new." Heavy wartime taxes may reduce savings rates and hence the accumulation of capital, but this interruption will be temporary unless the redistributive burdens of a national debt are carried into peacetime. With pay-as-you-go taxation "the ability of private people to accumulate, though less during the war, would have been greater during the peace than under the system of funding" (926).

One of the empirical anomalies observed from time to time in classical economics, and spelled out clearly by Thomas Chalmers, was that nations vanquished in war and evidently laid to waste were often in a few years more prosperous than the victors. (See, for example, discussion of the Chalmers paradox in Fawcett 1888, 30.) How could this be, if much of a nation's accumulated savings, its capital stock, had been destroyed? Part of the answer lay in Smith's explanation of the meaning of capital. What in fact was destroyed by war was current output, not capital stock. Capital, the means to replenish supplies of consumption and investment goods, remained intact. However, two additional explanations for the paradox were offered which deserve our notice, one on the supply side and one on the demand side of the market.

John Rae, that eccentric Scots emigrant to Canada, was led by his experience in the New World to test the theory of economic growth received from the classical economists against the evidence around him. And he found the theory wanting. In particular he postulated that capital increased in an advanced economy not simply by the process of saving, or not consuming, which received most attention from classical economists. Instead, he argued, economic growth depended on two processes: accumulation and invention. The latter was essential to provide the ever-changing forms in which savings could be embodied. Most important, the determinants of each one of the two processes were not the same. Indeed, "there are yet a set of causes, the effects of which, while they paralyze the exertions of the one, rouse the other to activity" (Rae [1834] 1965, 222). War was one of these causes, and its differentiated impact on accumulation and invention explained the Chalmers paradox as far as Rae was concerned. War did frequently reduce the propensity and capacity of citizens to accumulate (save), thus pointing toward a future decline in growth. However, war also stimulated the propensity to invent. The challenge of wartime and postwar conditions leads inventors to discover new and improved products and processes. Thus in terms of the effect on growth the unintended economic benefits of war might even exceed the costs.

> Whatever disturbs, or threatens to disturb, the established order of things, by exposing the property of the members of the society to danger, and diminishing the certainty of its future possession, diminishes also the desire to accumulate it. Intestine commotions, persecutions, wars, internal oppression, or outward violence, either, therefore, altogether destroy, or, at least, very much impair the strength of the effective desire of accumulation. On the contrary, they excite the inventive faculty to activity. The excessive propensity to imitation, which is natural to man, seems the only means by which we can account for this diversity of effects. Men are so much given to learning, that they do not readily become discoverers. They have received so much, that they do not easily perceive the need of making additions to it, or readily turn the vigor of their thoughts in that direction. . . . Whatever, therefore, breaks the wonted order of events, and exposes the necessity, or the possibility, of connecting them by some other means, strongly stimulates invention. The slumbering faculties rouse themselves to meet the unexpected exigence, and the possibility of giving a new, and more perfect order to elements not yet fixed, animates to a boldness of enterprise, which were rashness, had they assumed their determined places. Hence, as has often been remarked, periods of great changes in kingdoms or governments, are the seasons when genius breaks forth in brightest lustre. The beneficial effects of what are termed revolutions, are, perhaps, chiefly to be traced, to their thus wakening the torpid powers; the troubling of the waters they bring about, undoes the palsy of the mind. (222–23)

Rae did not reach the point of advocating war as an instrument of economic growth, but he was unequivocal in suggesting that benefits in the past from some wars had exceeded the costs.

> War itself, so great an evil to the individuals within the scope of its ravages, is evidently the only manner by which, in certain states of society, an amelioration can be induced. The destruction of the Roman Empire, and almost of the Roman race, by the barbarians, was, perhaps, ultimately, the most beneficial revolution ever brought about. Even in its minor consequences, this apparent evil

produces also much of real good. Without it, many of the most useful inventions might never have been either propagated, or improved. (255–56)

The policy message of Rae's observations was that it should be possible for clever government leaders to discover practices that would produce the benefits of war without the costs: "Wars and similar interruptions to intercourse, as has been repeatedly observed, are, in fact, one of the chief agents by which the arts have been made to pass from country to country. But the same benefits might have been produced by the gradual operations of the legislator, without the sacrifice in this way required, and it is the business of reason, watching events, to separate the good from the evil, and to search for plans of obtaining the one, and avoiding the other" (367). Rae ascribed the depression that followed the Napoleonic Wars in Britain to the misdirection of capital and labor and the absence of innovative leaders: "they have applied themselves largely to objects, the direct effects of the attainment of which are worse than useless to society" (312).

The contribution to understanding the costs and benefits of conflict from the demand side focused on the macroeconomic and adjustment problems that occurred in war and its aftermath. A modern economy, classical economists pointed out, simply could not adjust smoothly to or from the demands of war without substantial transitional costs. The costs of unemployment and production of the wrong goods had to be added to the familiar wastes of warfare. The depth and duration of the transitions would vary with the conditions, but there would surely be costs of forgone production from idle resources in all transitions, and these must be added to the waste of war material when making any cost-benefit calculation of conflicts.

Ricardo put it thus:

The commencement of war after a long peace, or of peace after a long war, generally produces considerable distress in trade. It changes in a great degree the nature of the employments to which the respective capitals of countries were before devoted; and during the interval while they are settling in the situation which new circumstances have made the most beneficial, much fixed capital is unemployed, perhaps wholly lost, and labourers are without full employment. The duration of this distress will be longer or shorter according to the strength of that disinclination which most men feel to abandon that employment of their capital to which they have long been accustomed. It is often protracted too by the restrictions and prohibitions, to which the absurd jealousies which prevail between the different States of the commercial commonwealth give rise.

> The distress which proceeds from a revulsion of trade, is often mistaken for that which accompanies a diminution of the national capital, and a retrograde state of society; and it would perhaps be difficult to point out any marks by which they may be accurately distinguished. ([1817] 1951, 265)

In cases where the economy required an adjustment period after warfare to permit "every capitalist to find his place" and to avoid a "revulsion," Ricardo was prepared to contemplate import duties to facilitate the transition, "decreasing in amount from time to time . . . for a limited number of years" (90, 266). An especially painful adjustment to and from war, Ricardo pointed out, was in the size of the labor force. Demands for military personnel during the war would lead to an increase in the population which after the war would become "redundant, and by its effect on the rest of the population, and its competition with it for employment, will sink the value of wages, and very materially deteriorate the condition of the labouring classes" (394).

In order for the citizenry to have before it all the precise data for calculating the costs and benefits of war, Ricardo insisted, war finance should be by taxation alone and in no part by borrowing: "When the pressure of the war is felt at once, without mitigation, we shall be less disposed wantonly to engage in an expensive contest, and if engaged in it, we shall be sooner disposed to get out of it, unless it be a contest for some great national interest" (186). He did not attend to Smith's concern that incentives for exertion could not be sustained with pay-as-you-go taxation in an all-out war, presumably because he believed that if the incentives were not present naturally there should be no war. An important additional benefit of full-cost taxation would be that price stability could be maintained and the costs of a postwar deflationary "revulsion" avoided: "The greatest advantage that would attend war-taxes would be the little permanent derangement that they would cause to the industry of the country. The prices of our commodities would not be disturbed by taxation, or if they were, they would only be so during a period when everything is disturbed by other causes, during the war. At the commencement of peace, everything would be at its natural price again" (189).

Although classical economists were prepared to concede that war could interrupt patterns of aggregate demand and might require some remedial action by government to restore employment in the right places, they would not concede that war could stimulate the economy to increase employment and growth through an increase in demand. John Stuart Mill slapped the hand of William Blake for making such a suggestion in 1823.

There is another and a still more mischievous effect, to which the conclusions of Mr. Blake, should they ever obtain vogue, could not fail to be made subservient. We have heard before now the fallacy of the universal glut adduced in justification of enormous taxation, of extravagant government expenditure, and particularly of wars. How convenient to all who are interested in these abuses, is such a theory as that of Mr. Blake! Here, they may say, is a portion of capital, which, if it remains in the hands of the producers, must lie dormant in the shape of goods, yielding no advantage to the owners: let the government take it, to be expended in hiring soldiers and sailors, and in purchasing naval and military stores; and a new demand will suddenly be created for all sorts of produce; prices will rise, the producers will be enriched, the labourers will obtain an increase of wages, industry will be vivified, and production itself will be stimulated by that very expenditure, which the people, in their "ignorant impatience of taxation," believe to be a calamity. (Mill [1824] 1965, 21–22)

How to Sustain National Defense?

Although Smith concluded that the economic case for offensive behavior declines over time for rich nations, especially as they enter the advanced manufacturing stage of development, the danger to those nations from attack increases. Their very prosperity, reflected in a rightward movement along the x axis in figure 1, attracts the attention of envious neighbors and extends the point in the economic progress of another nation up to which it is profitable to engage in war. This relationship may be visualized as increasing prosperity in the advanced nation causing a steady upward shift in the "spoils of war" function of a less developed nation (see figure 2). Smith offered numerous examples from history of how warfare had broken out under such conditions (when the spoils function rose above the costs function) and led to the fall of such advanced nation states as the Greek republics and the Roman Empire.

The challenge for a relatively developed nation, therefore, is to make certain that for its neighbors the perceived "cost of conflict" function shifts upward as rapidly as does the "spoils of war" function. This means, in essence, that advanced nations must sustain a credible and effective defense as a deterrent—a not inconsiderable problem, Smith observed. The difficulty was that if left to their own inclinations an economically successful people typically neglect their defense. Mistakenly they see their own pacific intentions reflected in their neighbors. "An industrious, and upon that account a wealthy nation, is of all nations the most likely to be attacked; and unless the state takes some new measures for the publick defence, the natural habits of the peo-

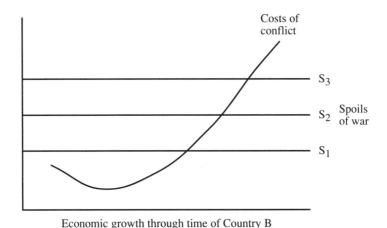

Figure 2. Adam Smith's understanding of the changing desirability of offensive warfare to a less developed nation (Country B) facing advanced neighbors

ple render them altogether incapable of defending themselves" (Smith [1776] 1976, 697–98).

The essential means to deter aggression, Smith believed, was a credible military force. This required, for a modern nation, both a standing army and a reserve militia. The former was needed because of the "skill and dexterity" required in the use of up-to-date munitions. Division of labor as well as discipline and obedience to authority were required for efficiency in the defense sector as in any other. The benefits of a standing army were its constant readiness for action and the luxury it gave the sovereign to tolerate dissent internally, knowing it could be quelled in a pinch. Indeed it was ironic, he noted, that the efficacy of such an authoritarian social unit as the military was crucial to the survival of liberal practices in a civilized society. With a tough and loyal military there was no danger that democratic controversy would get out of hand.

The costs of a standing army, Smith said, were two: first, its use of scarce resources, whose value rose with economic progress; second, the danger that if not controlled vigilantly it might subvert the government. Cost containment could be achieved by maintaining a reserve militia prepared to supplement the standing army in case of need and to constrain any unconstitutional behavior. However, a special problem with a militia was that it quickly lost its effectiveness in peacetime. To cope with this condition Smith went beyond the economist's traditional range of incentives. He advocated public exercises to maintain physical fitness, prizes to reward athletic prowess such as those at the Olympic Games, and cultivation overall of a "martial spirit" among the citizens. "But where every citizen had the spirit of a soldier, a smaller standing army would surely be requisite. That spirit, besides, would necessarily diminish very much the dangers to liberty, whether real or imaginary, which are commonly apprehended from a standing army" (786–87).

The question naturally arose among classical economists of whether pacifism could be an effective form of national defense and a means of ensuring international security. Strikingly, they thought not. Their appreciation of the strong economic motives upon which they believed aggressive intentions lay made them conclude that there was no alternative to making the perceived costs of war exceed the perceived benefit. Even John Stuart Mill, that peace-loving philosopher, was not soft on this point: "War may be stigmatized universally, and we are quite ready to give our vote for its abolition in a universal congress of mankind; but while the enemies of freedom are allowed to levy their vassals, embattle their slaves, and organize their dupes, assuredly the friends of freedom have a right to employ their own thews and sinews to check the onward flow of barbarism and tyranny" ([1837] 1989, 364).

Mill, who liked to look ahead to stationary states and conditions where all forces had been resolved, could conceive of a period ahead when some sort of international organization analogous to a domestic police force would guarantee the peace. But he did not see it coming any time soon.

> If it were possible, as it will be in time, that the powers of Europe should, by agreement among themselves, adopt a common rule for the regulation of wars of political opinion, as they have already adopted so many for the regulation of their private quarrels, it is easy to see what the purport of the agreement should be when a struggle breaks out anywhere between the despotic and the democratic principles, the powers should never interfere singly; when they interfere at all, it should be jointly, as a general European police, when the two parties are so unequal in strength that one can easily prevail, and keep the other down, things should be allowed to take their course. If parties are nearly balanced, and general anarchy or protracted civil war, is likely to ensue, the powers should interfere collectively, and force the combatants to lay down their arms and come to a compromise, and should send their own troops against the party that refused to do it. . . . It is simply the first step towards getting rid of war; a beginning towards doing for public wars what was done for private wars when tribunals were established to adjudicate the quarrels from which those wars arose, and a police to execute the decision. ([1837] 1989, 374–75)

Conclusions

This review of what some classical economists had to say about war and national security does not yield any startling surprises. They did what one might expect, which is to bring their models and their mindset to this particular applied area of their science and the policy questions it turned up. For the most part they treated the issue of conflict in familiar "economizing" ways. Sometimes, they postulated, it was profitable (when benefits exceeded costs) for one nation to attack another. The economist's primary task was to discover the conditions under which this situation occurred and contrive ways to change them. A secondary task for economists was to understand the behavior of the economy if war unhappily did break out and to advise on the efficiency questions that were presented therein. The most intriguing theoretical puzzle presented by conflict was the "Chalmers paradox" concerning the effect of war on economic growth. This paradox was solved by the theoretical advances of John Rae.

One contrast evident from this review is between the rich and suggestive reflections of Adam Smith, writing from a broad social-scientific perspective, and the more constrained approach of Malthus, Ricardo, and Mill, writing as they were with the limiting forces of a set of well-specified economic models. The appearance of Schumpeter's "Ricardian vice" may have had its costs in this applied field too.

References

Fawcett, Henry. 1888. *The Manual of Political Economy.* 7th ed. London: Macmillan.

Malthus, Robert. [1798] 1986. An Essay on the Principle of Population. In *The Works of Robert Malthus,* vol. 1. London: William Pickering.

———. [1826] 1986. An Essay on the Principle of Population. In *The Works of Robert Malthus,* vol. 2.

Mill, John Stuart. [1824] 1965. War Expenditure. *Westminster Review* 2 (July). Reprinted in *The Collected Works of John Stuart Mill,* vol. 4, *Essays in Economics and Society.* Toronto: University of Toronto Press.

———. [1837] 1989. The Spanish Question. In *Collected Works,* vol. 23, *Miscellaneous Writings.*

———. [1848] 1965. *Principles of Political Economy with Some of Their Applications to Social Philosophy.* In *Collected Works,* vol. 4, *Essays in Economics and Society.*

Rae, John. [1834] 1965. *Statement of Some New Principles on the Subject of Political Economy.* Edited by R. Warren James. Toronto: University of Toronto Press.

Ricardo, David. [1817] 1951. On the Principles of Political Economy, and Taxation. In *The Works and Correspondence of David Ricardo.* Cambridge: Cambridge University Press.

Senior, Nassau. [1836] 1938. *An Outline of the Science of Political Economy.* London: George Allen & Unwin.

Smith, Adam. [1776] 1976. *An Inquiry into the Nature and Causes of the Wealth of Nations.* Edited by R. H. Campbell and A. S. Skinner. Oxford: Clarendon Press.

The Economics of Defense in British Political Economy, 1848–1914

John K. Whitaker

Paucity is the most striking feature of British writing on the economics of defense in the late classical and neoclassical periods. The general economic treatises of the era pay little or no attention to the question and hardly recognize its existence. Even among treatments of public finance, only Bastable (1892) attempts a serious discussion of the cost of defense, devoting a chapter to the matter. The useful articles on the same topic in the two editions of *Palgrave's Dictionary of Political Economy* were supplied by Spenser Wilkinson, the doyen of British defense experts but hardly an economist. Apart from a few obiter dicta, some noted below, major economists such as J. S. Mill, Fawcett, Jevons, Marshall, Sidgwick, Edgeworth, Wicksteed, and Pigou ignored in their pre-1914 writings the entire range of issues raised by the existence of war and defense needs. It is only in the occasional writings of some lesser economists, writings typically viewed as more political than economic, that serious issues of defense economics are addressed, with interesting contributions by Walter Bagehot, Thomas Edward Cliffe Leslie, John Elliott Cairnes, and Robert (later Sir Robert) Giffen, the last being (at least among the mainstream) the economist most prolifically and consistently concerned with the interface of war and economics in our period.

I interpret the economics of defense as a branch of the theory of economic policy concerned with structural questions involving the appropriate *peacetime* organization of the economy and its defense sector. To use a distinction familiar from discussions of monetary policy, it is concerned with rules rather than discretion. Such a restricted conception excludes consideration of tactical issues of how best to conduct and finance an ongoing war.[1] It also excludes speculations on the causal interrelations between war and economic life. Thus I leave aside such

---

1. Thus, for example, a series of notes in the *Economic Journal* on the financing of the Boer War will be left aside. See Bastable 1900, 1901, 1902; Giffen 1901b; Hirst 1900; Price 1900. See also Giffen 1899. Pigou (1921) gives an excellent general treatment of the problems of organizing a war economy.

matters as Ruskin's (1866) strange paean to war as a civilizing force, or the period's literature—mainly socialist—on the economic causes of war, subsequently assessed by Robbins (1939). Despite such exclusions, no hard and fast line can be drawn between the economics of defense, or perhaps better the political economy of defense, and the more extensive range of topics that might be collected under some such portmanteau rubric as "war and economics."[2] Defense strategy for peacetime cannot be settled rationally without contingency plans for moving to a war footing should the need arise: strategy implies some prevision of future tactics. Moreover, since the size and effectiveness of the defense sector influence the likely incidence of war, some estimate of the probable cost of war is needed in order to judge how much peacetime defense procurement is worthwhile. For this reason Giffen's attempt to estimate ex post the costs of the Franco-Prussian War is described below, despite its lack of immediate bearing on defense decisions.

Of course, the incidence and cost of war depend, complexly, upon policy decisions that extend far beyond those of defense provision: upon policies concerning foreign trade, colonies, and treaty obligations, for example. But even where defense provision is concerned, it is by no means clear that greater provision implies greater security, because an arms race might be precipitated. Arms races were a prominent feature of the period, culminating in the Anglo-German Dreadnought competition in the decade or so before the "Great War" of 1914–18. But this feature of the problem does not seem—with the partial exception of Bagehot—to have been recognized as posing a new *analytical* problem. The tendency was to ask how Britain should react to given military developments abroad. The problem of defense provision was typically viewed as one of deciding how much in the way of defense resources should be provided in total and how these resources should be allocated in detail in order to ward off a given foreign threat. In this broad sense, the characteristic approach was thoroughly neoclassical, focusing on questions of optimal resource allocation among given ends.

A sketch of some contributions to defense economics in the classical era seems necessary as a prelude to discussion of the 1848–1914 period. After that I deal with four specific topics: (1) setting and controlling the level of spending for the defense sector (essentially the army and navy); (2) organizing the army; (3) organizing the economy outside the defense

2. The wider range of issues is dealt with, rather haphazardly, by Silberner (1946), who also covers the American and Continental literature: see also Silberner 1939. For further references on war and economics and useful bibliographies see Robinson 1900; Rosenbaum 1942; Anon. 1907; Mendershausen 1940. See McGuire 1987 for evidence that definitional issues still remain largely unresolved. Pigou (1921, chs. 1–2) gives a lucid overview of defense economics and the economic causes of war.

sector with an eye to defense; (4) calculating the cost of war. In conclusion I speculate on the reasons for the dearth of writing about defense matters by British economists in the era, almost two-thirds of a century, being reviewed.

Classical Views on Defense Economics

Writing towards the end of a century dominated by British involvement in major war, Adam Smith gave considerable attention to the economic implications of warfare, tracing the military effects of changing technology and increased division of labor. He plumped firmly, in his own age, for basing land defense upon a standing army rather than a militia, although he favored universal military exercises as a supplement or at least as an antidote to the dehumanizing effects of extreme specialization of labor. Under the dictum that "defence is of much more importance than opulence" ([1776] 1976, 1:464–65) he defended the Navigation Laws insofar as they protected the British merchant marine: a special case of the national-defense argument for protection, because war conditions transformed the merchant marine into a valuable naval asset. In an era in which war was largely a spectator sport he urged the practice of tax- rather than loan-financing of war expenditures in order to curb jingoism at home: sometimes avoidance of offense is the best defense.[3]

Ricardo extensively debated questions of war finance. The concept of "Ricardian equivalence" stems from this debate, although it was hardly espoused by Ricardo, who took a line similar to Smith's. With Britain no longer self-sufficient in food, Ricardo opposed the permanent protection on national defense grounds of agriculture, taking the view that a complete interruption of supplies from abroad was improbable given Britain's naval might and the likely existence of several neutral supply sources. He argued that domestic agriculture could be expanded if prolonged war occurred or seemed imminent, and he favored only temporary protection to alleviate the phasing down of agriculture after such an expansion.[4]

Ricardo's popularization of the theory of comparative costs, and his extolling of the benefits of international division of labor due to free trade, gave rise to a line of thought, well exemplified by Senior and McCulloch, that threw general doubt on the national security argument for protection and indeed predicted a decline in the incidence of war among advanced nations. Attacking a country's foreign customers harms the attacking country's own producers. Freedom of trade and

3. For Smith's views on defense see Smith 1776, bk. 6, ch. 2; bk. 5, chs. 1, 3; Bullock 1936, 121–29.
4. For Ricardo's views on defense see Silberner 1946, 16–36.

the resulting international economic integration were seen as creating strong incentives to avoid war while also providing the best ultimate potential for defense in a highly productive and wealthy economy. As Senior put the matter: "an attempt at commercial independence must infinitely increase the chances of a war to a nation by diminishing the incentives to remain at peace with her, and, by impoverishing her, must make her less able to support the wars to which it inevitably leads" (1828, 51; see also 49–50). As McCulloch asked, "can anything be more contradictory than the attempt to increase the defence or security of a country by enacting measures that must necessarily fetter and narrow its commerce?" (1843, 159–60).[5]

By the 1840s the general tenor of classical thought was firmly set in the direction of viewing war as irrational and destructive, as largely provoked by adherence to the false economic doctrines gathered under the label of mercantilism, and as lying largely outside the ambit of a political economy conceived as based on rational behavior.[6] The need for maintaining an effective army and navy was, of course, not denied, and the occasional national-security exception to free trade and laissez faire was conceded, if downplayed. Nevertheless war between civilized societies was seen as increasingly improbable and at variance with the entire spirit of the age.

Richard Cobden, an inveterate opponent of defense spending, became the most vocal and prominent exponent of such views after 1848. Thorold Rogers and the Cobden Club carried the tradition down to the twentieth century, when Norman Angell resuscitated it in his influential *The Great Illusion* (1911), albeit with much more emphasis on financial, as opposed to commercial, interdependence among nations.[7]

Setting and Controlling Defense Spending

The broad facts of the changing nominal level of defense spending by Britain over the relevant period are displayed in table 1. Deflation of nominal expenditures to obtain real expenditures is difficult, partly because of the conceptual problem of determining the appropriate deflator and partly because of a serious lack of adequate wage and price indices. For what they are worth, figures for the Sauerbeck-Statist price index and the Wood-Bowley money-wage index are included in the table. The defense of the British Empire was also supported by contributions from India, which financed much of the Indian army, especially

5. McCulloch did not dismiss the national-defense justification entirely and gave it more weight in the fifth edition (1864). See McCulloch 1843, 153–60; 1864, 109–11.
6. See Senior 1828, 42, and McCulloch 1864, 191, for statements that defense issues lie outside the bounds of political economy.
7. Cobden's views are scattered through Cobden 1867.

Table 1. British Military Expenditure, Prices, and Wages, 1850–1915

Year	Expenditure[a] (in millions of pounds)			Prices[b] (1867–77 = 100)	Money Wages[c] (1850 = 100)
	Army	Navy	Total		
1850	8.9	6.2	15.1	77	100
1855	13.8	13.7	27.5	101	116
1860	14.1	10.8	24.9	99	114
1865	15.0	10.9	25.9	101	126
1870	12.1	9.4	21.5	96	133
1875	14.0	10.5	24.5	96	154
1880	15.0	10.2	25.2	88	147
1885	18.6	11.4	30.0	72	149
1890	17.4	15.3	32.7	72	163
1895	17.9	15.5	33.4	62	162
1900	43.6	26.0	69.6	75	179
1905	36.7	35.5	72.2	72	175
1910	27.2	35.8	63.0	78	187
1915	28.9	51.6	80.5	108	—

Source: Mitchell and Deane 1962, 343–45, 396–98, 474–75.
[a]Based on Parliamentary Estimates
[b]Sauerbeck-Statist Wholesale Price Index
[c]Wood-Bowley index of average money wages, not allowing for unemployment

the native troops, and (to a small extent) from the self-governing dominions. (The respective contributions of India and the Dominions were £15 million and £2 million in 1890: see Wilkinson 1894.)

The most evident feature of the table is the secular rise in defense spending (note that only 1855, 1900, and 1915 were years of major war). As Bastable remarked, "It is as certain as any prediction in social matters can be, that no reduction in the military budgets of Europe will soon be made; on the contrary, there is every probability that this form of expenditure will go on increasing in the future as it has done in the past" (1892, 54). Along Smithian lines, Bastable attributed this secular growth to the progress of invention and the division of labor. But he also recognized the arms-race or game-theoretic aspect of the situation, quoting Montesquieu's oft-repeated observation that "a new disease has spread through Europe; it has seized our sovereigns and makes them maintain an inordinate number of troops—as soon as one State increases its forces the others at once increase theirs, so that nothing is gained by it except general ruin" (Bastable 1892, 59, from Montesquieu 1748, book 13, ch. 17). As already indicated, the interdependence of national defense policies tended to be glossed over, with Britain viewed as merely responding to developments abroad. At least this was true of military provision, the navy being widely regarded as a special case. However, Bagehot stands as an exception to this general rule, explicitly recommending that Britain adopt a "follower" policy in the arms-race game of strategy.

Bagehot (1862a, 1862b) published a remarkable discussion of the problems of determining and controlling defense spending under a democratic parliamentary government. The backdrop was the alarm raised by the military deficiencies revealed in the Crimean war of 1853–56, by the increasingly apparent military and naval ambitions of Napoleon III, and by the rapid change in naval technology as iron-hulled ships replaced wood-hulled ones. Naval expenditure had risen from £5.8 million in 1851 to £13.3 million in 1861, and something of a naval arms race between Britain and France was in progress. British military spending had also risen substantially: from £9 million in 1851 to £15 million in 1861.

Bagehot drolly punctured the notion that the determination of defense spending could be left to the advice of technical experts, overseen by a harried and distracted cabinet, ultimately driven by public opinion. Experts are prone to promote the latest innovation, regardless of cost, their recommendations often veering wildly as fresh innovations come over the horizon. Experts are also unlikely to be unanimous. If the British government backs the wrong faction of experts and its opponents back the right faction, all Britain's great expenditure will be in vain. The cabinet has neither the time nor the incentive to consider carefully the justification for any particular level and composition of defense spending, since in Britain this has never been a matter for careful parliamentary and political debate. Public opinion is insufficiently informed to provide guidance to politicians:

> the opinion of what is called the public is simply the opinion of average ordinary persons like myself, who have not paid any particular attention to the subject, and have no special information respecting it. Such persons have no obstinate opinion that twenty-eight millions sterling and no more are necessary for the defence of the country. They know they wish to be safe, and they are ready to pay whatever is necessary to make them safe; but they have no other notion on the subject. ([1862a] 1974, 49)

Even when the public has definite opinions, these are likely to fluctuate violently, because "A is very prone to believe because he thinks B believes, and C to acquiesce in what he imagines to be the accordant opinion of A and B" and so on (50).

The pursuit of the latest in defense technology, almost for its own sake and without regard to what other countries are doing, combined with the lack of reasoned public justification, promotes an expensive international competition in armaments by alarming foreign governments who fail to perceive Britain's intentions: "The really pacific *nature* of England is not comprehended anywhere abroad, because the considerations which regulate the amount of our armaments are only half divulged, and are supposed on the Continent to be in fact offensive, while they really and truly are defensive" ([1862a] 1974, 56).

The remedies proposed by Bagehot are basically two. The first is to adopt a "follower" strategy by changing the level and type of armaments only in response to changes initiated by foreign governments: "Unless you have some standard for your destructive constructions beside the state of science itself, you are launched on a chaos with no hope of a *kosmos*. The true test is the previous industry of competing nations. *Don't begin*. Unless some foreign nation has already made, or is actually making, some new things of the same sort, or something which requires this new sort to resist it, don't commence" ([1862a] 1974, 54). Such a policy, if perceived by foreign governments, would reveal that "our armaments are, as a mathematician would say, only *functions* of foreign armaments; that if foreign nations increase theirs, we shall as a principle increase ours, so that they will gain nothing" (56). Similarly, other countries would lose nothing from reducing armaments.

Bagehot's second remedy is to require that Parliament undertake a full discussion before approving each year's defense budget, a discussion involving detailed justification of each item and indicating "plainly and expressly . . . what foreign work ours was meant to oppose" ([1862a] 1974, 54). The overall level of defense provision would have to be justified by demonstrating "what is the maximum force which it is at all likely may be brought against us, and what is the disposable force with which we are prepared to meet it" (53). The inauguration of such a systematic annual debate would, Bagehot claims, concentrate the mind of the cabinet, help develop and inform parliamentary and public opinion, and, not least, allay foreign fears and resentments by making clear the reactive character of Britain's actions.

Bagehot did not pursue in detail the calculation of the naval and military forces necessary for defense, but he indicated some of the general principles involved for the naval case. He accepted fully the practically unanimous view (shared even by Cobden) that Britain must maintain absolute naval supremacy at all costs. Losing control of the seas would render Britain and her far-flung empire vulnerable to invasion or dismemberment. Continental nations ought to concede such naval supremacy to Britain, recognizing her unique position. Just what force should Britain be prepared to oppose? The home fleet alone would need to be as large as the combined fleet of any plausible coalition of opposed powers, and naval resources above this would be required for policing the world's oceans and protecting distant dependencies and coaling stations.

> We must have a defensive force equal to the attacking force. It is obvious that, as our fleet *must* be distributed, and theirs *may* be concentrated, ours should be much larger than theirs. . . . Equality in figures is inferiority in reality. France, too, may not be alone. A coalition between her and any other great naval power may not be likely, but it is possible; it is within those fair limits of reasonable probability which should regulate our measures of precaution. The Stock Exchange was excited not very long since to its inmost capitalists by a rumour that there was a general combination between France and Russia . . . we should take *some* precaution against a contingency of which the very anticipation is so dangerous and so fatal. ([1862b] 1974, 61)

The notion that the British navy should be maintained at a level equal to the combined forces of the two next-most-powerful naval powers— the so-called two-navy rule—was to become an axiom of popular thinking about defense in the decades leading up to the Great War of 1914– 18.[8] Robert Giffen, writing in 1901, fully accepted the general line of thought: "The condition of the British Empire without command of the sea is hardly conceivable. We should then be at the mercy of any Power which had such command. Our communications could not be maintained. We should be liable to blockade at home and to the ruin of our foreign commerce, nor could we keep India or any other dependency by force" ([1901a] 1904, 243). Giffen saw the two-navy rule as simplistic but as providing a reasonable initial basis for judging the adequacy of naval provision. Such a clear-cut basis was entirely lacking in the case of military provision, and Giffen's contribution was to attempt a reasoned justification—a "business estimate," as he termed it—for military manpower requirements.[9] He did so without reference to Bagehot's ideas. Giffen was, of course, not the first individual to analyze matters of such centrality to British defense debates, just as Bagehot was not the first to discuss naval needs.[10] But their contributions seem to have been the only efforts in the period by writers with stature as economists to approach the question of overall defense requirements.

---

8. The adherence to such a rule probably helped fuel the Dreadnought race with Germany in the decade before 1914. For the background see Marder 1961; Padfield 1974.

9. Giffen's invocation of a "business estimate" may well have been a reaction to the discussion of Dilke 1900, in which Giffen participated. There were several allusions there to what a businessman might do to rationalize defense.

10. For background on the character of the British armed forces of this era and on the public debates and political forces impinging upon them see, for example, Marder 1940, 1961, and Ranft 1977 on the navy and Hamer 1970, Harries-Jenkins 1977, Skelley 1977, and Spiers 1980 on the army.

Britain's unique island position and her extensive but scattered empire called for a unique naval provision. The same factors differentiated her military needs from those of the great Continental powers, facing each other with massed armies across extended land frontiers. Seaborne invasion was the threat to Britain, and it could hardly be on a massive scale providing that Britain maintained naval supremacy. Apart from the special case of India, where the Russian threat was hardly imminent due to the hard terrain and intractable hill tribes, defense of the overseas empire called primarily for mobile forces ready to meet attacks of moderate scale, probably also seaborne. Treaty obligations and political considerations might require an expeditionary force capable of fighting on the Continent, but there was no need to replicate the military might of the great Continental powers.

Giffen's "methodology" was unsophisticated and consisted merely of a detailed classification of the various needs to be provided for with a commonsense guess at the minimum troop requirement to meet each need. His estimates of total *peacetime* manpower requirements were 110,000 for the United Kingdom (40,000 being kept in Ireland, where insurrection or invasion seemed likeliest) and 160,000 for the Empire (70,000 being kept in India, supported by an additional 125,000 native troops), together with 90,000 recruits in training and a trained reserve of 160,000 men able to move rapidly to a war footing.[11] The total peacetime manpower requirement of 360,000 troops and 160,000 reserves exceeded considerably the 250,000 troops and 90,000 reserves actually available but still fell far short of the vast armies of the Continent.[12]

The significance of Giffen's contribution lies not so much in the details of his calculations and justifications as in the fact of his attempting to think systematically and quantitatively about overall defense needs, thus providing a basis for further rational discussion. The weakness of his approach was his reliance on an estimate of "need" independent of cost considerations. Marginal ideas were absent from his thinking. In extenuation it should be stressed that his concern was with minimal defense requirements, where "the profit to be derived . . . in the security of social order and freedom from international disturbance is so overwhelmingly great that is worth the price and more" ([1901a] 1904, 262). He urged that, in line with engineering practice, a large additional margin should be added for "under-estimates and the unforseen" (256), and in setting such an insurance margin we might imagine that more explicit cost-benefit balancing would have seemed appropriate. The

11. Britain's long-established militia, volunteers, and yeomanry were dismissed widely as of trivial military value.

12. In 1910 Britain could mobilize rapidly an army of 300,000 men against France's 1.2 million or Germany's 1.8 million. See Wilkinson 1925.

general need for such balancing had already been clearly stated by Sidgwick, although without specific reference to defense spending:

> We cannot properly take governmental expenditure as something of which the amount is fixed prior to the consideration of the methods of supplying it and their effects. Practically, no doubt, the problem of finance is often presented to a statesman in this simplified form: but theoretically we must regard both expenditure and supply [of revenue] as having at least a margin within which the restriction or enlargement of either must partly depend on the effects of the corresponding restriction or enlargement of the other; within which, therefore, the gain secured to the public by an additional increment of expenditure has to be carefully weighed against the sacrifices inevitably entailed by the exaction of an additional increment of supply. This remains true even if the sphere of Government be restricted to the "individualistic minimum." . . . No doubt it is the worst possible economy not to make adequate provision for the necessary and acknowledged functions of Government; but adequacy in such cases cannot be defined by a sharp line. Most Englishmen are persuaded that they at present enjoy very tolerable protection of person and property against enemies within and without the country; but it would be difficult to argue that our security would not be enhanced by more and better-paid judges and policemen, or more and better-equipped soldiers and sailors. (1883, 543–44)

Considerations of cost were not entirely absent from Giffen's thinking. If Britain were to continue to rely on its traditional system of voluntary recruitment, rates of military pay would have to be increased substantially to accomplish the desired manpower increase. Indeed current pay was inadequate to maintain even the current establishment at acceptable quality. Giffen proposed that the total remuneration in cash and kind of the common soldier be raised to equal the average industrial wage. Together with the needed expansion in numbers, this would require an increase of one-third or more in the annual military budget, a large increase but manageable, to Giffen's mind, in the light of rapidly growing national income and wealth.

Army Organization and Cost: Voluntarism versus Conscription

The insufficient size, high cost, and organizational inadequacies of the British army were a continued source of public concern throughout our period.[13] Prussia's spectacular military successes against Austria in

13. See Hamer 1970.

1866 and France in 1870 helped precipitate a debate on the cost and organization of the British army, evoking interesting contributions from Cliffe Leslie (1867) and Cairnes (1871). Since the two presented virtually identical views, the same general description serves for both.

Three military "systems" are distinguished: that of voluntary recruitment with an extended period of service (the British model), that of conscription for an extended period by lottery with paid substitution permitted (the French model), and that of universal military obligation with a limited period of initial service followed by an extended reserve obligation (the Prussian model). The first two systems produce what are in effect "standing armies," the latter a "national army," resembling in its high ratio of trained reserves to active troops the old-style militia discredited by Adam Smith. However, both our authors demur from Smith's preference for a standing army over a militia and opt firmly for the national-army model.

An important ground for preferring a national army is that it will avoid the development of a military caste, out of tune with the dominant feelings of the nation, a caste prone to adventurism and to serving as a tool of autocratic elements in society. Moreover, in order to put the whole army in the field, reserves will have to be called up, withdrawing suddenly a large fraction of the economically active population from civil life at enormous opportunity cost. This cost will make even more unlikely the use of such an army for military adventurism, although the army will be immensely effective in defending hearth and home against invasion.

It had to be conceded, especially after 1870, that the imputed pacific tendencies were hardly manifested by Prussia's national army. This was accounted for by Prussia's peculiar history and constitution, together with the rather long period of initial service (three years) that introduced a large "standing" component. The Swiss army, in which a universal military obligation seldom required more than 180 days total training over a twenty-five-year period of eligibility for call-up, was put forward as a closer approximation to the national-army ideal.

Whatever the political and strategic advantages attributed to a national army, cost considerations alone made it the only adequate basis for defense in a world in which large armies could be mobilized rapidly and transported en masse, as by Prussia in 1870, and in which economic and civil life was increasingly vulnerable to disruption. Once invented, the national army was a device all countries would be forced in self-defense to adopt. Whatever its innate pacific tendencies, such an army could become an aggressive instrument in the hands of an autocratic government, and the sheer scale of numbers it could bring into the field at short notice could be matched by a standing army only at crushing cost, especially if the standing army relied on voluntary enlistment, as Britain's did. In urging this, both Leslie and Cairnes seem to have assumed implicitly that Britain must match the manpower of the Continental powers to a greater extent than Giffen later called for.

Of the three military systems, the British was much the most expensive. Cairnes ([1871] 1873, 205) calculated that the cost of a soldier was £100 a year in Britain, £41 a year in France, and £29 a year in Prussia. Voluntary enlistment was expensive, partly because an enlistee's full opportunity cost had to be covered in cash and kind and partly because the progress of society made the soldier's trade less and less reputable, calling for an ever-larger compensating differential over civilian employment and biasing recruitment towards those too brutalized to care and hence of low efficiency. Both authors recognized clearly that compulsory military service involved what was in effect a tax on those forced to serve, and that an allowance for this implicit tax should be added to the explicit defense outlays borne by the government if the true cost of defense was to be calculated.[14]

> Where the services of the citizen during his career in the ranks are rated at less than their proper worth, the burden is merely transferred from the nation in its corporate capacity to the individuals who endure the loss; and as this is probably more or less the case with all armies raised by compulsory recruiting, this circumstance should undoubtedly be taken account of in considering the cost of such armies. (Cairnes [1871] 1873, 212)

> To the real cost of the French army we must add, then, not only every shilling above a soldier's pay which each actual soldier could have earned in a civil occupation, but also the lost value of all the indirect and distant results of invention and special productive capacity. (Leslie [1867] 1879, 137)

As the latter passage indicates, a full comparison of the costs of alternative military systems must extend to far-ranging consequences. An extended period of active service tends to ruin a man for civil life, producing an "old soldier" who needs a pension and generally has a corrupting influence on society.[15] On the other hand, a shorter period of

14. It should have been noted (but was not) that when paid substitutes are accepted the implicit tax is replaced by the explicit payment from substitutor to substitutee. For subsequent considerations of the relative costs of different types of army see Dilke 1891, 1900; Wilkinson 1894, 1909, 1925.

15. See Leslie [1867] 1879, 137–38, for a strong statement along these lines. A modern labor economist might observe that pay and pensions do not represent separate and additive costs and that one may substitute to some extent for the other, since it is the overall package that must compete with civilian alternatives. This fact complicates calculation of the implicit tax borne by conscripts. Bastable (1892, 62) gives the most general definition of the latter, as the amount conscripts would pay to escape military service.

service allows soldiers to return to economic activity, perhaps with increased strength and discipline, but also with less industrial skill and initiative than they would have acquired without the interruption for military service.[16] Also technical progress might be retarded by "the loss of all the men of superior industrial or intellectual power [that conscription] spoils for their natural pursuits" (Leslie, 137; see also 138–43).

Britain's unique situation must in any case preclude sole reliance on conscription: "The immense distance of several of the regions the British soldier must serve in, and the bare cost of moving troops backwards and forwards, render the service necessarily both one of some length, and one which the citizens of a free country could not be compelled to perform" (Leslie [1867] 1879, 145). Such considerations called for a dual system, with a long-service army for overseas and a short-service national army (supported by a long-service cadre of officers) at home. This might be accomplished by reform of the already existing but hopelessly ineffective yeomanry, militia, and volunteers, who merely indulged in military amusements. But some element of compulsion would probably be required to reassure the willing that "the common burden shall not be shirked by any" (Cairnes [1871] 1873, 233).

Despite such arguments Britain was to continue its sole reliance on voluntary enlistment until well into the Great War of 1914–18. But the question of voluntarism versus conscription continued to be aired periodically.[17] Sidgwick saw some merit in the argument that military service ought to be undertaken "from patriotism or a sense of duty, rather than from mercenary motives and a taste for the incidents of the painful business of mutual slaughter" (1883, 545), but he argued for compulsory service mainly on economic grounds. To maintain a large volunteer army, the rates of pay must be high, so that "the burden of taxation requisite to provide for such an army may easily be less endurable than the burden of compulsory service" (545). Bastable concurred that "when the duty of military service is general and enforced without favouritism the sacrifice entailed by it will probably be less felt than if the large amount of additional funds needed under voluntary enlistment had to be levied through taxation" (1892, 61). Giffen, however, argued that preserving the morale of conscripts required that their remuneration not be kept below the civilian average ([1901a] 1904, 261). In favor of voluntarism, Sidgwick (1883, 545) noted that it is more efficient in selecting for military service those whose opportunity cost as civilians is low (although, as Cairnes and Leslie might have observed, by con-

16. There is a risk of double counting. If the implicit tax borne by conscripts is properly calculated, it should in principle already allow for changes in human capital.

17. For example, Wilkinson (1909) makes a strong plea for the British adoption of a national army. See also Giffen 1906.

centrating recruitment on the lowest class this sacrifices the supposed political virtues of a truly national army). Finally, it was observed (Bastable 1892, 62; Dilke 1900, 422) that Britain's high per capita income was an important factor, perhaps as important as reliance on voluntarism, in making absolute cost per soldier much higher for Britain than for the Continental powers.

The period's discussion of the costs of alternative military systems was inconclusive and failed to produce a suitable analytical framework, although many of the requisite general insights were arrived at. Conscription clearly tended to lower explicit costs to the government, but it was recognized that a more general concept of social cost was the relevant one and that no clear presumption of conscription's lower *social* cost per soldier was or could be established. A preference for a national army on economic grounds would have to be justified by its ability to maintain trained reserves at low cost and to maintain in arms during peacetime a smaller fraction of the population than a comparable standing army would require. However, the issue of fundamental army reform never entered seriously into Britain's political agenda. Germany's increasing militarism made the Prussian model seem unappealing and the Swiss model appear ineffective. Britain's naval bulwark came to seem ever more vital and engrossed public and political attention. The mass mobilization of a Continental-style army had to be invented almost from scratch after 1914.

Organizing the Civilian Economy with an Eye on Defense

National-defense justifications for deviating from laissez faire and free trade, although recognized in principle in the 1848–1914 era as they had been in the preceding one, continued to be downplayed in practice and received very little attention. The most general statement is that provided by Sidgwick in the course of his influential treatment of the functions of government:

the needs of war may furnish decisive considerations in favour of measures which would otherwise be inexpedient—although they are not unlikely to be advocated on other than military grounds. Thus a government may reasonably undertake for military reasons the construction of railways commercially unremunerative; or may control the arrangement of a system of railways which it would otherwise leave to unrestricted private enterprise. Again, similar reasons have often been urged for the protection of native industry in certain departments; and certainly, where there is a reasonable probability that a government would find serious difficulty in obtaining, should it be involved in war, any part of the supply of men or things required for the efficient conduct of the war, it is obvious that some kind of provision should be made in time of peace for meeting this difficulty. . . . On similar grounds we cannot say positively that it can never be expedient for a country situated as England is to secure itself by protection to native agriculture against the danger of having its necessary supply of food cut off by a maritime blockade. (1883, 428–29)

Defense of mother country and empire was doubtless an element fueling British debates on protection and imperial preference, debates that reached a crescendo in the last decade of the 1848–1914 period. But the disregard of such considerations in the contributions made by economists to the debate is remarkable, this being the case even for such heterodox economists as Ashley and Cunningham.[18]

In Ricardo's era, securing British self-sufficiency in food and raw materials may have been a feasible option, although not one Ricardo recommended. By the opening of the twentieth century Britain's dependence on imports of these essential commodities was so great that autarky could not be considered seriously. Given the growth of Germany's navy and imperial ambitions, this fact gave rise to a serious public concern with the problem of safeguarding essential imports and ensuring an adequate food supply for the populace in time of war.[19]

Again, the remarkable fact is that economists took no real part in the debate despite being explicitly urged to.[20] The public concern helped lead to the establishment of a royal commission to deal with the question of the supply of food and raw materials in time of war. Henry Cunynghame, a civil servant and amateur economist, was a member, and Walter Layton, later a Cambridge economist but now only a neophyte hoping to embark soon on the Cambridge Tripos, was the assistant secretary. But no established economists gave evidence or presented memoranda, apart perhaps from Charles Booth, who appeared as witness in his role of shipowner and social inquirer rather than that of economist.[21] Cunynghame had, indeed, approached Alfred Marshall about the questions involved, inviting him to present testimony to the commission. Marshall

18. See, for example, Ashley 1903; Cunningham 1904, 1911; Hobson 1904; Money 1903; Pigou 1904, 1906; Smart 1904.

19. See the articles listed under Food Supply in the pertinent volumes of *Poole's Index* and the *Reader's Guide to Periodical Literature* (Fletcher and Poole 1902, 1938; Guthrie 1905, 1910).

20. See the notes on periodical literature in *Economic Journal* 12 (December 1902): 586, which says of Wilkinson 1902 that it "urges economists to make a careful forecast of the economical conditions that would accompany such a war as might threaten our food supply." Also see Fremantle 1903.

21. The commission did include two other dabblers in economics: A. J. Balfour and Henry Chaplin, a bimetallic proponent. H. Llewellyn Smith gave statistical evidence on behalf of the Board of Trade. See Royal Commission 1905.

declined, feeling himself "no authority on either agricultural or military questions," although observing that the commission's topic had been on his mind for many years (Pigou 1925, 447). He nevertheless provided Cunynghame with some suggestions for a scheme to subsidize the storage of wheat reserves in Britain. Cunynghame and others urged variants of such a scheme on the commission, and they did receive extensive consideration, although at best lukewarm endorsement. Marshall's name was not mentioned.[22]

Cunynghame's variant scheme was the most ingenious. He proposed levying on wheat an import duty that was to be rebatable, wholly or in part, as a function of the length of time the wheat was held in bond, four months being suggested as the period earning a full rebate. Importers would have an incentive to keep the wheat stored in a bonded storage facility for the full four months unless the current price was rising rapidly, in which event wheat would be withdrawn from bond, thus restraining the price rise. One criticism raised was that speculative price increases, occurring in anticipation of war, might deplete stocks before war even began (although it would seem more likely that the withdrawn stocks would continue to be held elsewhere than that they would be consumed immediately).

The commission devoted considerable attention to estimating probable increases in the prices of food and raw materials following upon an outbreak of naval warfare, and to analyzing the effects of such price increases on the position of the working classes. That such important matters could be considered without invoking economists as expert witnesses testifies to one or both of two things. Either economists as a group were not particularly interested in the commission's task. Or the public standing of the economics profession was not yet such as to make the involvement of full-time economists seem essential.

Giffen on the Cost of War

Giffen's pioneering study (1872) of the costs of the eight-month-long Franco-Prussian war of 1870–71 is significant more for its conceptual framework than for its numerical estimates, which are frequently cavalier and at best rough and ready given the inadequacies of the available data. Nevertheless the orders of magnitude obtained are of considerable interest.

Giffen divides costs into direct and indirect. Direct costs are the value

---

22. See Royal Commission 1905, 1: 45–52, 133–45, 3:327. The commission's report was firmly premised on the assumption that Britain would retain naval superiority but not the ability to shepherd every merchantman safely to port. A note on the report appeared in *Economic Journal* 15 (December 1905): 609–16 (see also September 1905: 454).

Table 2. Costs of the Franco-Prussian War (in millions of pounds)

	France	Germany
Direct costs		
Government outlays for war	120	60
Destruction of capital	6	—
Requisitions by army of occupation	38	—
Military pension obligations	5	5
Subtotal	169	65
Indirect costs		
Loss of income	150	50
Loss of organizational capital, etc.	112	—
Loss of human capital	102	30
Subtotal	364	80
Total	533	145

Source: Based on estimates presented in Giffen [1872] 1904.

of physical capital destroyed plus government outlays for war purposes. The latter include the capital value of additional military pensions obligated by the war and the value of requisitions from the French populace by the German army of occupation. Direct costs would have been the only costs had the belligerents been able "to carry on their war operations without a stoppage of industry and production, and by hiring soldiers from distant countries with which they had no other relations" (Giffen [1872] 1904, 13). Indirect costs comprise temporary losses of civilian income due to military conscription or wartime disorganization of business, plus permanent losses of the organizational and goodwill capital of businesses induced by wartime dislocation. Identification and estimation of these permanent losses seems particularly hazardous and uncertain. Giffen also calculates the loss of human capital due to war-induced mortality but is reluctant to attach significance to the result. (Each life lost is valued at the cost of an annuity that is equal to the average wage and purchased at age twenty-five).

Giffen's rough estimates of the costs to the belligerents, all costs being expressed in pounds sterling, are summarized in table 2. France, whose territory was subject to combat, occupation, and the ravages of the Paris Commune, bore much greater costs than Germany. To Germany, the war was one fought on foreign soil with minimal domestic disruption apart from the considerable extraction of military reserves from their normal civilian occupations. In the peace settlement, Germany exacted reparation payments of £200 million from France and annexed Alsace-Lorraine. Giffen estimated that the ceding of Alsace-

Lorraine was equivalent to the loss of £64 million capital to France.[23] Thus, taking the overall war costs shown in table 2 and adjusting for reparations and annexation, the net cost of the war to Germany becomes *negative* to the tune of £119 million while France's net cost rises to £797 million. These amounts should be compared to prewar figures for national income per year of about £600 million for each country. Germany, by an eight-month war involving little destruction of German property and limited loss of German life, had made a net profit of some 20 percent of a year's national income—an ominous sign that ruthless exaction of reparations might turn war into a paying proposition for a country prepared to undertake a preemptive strike.

Giffen estimated the reduction in consumption during the war as £88 million for France and £25 million for Germany. Subtracting from each country's postreparation war costs the consumption it has sacrificed yields an estimate of the net change in the country's national wealth consequent on the war: that is, a loss of £709 million for France and a gain of £144 million for Germany. These figures estimate the deviations from what national wealth would have been at the time peace was concluded had there been no war, so that saving would have continued at normal peacetime levels.

Countries other than the belligerents were also affected by the war, but Giffen judged the consequent costs and benefits too minor and imponderable to estimate meaningfully. Considering the war's impact on international capital markets, he was impressed by the slightness of the effects, discerning no sustained changes in world interest rates. From a global viewpoint the economic disturbance due to the war was minor. Even devastated France might recoup its wealth loss surprisingly rapidly:

> all the chances are that the past rate of saving will be greatly increased. The anxiety of each individual in a nation which is habitually thrifty will assuredly be to make up for the storm which has passed over them by the most desperate industry and saving. They will seek in a year or two not only to recover lost ground, but to place themselves at the point of prosperity which they had looked forward to reach at a given period of their lives. ([1872] 1904, 49)

This prediction was to be largely borne out by events.

Giffen's pioneering study of the costs of war is crude and lacks a unified social-accounting framework.[24] Nevertheless his adroitness in

23. This figure reflects primarily the loss of Alsace-Lorraine's contribution to the unchanged fixed cost of France's central government. Transfer of territory considerably complicates the conceptual problem of defining each country's war costs.

24. In a classical vein, Giffen (1872) regards even domestically held national debt as a

steering a sure path among the many pitfalls, and the sheer audacity of his effort, must excite admiration. He later returned to the theme of the economic costs of war and defense (see Giffen 1900, 1901b, 1901c, 1901d, 1902), concluding once more that the affluence and power of accumulation of advanced societies make the costs of defense and war quite tolerable, often surprisingly light, so long as combat does not disrupt the civilian sector. But his early essay contains by far his most remarkable contribution to the topic.

Concluding Reflections

Some basic defense issues were addressed by economists in the 1848–1914 period, and some progress was made in articulating thought about them and providing appropriate frameworks for their analysis. In some ways the modernity of the discussions about the adoption of new defense technology, controlling defense spending, and voluntarism versus conscription, is surprising. Nevertheless economists' discussions on defense-related issues lay well outside the mainstream of the subject and seem hardly to have entered the consciousness of most major economists of the era, or, presumably, of the aspiring young professional economists who now began to appear on the scene.

How are this neglect and lack of interest to be accounted for? One possible line of explanation would be to argue that the century after Waterloo was unprecedentedly peaceful, so that public attention, and with it economists' attention, turned from war to peace. It is true that extended major European wars did not occur, yet the view of the nineteenth century as predominantly peaceful is easily overstated and was strongly controverted by Leslie as early as 1860 (see 1860a, 1860b). After 1870 one had to be something of an ostrich to fail to observe the fact that Europe was turning into an armed camp. Military and naval issues became prominent in British popular consciousness and debate, and it would be difficult to argue that British economists evaded defense issues because of their unimportance or a lack of public concern about them.

An alternative line of explanation would emphasize the internal dynamics of the discipline of economics as it became professionally self-conscious and sought to establish claims to legitimacy as *the* authority on certain central concerns. Preoccupied as its practitioners were with working out long-run value and distribution theory, other issues, seen as

---

liability in the national balance sheet. This can be reconciled with his calculations by recognizing that he assumes tax-financed government expenditure is entirely at the expense of private consumption whereas bond-financed government expenditure is entirely at the expense of private investment. Thus an increase in national debt represents an equal sacrifice of private capital. See also Giffen [1901d] 1904, 295–96, 298–99.

only peripheral to the subject, might be expected to suffer neglect. There may be some truth to such arguments in the case of someone as unworldly as Edgeworth, yet the bearing on economists such as Marshall and Jevons, both of whom had a strong interest in applied questions, seems remote. Moreover, by the turn of the century many of the young professionals who had been newly trained to the subject were embarking on a substantial program of applied studies (see Jha 1963). It seems puzzling that some of their efforts were not turned to questions of defense. But in support of the general line of argument it should be conceded that there was a tendency to view detailed discussions of defense issues as more politics than economics. Cairnes's 1871 article, for example, was reprinted as one of his *political* essays and not included in his economic essays. Leslie's 1867 article was eliminated from his collected essays when the second edition narrowed the scope from "political and moral philosophy" (Leslie 1879) to "political economy" (1888).

Even if professional preoccupations did not blind economists to the existence of defense issues, it might be argued that their vocation caused them to perceive these issues in a peculiar way, a way that made the problems seem less pressing and important. In other words, it induced economists to adhere to the Cobdenite position that war was irrational and hence that it was almost unthinkable that civilized nations would actually resort to it. Even Giffen, the economist who most concerned himself with defense matters, came close to such a position (see Giffen 1907). In an interesting anticipation of Angell (1911), Giffen stressed that the great commercial and financial interdependence of the advanced nations could make disruption due to hostilities enormously costly to all parties. But rather than draw the Cobdenite conclusion that all nations would, in consequence, voluntarily refrain from war, Giffen argued for deterrence. Defense should be, not emasculated, but made so compelling that an aggressor would face even greater and more prohibitive costs.

The Cobdenite argument that given a universal and inviolable commitment to free trade, war can yield no economic benefit to the victor though acquisition of territory or access to markets is largely incontrovertible—only "largely" because, for example, a budget surplus levied on acquired territories might help support the original territories. But the proviso about free trade is an important one. Gaining control of, or access to, hitherto protected markets can bring economic gain. By the opening of the twentieth century it was difficult to believe that free trade was the norm, and increasingly difficult to see national ambitions as primarily driven by economic considerations, even though Kaiser Wilhelm was no Hitler. The economic disruption due to war, as highlighted—perhaps exaggerated—by Angell, undoubtedly served as a deterrent, as did the prospect of loss of life and capital due to hostilities. Yet even leaving aside the ominous possibility of reparations, it was increasingly difficult to argue that there could be no long-term national (as opposed to cosmopolitan) gains, economic or noneconomic, that could induce a nation to embark on war despite large short-term costs. Deterrence sought to raise these costs sufficiently to eliminate any incentive to incur them—that was Giffen's 1907 position.[25] The alternative, as Leslie had hopefully urged (1860b), was the institution of some kind of supranational system of arbitration and conflict resolution, an idea that was to come into prominence only in the 1920s.

The British defense debates of the period had a large peculiarity that may help account for the limited participation of economists. This was the overwhelming preoccupation with naval might. The need for Britain to control the seas seems to have been an unquestioned axiom of all thinking about defense. Once the transition from sail and timber to steam and iron was firmly accomplished, naval issues seem to have boiled down to the simple question of whether Britain had enough ships, and the answer tended to be found in some simple rule of thumb, such as the two-navy rule. Perhaps because belief in Britain's naval supremacy was so strong, the navy was never seriously put to the test of combat during the century after Waterloo, so that deficiencies were not made manifest (as they were by the army's not infrequent debacles).[26] With the navy largely removed from controversy, and with the cost of meeting naval needs apparently driven by a fixed reaction function generated by considerations of naval strategy, there was not much left for economists to grapple with. Military reform, of course, provided ample scope for economic analysis, but the army was outranked by the Senior Service, not only nominally but also in public priorities and concern. Thus the incentives for economists to address defense issues were attenuated.

References

Angell, Norman. 1911. *The Great Illusion.* New York: Putnam.
[Anon.] 1907. *A Library of Peace and War.* Darlington, England: Speaker Publishing Co.
Ashley, W. J. 1903. *The Tariff Problem.* London: King.

25. Mention might also be made of a much earlier discussion by Fawcett (1888, 30–32), who recommends deterrence through the announcement of a retributive intention to devastate an attacker's fixed capital, thus precluding his rapid postwar recovery.

26. Economists may like to note that while at Eton, the youthful R. G. Hawtrey published a severe criticism (1897) of naval speed trials, producing a heated reply (White 1897) that took, in a postscript, the rather curious position that a reply would not have been deigned had the writer been aware that the criticisms came from a schoolboy. Hawtrey does not seem to have followed up this early interest.

Bagehot, W. [1862a] 1974. *Count Your Enemies and Economise Your Cost.* London: Ridgway. Reprinted in Bagehot 1974.

———. [1862b] 1974. The Limits of Defense Outlay: Mr. Cobden's Three Panics. *The Economist* 20 (26 April): 449–50. Reprinted in Bagehot 1974.

———. 1974. *The Collected Works of Walter Bagehot.* Vol. 8, *Political Essays.* Edited by N. St. J. Stevas. London: The Economist.

Bastable, C. F. 1892. *Public Finance.* London: Macmillan.

———. 1900. Note on the Budget of 1900. *Economic Journal* 10 (June): 208–10.

———. 1901. The Budget of 1901. *Economic Journal* 11 (June): 224–25.

———. 1902. The Budget of 1902. *Economic Journal* 12 (June): 261–63.

Bullock, J. 1936. *Economic Essays.* Cambridge: Harvard University Press.

Cairnes, J. E. [1871] 1873. Our Defences: A National or a Standing Army? *Fortnightly Review,* o.s. 15 (February): 167–98. Reprinted in his *Political Essays.* London: Macmillan.

Cobden, Richard. 1867. *The Political Writings of Richard Cobden.* London: Ridgway.

Cunningham, W. 1904. *The Rise and Decline of the Free Trade Movement.* London: Clay.

———. 1911. *The Case against Free Trade.* London: Murray.

Dilke, Sir Charles W. 1891. Statistics of the Defence Expenditure of the Chief Naval and Military Powers. *Journal of the Royal Statistical Society* 54 (March): 1–21.

———. 1900. The Defence Expenditure of the Empire. *Journal of the Royal Statistical Society* 63 (September): 410–20.

Fawcett, H. 1888. *Manual of Political Economy.* 7th ed. London: Macmillan.

Fletcher, W. I., and M. Poole, eds. [1902] 1963. *Poole's Index to Periodical Literature: Fourth Supplement (1887–1901).* Reprinted, Gloucester, Mass.: Smith.

———. [1938] 1963. *Poole's Index to Periodical Literature: Fifth Supplement (1902–1906).* Reprinted, Gloucester, Mass.: Smith.

Fremantle, E. R. 1903. Our Food Supply and Raw Materials in War. *Fortnightly Review,* o.s. 79 (February): 355–58.

Giffen, R. [1872] 1904. The Cost of the Franco-German War. Privately printed. Reprinted in Giffen 1904 (also reprinted in Giffen 1880).

———. 1880. *Essays in Finance.* London: Bell.

———. [1899] 1904. Consols in a Great War. *Economic Journal* 9 (September): 353–64. Reprinted in Giffen 1904.

———. [1900] 1904. Some Economic Aspects of the War. *Economic Journal* 10 (June): 197–207. Reprinted in Giffen 1904.

———. [1901a] 1904. The Standard of Strength for Our Army: A Business Estimate. *Nineteenth Century and After* 49 (June): 931–48. Reprinted in Giffen 1904.

———. 1901b. Further Notes on Economic Aspects of the War. *Economic Journal* 11 (March): 1–11.

———. 1901c. City Notes. *Economic Journal* 11 (September): 455–57.

———. [1901d] 1904. Are We Living on Capital? Address to the Institute of Bankers, 22 May. Reprinted in Giffen 1904.

———. [1902] 1904. A Financial Retrospect, 1861–1901. *Journal of the Royal Statistical Society* 65 (March): 47–75. Reprinted in Giffen 1904.

———. 1904. *Economic Inquiries and Studies.* 2 vols. London: Bell.

———. 1906. Is the British Empire Safe? A Note on National Service. *Nineteenth Century and After* 59 (April): 543–45.

————. 1907. English Commerce in a Naval War. *Nineteenth Century and After* 62 (August): 177–86.

Guthrie, A. L., ed. 1905. *Reader's Guide to Periodical Literature*. Vol. 1, *1900–1904*. Minneapolis: Guthrie.

————. 1910. *Reader's Guide to Periodical Literature*. Vol. 2, *1905–1909*. Minneapolis: Guthrie.

Hamer, W. S. 1970. *The British Army: Civil and Military Relations, 1885–1905*. London: Oxford University Press.

Harries-Jenkins, G. 1977. *The Army in Victorian Society*. London: Routledge & Kegan Paul.

Hawtrey, R. G. 1897. The Speed of Warships. *Fortnightly Review,* o.s. 68 (September): 435–44.

Hirst, F. W. 1900. The War Budget. *Economic Journal* 10 (March): 105–8.

Hobson, J. A. 1904. *International Trade: An Application of Economic Theory*. London: Methuen.

Jha, N. 1963. *The Age of Marshall*. Patna: Novelty.

Leslie, T. E. C. [1860a] 1879. The Question of the Age—Is It Peace? *Macmillan's Magazine* 2 (May): 72–88. Reprinted in Leslie 1879.

————. [1860b] 1879. The Future of Europe Foretold in History. *Macmillan's Magazine* 2 (September): 329–38. Reprinted in Leslie 1879.

————. [1867] 1879. The Military Systems of Europe. *North British Review* 47 (December): 210–30. Reprinted with some deletions in Leslie 1879.

————. 1879. *Essays in Political and Moral Philosophy*. London, etc.: Longmans Green.

————. 1888. *Essays in Political Economy*. London, etc.: Longmans Green.

McCulloch, J. R. 1843. *Principles of Political Economy*. 4th ed. London: Longmans Brown Green & Longmans.

————. 1864. *Principles of Political Economy*. 5th ed. Edinburgh: Black.

McGuire, M. C. 1967. Defence Economics. In *The New Palgrave: A Dictionary of Economics,* edited by J. Eatwell, M. Milgate, and P. Newman. London: Macmillan.

Marder, A. J. 1940. *The Anatomy of British Sea Power: A History of British Naval Policy in the Pre-Dreadnought Era, 1880–1905*. New York: Knopf.

————. [1961] 1978. *From the Dreadnought to Scapa Flow: The Royal Navy in the Fisher Era, 1904–1919*. Rev. ed. London: Oxford University Press.

Mendershausen, H. 1940. *The Economics of War*. New York: Prentice-Hall.

Mitchell, B. R., and P. Deane. 1962. *Abstract of British Historical Statistics*. London: Cambridge University Press.

Money, L. C. 1903. *Elements of the Fiscal Problem*. London: King.

Montesquieu, Charles Louis de Secondat. 1748. *De l'esprit des loix*. Geneva. Translated as *The Spirit of Laws*. London: Nourse & Vaillant, 1773. Many subsequent editions.

Padfield, P. 1974. *The Great Naval Race: The Anglo-German Naval Rivalry 1900–1914*. New York: McKay.

Pigou, A. C. 1904. *The Riddle of the Tariff*. London: Johnson.

————. 1906. *Protective and Preferential Import Duties*. London: Macmillan.

————. 1921. *The Political Economy of War*. London: Macmillan.

————, ed. 1925. *Memorials of Alfred Marshall*. London: Macmillan.

Price, L. L. F. R. 1900. Some Economic Consequences of the South African War. *Economic Journal* 10 (September): 323–39.

Ranft, B. 1977. *Technical Change and British Naval Policy 1860–1939*. London: Hodder & Stoughton.

Robbins, L. C. 1939. *The Economic Causes of War.* London: Cape.
Robinson, E. V. 1900. War and Economics. *Political Science Quarterly* 15 (December): 581–628.
Rosenbaum, E. M. 1942. War Economics: A Bibliographical Approach. *Economica,* n.s. 9 (February): 64–94.
Royal Commission. 1905. *Report of the Royal Commission on Supply of Food and Raw Materials in Time of War.* 3 vols. Cd. 2643–5.
Ruskin, J. [1866] 1873. *A Crown of Wild Olive: Four Lectures on Industry and War.* 4th, expanded ed. London: Smith Elder.
Senior, N. W. 1828. *Three Lectures on the Transmission of Precious Metals from Country to Country and the Mercantile Theory of Wealth.* London: Murray.
Sidgwick, H. 1883. *Principles of Political Economy.* London: Macmillan.
Silberner, E. 1939. *La guerre dans la pensée économique du XVIe au XVIIIe siècle.* Paris: Sirey.
———. 1946. *The Problem of War in Nineteenth Century Economic Thought.* Princeton: Princeton University Press.
Skelley, A. R. 1977. *The Victorian Army at Home: The Recruitment and Terms of Conditions of the British Regular, 1858–99.* London: Croom Helm.
Smart, W. 1904. *The Return to Protection.* London: Macmillan.
Smith, A. [1776] 1976. *An Inquiry into the Nature and Causes of the Wealth of Nations.* London: Strahan & Cadell. Glasgow edition, edited by R. H. Campbell, A. S. Skinner, and W. B. Todd. London: Oxford University Press.
Spiers, E. M. 1980. *The Army and Society, 1815–1914.* London: Longmans.
White, W. H. 1897. The Speed of Warships: Reply. *Fortnightly Review,* o.s. 68 (October): 606–16.
Wilkinson, H. Spenser. 1894. Defence, Cost of. In *Dictionary of Political Economy,* edited by R. H. I. Palgrave, vol. 1. London: Macmillan.
———. 1902. Does War Mean Starvation? *National Review* 40 (November): 472ff.
———. 1909. *Britain at Bay.* New York: Putnam.
———. 1925. Defence, Cost of. In *Palgrave's Dictionary of Political Economy,* edited by H. Higgs. London: Macmillan.

British and American Economists and Attempts to Comprehend the Nature of War, 1910–20

William J. Barber

War is an unpleasant subject—and particularly so for economists whose professional predisposition is to view warfare as the antithesis of what their discipline is about. It is much more congenial to analyze efficiency in production than efficiency in destruction, and much more agreeable to think about the economics of welfare than the economics of warfare.

Nevertheless, even before the guns of August 1914 sounded, a number of economists of high professional standing anticipated Clemenceau in holding that "war is too serious a business to be left to the generals." In their view economic research and analysis, professionally conducted, could make an important contribution to the minimization—if not the elimination—of friction between nation-states. This paper traces the odyssey of important contributors to this discussion and their critics as they sought to cope intellectually with the threat and, later, the reality and the aftermath of the First World War.

The Context of the Debate about the Economics of War, 1910–13

In the early years of this century much of the agenda of discourse on the economic implications of war was set, initially, not by an economist but by a journalist: Norman Angell.[1] With the publication of *The Great Illusion* in 1910 Angell confidently pronounced that war between modern industrial states was an exercise in economic futility. This conclusion, he maintained, was inescapable in light of the basic facts of the evolution of the international economic system. All major countries were interlocked in a network of interdependence: none could afford the

---

1. Born in England in 1872, Angell at the age of seventeen emigrated to the United States, where—after an unsuccessful attempt to establish a homestead claim—he drifted into journalism. He returned to Europe in 1897 and became manager of the continental edition of the *London Daily Mail.* Concerned about the war fever then building up, he produced a monograph in 1909, entitled *Europe's Optical Illusion,* to demonstrate the economic folly of war. Initially this document (which he had underwritten from his own pocket) got little notice. A retitled and expanded version of the argument, published a year later, established his reputation.

derangement of markets that would accompany the outbreak of armed hostilities. Each was dependent on imports for essential supplies, and each required outlets for exports to sustain prosperity. Similarly, the delicate machinery of international finance brought countries closer together. The major European powers had become exporters of capital and, as creditors, could not afford to put assets held abroad at risk. In short, the boundaries of nation-states had largely lost their relevance in a world in which economic activity transcended political jurisdictions.[2]

Contained within this vision was a presupposition that motives which had impelled countries toward war in the past no longer had meaning. Territorial aggrandizement had ceased to be feasible. The misguided ideologies of an early mercantilist era should be discarded: an expanding world economy with an ever-widened division of labor would bring benefits to all. Moreover, the conception that any country could gain from war should be scrapped as an "illusion." The nominal victor would be bound to lose from the disruption of normal economic activity. Nor could it recoup losses by claiming "spoils" from the vanquished.

In an earlier age that outcome might have been possible when the power prevailing on the battlefield could commandeer assets in kind. In the modern world, on the other hand, an indemnity would be a monetary transaction. If the transfer were to be effected, the recipient country would end up behind. Its home prices would rise, causing it to lose export markets and to suffer unemployment. Angell was persuaded that the French indemnity payment to Germany after the Franco-Prussian War demonstrated the truth of this proposition. The French economy had prospered in the later 1870s and the German economy had not. The prospect that a military winner could profit through "tribute" was mistaken.[3]

It should be noted, however, that even some commentators sympathetic to Angell's general position found his treatment of this point technically deficient. One of these was Horace Hadley O'Farrell, who had been commissioned to analyze Angell's contentions by a British philanthropy committed to promoting the cause of peace. O'Farrell concluded that differential performance of the French and German economies in the 1870s could be attributed primarily to broader influences in the world economy, rather than to the transfer of indemnities. In addition he argued that the possibility that a victorious country might gain from exacting "tribute" should not be excluded. But a favorable result turned on special circumstances: (1) the defeated country would have to be rich; (2) its defeat would have to be total; and (3) the military

---

2. See Angell 1912.
3. Angell 1912, part 1, ch. 6.

conflict would have to be brief. These conditions had been satisfied at the end of the Franco-Prussian War, but O'Farrell thought it improbable that they could be replicated.[4]

Angell did not argue that war between industrial powers was impossible. (A number of his critics, incorrectly, alleged that he had done so.) To the contrary, he regarded the outbreak of war as a real and present danger: *The Great Illusion* was inspired by his alarm over the possibility that Anglo-German competition in naval construction, and the jingoistic public attitudes that accompanied it, might provoke disaster. His central point was that war was not inevitable. And, in the context in which he wrote, that conclusion was arresting. Conventional wisdom at the time held that wars were rooted in the "natural" order of things and unavoidable in view of combative instincts inherent in the human condition.[5] Angell explicitly rejected that position. To his way of thinking, human behavior was not immutable: it could be conditioned through rational discourse that spoke to man's higher nature. He saw it as his mission to be a part of the conditioning process.

In the first decade of the twentieth century another body of doctrine did, however, maintain that war between industrial countries was impossible. Arguments from the Left, influenced by Marxian thought, insisted that workers (who could be expected to bear the brunt of a war's combat risks) would not fight their "class brethren" in other countries. Their real enemy was capitalist "exploiters" at home. Members of the proletariat, according to the official line of the Socialist International, would go "on strike" if asked to bear arms against their own. Angell and many of those like-minded were aware of this doctrine but found it unacceptable. Even if peace between nations might thus be maintained, the price in domestic class warfare would be too high. Angell thought he saw the way to achieve harmony within nations, as well as between them. This could be accomplished by reducing military budgets. The resulting "peace dividend"—to borrow from the vocabulary of a later day—would free up resources for domestic social uplift.[6]

Angell's works attracted attention. *The Great Illusion* became an international best-seller in the years before 1914. His work received philanthropic support in Britain and in the United States. The Carnegie Endowment for International Peace—founded in 1910 with a grant of $10 million from Andrew Carnegie—aided in spreading his message by subsidizing the distribution of a German edition.[7] In his autobiography,

4. See O'Farrell 1913.
5. For a discussion of prevalent public attitudes toward war in this period see Clarke 1966, esp. chs. 3–4.
6. This argument is developed in Angell 1914a, a pamphlet published by the American Association for International Conciliation.
7. See Carnegie Endowment 1913–14, 78–79.

published when he was seventy-nine years of age, Angell maintained that "we could have diluted Prussianism sufficiently to have rendered it much less dangerous" if there had been "five years in which to work among young Germans."[8]

Closer to home, Angell had an immediate impact on the thinking of a generation of younger economists, especially at the University of Cambridge. John Maynard Keynes, a Fellow of King's College, arranged for him to speak to its Political Economy Club, and a War and Peace Society was organized soon thereafter to provide a continuing forum for the discussion of his views.[9]

The Economics of War as
an International Research Enterprise

In 1911 the Carnegie Endowment for International Peace launched an unprecedented initiative in spurring economists to address the problem of war. The Endowment took as its charge "to promote a thorough and scientific investigation and study of the causes of war and of the practical methods to prevent and avoid it" and appointed Columbia University's John Bates Clark as director of the Division of Economics and History to press this work forward.[10] Clark brought impressive credentials to this assignment. His pioneering contributions to the development of marginal productivity theory had won him international prestige. In his professional activities he had displayed keen interest in applying economic theory to practical problems, most notably in the promotion of "industrial peace." Moreover, he had already extended this line of thought to questions of conflict resolution between nations in presentations to the American Association for International Conciliation.[11]

With funding provided by the Carnegie Endowment, Clark gathered economists from twelve countries to meet in Bern, Switzerland, in August 1911 to discuss the "economic causes and effects of war." In the background memorandum prepared for distribution to participants he wrote that "the largest of all the issues which our subject embraces is whether there are natural forces which of themselves decisively work in the direction of peace. Do economic movements make for the result which the world desires, or do they not? Without measuring the speed

8. Angell 1951, 172.

9. In *To the American Student* (1914b) Angell wrote that a "movement" for the dissemination of his doctrine had been formed in England, with some fifty societies and clubs, of which the "most important" was the Cambridge University War and Peace Society. (This pamphlet was distributed by the American Association for International Conciliation.)

10. See Carnegie Endowment 1911a.

11. See Clark 1910.

with which they are working, we need first to be assured as to its direction." Even to raise this as a question suggested that Angell's conclusions should be tested by analysis, not accepted on faith. There was more and important work to be done. But in deciding the issue between war and peace Clark was convinced that "nothing can do as much . . . as economic research."[12]

The program Clark outlined was ambitious. High priority was assigned to assessments of the costs of war—with attention not just to expenses measurable in the public accounts but also to the destruction of human and physical capital, impairment of labor efficiency, and costs imposed on neutral parties. He recommended inquiry into the efficiency of military budgets in times of peace, suggesting that the size of military establishments might be subject to a law of diminishing returns. In addition he indicated that the tradeoffs between increased military spending and public outlays for social purposes should be better understood, and asked: "Does not the need of more and more revenues for institutions of peace contract to a degree that is worthy of attention the natural limit of expenditures for possible warfare?" He further called for research into the dynamics of economic, political, and social change and their implications for possible international disputes and their resolution. This line of investigation should include study of the differing interests and attitudes of various social classes in cooperation, both within countries and between them.[13]

This agenda did not presuppose that social harmony was a natural state of affairs. It did presuppose that rival parties would act in pursuit of their own interests. From that premise it followed that economic research could help to smooth frictions and to promote harmony by insuring that actual (or potential) rivals were accurately informed about the relevant costs and benefits of alternative courses of action.

Clark assembled a formidable array of talents to review this research strategy at the 1911 conference in Bern. In addition to Clark, those present were:

United Kingdom: Francis W. Hirst, editor of *The Economist,* and George Paish, editor of *The Statist*

France: Paul Leroy-Beaulieu, Professor of Political Economy at the Collège de France, and Charles Gide, Professor of Economics in the University of Paris

Belgium: Henri La Fontaine, member of the Belgian Senate

The Netherlands: H. B. Greven, Professor of Political Economy and Diplomatic History in the University of Leyden

12. Carnegie Endowment 1911c.
13. Carnegie Endowment 1911c.

Italy: Luigi Luzzatti, Professor of Constitutional Law in the University of Rome and Prime Minister of Italy, 1908–11, and Maffeo Pantaleoni, Professor of Political Economy in the University of Rome

Germany: Lujo Brentano, Professor of Economics in the University of Munich, and Theodor Schiemann, Professor of the History of Eastern Europe in the University of Berlin

Austria: Eugen von Böhm-Bawerk, president of the Imperial Academy of Sciences at Vienna and former Austrian Minister of Finance, and Eugen von Philippovich, Professor of Political Economy in the University of Vienna

Switzerland: Eugene Borel, Professor of Public Law in the University of Geneva

Denmark: Harald Westergaard, Professor of Political Science and Statistics in the University of Copenhagen

Japan: G. Ogawa, Professor of Political Economy in the University of Kyoto, and Baron Sakatani, formerly Minister of Finance.

Paul S. Reinsch, Professor of Constitutional Law in the University of Wisconsin—then a visiting professor at the University of Berlin—was also in attendance.

A few words are in order about the composition of two of the national delegations. The British team, unlike the others, lacked a representative from the academic community. (Professor Alfred Marshall of Cambridge University had been invited, but declined for health reasons.) Hirst and Paish had other competences to recommend them. Both were skilled publicists (and potentially influential opinion-makers), and both were sympathetic to the idea that warfare was futile. Hirst was on record in urging that prize-taking at sea be outlawed by international agreement: such a step, he had argued, was needed to take "profits" out of naval warfare. He had also maintained that nations could ill afford to suspend normal commerce (excluding contraband), even between themselves, in the event of hostilities. Military operations would mandate massive additions to the public revenues, and they could be obtained only when standard business could generate tax receipts.[14] For his part, Paish addressed particularly the contribution of international investment to the growth of interdependence between countries.[15]

While those selected for the British contingent assured that peace

14. See Hirst 1909 and 1910.
15. "Experience of the benefits of increasing dependence of nation upon nation, which has been gained in the last century from the removal of physical barriers which used to divide them, and from the supply of capital by one country to another, affords some idea of the great well-being to which the whole world will attain in the years that are yet to come from the ever growing movement towards the economic unity of the race" (Paish 1912, 58).

advocacy would get a hearing at Bern, the organizers must have been aware that the composition of the German delegation posed a problem of some delicacy. Professor Gustav von Schmoller of the University of Berlin was on the invitation list but did not attend. Though a major figure in the German academic establishment and one of the most prominent of the *Kathedersozialisten* ("socialists of the chair"), Schmoller had been a prime mover in organizing support from the professoriate for von Tirpitz's naval expansion program in the 1890s. His presence at the conference might not have made for a congenial "mix." Lujo Brentano of the University of Munich—although he too had endorsed expansion of the German fleet—was different. In his writings Brentano had linked his economics more closely with British "free trade" theory than with the protectionist nationalism espoused by most of his colleagues. He had developed a reputation as an Anglophile and indeed had advised Schmoller in 1897 that his endorsement of a larger German navy was based on the expectation that it would aid German commerce by making it more secure, and that it would not be a program to rival Britain.[16] The second German delegate at Bern, Theodor Schiemann, brought expertise as a student of the history of Eastern Europe. Clark was to characterize Schiemann's "attitude toward war and peace" as "extremely unlike that of the ordinary member of a peace society."[17]

The upshot of the 1911 gathering in Bern was an agreement on the part of the participants to carry forward an active research program—assisted by younger economists in their respective countries—into the economics of war. Clark anticipated that the conference might "easily become a more or less permanent quasi-faculty holding periodical though not too frequent meetings."[18] The next round of discussions was scheduled to be held in Switzerland in August 1914.

Heterodox Economics and the Understanding of War

Clark and most of those who had joined him at Bern represented "establishment" economics as it was understood in the early years of the twentieth century. But then as now, economists did not speak with one voice. In the opinion of a number of them in Britain and America, the aspirations of the Carnegie Endowment's research program were out of touch with basic realities governing economic life.

Most of the American and British representatives of perspectives rivaling the orthodox neoclassical one had made some intellectual contact with the German historical school's approach to the economic

16. For a discussion of these points see Sheehan 1966, esp. 178–86.
17. Carnegie Endowment 1911b, 2.
18. Carnegie Endowment 1911b, 6.

process. Their attention was focused on the dynamics of larger historical change, rather than on the analysis of rational decision making. In
this reading, the central fact of the relationships between nation-states
was one of latent friction, not latent harmony.

In Britain William Cunningham, an economic historian of the University of Cambridge, was influenced by this point of view. Though originally a proponent of free trade, he had shifted position by 1911, when
he produced *The Case against Free Trade,* a pamphlet in which he
concluded that international competition was more likely to produce
conflict than concord and that those who expected a regime of peace to
be generated from economic "interdependence" were misguided. Britain, to be sure, depended on foreign trade for its prosperity, but it should
solidify its commerce within the Empire through preferential tariffs.[19]

An analogous line of thinking was developed by W. J. Ashley, Professor of Economic History in the University of Birmingham. When the
war came, he was better prepared to cope with it intellectually than were
many of his colleagues. Its outbreak was a "special and personal grief":
he had studied in Germany and had been awarded an honorary degree
by the University of Berlin.[20] Nevertheless he could comprehend it. He
was acquainted at first hand with German economists who had supported the expansion of the fleet. But he faulted his German friends for
their "conceit" and their "inability to understand the point of view of
other nations." It seemed "impossible" for them to "realize that a
nation which proposed to have both the strongest army and the strongest navy in the world was not going the best way to work to promote a
peaceable temper either in itself or in others."[21] The root of the matter
was the "German phase of self-glorification," which he had hoped
would pass away. He acknowledged that he had been mistaken in ascrib-
ing to Germany "a reserve of statesmanship and cool sense which it is
now apparent that it did not possess."[22] With "conceit," not reason,
driving German policy, the task at hand was to assure Allied victory. He
anticipated that the war might have one salutary consequence: it would
strengthen ties within the British Empire.

In the United States, Columbia University's Edwin R. A. Seligman
forcefully challenged the "latent harmony" premise imbedded in orthodox economics. His debt to the German historical school was apparent
in his *Economic Interpretation of History,* originally published in 1902.
Subsequently, in 1915, he extended this line of thought to the interpretation of war. "[I]f the modern age is essentially a capitalist age," he then

19. For a discussion of Cunningham's thought see Silberner 1946, 201–4.
20. Ashley 1914, 3.
21. Ashley 1914, 5, 6.
22. Ashley 1914, 6.

wrote, "why should we not, in the face of the international aspects of capitalism, have a growth of internationalism rather than nationalism? Why should we not be on the brink of that era of universal free trade, of permanent peace and of international brotherhood for which Adam Smith and the Manchester School so valiantly contended?"[23] The reason that had not happened, Seligman maintained, could be traced to unevenness in the stages of economic development in the main contesting powers. Britain had set the pace in capitalist economic development, while Germany had been the latecomer. This made antagonism—particularly over outlets for capital export to the less developed parts of the world—virtually inevitable. The war should thus be seen as rooted in the forces of history. Lasting peace could not be achieved through appeals for "rational calculations" by the belligerents but would come only when all nations of the world had advanced to the same economic level. Attempts to assign praise or blame to the various parties in the current conflict were beside the point. As Seligman saw matters, "How bootless is it to attempt to estimate from the blue book or the yellow book which statesman or set of statesmen is responsible for the particular action that led to the declaration of war! If the war could have been averted now, it was bound to break out in the more or less immediate future."[24]

An even more pointed dissent from the doctrine that warfare could be studied in the mode of conventional rational discourse flowed from the pen of Thorstein Veblen. His *Imperial Germany and the Industrial Revolution* (1915) was little read at the time (though it enjoyed a revival in the late 1930s). From his idiosyncratic perspective, friction was inherent in the contrasting cultural settings of industrialism in Germany and Britain. As the latecomer, Germany could imitate the technology of machine-age capitalism. Its industrial growth rate could thus be accelerated. But there was a mismatch between its emergence to industrial maturity and the immaturity of a political culture dominated by the disciplines of a dynastic state. Thus the fruits of industrial productivity could be allocated to warlike purposes. Echoing themes that he had set out earlier in *The Theory of the Leisure Class,* Veblen noted that Britain was well practiced in the techniques of wastefulness. Its business community knew how to restrict outputs in the interests of maximizing profits and how to suppress innovation to preserve capital values. Moreover, its leisure class was accomplished in the practices of "conspicuous consumption" and of withdrawal from socially productive work in favor, for example, of travel and sport. In these respects, German culture

23. Seligman [1915] 1925, 164.
24. Seligman [1915] 1925, 172.

was different. Social conventions to support wastefulness in private behavior had not yet been deeply ingrained. And this offered wider scope for the imperial government to "[divert] to warlike waste what would otherwise have gone into conspicuously wasteful living." Similarly, Germany had lagged in the cultivation of sports. The "sporting blood . . . of the idle classes" could be channeled instead into the military service, a phenomenon which had "doubtless contributed to the growth of an aggressive war spirit."[25]

The clash in cultural styles that Veblen identified could readily be invoked to account for the fact of war. But that clash, as he analyzed it, was not amenable to resolution through rational negotiation. Friction was inherent in the nature of the "business system" and in the differences in the cultural settings into which it had been assimilated. Veblen's iconoclasm toward "standard" economics did not end there. He also took aim at "peace advocates" interested in measuring the costs of war. Their approaches to this issue rested on misconceptions. In his view, "the gravity of the material destruction involved may readily be overrated." Real as the devastation might be, recuperation could be speedy. In his words: "In time of stress, as in a season following warlike devastation, the conventions governing the necessary consumption of decent superfluities are likely to be seriously demoralised, so that this 'unproductive' consumption will be greatly reduced for the time being. At the same time, and on similar grounds, the conventionally decent avoidance of productive work . . . will also fall somewhat into abeyance."[26]

Veblen was still more heretical in his treatment of the human losses of war. He insisted that a distinction be drawn between the "aggregate loss of life" and the loss of "economically valuable personnel." In his view commissions in the officers' corps in both Britain and Germany were awarded primarily to members of the "well-to-do classes": "officers commonly are gentlemen, in the several senses which that word conveys; and gentlemen commonly have no industrial value. Indeed, as bears on the net industrial efficiency of the community they have appreciably less than no value, being typically unproductive consumers. The mortality among officers may therefore be set down as net gain, in the economic respect."[27]

25. Veblen [1915] 1939, 245, 257.
26. Veblen [1915] 1939, 273.
27. Veblen [1915] 1939, 277. This reading was sharply at odds with that derived from standard economic theory. In the view of John Bates Clark, for example, the destruction of war "works selectively, killing and disabling the most productive workers, and, by this effect, it will lessen the average *per capita* efficiency of a people" (Clark 1916, 88).

Some Wound-Bandaging after
the Guns of August 1914

The second meeting of the Carnegie Endowment's International Research Committee was to convene at Lucerne, Switzerland, on 5 August 1914. Only four committee members—two from Japan, one from Holland, and one from the United States—managed to attend.[28] The original dream of enlisting a "quasi-permanent faculty" of economists to enlighten the world on the hazards of war seemed to have gone up in gunsmoke. No formal business could be conducted. Those present expressed a hope that the conference might be reconvened in Lucerne during the summer of 1915, "provided that conditions in Europe should permit."[29]

Despite the dismaying turn of events, the war—in Clark's judgment—provided a new opportunity to put economic research to work to advance the long-term objective of world peace. In October 1914 he proposed to the trustees of the Carnegie Endowment that they commit funds for the preparation of a comprehensive economic history of the war and its effects. "The war is a terrifically costly laboratory for the study of war," he wrote, "but as a rich source of data for conclusions of inestimable value, it is simply invaluable."[30] At the same time, it was self-evident that the program of investigations projected in 1911 was no longer feasible. Difficulties in international communication, along with preemption of the time of many potential contributors by other duties, meant that most manuscripts could be neither produced nor delivered. But there was a further difficulty which the Endowment's Executive Committee addressed obliquely in its report for 1915. Noting that some manuscripts had been received with contents of "such a nature that their publication might cause resentment or ill-feeling in other countries," the committee held that publication of potentially controversial material should be suspended.[31] Among the manuscripts suppressed were two prepared under the direction of Francis W. Hirst. A study dealing with the law of prize was also rejected on grounds that it might reflect "unfavorably" on the actual conduct of the British Navy.[32]

The outbreak of war had obliged Norman Angell to reallocate his energies. In the first days of August 1914 he was busy drafting manifestos urging British neutrality, but that activity terminated with Britain's declaration of war on 5 August. The year 1915 found him in the

28. Carnegie Endowment 1915, 22.
29. Carnegie Endowment 1914.
30. Clark, as quoted in Marchand 1972, 165.
31. Carnegie Endowment 1915, 24.
32. Marchand 1972, 172.

United States, where he called upon Americans to recognize that—given the interdependent character of international economic life—they could not stand totally aloof from the conflict. The United States, in his judgment, needed to develop a foreign policy through which its resources could be brought to bear in producing a lasting peace. This was not an appeal for American intervention as a belligerent. But it was an appeal for increased American preparedness. In his conception the goal to be sought was the creation of an international council formed from a concert of nations—he then had in mind the United States, the Allies, and other neutrals for membership. This should be designed as a "League to Enforce Peace," and Angell helped to stimulate the formation of citizens' organizations by this name to gather support for the idea. Such activity did not bear immediately on the war itself. It spoke instead to the need for preparatory thinking on the architecture of a postwar international order in which peace could be preserved. The war brought Angell some unpleasant personal experiences, particularly in Britain (where his patriotism was called into question). Even though he had not been prepared for what had happened, he managed to adjust to its shock and drew satisfaction from knowing that his ideas got a hearing at the Wilson White House.[33]

Among the veterans of the 1911 Bern conference Francis W. Hirst suffered the most severe psychic wounds. Still convinced of the folly of war and embittered by its onset, he stayed on as editor of *The Economist* until 1916, when he could no longer reconcile his convictions with the expectations of his audience. In his valedictory leading article, he wrote: "Since the war began, the function of an editor who believes that truth and patriotism ought to be reconciled has been difficult and even hazardous."[34] In 1915 he published *The Political Economy of War,* in which he foresaw nothing but the direst economic consequences from the continuation of hostilities. Quite apart from the intolerable destruction and economic derangement, the governments of belligerent states had burdened their peoples with debts threatening the very survival of their economic systems. Oppressive taxation strangling normal economic life was in prospect; alternatively, governments would repudiate payment (which he regarded as unacceptable confiscation of the property of creditors). The only "tolerable prospect for Europe in the long years of industrial and commercial depression that lie ahead" would be a regime in which states would abandon "by mutual consent the system of conscription and be content for a long time to come with a very small ex-

---

33. See Marrin 1979, esp. ch. 3.
34. As quoted in the entry for Francis W. Hirst, *Dictionary of National Biography, 1951–60,* ed. E. T. Williams and Helen Palmer (Oxford: Oxford University Press, 1971), 482.

penditure upon armies and navies."[35] "[R]eason," he submitted, "must be summoned to save Western Europe from social and economic ruin." He added the hope that "perchance the new world may recall sanity to the old."[36]

The course of events also ran counter to the expectations of another alumnus of the Bern research team of 1911. As late as July 1914 Lujo Brentano at the University of Munich continued to hold that the conditions of modern economic life made war, or at least a prolonged war, impossible.[37] But he made a better adjustment than Hirst did to his country's dominant temper. Recovering from surgery in August 1914, he was absent from the patriotic rallies of those emotion-packed days, though he later spoke with pride about the national solidarity demonstrated by the German working class. Along with most of his compatriots Brentano took the view in the early stages of the fighting that Germany was engaged in a defensive struggle against France and Russia. He found Britain's entry disheartening. In the autumn of 1914, however, he allowed his name to be used in support of a manifesto denouncing charges of German atrocities and denying that Belgian neutrality had been violated. This act ruptured a number of his friendships in Britain and France. Even so, British commentators reviewed his wartime writings charitably. In September 1915, for example, Keynes reported to readers of *The Economic Journal* on Brentano's contribution to a *Kriegsheft* prepared by German economists, in which Brentano had addressed the importance of avoiding recurrence of war. What was needed, Brentano argued, was "internationalisation of the sea" and a "union between civilised peoples" to insure that "such misfortunes as those which the world now suffers" would not be repeated.[38] (These recommendations were not all that different from those Angell was pressing at that time.) Similarly, F. Y. Edgeworth, when commenting in June 1917 on war-related literature produced by German economists, spoke favorably about Brentano's counsel to his countrymen to avoid indulging in "hate," even if Britain had behaved "abominably," and about his desire to build durable peace by abandoning "all trade enmity."[39] Though Brentano remained loyal to the German cause—and

35. Hirst 1915, 303.
36. Hirst 1915, 319.
37. According to his biographer, Brentano "confidently demonstrated" this to his students at that time (Sheehan 1966, 187).
38. See Keynes 1915, 447–48. Keynes's overall assessment of the *Kriegsheft* was that it demonstrated that "Germany and Germans are not so different from the rest of the world as our daily Press would hypnotise us into believing. . . . the general note is of moderation, sobriety, accuracy, reasonableness, and truth."
39. Edgeworth 1917, 247, 248. Edgeworth added: "Professor Brentano insists strongly on the freedom of the seas, in immunity of merchant ships (not carrying contraband) from

put his pen at the disposal of the German Foreign Office in 1917 to explain his country's position to neutral nations—he was still "moderate" within the spectrum of German opinion at the time. In mid-1918 he attempted to mobilize support for an immediate end to hostilities, without territorial changes, and called for the democratization of the Reich.[40]

Military Stalemate and a New Context for the Invocation of Rationality

When war was declared, the conventional wisdom held that the conflict would be brief. It might not be "over by Christmas," as the press in the belligerent countries had proclaimed, but it still seemed reasonable to expect that hostilities would not be protracted. This expectation had been nourished by prewar arguments about the high degree of interlocking interdependence in modern economies, which implied that the economic disruptions accompanying mass mobilization would preclude sustained combat engagements.

At least by the end of 1915 battlefield reality seemed to provide unambiguous evidence that Ivan Bloch, a French writer, had produced, in 1900, a far more prescient analysis of the course of a future war than had any of his contemporaries. Bloch had then argued that developments in military technology and in social organization meant that it would likely be fought, not as a contest of movement and maneuver, but as one between armies entrenched in fixed positions. He accurately predicted that in the next conflict the shovel would be as important as the rifle and that victory through decisive breakthrough would elude the contending parties.[41]

Perhaps paradoxically, the stalemate on the western front rekindled some hope that economists might contribute to hastening the end of hostilities. In the United States, John Bates Clark took up this theme at the annual meeting of the American Economic Association in December 1915. He then asked: "Are there any clear economic principles which will determine the length of the war?" As an answer to this question, he proposed a formula, derived from the teachings of economics, to identify "a natural period beyond which beings endowed with reason should not be expected to prolong a war."[42]

In working through this analysis Clark began by recognizing what he

---

capture by an enemy. But he hardly realises the difficulty which an English patriot feels about entering into an agreement for this purpose with a Power so strong and so unscrupulous as Germany" (248).

40. See Sheehan 1966.
41. For a discussion of Bloch's analysis see Clarke 1966, 134.
42. Clark 1916, 89.

took to be the "decisive fact" about the present war: it was essentially a contest of "attrition." Military ingenuity and individual acts of heroism no longer had the significance for the outcome that they might once have possessed: "a long war carried on in modern trenches by disciplined troops is far less capricious in its results." This provided a starting point from which to determine when contesting parties might find it worthwhile to strike a bargain. Two assumptions were necessary: (1) that wastage of men and munitions approached equality for both combatants (a presumption which seemed to be reasonable in a war of attrition); and (2) that the rival parties acted on the basis of rational self-interest. This way of looking at matters meant that the prospects of a settlement could be analyzed in the mode of a marginal-cost–marginal-benefit analysis.[43]

This approach to the stakes of war was obviously removed by a considerable distance from the prewar argument of the Angellites that "war could not pay." In Clark's assessment a prospective victor could anticipate genuine gains in territory and/or in money. But those "benefits" needed to be weighed against the "costs"—in terms of sacrifices of "life, treasure, future efficiency, both economic and military"—of prolonging the conflict. The stronger party might anticipate major gains from total victory, but it was in its interest to deduct the costs of such success from the terms it might ultimately exact, and to offer terms to the weaker on that basis. Similarly, it was in the interest of the weaker party—recognizing that prolongation of the war would result in more onerous exactions as well as additional costs—to accept them.

In Britain, F. Y. Edgeworth, Professor of Political Economy in the University of Oxford, reasoned along similar lines. The science of economics, he maintained in 1915, had something useful to say about "rendering the ends for which war is waged less desirable."[44] In his reading, there was a close analogy between the rival claims of self-interested parties in an industrial dispute and those observable in contention between nations. Edgeworth asserted that "between two self-interested parties there will be war when either has a clear prospect of obtaining advantage thereby" and that "one party without the consent of other party will resort to operations of which the probable result is to make the other party offer better terms than he was at first disposed."[45] (On this point he took explicit issue with Norman Angell's doctrine that

43. Clark noted that his rational calculus required him "to leave out of account every sentiment of love or hate, of gratitude or revenge, and consider that the regard for justice is qualified to the vanishing point by an assumed right of conquest. . . . The calculation to be made is so pitiless and remorseless that one regards himself as something of a barbarian for making it in theory, and yet it isolates dominant forces which actually will have play in the time and the manner of ending the war" (1916, 90).
44. Edgeworth 1915, 4.
45. Edgeworth 1915, 26–27.

alleged that gains by a nominal victor were "illusory.") In warfare, as in industrial disputes, the contesting parties should be mindful to maximize their own utility. Self-interested nations should ask themselves how favorable the terms secured by military success would really be after "account [had been] taken of the cost at which they are procured."[46] Thus, "even after the resort to arms there still remains an indeterminate tract of possible conventions, a *range* of arbitration, requiring resort to negotiation." But, Edgeworth cautioned, one should not expect the belligerents to assess their interests solely in terms of gains or losses of "tangibles." Nonmaterial objectives—such as "prestige," "position," "national honour"—were real, even though they resisted ready quantification. "Why," he asked, "should we suppose that independent peoples will be indifferent to such aims when we find work-people ready to strike for the recognition of their union or other mark of dignity?"[47]

Edgeworth was less direct than Clark in attempting to specify the conditions required for a negotiated settlement to the war then under way. At the analytic level, however, their thought proceeded along parallel lines. Edgeworth applauded Clark's analysis and "its tendency to clarify intellects and cool animosities."[48]

Factors Conditioning the War's Duration from Other Perspectives: Gustav Cassel and J. M. Keynes in 1916

In a quite different fashion an appeal to rational economic calculation—i.e., one based on pertinent "facts"—was issued in 1916 by Gustav Cassel, Professor of Economics in the University of Stockholm. Cassel spent three weeks in Germany in March 1916, at the invitation of the German Foreign Office, which had asked him to prepare a report on his findings for an English-language readership. He believed that governments of the Entente countries had underestimated Germany's economic capacity. This mistake should be corrected. "I wish to press home my view," Cassel wrote, "so that at any rate a prolongation of the war with its attendant misery for the whole of humanity may not be forced upon the world merely owing to continued miscalculations regarding Germany's economic power of resistance."[49] Cassel suspected that Allied planning had been the victim of "illusions," with unfortunate consequences. The main one derived from "the exaggerated idea people have regarding foreign trade under modern economic conditions. This

46. Edgeworth 1915, 28.
47. Edgeworth 1915, 30–31.
48. Edgeworth 1917, 249.
49. Cassel 1916, 80.

view is natural to England and to a certain extent justified by conditions. But as for the other great nations, it is mainly a popular illusion."[50]

In Cassel's estimation German productive capacity—despite more than a year and a half of war—had been maintained at nearly normal levels. Despite heavy claims on manpower by the armed forces, the aggregate input of labor had been little diminished. This outcome had been achieved through greater use of overtime, heavier labor force participation by women (as well as by the young and the old), and the assignment of some 1.2 million prisoners of war to the work force. Supplies of essential commodities had been maintained, augmented by resources mobilized in captured territories. Civilian consumption had been reduced; even so, "people in general do not seem to be suffering from economic difficulties." Cassel asserted that "there is no doubt that it is possible for Germany to make further restrictions, and thus still more increase its war funds."[51] The phenomenon of war, it thus appeared, had given the lie to the notion that a modern economic system was highly vulnerable to the interruption of normal channels of trade; the allied governments would be well advised to revise their thinking accordingly.

Cassel's estimate of Germany's economic capacity may have been somewhat overgenerous. However, his suggestion that British appraisals had typically underestimated Germany's capacity for economic survival was on target. Insight into British thinking at the time can be gleaned from Keynes's commentaries as an "insider" at the Treasury. Keynes certainly believed that the burdens of war had placed a severe strain on the German economy—as they had on the British economy as well. In January 1916 he wrote: "No country and no resources can support the present strain for very long. But Germany is six months nearer the edge than we are."[52]

Keynes's official preoccupation was with the efficient allocation of British resources under wartime constraints. He did not have to be instructed by Cassel about the differing economic structures of Britain and Germany and their implications for support of the war. Unlike Germany, Britain was heavily dependent on access to world markets. Three courses of action (or some combination thereof) were available to provide finance for its import requirements: earnings from exports (then substantially diminished by domestic claims on the resources of export industries and by the hazards of commerce at sea); borrowing from

50. Cassel 1916, 76–77.
51. Cassel 1916, 46, 75.
52. This observation appeared in a letter to the editor of the *Daily Chronicle,* 6 January 1916, signed "Politicus," but there is no doubt that it was Keynes's. See Keynes 1971, 16:161.

abroad, primarily from the United States; and the sale of British assets held overseas. By 1916 the British war effort had become heavily dependent on loans from the Americans. To sustain the country's creditworthiness, maintenance of gold convertibility of sterling at a pegged exchange rate was regarded as imperative.[53] Within this framework of thinking, the success or failure of Britain at war turned on the adequacy of its gold reserves to defend convertibility of the pound.

From Keynes's perspective Britain's position in international finance had significant implications for military strategy. In his view in January 1916, the buildup of a seventy-division army—then being urged by the War Office—invited the risk that the Allies might actually lose. Britain's resources were already stretched. A further draft on manpower for the military would be at the expense of domestic production and would add to claims on foreign exchange for equipment and supplies. This additional spending abroad might well compromise the nation's credit and provoke financial catastrophe. In that event, the country would no longer be able to underwrite external expenditures of its allies. Keynes summarized his view of the situation as follows:

> The governments of Russia, Italy, Belgium and Serbia are mainly dependent on us, and the government of France is partly dependent on us, for such supplies of food and the material of war as they need to purchase from abroad. . . . If at the beginning of the war we had immediately mobilised between 3 and 4 million men, we could not also have financed our allies without suffering by now as great an exhaustion as Germany's; and if we had armed these men, the Russian army must have continued indefinitely to go without. If we had exhausted our resources upon our army, Italy would not have joined us, Russia might have been driven into a separate peace, and France and ourselves might have been overwhelmed by the pressure of the entire forces of the enemy. . . . Nothing but the fact that we remained content for a considerable time with an army of reasonable size, has deprived Germany of victory. Nothing but military megalomania on our part can still save her from defeat.[54]

The economic logic Keynes used to diagnose the situation in early 1916 may have been analytically solid. But it should also be noted that something else was at stake in these efforts at persuasion. Keynes personally was adamantly opposed to military conscription, and it was

53. At the outbreak of the Second World War, Keynes observed that the imposition of exchange controls (which were applied immediately in September 1939) would have been unthinkable in 1916 and 1917. He wrote on 24 September 1939 about the World War I experience: "Complete control was so much against the spirit of the age that I doubt if it ever occurred to any of us that it was possible" (Keynes 1971, 16:210).

54. Keynes 1971, 16:159. Keynes developed a similar line of argument in a talk to the Board of the Admiralty, 15 March 1916 (Keynes 1971, 16:184–88).

self-evident that the ranks of an enlarged army could not be filled through voluntary enlistments. Other views prevailed in the 1916 debate over the conduct of the war. The Conscription Bill was passed and military appropriations escalated. The bankruptcy which Keynes feared from these measures was only narrowly averted in December 1916. With America's entry into the war in April 1917, external financial constraints on the British war effort were considerably eased.[55]

Shifting Attitudes with
American Intervention, 1917–18

Hopes that improved understanding of economic realities would avert war or, failing that, induce belligerents to shorten it had obviously been battered in the flow of events. Even so, some of the patronage of the Carnegie Endowment for economic scholarship was carried on through 1916 with a semblance of "business as usual." But the research program charted at Bern had largely been scrapped in favor of laying the groundwork for the ultimate definitive economic history of the war.[56]

Contact was maintained with members of the original Research Committee, who were on both sides of the trench lines. In his report as director of the Division of Economics and History in 1916, Clark noted that Hirst in the United Kingdom, Gide in France, and Pantaleoni in Italy were gathering materials for the war history. Similarly, Brentano and Schiemann in Germany and von Philippovich and von Wieser in Austria had undertaken to perform similar work in states of the Central Powers.[57]

Attitudes toward any form of collaboration with nationals of the Central Powers changed abruptly with America's declaration of war in April 1917. Representatives of Germany and Austria were dropped from the Committee of Research, and the trustees of the Endowment unanimously passed a resolution at a meeting that month declaring "their belief that the most effectual means of promoting durable international peace is to prosecute the war against the Imperial German Government to final victory for democracy, in accordance with the policy declared by the President of the United States."[58] In November 1917—after it had been learned that the German government had informed its people

55. For an account of Keynes's personal anguish at this time see Skidelsky 1983, esp. ch. 13.

56. Two of the studies projected in the original project design did, however, appear in 1916: Josef Grunzel's *Economic Protectionism* (which had been edited by Eugen von Philippovich in Vienna) and Arthur Girault's *Colonial Tariff Policy of France* (edited by Charles Gide in Paris). In the judgment of reviewers in the professional journals, neither of them seemed to have much pertinence to what was then going on in Europe.

57. Carnegie Endowment 1916. It should be noted that Friedrich von Wieser of the University of Vienna had been added to the Austrian research committee, replacing Böhm-Bawerk, who had died in 1914.

58. Carnegie Endowment 1918a, 19.

that American opinion was seriously divided about prosecution of the war—the trustees reaffirmed their April resolution and supplemented it with stronger language: "The path to durable international peace on which the liberty-loving nations of the world would so gladly enter, is now blocked by the blind reliance of Germany upon the invincibility of German military power and upon its effectiveness as an instrument of international policy. This reliance must be broken. . . . It can only be broken by defeat."[59] For his part, Clark informed his British colleagues through the pages of *The Economic Journal* of his support for the League to Enforce Peace, explaining that it was "as far as possible from being a stop-the-war organisation" and adding that "since the entry of the United States into the conflict the League has become openly a win-the-war society, and will use every ounce of energy it possesses to help in securing a victory for the Allies' cause."[60]

Meanwhile, in his capacity as director of the Division of Economics and History, Clark stepped up the pace of its research planning. A host of new studies was commissioned, with particular attention to the impact of economic mobilization on specific sectors and industries. The exigencies of war, in Clark's view, had created a form of "quasi-socialism" which had implications for industrial organization and for the distribution of incomes after the war. Specialized economic study would thus have to face a further challenge in light of problems which would be the war's legacy: namely, that of promoting peace within nations, as well as between them. Clark hoped that "research may show that the economic measures which war has forced on the several states engaged in it, even though they may not be permanent, may point the way toward an industrial system that will be, in some respects, new and will be good enough from the laborer's point of view to render genuine collectivism unnecessary, even if it were practicable." Genuine democracy, in his view, required "cooperation of different industrial classes in activities of peace" and "exclude[d] a ruinous proletarian war on capital, as to the effects of which Russia is giving an object lesson."[61]

Versailles and After

Appeals to rational economic calculation to avoid war or to terminate it had fared badly between 1910 and 1918. But could a treaty of peace succeed in producing the conditions which would banish thereafter a repetition of the carnage of 1914–18?

Keynes produced the contemporary commentary which was most widely read on the handiwork of the negotiators in Paris. His *Economic*

59. Carnegie Endowment 1918a, 19.
60. Clark 1917.
61. Carnegie Endowment 1918b, 109.

Consequences of the Peace was a vitriolic denunciation of what he took to be the surrender of reason to vindictive passion in the settlements drafted by the Big Four powers. The treaty, in his judgment, was both immoral and unworkable. Its reparations clauses imposed conditions on Germany which could not be met, and even the attempt to enforce them would doom Europe to a future of economic disorder. This work— though filled with emotive rhetoric—was ultimately an appeal for a rational revision of the treaty to bring its terms closer to the requirements of international economic reconstruction.[62]

Keynes's views on the Treaty of Versailles were echoed by Norman Angell, who found it incredible that the Allied negotiators would construct a settlement so contrary to "elementary considerations of self-interest" of their own countries. The result could only be damage to the victors when they insisted on indemnities from the defeated. Angell held in 1921 that his original position on the economic harm which the payment of "tribute" would bring to the recipient country was then being validated by events; he cited *The Economic Consequences of the Peace* in support. Altogether, the war and its aftermath meant, in Angell's judgment, that the arguments of *The Great Illusion* had stood the test of time. He acknowledged, however, that the original message required modification on one point: he had earlier believed that economic interdependence would preclude prolonged hostilities. The ability of the German economy to withstand isolation and blockade for the better part of four years was something he had not been prepared for. He had underestimated the ability of a country to carry on by "living upon capital." But this technique for survival could not be continued indefinitely. The "underlying process of disintegration" was bound to become apparent—as it did in mid-1918—and then "the whole structure went to pieces." The moral of the tale was the same as it had been in 1910: as an economic exercise, warfare was futile. But in light of the inability of the Allied powers to act on the principle of economic interdependence at the peace conference, it was now more urgent than ever to expose this folly.[63]

62. It should be noted that Keynes did not oppose all reparations claims against Germany. In early 1916 he had collaborated with W. J. Ashley (then at the British Board of Trade) in preparing a memorandum on the feasibility of reparations to repair damages in territories overrun by the enemy (see "Memorandum on the Effect of an Indemnity," 2 January 1916, in Keynes 1971, 16:313–34). This document reviewed the standing literature on the economic impact of the transfers following the Franco-Prussian War and concluded that an indemnity could be beneficial to the recipients. Keynes's attack on the reparations clauses in *The Economic Consequences of the Peace* was directed primarily at claims on Germany beyond those suffered in occupied territories and at mistaken assumptions about Germany's capacity to meet them.

63. See Angell 1921, esp. 15–19, 290–301. Keynes gave his enthusiastic endorsement to this book, informing Angell that he thought it "extremely good" and that he had "read it with the greatest satisfaction and agreement" (quoted in Angell 1951, 153).

American economists appraising the peace treaty were less concerned about the implications of reparations—the United States government had made no claims for indemnities—and more concerned about the fate of the covenants pertaining to the creation of the League of Nations. Clark, for example, was bitterly disappointed by the failure of the United States Senate to ratify the treaty. In his view the prospects for peace hinged fundamentally on the capacity of such an international organization to enforce it: the failure of the American government to take up membership was a missed opportunity with potentially tragic implications.[64] Even E. R. A. Seligman—who had earlier written about the inevitability of warfare between countries at differing stages of economic development—held that America's decision to stand apart from the League of Nations had increased the risk of a future war. In the version of his essay "The Economic Interpretation of War" republished in 1925, he appended a note deploring the shortsightedness of the American government's posture of isolation.[65] It remains debatable whether or not the American electorate could have been conditioned to support the Treaty of Versailles in 1920. But there can be little question that Keynes's *Economic Consequences of the Peace*—with its characterization of President Wilson as the naive Presbyterian who had been "bamboozled" by cynical politicians of the Old World—did not enhance such a prospect.[66]

Among the American commentators on the economic implications of Versailles one voice stood out for the singularity of its dissent from all of the standard positions. Thorstein Veblen, remaining in character, offered views which were distinctly different. The negotiators had compromised the prospects for future peace, he maintained, but not for the reasons that others had identified. Their fundamental flaw was that they had been informed by a spirit of outdated "mid-Victorian liberalism" which had attempted to restore the status quo ante in economic affairs. In Veblen's terms they had attempted to make the "world safe for absentee ownership." This, in his judgment, was a formula for continued international friction and for the suppression of healthy economic progress. The course of true "rationality" in the economic or-

64. In one of his last published writings Clark renewed his appeal for a credible international body which would apply force—both military and economic—to deter a potential aggressor (see Clark 1935).

65. Seligman then wrote: "The argument . . . discloses the futility of America's aloofness from the League, in vain reliance on the traditional doctrine of political isolation. If the League does not succeed in controlling the present phase of nationalism, the 'isolation' of the United States will be impotent to protect it from being dragged into the next war. In the meantime our abstention from the League and our deplorable refusal to help in creating a world code of civilisation or in developing international cooperation may well become the chief factor in bringing about the next world war" ([1915] 1925, 179).

66. On this point see Blitch 1991.

der—in his reading of matters—would have been to prepare for a future in which the technical expertise of the engineers would guide the processes of production. But a different outcome could hardly have been expected from a group of negotiators trained to think in terms of the economic doctrines of the past.[67]

On the vexed question of Allied claims against Germany, Veblen was no less heretical. In his view the Germans had been let off too lightly. The victors had wasted an opportunity to produce a revolutionary change in the German economic order—one which might have been forced by more stringent claims on the country's resources. Instead the interests of its absentee owners had been protected. (He suggested that one of the reasons for this outcome was the interest of the Allies in maintaining the established order in Germany as a bulwark against Bolshevism.)[68] Moreover, the entire debate over indemnity had been blurred by confused thinking. Germany could easily have been made to pay through a simple mechanism: German holders of public debt—at the national, state, and municipal levels—should have their rights revoked, and the interest which they would otherwise have received could be transferred as reparations.

The Renewed Attempt to Mobilize Economic Knowledge in the Interests of Peace

In 1923 John Bates Clark reported on the expanded program of research sponsored by the Carnegie Endowment for International Peace:

At an immeasurable and tragic cost the world [war] provided the data for a kind of knowledge that, on its face, should work decisively against a repetition of the ruinous conflict. The peace, however, actually finds humanity in more imminent peril of further war than it faced at any time in the preceding century. Evil impulses are at work which reason and the spirit of humanity will find it hard to meet; and yet the appeal to reason is the great resource for this purpose, and one thing which strengthens the appeal is a knowledge of the economic facts connected with the recent struggle.[69]

With these words, Clark set out the rationale for an enlarged economic and social history of the war. Some 150 volumes were then projected on the wartime experience of fourteen countries. Editorial boards had been formed in all of the belligerent countries as well as in a

67. See his essays entitled "Peace," "Dementia Praecox," and "Between Bolshevism and War," reprinted in Veblen 1934.
68. This theme comes through in his review of Keynes's *Economic Consequences of the Peace* (Veblen 1920).
69. Carnegie Endowment 1923, 90.

number of neutral ones. Germans and Austrians had rejoined the fold. (None of the original representatives of these countries from the days of the Bern conference of 1911 were included in their teams, however, though some of them were still alive.)

When the Economic and Social History Project was suspended in 1933, 132 volumes had been published. As promised, their scope was sweeping, with coverage that included seventeen countries or groups of countries (such as the Scandinavian states). Works attempting to estimate the costs of the war were prominent in the lists. They were accompanied by detailed monographic studies of the reorganizations of key industries to cope with the demands of war. Officers of the Carnegie Endowment took pride in the abundant commentary from reviewers about the spirit of scientific detachment with which the authors approached their tasks.

Economic scholarship with its appeal to reason was a frail reed in the winds of hatred that blew again in the late 1930s. Though it could not forestall the Second World War, it is just possible that some of the insights generated in the *Economic and Social History of the World War* later made logistical mobilization more efficient.

References

Angell, Norman. 1912. *The Great Illusion: A Study of the Relation of Military Power in Nations to Their Economic and Social Advantage.* 3d ed. New York and London: G. P. Putnam's Sons.

———. 1914a. *To the American Business Man: An Open Letter.* New York: American Association for International Conciliation. March.

———. 1914b. *To the American Student: An Open Letter.* New York: American Association for International Conciliation. March.

———. 1921. *The Fruits of Victory: A Sequel to "The Great Illusion."* New York: Century.

———. 1951. *After All: The Autobiography of Norman Angell.* London: Hamish Hamilton.

Ashley, W. J. 1914. *The War and Its Economic Aspects: A Lecture to the Workers' Educational Association at the University of Birmingham* [18 November]. Oxford: Oxford University Press.

Blitch, Charles P. 1991. The Reception of Keynes's *The Economic Consequences of the Peace* in the United States. In *Perspectives on the History of Economic Thought,* edited by William J. Barber, vol. 6. Aldershot: Edward Elgar.

Carnegie Endowment for International Peace. 1911a. Articles of Association. As reported by Elihu Root, President of the Board of Trustees (20 May).

———. 1911b. [John Bates Clark]. Report of the Director of the Division of Economics and History (26 October).

———. 1911c. [John Bates Clark]. Suggestions as to Possible Questions for Investigation. In 1911b above.

———. 1913–14. Report of the Acting Director of the Division of Intercourse and Education.

————. 1914. Report of the Meeting of the Committee of Research of the Division of Economics and History (August; Lucerne).

————. 1915. Report of the Executive Committee.

————. 1916. [John Bates Clark]. Report of the Director of the Division of Economics and History (22 March).

————. 1918a. Report of the Executive Committee.

————. 1918b. [John Bates Clark]. Report of the Director of the Division of Economics and History (20 March).

————. 1923. [John Bates Clark]. Report of the Director of the Division of Economics and History (21 March).

Cassel, Gustav. 1916. *Germany's Economic Power of Resistance.* New York: The Jackson Press.

Clark, John Bates. 1910. An Economic View of War and Arbitration. *International Conciliation,* July.

————. 1916. The Economic Costs of War. *American Economic Review Supplement* (March).

————. 1917. [Communication on the League to Enforce Peace]. *Economic Journal* 27 (September): 441–44.

————. 1935. *A Tender of Peace: The Terms on Which Civilized Nations Can, If They Will, Avoid Warfare.* New York: Columbia University Press.

Clarke, I. F. 1966. *Voices Prophesying War, 1763–1984.* London: Oxford University Press, 1966.

Edgeworth, F. Y. 1915. *On the Relations of Political Economy to War: A Lecture.* Oxford: Oxford University Press.

————. 1917. Some German Economic Writings about the War. *Economic Journal* 27 (June).

Hirst, Francis W. 1909. The Logic of International Conciliation. *International Conciliation,* January.

————. 1910. The Capture and Destruction of Commerce at Sea. *International Conciliation,* November.

————. 1915. *The Political Economy of War.* London: J. M. Dent & Sons.

Keynes, John Maynard. 1915. The Economics of War in Germany. *Economic Journal* 25 (September).

————. 1919. *The Economic Consequences of the Peace.* London: Macmillan.

————. 1971. *The Collected Writings of John Maynard Keynes.* Vol. 16. Edited by Elizabeth Johnson. London: Macmillan.

Marchand, C. Rowland. 1972. *The American Peace Movement and Social Reform, 1898–1918.* Princeton: Princeton University Press.

Marrin, Albert. 1979. *Sir Norman Angell.* Boston: Twayne.

O'Farrell, Horace Hadley. 1913. *The Franco-German War Indemnity and Its Economic Results.* London: Harrison & Sons.

Paish, George. 1912. International Investments and Their Important Influence upon International Unity. *International Conciliation,* January.

Seligman, Edwin R. A. [1915] 1925. An Economic Interpretation of the War. In *Problems of Readjustment after the War.* Reprinted in *Essays in Economics.* New York: Macmillan.

Sheehan, James J. 1966. *The Career of Lujo Brentano: A Study of Liberalism and Social Reform in Imperial Germany.* Chicago: University of Chicago Press.

Silberner, Edmund. 1946. *The Problem of War in Nineteenth Century Economic Thought.* Translated by Alexander H. Krappe. Princeton: Princeton University Press.

Skidelsky, Robert. 1983. *John Maynard Keynes: Hopes Betrayed, 1883–1920*. London: Macmillan.

Veblen, Thorstein. [1915] 1939. *Imperial Germany and the Industrial Revolution*. New York: Macmillan. Reissued with an introduction by Joseph Dorfman. New York: Viking Press.

———. 1920. Review of *The Economic Consequences of the Peace*, by John Maynard Keynes. *Political Science Quarterly* 35 (September).

———. 1934. *Essays in Our Changing Order*. Edited by Leon Ardzrooni. New York: Viking Press.

Thorstein Veblen on War, Peace, and National Security

Jeff E. Biddle and Warren J. Samuels

It would be inaccurate to say that the topic of war has been neglected by the mainstream economists of the past century. Armed conflict and preparation for possible armed conflict have given rise to situations that could fruitfully be discussed under the headings of resource allocation, macroeconomic stabilization, or public finance; and mainstream economists have participated in such discussions. But the subject of war has never become a part of mainstream economic theory qua theory, nor has the study of the nature, causes, and consequences of war been perceived as central to the study of the economic system.

One probable reason for this state of affairs is the relatively narrow conception of what constitutes the economy and the intellectual discipline of economics held by the mainstream economists of this century, a conception that focuses on the market mechanism and its operation. Further, mainstream economic theory has been organized around the concept of equilibrium, with equilibrium being implicitly if not explicitly associated with notions of normalcy and/or harmony. A serious study of war in this framework would require a preconception of war as normal, or as the eventuality towards which human activity gravitates. Such a preconception would be at odds with the basic presumptions of rational behavior and human progress that have been a part of mainstream economics at least since the time of Smith.

So, war enters mainstream economic analysis chiefly as an exogenous force, an aberration that disturbs equilibrium, to be analyzed only with respect to its effect on equilibrium. And it is for this reason that much of what falls under the rubric "economics of war"—for example, studies focusing on resource allocation during wartime, or war finance—could with only minor changes pass for economic analysis of a state-run effort to colonize the moon.

The objective of this essay is to examine the analysis of the topics of war, peace, and national security produced by an economist who worked outside the mainstream, Thorstein Veblen. Veblen, who lived as an adult through World War I and the various conflicts born of turn-of-the-century imperialism, discussed the topic of war in several books, articles, and book reviews, many of which were related in some way to the First World War. In particular, *Imperial Germany and the Industrial Revolution* (1915), conceived before and published shortly after the outbreak of the war, was an examination of the causes of Germany's emergence as an aggressive and formidable war power. On the eve of America's entry into the war Veblen wrote *An Inquiry into the Nature of Peace and the Terms of Its Perpetuation* (1917), an entire volume devoted to questions of war and peace.

Like other economists writing on war, Veblen examined questions of war finance, the economic costs of war, and the impact of war on product and financial markets. But the bulk of his writing on war, and the ideas with which we shall be mainly concerned, dealt with broader questions of the causes and consequences of war, questions seldom addressed by economists of his day or since. In particular Veblen undertook a theoretical analysis of the manner in which armed conflict emerged from the ordinary processes of life in modern human societies, and of the impact of armed conflict on the habits of thought and patterns of behavior of those directly or indirectly exposed to it.

An important reason for Veblen's rather extensive treatment of war is his "evolutionary" approach to economics. He regarded social and economic institutions as both the result of and efficient factors in an ongoing process of social evolution, a Darwinian process of variation and selection involving human aptitudes and patterns of belief and behavior. Thus the organizing principle behind Veblen's theorizing was not equilibrium but cumulative causation. His evolutionary outlook also implied a very broad conception of economics, one which went beyond consideration of the price mechanism to include questions of the organization, operation, and development of the institutions that socialize the individual and shape his beliefs, including those that form and operate through the market. This broader conception of what constituted economics made room in Veblen's theories for questions of war, while his commitment to a "post-Darwinian" mode of analysis helped to draw his attention to such questions.

The notion of life-or-death struggle as a mechanism of selection is central to the Darwinian concept of evolution, and armed conflict is arguably the form of human struggle that most obviously acts to selectively preserve or eliminate societies and patterns of social behavior. The adoption of the Darwinian metaphor for explaining economic development thus sets the stage for a consideration of the part played by war in that development. One finds such discussions, for example, in the works of A. T. Hadley, Thomas N. Carver, and Simon Patten, all of whom attempted evolutionary analyses of economic development and the first of whom was otherwise so orthodox that he acquired the appellation "Old School" Hadley.[1] Frank Taussig was another orthodox economist who produced a joint analysis of war and economic activity with Darwinian overtones. He wrote of an instinct of domination inherited from our "savage ancestors" and asserted that power over others had been the keynote of political and economic history (Taussig 1929, 2:494). Societies developed institutions through which the instinct of domination could be channeled, institutions which were often, but not necessarily, warlike or predatory. Indeed Taussig's defense of capitalism was that it provided a constructive channel for the instinct of domination. "Better that we should have Napoleons of industry," he wrote, "than the blood-guilty Napoleons of history" (1930, 129). Of all the self-consciously evolutionary economists of the late nineteenth and early twentieth centuries, however, Veblen offered the most extensive treatment of the relationship between war and economic activity. It is worth examining his effort because it stands as an example of what can emerge when the economic analysis of war is conducted by an economist who has abandoned the principle of economic equilibrium in favor of that of economic evolution.

Other, more idiosyncratic aspects of Veblen's basic approach to socioeconomic analysis, besides his adoption of the evolutionary viewpoint, contributed to his interest in questions of war and national security and give his analysis of those questions a distinctive tone. For example, certain of his fundamental assumptions relating to the prevalence of predation in human interaction led him to see an intimate relationship between warlike activities and more pacific pursuits. In his eyes war and other activities related to national security were manifestations of the same socioeconomic processes that underlay ordinary commercial life; they were neither exogenous nor aberrational. Also, it was not in Veblen's nature to accept uncritically the conventional homilies and preconceptions of nationalistic and economic ideology. While others might have been willing to accept the portrayal of commerce as a constructive intercourse among and between citizens of peace-loving nations, to him neither the polity nor the economy were necessarily benign.

Before presenting a detailed account of Veblen's views on war, some further prefatory remarks are in order. First, for Veblen "national defense/security" is a euphemism, and neither a given nor a necessarily honorific concept. The activities that from one point of view represent national defense can from another be clearly identified as aggression;

1. See, e.g., Hadley 1897, 20–22, 36–38. On Patten, Carver, and other economists of this period whose writings had evolutionary components see Spengler 1956.

such activities are necessarily present in a world in which each nation's "freedom to" correlates with the negation of another's "freedom from."

Second, several critical tensions in Veblen's analysis, identified below, remind us that his mode of analysis is characterized by neither teleology nor determinate solutions. He is content to identify the major forces at work, together with the possible lines of development which their various concatenations might produce. He took delight in puncturing the essentialist and inevitabilist explanations of phenomena and trends produced by writers engaged in either wishful thinking or presentist rationalization—in part because he stressed the ex ante problematicity of developments, in part because he liked to debunk high-flown pretense.

Third, Veblen's descriptions of reality (like those of any writer) combine elements of the objective and the normative. It is clearly normative to describe English and French culture as more "civilized" than German culture, which is characterized by relics of "feudalistic barbarism" (1915, 162–63, 231). Veblen also favored the Allies over their German opponents in World War I (e.g., 1915, 250). One of his more familiar normative sentiments shows through in his statement that the settlement of the war should have been entrusted to "reasonably unbiased production engineers, rather than to awestruck lieutenants of the vested interests" (1934, 419). Another example is his frequent argument that war benefits only certain business and political interests while the entire cost is borne by the common man. All such statements are examples of the economic analyst substituting his perceptions and/or judgments for those of economic actors.

At the same time it should be noted that Veblen's emphasis on the cultural relativity of value judgments included self-referential elements. So, for example, when he characterizes the abandonment of medieval institutions for those of more recent vintage as an advance, he adds the qualifying statement that "such an appraisal, however, is a matter of taste and opinion, in which the habituation embodied in this modern cultural scheme is itself taken as a base-line of appraisal and could, therefore, not be accepted as definitive in any argument on the intrinsic merits of this culture in contrast with any other" (1915, 258). The advance spoken of is thus an advance only on the terms of modernity itself—and Veblen was clearly in several important respects a creature of what he termed modern, mature, civilization.[2]

Fourth, in Veblen's writings on war, as in all his writings, straightforward analysis is mixed with irony and sarcasm. And, as with his other writings, it is not always clear whether the irony and sarcasm perceived

---

2. See Samuels 1990 for a discussion of this point.

by the reader was intended by the author. It seems likely, for example, that analysis of the costs and benefits of war in the concluding chapter of *Imperial Germany* was meant in part as a satire of similar exercises undertaken by more orthodox economists of the day.[3]

Finally, our goal is a summary of the main arguments found in Veblen's many writings on war and peace. It is not within our intended objective to offer a critique of Veblen's ideas on these matters.

The Roots of War: Nationalism, Patriotism, and the Nation-State System

Central to Veblen's writings on war are his discussions of the related phenomena of patriotism and nationalism. He describes patriotism and nationalism variously as sentiments, spirits, habits of thought, and so on. They are acquired through and persist as a result of habituation, although Veblen believed that there was an inherent susceptibility to such sentiments among the European peoples. The institution upon which these sentiments converge in modern times is the nation-state. Patriotism and nationalism act through the nation-state system to create armed conflict, and armed conflict has historically helped to strengthen and perpetuate both patriotic and nationalistic sentiments and the nation-state system.

For Veblen, as for many other writers, the psychology of nationalism centers on individuals' identification with the nation in which they are born or in which they come to reside. It involves a conception of and a concern with a national honor or prestige. A challenge to this prestige is a serious affront to the individual, and an increase in it is counted as positive gain (1917, 27–28). Although the national prestige is metaphysical in nature, it is tied to certain observable situations and events. Which situations and events, and their weights in the calculation of the national honor, depends on prevailing sensibilities; but they could include the size of the national territory, the wealth of the sovereign, the effectiveness of the army, the profitability of the nation's business interests, and so forth.

Nationalism gives the individual an interest in the otherwise irrelevant activities of fellow nationals. An individual will count a gain by a

3. For example, Veblen argued that the economic cost of war in terms of human life was usually overstated. The traits that made an enthusiastic and successful soldier generally also impaired efficiency in the industrial environment created by machine technology, so that those who volunteered for war were likely to be those who were less productive in times of peace. Officers tended to come from among the aristocracy and "the buccaneering scions of the leisure classes"; the lower ranks came disproportionately from among the community's pugnacious delinquents. Casualties among these groups had little effect on society's efficiency; in fact the loss of an officer, who in peacetime was probably an unproductive consumer after the fashion of the leisure class, might represent a net economic gain to society (Veblen 1904, 395–97; 1915, 268–70).

compatriot at the expense of an alien as a gain to himself, by virtue of its positive effect on the national prestige. There need not be any material link between the welfare of the individual and that of his compatriots for this mechanism to operate. Indeed the individual acting under the influence of nationalism will undergo material sacrifice to secure the good fortune of an otherwise unknown compatriot, under the perception that by such action the national prestige will be bolstered. Striking but common examples of this are the willingness of the common man to go to war to advance the personal ambitions of his sovereign or to redress some perceived affront to the representatives of his nation's business interests.

The patriotic animus, an outgrowth of nationalism, is the desire to advance or preserve the prestige of one's own nation relative to the prestige of other nations. It is an invidious animus, as well satisfied by an absolute advance of the prestige of one's own nation as an absolute decline in that of neighboring nations. Success on the part of a nation's commercial interests can give vent to the patriotic impulse, but it "finds its full expression in no other outlet than warlike enterprise; its highest and final appeal is for the death, damage, discomfort, and destruction of the party of the second part" (Veblen 1917, 33). The sense of patriotism biases an individual towards any proposed measure that can be argued to increase national power and prestige (or decrease that of a rival nation), however specious the argument may be (67).

Veblen regarded the patriotism and nationalism of his own day as the result of centuries of human life within a tightly knit institutional scheme centered on status emulation, a scheme that reached its most perfect form during the Middle Ages. In general, feudal habits of thought ran in terms of status hierarchies and invidious distinctions. Individuals were cognizant of and jealous to advance or preserve their positions in the hierarchy. Status, always figured in relative terms, was first associated with the real or apparent ability to best others through force, later coming to be associated with the possession of wealth as well. Interpersonal relations were infused with punctilios of dominance and servility to which great importance was attached. Nationalism and patriotism represent the working out of these medieval habits of thought on the level of collectives, in accordance with an instinct of group solidarity that Veblen believed to be a part of the hereditary endowment of the European peoples.[4] Each nation's prestige relative to others in an interna-

---

4. Descriptions of how nationalism and patriotism developed out of the instinctive sense of group solidarity can be found in Veblen 1904, 288–89; 1915, 45ff.; 1917, 48–52. This process and the similar process of the "contamination" of the instinct of workmanship (described in Veblen 1899) were interrelated and important aspects of Veblen's portrayal of the European peoples' "fall from grace."

tional status hierarchy is a matter of great importance, with national prestige linked to measures of a nation's effective force or wealth. Relations between different nations (or citizens of those nations) involve precise formalities reflecting relative national status, and a failure by one party to adhere to form is perceived as an affront to the honor of the nation of the other.

The mere process of life within medieval institutions served to preserve patriotism and nationalism along with the rest of the preconceptions upon which those institutions rested. Through this nondeliberative socialization it became second nature for the common man to regard the national honor as something of great moment, to identify national honor with the ambitions of the sovereign, to regard outsiders with hostility and distrust, to see the use of force against outsiders and to the benefit of the national honor as necessary and desirable. This is not to say that the socialization of the common man in the ways of nationalism was always nondeliberative. Veblen noted frequently the ability of leaders to generate or exacerbate nationalistic tendencies, if they believed that such action would secure the backing of the common man for an enterprise, often warlike, designed to advance the leaders' personal ambitions.

Veblen claimed that the habits of thought and patterns of behavior prevalent in his day retained many of the predatory characteristics that set the tone of feudal times. In particular, nationalism remained an important part of the fabric of life. Certain aspects of modern life instilled in the individual a sense of national honor along with the desire to advance it through belligerent action against other nations; and leaders continued to play on the sentiments of the underlying population to secure personal advantages.[5]

Preparation for war and warfare itself, especially successful warfare, had a particular potency for invigorating nationalistic sentiments. They did so directly, by increasing the sense of national solidarity and magnifying hostility towards outsiders, and indirectly, by invigorating the feudal habits of thought of which nationalism and patriotism were an integral part. Thus Veblen wrote that "warfare . . . has always proved an effective school in barbarian methods of thought" and "warlike enterprise nourishes a harmonious national hatred of all outsiders, and military discipline induces a virtuously servile temper and an unreasoning obedience to constituted authority" (1904, 393; 1934, 446–47). War also

5. On the position of patriotism and nationalism in the network of medieval habits of thought see Veblen 1915, ch. 3, or 1917, 306–8. The survival of barbaric habits of thought in modern times is a theme found throughout Veblen's work (see, e.g., 1899, ch. 1). On the deliberate manipulation of nationalistic sentiments by both feudal and modern political leaders see Veblen 1917, 3, 21, 35, 189, 226, 307. The manipulation of psychic states by political and other power players was also emphasized by Pareto.

served as a psychic balm: "the disciplinary effects of warlike pursuits and warlike preoccupations" could be relied upon to "direct the popular interest to other, nobler, institutionally less hazardous pursuits than the unequal distribution of wealth or of creature comforts" (1904, 392–93).

The nation-state system was another aspect of modern life that served to preserve nationalism. To "the conception of cultural solidarity within the nation" corresponded a "consequent aliency between nations." Indeed one of the central themes of *The Nature of Peace* is that the nation-state system is the necessary and sufficient condition for the existence of war as it has come to be known. The ultimate consequence of the existence of national establishments is the preservation of nationalistic animosities, and these animosities create a need for such establishments as providers of "common defense." "Taken in the large, the common defense of any given nation becomes a detail of the competitive struggle between rival nationalities animated with a common spirit of patriotic enterprise and led by authorities constituted for this competitive purpose." National establishments are coercive in nature, and in that they are, they act to preserve elements of the feudal mentality. Without nation-states there would be no patriotic devotion, no ambitious governmental establishments, and no serious international aggression (1917, 61). Veblen is asserting more than the tautology that without nations there would be no international war; he is arguing that the very existence of nations causes war. The existence of nation-states generates the problem of international order, that is to say, of peace on which/whose terms, which frequently enough leads to war.[6]

The interlocking and mutually reinforcing relationship between the nation-state system, nationalism, and war is suggestive of a vicious cycle, and by Veblen's estimation such a vicious cycle operated throughout the Middle Ages and on the continent of Europe through the sixteenth and seventeenth centuries. But he also identified forces that could break the cycle, or at least hamper its operation. Of primary importance historically was the mere cessation of hostilities. Without the persistent habituation provided by war and threat of war, the system of preconceptions supporting nationalism, patriotism, and unquestioning obedience to constituted authorities would begin to decay as the common man reverted to habits of thought more consonant with his basically peaceful and independent nature.[7] Conversely, Veblen seemed

6. This is the international version of what Spengler (1948) called the Problem of Order, namely, the ongoing necessity to resolve conflicts between freedom and control, between continuity and change, and between equality and hierarchy.

7. Veblen argued that during the longest segment of their race history the European peoples lived in small, anarchic bands practicing the principle of Live and Let Live. The process of natural selection had produced in these peoples a human nature that was basically peaceable and insubordinate. In the absence of countervailing habituation this

to believe that in the absence of a geographical or historical accident serving to remove some segment of the community of nations from the cycle of hostilities, the cultural forces that offered a way out of the cycle could not have emerged (1904, 304–6, 361–62).

Veblen argued that the roots of the decay of feudal preconceptions could be found in Elizabethan England. England's geographical isolation allowed its people a respite from international strife, and over the course of generations of relatively peaceful existence feudal habits of thought began to fall by the wayside. They were replaced by the more individualistic, insubordinate habits of thought idealized in the notions of natural right and natural liberty. At the same time the industrial arts were able to develop unhindered, fueled by and reinforcing the development of a set of materialistic and mechanistic preconceptions (1915, 100–108). These processes laid the groundwork for the two systems of institutions Veblen referred to as business enterprise and the machine process. Life within both sets of institutions served to modify or eliminate predatory habits of thought and behaviors. It is a well-known theme of Veblen's that the habits of thought engendered by the machine process were matter-of-fact, unpatriotic, undevout, and skeptical of all but scientific authority. The pecuniary institutions of business enterprise also tended to turn men's attention away from war and politics and towards trade and industry. Veblen believed that under the appropriate circumstances, however, the habits of thought peculiar to the system of business enterprise could come into interaction with the more archaic feudalistic preconceptions to produce an extremely bellicose temper among the population, a possibility to be discussed further below.

The Dynastic State and the Modern State

The historical development of the machine process and business enterprise out of and in opposition to feudal institutions, and the unevenness of that development, provided Veblen with the basis for a dichotomy which was central to his analysis of war: the dichotomy between the dynastic state and the modern state. He offered descriptions of "the dynastic state" and "the modern state" as ideal types: the dynastic state was one in which prevailing patterns of behavior and habits of thought remained close to the feudal model; the modern state was one in which the machine process and business enterprise had made substantial headway against feudal or predatory habits of thought. In Veblen's view Germany and Japan came the closest to his model of the dynastic

---

inherited human nature would assert itself in any society made up of people of this race. Lest he be accused of engaging in conjectural historiography, Veblen cited contemporary archaeological evidence in support of his argument (e.g., 1915, chs. 1–2).

state, while the most nearly modern states were the English-speaking nations. The states he characterized as "dynastic" were all in fact states in which rulers came in succession from the same family, but his descriptions of the dynastic state make it clear that what made a state "dynastic" was its attitude and mode of behavior, established by its rulers, and not the manner in which those rulers were chosen (see 1915, 64, 79, 160, 224; 1917, 82). Thus, for example, the Stalinist Soviet Union could readily be designated a dynastic state in Veblen's sense of the word, notwithstanding the absence of the czar.

The dynastic state is variously described by Veblen as predatory, militarist, competitive, and rapacious. It emphasizes national discrepancies, it believes in national prowess and prestige. In the dynastic state intense national pride is shot through with envy and distrust of other nations. Its patriotic statesmen seek in real and imaginary grievances the "raw materials for the production of international difficulties" (1917, 71). If this is conspicuously the Germany of 1870, 1914, and eventually 1939, most if not all other nation-states have exhibited from time to time certain of these characteristics, their own preconceptions of identity and other rationalizations of policy notwithstanding.[8]

Veblen also incorporated certain structural features in his description of the dynastic state. The masses were held in usufruct by a centralized and irresponsible autocracy exercising coercive personal rule. There was an identification of self and nation with ruler. "The habit of authority and unquestioning obedience has been so thoroughly ingrained," he wrote, "that subservience has become a passionate aspiration with the subject population" (1915, 78–79). In 1915 he wrote that "to the Japanese government, or 'state,' the country, with its human denizens, is an estate to be husbanded and exploited for the state's ends, which comes near to saying, for the prestige of the Mikado's government. . . . In effect the people at large are the government's chattels to be bred, fed, trained, and consumed as the shrewd economy of dynastic politics may best require" (1934, 249). He commonly discussed the international, predatory, and domestic hierarchical features of the dynastic state together, making it clear that they were integral parts of the same package.

Veblen's idealized modern state was (ostensibly) democratic, peaceful, and cosmopolitan. He linked it to post-Enlightenment values such as liberalism, rationalism, individualism, and the system of natural rights. Its ideals included representative government, self-help, and

---

8. "In the current German conception, e.g., . . . peace appears to be of the general nature of a truce between nations, whose God-given destiny it is, in time, to adjust a claim to precedence by wager of battle. . . . The conception of peace as a period of preparation for war has many adherents outside the Fatherland, of course" (Veblen 1917, 299–300).

local autonomy. Its people had materialistic rather than spiritual habits of thought, and a mechanistic conception of logic. The modern state was decidedly not what the dynastic state was.

Veblen drew a sharp contrast between the two states with regard to questions of peace and war. Peace, in the modern state, is not seen as a time during which to prepare for war, but "has come to stand in the common estimation as the normal and stable manner of life, good and commendable in its own right" (1917, 300). "In point of fact, the democratic commonwealth is moved by other interests in the main, and the common defense is a secondary consideration. . . . It is otherwise with the dynastic state, to the directorate of which all other interests are necessarily secondary, subsidiary, and mainly to be considered only in so far as they are contributory to the nation's readiness for warlike enterprise" (1917, 228–29).

But there is a tension in Veblen's treatment of the modern state. Along with all his distinctions between the modern and the dynastic state, and his subtle and not-so-subtle expressions of approval for characteristics he associates with the modern state, he sends the clear message that the dynastic state and the modern state are not so different after all. The differences are those of degree, not kind, we are told; the two types of states do not represent a divergence, but a "differential in point of cultural maturity"; the "practical attitude towards the constituted authorities is by no means widely different" in the two types of state, and so forth (see 1915, 57–58, 100, 104, 166; 1917, 10, 100). Veblen's assertions of the similarity between the two types of states rest on a few basic premises. First, both types of state have evolved out of the institutional environment of feudalism, and both retain predatory characteristics of the ancient regime, "though not in an equal degree of preservation and effectiveness" (1917, 10). Second, the prevailing institutions in both types of state are such that fruits of the common man's labor flow to a relatively small and unproductive ruling elite. Third, the modern state remains after all a state, and thus a focal point for patriotic sentiments. The common man in the modern state does value peace, but it must be "peace with honour" that is, national honor (1917, 301). In the modern state nationalistic sentiments are allied not with an aristocratic warrior caste but with the interests of the newer ruling classes ("gentlemen investors" in England, "business interests" in America). The new ruling classes, like the old, can and do manipulate such sentiments, and a frequent consequence of this manipulation is war.

The bottom line for Veblen regarding the dynastic and the modern states is that the ordinary processes of life in both tend to lead to armed conflict between nations. The differences in the goals and habits of thought across the two types of states mean that the paths they take to conflict may differ in detail, but the final outcome is the same.[9]

Two Paths to War

The previous sections have dwelt mainly on the aspects of modern society that Veblen believed to be derivative of predatory habits of thought persisting from feudal times. He is better known for his analysis of what he held to be the two major socializing forces of his own day: the pecuniary and industrial employments, or the machine process and business enterprise. His discussions of the causes and consequences of war in recent times and the chances for peace in the future deal with the way in which these three forces—the predatory, the pecuniary, and the technological—interact to generate both socialized persons and the phenomena of history, including the dynastic state and the modern state. Veblen allowed of several relationships between the three forces, precluding a definitive prediction of the future course of events. So, rather than attempting such predictions, his practice was to outline a range of possibilities, attaching to each a (sometimes vague) assessment of its probability. In this section we describe some of the patterns of interaction he identified and their relevance for questions of war and peace.

War and the Dynastic State

As discussed above, warlike activities were considered a normal and suitable aspect of life by the people and leaders of the dynastic state. The leaders saw war as both an honorific activity and an effective instrument for the accomplishment of their goals. The people embraced the values of their leaders and supported their bellicose adventures with an unquestioning loyalty. If the dynastic state was not involved in an act of international aggression, it was planning one. Even in the modern era, when proper form demanded that the spokesmen of the dynastic state join in the general diplomatic disavowal of aggressive aims, they developed the notion of the "defensive offense," or preemptive strike against a threatening neighbor, allegedly intended solely for the protection of the homeland (Veblen 1915, 254–55).

9. For example, a dynastic state practices protectionism in order to promote self-sufficiency, an attribute held to be of great value in time of war. The common man gladly undergoes the material deprivation thus caused for the sake of king and country. The modern state practices protectionism at the urging of its business interests, which gain thereby competitive advantages against foreign interests. The common man supports this policy because of his groundless belief that he shares in the good fortune of his nation's business interests. In either case the policy of protectionism by one nation leads to retaliation by others and to a subsequent increase in animosity between nations and partisan solidarity within nations, both of which increase the prospects that what began as an economic conflict will ultimately be settled by force of arms.

Despite their basically feudal complexion, the dynastic states were not untouched by pecuniary and technological forces. Leaders in some dynastic states early appreciated the potential for turning new developments in machine technology, communication, and transportation to their advantage and used this advantage to expand their states and consolidate their rule (Veblen 1915, 76, 170). Technological changes allowed for more effective indoctrination of the populace with militant nationalism and enabled more coercive control to be exercised over larger areas (1917, 15–21). The new technology could be applied to the art of war in the form of new weapons, more effective systems of logistical support, etc.; and the dynastic states pursued such applications with a vigor unmatched by their modern counterparts (1915, 48, 247–48).

More importantly, the new technology considerably expanded the productive potential of the dynastic state that employed it. And in the dynastic state there was little to prevent the bulk of this expanded potential from being employed to enhance military capability. The common people were accustomed to a low standard of living, leaving a relatively high margin of production above cost. Further, the common man of the dynastic state, as a result of centuries of habituation to the feudal mindset, regarded as natural and desirable the policies that directed this disposable margin towards the aggrandizement of the dynasty rather than the improvement of his material welfare (1915, 47–48). The combination of the time-honored "fanatical loyalty of feudal barbarism" with the possession of modern technology made the dynastic state a formidable warlike force indeed (1917, 200).[10]

Historically, according to Veblen, the borrowing of machine technology by the dynastic states also involved a partial adoption of the institutions of business enterprise, which led to the growth in the dynastic state of commercial interests sometimes more preoccupied with the profitability of their business concerns than the advancement of national honor. He argued that dynastic leaders could easily ensure the loyalty of the commercial classes with arguments that the extension of imperial dominion would bring increased opportunities for profit (1917, 199).

This did not mean, however, that the borrowing of institutions of business enterprise was unproblematic for the dynastic state. Veblen noted that loyalty which came only at a price was far short of "that spirit of enthusiastic abnegation that has always been the foundation of a prosperous dynastic state" (1915, 99–100), an observation that underscores his larger point that business enterprise engendered habits of thought contrary to the ideals of the dynastic state. Under the discipline

10. Veblen makes this argument often, in particular with respect to Germany and Japan (e.g., 1934, esp. 251–52).

of business enterprise, concern with profitability and one's own pecuniary status moved to the foreground, partly displacing concern with the glory of the sovereign. As business enterprise took firmer hold, the commercial interests, observing the exploits of their counterparts in the more modern commercial states, required wider margins of profit to be satisfied. The common man, emulating the behavior of the growing commercial classes, became more concerned with his own material well-being and less willing to foot the bill for dynastic projects. The leaders of the dynastic state found themselves having to direct part of the disposable margin towards these groups to ensure their loyalty, leaving less for dynastic purposes. Veblen stressed the long-run nature of this process, and the persistence of predatory habits of thought in the face of it, but also noted that it was becoming a source of perplexity and concern for the dynastic statesmen of his own day (1915, 190–203).

More problematic for the dynastic state in the long run was its dependence on machine technology. The leaders of the dynastic state were well aware that in the modern world dynastic prestige could only be maintained through proper use of the nation's material resources and that "technology and industrial experience, in large volume and at high proficiency, are indispensable to the conduct of war . . . as well as a large up-to-date industrial community and industrial plant to supply the necessary material of this warfare" (1934, 255–56). But experience with the technology of modern industry, even more so than with business enterprise, bred habits of thought alien to those on which the dynastic state rested. Those who worked in close contact with the processes of modern technology came to view the world in mechanistic, materialistic, impersonal terms and lost respect for institutions, explanations, and justifications that did not run on such terms. Appeals to tradition, to natural or divine rights, to hereditary authority, and so on ceased to influence these workers. The habituating influence of technology undermined both dynastic and pecuniary habits of thought, including nationalism and patriotism.[11]

The deliberate maintenance of a patriotic and warlike temperament in the population, ultimately through recourse to war, could fortify predatory habits of thought against the decaying influence of business enterprise and the machine process. But there was a catch here as well. Just as the use of modern industry inculcated in the workforce a particular way of looking at the world, the effective use of machine technology required workers with such a world view. If war and warlike activities reversed the cultural tendencies set in motion by technology, they also

---

11. This is a familiar theme in Veblen: see 1904, 310, 372–74; 1915, 223–27; or 1917, 197–98, 313–14. On the long-run nature of the impact of both pecuniary and technological forces on archaic habits of thought see Veblen 1915, 242; 1917, 192–95.

cut into the technological efficiency of the workforce, thereby diminishing the warlike effectiveness of the dynastic state.[12] Veblen thus wrote that "the Imperial State . . . may be said to be unable to get along without the machine industry, and also, in the long run, unable to get along with it; since this industrial system in the long run undermines the foundation of the State" (1915, 262).[13]

Veblen's analysis of what he called the "dilemma" of the dynastic state by no means implied that such states were destined to pass peacefully from the face of the globe. It was meant mainly to suggest the factors that would determine the success or failure of a dynastic state's inevitable aggressive actions, with a tongue-in-cheek implication that the shrewd dynastic statesman could calculate and chart the positive and negative effects of the industrial system on the warlike capacity of his own nation and rival nations, and strike when his advantage was the greatest.[14]

But strike he would, whether optimally or not. As long as dynastic states existed there was no hope for neighboring states of a more modern complexion to enjoy the lasting peace they professed to desire. Their justifiable fear of aggression required them to maintain military establishments. Military establishments, and the ever-present possibility that hostilities would break out, acted to preserve predatory habits of thought in the modern states. As long as dynastic states existed there would be international war, and as long as war remained a feature of life the predatory habits of thought that supported it would prevail against the influence of the pecuniary and technological forces, perhaps leading ultimately to a general cultural retrogression.

War, Imperialism, and the Modern State

The presence of dynastic states made war inevitable, but dynastic states were not necessary in order for war to exist. Veblen provided an analysis of the way in which the ordinary processes of life in a world of

12. Veblen argued in 1915 that the decay in the industrial efficiency of the population due to habituation was perhaps the most important cost of war. He would shortly change his assessment of the effect of warfare on habits of thought, but not his opinion that commentators tended to overstate the economic costs of war relating to the destruction of property and capital equipment. A nation's most important economic resource, he claimed, was its stock of technical know-how. This stock was a possession of the community at large and was not diminished by the destruction of the pieces of machinery in which it might be embodied. It was damaged, however, when the community at large was subjected to habituation that undermined the preconceptions conducive to technical efficiency and scientific advance (1915, 258–64).

13. See also Veblen 1917, 311–12.

14. Veblen estimated that Germany had waited a bit too long to launch its defensive offense to start World War I, whereas for the Japanese the optimal time lay "within the lifetime of the generation now coming into maturity" as of 1915 (see 1915, 251–54; 1934, 264–66).

modern nation-states led to war. This analysis, presented first in 1904 in *The Theory of Business Enterprise,* also represented the essence of his theory of imperialism as an economic and political phenomenon.

Veblen's modern state was controlled by business interests, so that considerations bearing on the pecuniary profitability of the nation's business establishments guided the making of policy. This is not to say that there were not in both the governmental and military establishments of such states leaders who embraced the ideals of dynastic dominion or that these ideals had no place in the minds of the business community. There was in the modern state, as in the dynastic state, a tension between the commercial interests and the dynastic interests over the ends towards which resources would be directed, but in the modern state the business interests had the upper hand (1904, 285–86, 394).

The government of the modern state was representative, and its policies on behalf of business enjoyed popular support. The system of property rights through which the commercial classes achieved their wealth and power were part of the unquestioned cultural heritage of the modern state. Also, the preconceptions reinforced by exposure to the pecuniary institutions that dominated the modern states included a presumption that those who amassed the most pecuniary wealth were the most deserving of honor and esteem and the most fit to guide the fortunes of the nation. Popular support of the business government rested on patriotism as well, a patriotism linked to a "commercial nationalism" in which the nation's prestige was tied to the profitability of its business interests. The common man of the modern state wanted the business interests of his nation to be more profitable than, and to succeed at the expense of, the business interests of other nations. He wanted his nation's businessmen to be given preferential treatment by the governments of other nations, and a failure on this score led to considerable patriotic indignation. Veblen believed that a reasoned analysis would reveal little or no relationship between the way in which a nation's business interests were treated abroad or their success in international commerce and the material well-being of the average citizen of that nation, but the patriotic impulse was not based on reason. The common man simply assumed that he and the national honor he prized somehow benefited from gains accruing to his nation's businessmen, and enthusiastically supported government policies to secure such gains (1904, 286–92; 1917, 66–78).

The businessman regarded the powers and functions traditionally associated with the state in the same way that he regarded all else falling within his view: as instruments to be used in his competitive quest for pecuniary gain. Unlike the dynastic statesman, he was not interested in war first and foremost; in fact he preferred a peaceful environment in which to conduct his business. But he would support a breach of the peace if he believed that it would lead to the establishment of a new peace on terms more favorable to his interests (1904, 293, 296).

Acting through the instruments of government, the businessmen of the modern state created competitive advantages for themselves in the form of tariffs against foreign competitors and subsidies for domestic interests, both of which did their part to increase the level of international animosity. There were also situations in which the business interests found the military capacity of the state to be of use. Military force was sometimes necessary, for example, to create in less developed parts of the world an environment suitable for doing business.[15] In addition, when business interests of two or more nations met in a less developed part of the world, military force was often the final arbiter of conflicts over terms on which the market would be shared. Thus were colonial wars and imperialistic conflicts born (1904, 295–96; 1917, 156).

It was not only in the colonial arena that the business interests of the modern state met. Given the international nature of modern commerce, modern businessmen aggressively sought markets in and favorable terms of trade from other countries. And they called upon the powers of the state, including the military power, to aid them in or to protect themselves against such incursions: "In international competition the *ultima ratio* is, as ever, warlike force, whether the issue be between princes of the grace of God or princes of ownership" (1904, 294). The businessmen did not necessarily want war in these situations but wanted to be able to point to a warlike establishment large enough to constitute a credible threat during negotiations. And warlike strength being assessed in relative terms, this desire of the business interests could draw the modern nations into an arms race (295–98).

Veblen believed that in using the mechanism of the state as a tool for gaining a competitive edge the business interests of the modern state might get more than they bargained for. Commercial warfare, whether involving tariffs, threat of war, or recourse to war, was accompanied by intensified nationalistic and patriotic sentiment in the population and by a general rehabilitation of dynastic habits of thought. As a result of this

15. "The advanced nations of Christendom are proselyters, and there are certain valuable perquisites that come to the business men of those proselyting nations who advance the frontiers of the pecuniary culture among the backward populations. There is commonly a handsome margin of profit in doing business with these, pecuniarily unregenerate, populations, particularly when the traffic is adequately backed with force. But, also commonly, these people do not enter willingly into lasting business relations with civilized mankind. It is therefore necessary . . . that they be firmly held up to such civilized rules of conduct as will make trade easy and lucrative. To this end armament is indispensable" (Veblen 1904, 295).

sentiment policy would come more and more to reflect the dynastic outlook, and the aggressive national policy begun to advance business interests would be turned to the achievement of dynastic ends. Instead of temporary wars to establish more favorable terms of trade, the state would enter into a long-term program of war for dynastic dominion, one to be pursued whether or not it happened to be a good business proposition and all the way to the point of economic collapse if not military destruction (1904, 297–99, 398–400).

Why, Veblen asked, would the business community allow the situation to get out of control? His answer looked to the individualistic nature of private enterprise: "business enterprise is an individual matter, not a collective one. So long as the individual business man sees a proximate gain for himself in meeting the demands for war funds and materials . . . that go with military politics, it is not in the nature of the business man to draw back . . . regardless of what the ulterior substantial outcome of such a course may be in the end" (1904, 301). War was good for the individual businessman. The businessman had no trouble securing lucrative terms when negotiating government contracts.[16] He sensed in war an enterprise in which he could get "something for nothing," a chance to enlarge his profits while the common man paid the cost of war.

There is another reason that businessmen as a class looked with favor on an increase in warlike fervor. The socializing forces associated with modern technology were at work in the modern state, and in addition to eroding the faith of the workers in the verities held over from the feudal era, they undermined the natural-rights ideology upon which business control of the state and its resources was based. Veblen did not contend that the businessmen fully understood the nature of these forces and their interactions, e.g., that they linked the increased dissension and restiveness among the working classes to the cultural effects of the machine process. But Veblen's businessmen did appreciate that workers in a patriotic state of mind were less disruptive and less concerned with matters relating to their material well-being (the "psychic balm" function of war mentioned earlier). Unfortunately for the businessmen the increased loyalty they noticed in the workers was a loyalty not to business principles and business rule but to the aims and policies of the dynastic politicians (1904, 392–94).

The foregoing constitutes Veblen's analysis, as of 1904, of imperialism. The only key component added to the theory in subsequent years was his discussion of the dynastic state, the imperialistic activities of

---

16. Veblen (1904, 296) supports this view by noting that government procurement is plagued by what is now known as a principle-agent problem, leading to shirking and malfeasance by government officials.

which follow straightforwardly from its fundamental nature. His approach to imperialism is, economically, broader than Lenin's and also encompasses Schumpeter's political theory of imperialism.[17] Veblen combined political and economic interpretations of imperialism because he saw that in the modern capitalist nations the nominally political and the nominally economic are two aspects of the same social process, which may be called the legal-economic nexus: "Business competition has become international, covering the range of what is called the world market. In this international competition the machinery and policy of the state are in a peculiar degree drawn into the service of the large business interests . . . the business men of one nation are pitted against those of another and swing the forces of the state, legislative, diplomatic, and military, against one another in the strategic game of pecuniary advantage" (1904, 292). Whereas for Taussig the Napoleons of industry were a reasonable substitute for the bloodthirsty Napoleons of history, for Veblen (as for Hobson, Hilferding, and others) the latter phenomena could, and often did, follow upon the former.

World War I and
the Prospects for Lasting Peace

Shortly before America's entry into World War I, Veblen wrote *An Inquiry into the Nature of Peace and the Terms of Its Perpetuation,* an examination of the causes of war and the necessary conditions for a lasting peace. We have already outlined his analysis of the causes of war. His prescription for lasting peace followed from that analysis. A lasting peace could not be established until dynastic states no longer sought dominion and nationalism died out in the modern states. A lasting peace required first that the ongoing war end with the invasion and unconditional surrender of Germany and the establishment of democratic institutions therein by the victors following the destruction of all vestiges of imperial rule and aristocratic power and authority (1917, 239–44, 258).[18] Next, the formation of a league of pacific nations, with a

17. For Lenin imperialism arose from the need to export surplus capital; for Schumpeter, from the machinations of domestic politics as different groups attempted to manipulate nationalistic sentiments to capture state power. Veblen's theory does include Lenin's argument: e.g., "It is also a matter of course that the effective growth of the foreign market has not kept pace with the growing productive capacity. . . . the quest of markets has been one of the leading incentives to [German] colonial policy" (Veblen 1915, 196).

18. The only alternative foundation of a lasting peace, Veblen insisted, would be submission by the modern states to the rule of the German dynasty. He devoted a chapter of *The Nature of Peace* to describing possible material benefits and costs of such a submission. The alleged benefits followed from the elimination in the subject nations of the fear of invasion and the need to support a military establishment, and from the expectation that Germany would treat the subject peoples as productive chattel, not allowing their standards of living to fall below the level making for an optimally efficient

new Germany admitted as a member on equal terms—although the German people would have to be monitored until enough time had passed for them to unlearn their predatory habits of thought. Within the league of pacific peoples all sources of national jealousy and national discrimination were to be removed (217, 276–77). This would require a regime of free trade between nations, conversion of colonies into self-governing commonwealths, the end of constitutional monarchies and any other remaining vestiges of feudal government, and what Veblen referred to as the "neutralization of citizenship." The latter phrase referred to a policy in which all people living or operating within the borders of a national jurisdiction would be treated equally under the laws of that jurisdiction, regardless of their nation of birth.[19]

Veblen held that his proposal for what he called "peace by neglect" was very simple in principle, requiring mainly the dismantling of existing policies regarding international intercourse, which were invidious in nature and which kept alive international jealousies and competition. The material benefits of the proposed arrangement were clear: the nations stood to save the cost of maintaining separate defense establishments (there would be one defense force for the entire league to deal with dynastic powers still outside the fold, which would not represent a serious threat once Germany was neutralized), and the benefits of replacing protectionism with free trade would be realized as well (1917, 215, 281–82, 336–37; 1934, 377–78, 381).

However, Veblen realized that much in the way of habit and vested interest stood in the way of his proposals, however simple and generally beneficial they might appear in the light of reasoned analysis.[20] The modern states were controlled, after all, by their business interests, who

---

workforce. He argued that many workers in the modern states currently lived below that level. Although he ruled out peace by submission as even a remote possibility (the pugnaciously independent nature of the common man in the modern states would prevent it, in spite of the material benefits it might offer), and although he probably conducted his cost-benefit analysis with tongue in cheek, his willingness to speculate on the possibility created controversy (Dorfman 1934, 381).

19. Veblen hoped to forestall the process by which governments became embroiled in the pecuniary competition of their respective business interests. He also summarized the policy of his proposed league with the principle that "the community will no longer collectively promote or safeguard any private enterprise in pursuit of private gain beyond its own territorial bounds," describing this as "an unreserved extension of the principles of free trade, but with the inclusion of foreign investments as well as commercial traffic" (1934, 376, 381). A full account of his proposal for the pacific league is Veblen 1934, 347–82. He believed that free trade made for peace not only by removing a source of international contention but also by making nations economically more dependent on one another (1917, 207–8).

20. *The Nature of Peace* begins with a rejection of the argument that a reasoned explanation of the costliness of war could persuade a nation to take the steps necessary for lasting peace. See Barber 1991 for some of the history of this argument.

had put in place the whole apparatus of tariffs, subsidies, preferments, and so forth for their own benefit (1917, 289–90, 297). The common people still attached great importance to the trappings and instruments of nationhood, citizenship, and national rivalry. The people of the Allied states, whipped into a vengeful fury by the war experience, would have trouble accepting even a reformulated German state as an equal partner in a league of nations. Accordingly, Veblen's assessments of the chances of a peace settlement along the terms he proposed involved phrases ranging from "uneasy doubt" to "beyond reasonable hope" (203–5, 219).

Still, one occasionally detects in *The Nature of Peace* a cautious optimism on Veblen's part, stemming mainly from his belief that the cultural impact of World War I would be fundamentally different from that of any previous war. Habits of thought in the modern states, under the discipline of the machine process and business enterprise, had been drifting away from the notion of war as a glorious or desirable enterprise to that of war as a necessary evil, to be endured only in defense of the national integrity. Two years of observing the devastating consequences of a war fought with the devices of modern technology hastened this drift of sentiment. Moreover, Veblen argued, the new technology of war shifted the advantage to the offensive and gave states with aggressive designs an ability to strike almost anywhere on the globe. Nations wishing to avoid war faced the almost impossibly costly task of establishing a military force adequate to deter or defend against aggression. It was to the feeling that only by banding together could the pacific nations afford to provide an adequate defense against aggressors that Veblen attributed much of the sentiment being expressed for some sort of league of peaceful nations (1917, 103–6, 202–3, 219–24). As the war continued, people would become more persuaded of the costliness of war in general and the danger posed by the continued existence of the dynastic states, and would thus be more willing to make what they perceived to be sacrifices in order to achieve a lasting peace (297).

There was a second important change in Veblen's view on the cultural impact of war that contributed to his guarded optimism. Prior to World War I, he had argued that the experience of war served to rehabilitate predatory sentiments to the detriment of the more peaceable and industrially serviceable habits of thought associated with the machine process, so that the people of the modern state would emerge from war industrially less efficient, but with their patriotism and loyalty to constituted authorities intensified. In *The Nature of Peace* he stated that this had changed. War had become a technological matter, with victory going to the nations best able to produce the machines of war and employ them effectively in the field. The successful soldier was familiar and comfortable with the mundane ways and means of modern technology, and the successful officer approached war as an impersonal technological project. "The discipline of the campaign," Veblen now believed, "is not at cross purposes with the ordinary industrial employments of peace . . . [it] does not greatly unfit the men who survive for industrial uses . . . or break the continuity of that range of habits of thought which . . . the technological order induces" (1917, 304). War still inculcated acrimonious patriotism and unquestioning obedience among the participants, but it no longer impaired their technological efficiency (305).

This new aspect of war had an implication for the chances of a lasting peace. By Veblen's reckoning, the British would set the tone in any peace negotiations. At the onset of the war Britain was ruled, and its armies were led, by well-bred gentlemen. Such gentlemen, respectful of the monarchy, proud of the empire, and having a vested interest in the colonial system and protectionism, could never conceive of a league of nations that called for the elimination of such arrangements. But, Veblen argued, the war was undermining the authority of the British ruling class. The characteristics bred into the British gentleman—gallantry, humanity, liberality—proved a handicap on the modern battlefield, where ferocity and technological ability carried the day. As a result gentlemanly officers were dying at a disproportionate rate while common men with matter-of-fact mindsets were moving through the ranks into positions of command. A similar process of "discredit and elimination" was occurring on the home front among the officials responsible for the conduct of the war, as it was discovered that gentlemanly methods were no longer appropriate in the conduct of modern war (1917, 245–48).

The rule of the British gentlemen rested on the underlying population's faith that those gentlemen were best qualified to rule. The war was simultaneously undermining that confidence and throwing into authority competent replacements from among less privileged classes. At the same time the habits of thought bred of technological experience, which led men to question the rights of property and hereditary class distinctions, were undisturbed by the war. Veblen speculated that a further erosion of faith in the sanctity of existing property relations might occur as the people at large observed war production taking place—materials produced and delivered, even across international boundaries—without the benefit of the pecuniary formalities that were held to be indispensable to the conduct of analogous industrial operations during peacetime (1917, 250–54).

Thus Veblen believed that the war had set in motion forces conducive to the establishment of a lasting peace. If the war persisted long enough, the people and perhaps the rulers of the modern states would be in a frame of mind to make sacrifices for lasting peace. Furthermore, should the war continue to undermine faith in the existing order and fortify the materialistic habits of thought in the populations of the modern states, they might no longer regard the elimination of protectionism, constitutional monarchy, colonial ambitions, and other trappings of the nation-state system as a very serious sacrifice. The chances of this were slim, but, as Veblen noted on several occasions, the longer the war persisted, the greater the chances would become (1917, 256–57, 276, 294, 305–6).

It is hard to know how serious Veblen was in all this. He devoted enough space to his discussion of the possible contribution of the war experience to the chances of lasting peace to imply that he did not consider it an idle matter. Yet he almost invariably included in such discussions language downplaying the importance of the forces being described and the probability of their having an impact on people's habits of thought. It is true that an attribution of importance to the habituating effect of the war experience would run counter to his general position that major changes in preconceptions could occur only over the long run. However, in *The Nature of Peace* he at one point includes in a statement of this position the qualifying clause "but it should be also noted that events are [now] moving with unexampled celerity, and are impinging on the popular apprehension with unexampled force" (1917, 233–34).

All this aside, there is no shortage of pessimism to be found in *The Nature of Peace*. Veblen argued that if the war was of insufficient length to substantially alter existing habits of thought, leaving the business interests and gentlemen investors in control in the modern states, any peace settlement would necessarily be merely an armistice, and any league of pacific nations would be ineffectual.

The tone of the peace settlement would be set by the gentlemanly British government, which could not countenance the complete destruction of the German ruling establishment (1917, 275). Being mainly of a pecuniary frame of mind, the statesmen would seek to satisfy popular demands for "justice" by levying a pecuniary penalty on Germany—a trade boycott, reparations, perhaps some confiscation of colonies or territory. The burden of the penalties would fall, as all economic burdens tend to fall, on the common man, leaving untouched the ruling classes, on whom Veblen laid the blame for the war.[21] Also, such a

21. Veblen argued that the German people were held in usufruct by their leaders, "unremittingly, and helplessly, disciplined into a spirit of dynastic loyalty" with their chief fault being "an habitual servile abnegation of those traits of initiative and discretion in a man that constitute him an agent susceptible of responsibility or retribution." Thus it would be "a pathetic mockery to visit the transgressions of their masters on these victims of circumstance and dynastic mendacity, since the conventionalities of international equity will scarcely permit the high responsible parties in the case to be chastised with any penalty harsher than a well-mannered figure of speech" (1917, 268–69).

settlement would "play into the hands of militarist interests by keeping alive the spirit of national jealousy and international hatred, out of which wars arise" (267; see also 275).

Should the allied victory not be decisive enough to force Germany and the other imperial powers into the league, the world would become "a coalition of nations in two hostile groups, the one standing on the defensive against the warlike machinations of the other . . . it would also involve a system of competitive armaments . . . in other words . . . a virtual return to the status quo ante" (1917, 237; see also 84–85). Veblen noted presciently that should Germany not be adequately pacified, Germany and Japan were "bound to come into a coalition at the next turn, with whatever outside and subsidiary resources they can draw on; provided only that a reasonable opening for further enterprise presents itself" (238). Even if Germany was pacified and brought into the league, ongoing discussions among representatives of the Allies involved a proposed league in which national discriminations and jealousies would be preserved.[22] A peace based on such a league, even in the absence of dynastic states, would be a precarious one, for reasons we mentioned in the preceding section (202–3, 302–3).

Veblen was willing to speculate, however, on what might occur if such a league of pacific nations as was then being contemplated by the Allies were able to form, and enjoy, through some fortunate circumstance, an extended period of peace. Gradually, as the conditioning force of the machine process worked unhindered by seasons of war-inspired patriotic frenzy, materialistic habits of thought would take a firmer hold. Nationalistic sentiments and the related system of national discriminations would fall away, and Veblen's ideals of free trade and the neutralization of citizenship would approach reality. However, the discipline of the machine process undermined not only the predatory preconceptions but also the natural rights preconceptions upon which the business interests' control of government was based. In the absence of concerns about national integrity and maintaining defense against possible invasion, the attention of citizens would turn increasingly to their material well-being. The common man, well-schooled in the discipline of the machine, would begin to question the institutions which kept the nation's wealth out of his hands, and animosity between the commercial classes and the rest of the population would intensify.

The intensification of class animosity, Veblen argued, was the result of lasting peace but also a source of its disruption. If, as was likely, increasing class animosities erupted into civil disturbances against es-

---

22. "What the peace makers might logically be expected to concern themselves about would be the elimination of these discrepancies that make for embroilment. But what they actually seemed concerned about is their preservation" (Veblen 1917, 302).

tablished business governments, it was conceivable that the resources of the pacific league would be employed to restore order. And if, in the nations where the habituating effects of the machine process were most advanced, businessmen's governments were replaced by governments more in accordance with the preconceptions of the common man, the return of international hostilities "undertaken . . . by the more archaic, or conservative, peoples to safeguard the institutions of the received law and order against inroads from the side of the iconoclastic ones" was the likely outcome (1917, 316–30).[23]

In this last bit of analysis, found in the final chapter of *The Nature of Peace,* Veblen revealed his hand on the question of war and peace. A reader of the book gathered first that the elimination of dynastic states was a necessary condition for lasting peace, a prospect few in his audience would have found objectionable. A second necessary condition was the institution of free trade and the neutralization of citizenship—both fairly substantial changes from the status quo, but changes that would meet with the approval of many cosmopolitan thinkers of Veblen's day, including a large number of his fellow economists. Only in the closing pages did the reader find that these conditions are necessary but not sufficient for the establishment of a lasting peace. Ultimately the establishment of a lasting peace would require the dismantling of the entire system of private property rights upon which modern capitalism was based. That the book is arranged in this way, with the potentially most controversial material at the end, may be a coincidence; it was not ordinarily Veblen's style to avoid shocking his audience. But it is at least possible that he did this purposely in an attempt to increase the chance that people would give most of his arguments a fair reading rather than dismissing the book immediately as repugnant radicalism, an attempt born of his belief that at a critical juncture in history he could make a constructive contribution to the cause of lasting peace.[24]

Veblen and the Versailles Treaty

Veblen was disappointed if not disillusioned by the Versailles Treaty, criticizing it in several essays with a bitter, vitriolic style that stood in stark contrast to the more constructive and sometimes optimistic tone of his writings during the last two years of the war. The treaty confirmed the fears he had expressed in *The Nature of Peace.* It was written, he

23. Veblen 1917, 330.
24. Reviewers of the book commented on the placement of the controversial material at the end and responded more favorably to the arguments at the beginning. The book was widely noticed; among other things, the Carnegie Endowment for International Peace purchased five hundred copies for free distribution to schools. Veblen's reaction to the reception of his book: "Now they are beginning to pay attention to me" (Dorfman 1934, 370–71).

said, in "the best and highest traditions of commercialised nationalism."
The peacemakers had sought to establish peace by restoring the environment of dissension and national ambition out of which war arose.
The treaty was a "screen of diplomatic verbiage behind which the Elder
Statesmen of the Great Powers continue[d] their pursuit of political
chicane and imperialistic aggrandisement" (1934, 415–16, 424, 463).

The war had been brought to a premature conclusion, with Germany
being spared the ordeal of a devastating invasion. The ruling classes of
Germany were left relatively unscathed "under a perfunctory mask of
democratic forms," and their military leaders were able to return home
as war heroes. This hasty consummation of the Allied war effort was a
direct result of the Russian revolution. The statesmen of the Allied
powers, or rather the business interests to whom they answered, saw in
the Bolsheviks a threat to the established order, and their primary
concern by 1918 was the suppression of Soviet Russia. This suppression
was to be accomplished in part by rehabilitation of a reactionary regime
in Germany as a bulwark against the spread of Bolshevism. The aspects
of the treaty relating to German indemnity were irrelevant, a diplomatic
bluff designed to distract those in the victorious states who clamored for
vengeance. Veblen predicted that none of the indemnifying clauses
would be lived up to. The Great Powers would not enforce upon the
restored German government any penalty that might weaken its ability
to resist radicalism at home or Bolshevism abroad.[25]

The Versailles treaty, Veblen concluded, offered only the "twilight
peace of the armistice, . . . made up of alarms and recrimination, of
intrigue and hostilities, . . . hedged about with fire, famine, and pestilence" (1934, 459).

Conclusion

Our objective in this article has been to identify what Thorstein Veblen
had to say about matters related to war. It is clear that he brought to bear
on his analysis his own subjective, even normative preconceptions. In
particular, his preoccupation with the pecuniary/industrial dichotomy
clearly influenced (some might say distorted) the pattern of emphasis in
his discussions of causes and consequences of war. Yet once one adjusts
for this and other subjectivities, and for his contentious style, there
remains a substantial body of analysis untainted by sentiment, emotion,
or personal loyalty. Whether or not one agrees with Veblen in detail or in
the whole (and there is no assumption here that he was fully correct in
either regard), his treatment of war and national security is a remarkable
and indeed prescient (to which attribute we shall return) achievement.

25. He makes these arguments repeatedly in a series of essays reprinted in Veblen
1934, 399–470.

Veblen understood that every society constituted an ongoing set of answers to the question "Order on which/whose terms?" In his treatment of war and the possibility of peace he identified and considered the correlative question, "Peace on which/whose terms?" The result was no mean accomplishment, combining a high level of theoretical generalization with a ready handling and interpretation of extensive historical data, all expressed through his marvelous command of the language.

One suspects that Veblen did not think the chances of permanent peace were or are great. This is a conclusion supported, alas, by subsequent historical evidence.

Veblen's analysis, cynical or otherwise, supports the view that terms such as *national defense* and *national security* are, when objectively considered, euphemisms for the inevitable state of affairs under the predatory nation-state system, as well as the ideological and material interests that cloak themselves in the discourse of patriotism. But for most people it is difficult if not impossible to be objective about war.

The key practical question must become the normative status ascribed to particular wars and warlike situations. The three-quarters of a century since the publications of *Imperial Germany* and *The Nature of Peace* have seen World War II, the Korean and Vietnamese wars, the Cold War with its heated elements, and a host of other conflicts. There are evident tensions between warriors on both sides of each conflict as to their respective normative status, just as there is tension in the United States over the nature of the nation's involvement in various wars— whether the actions of the United States constituted aggression or defense, whether a war effort was noble, ignoble, or simply ill-advised. It is difficult to differentiate between war as a derivative of the nation-state system and predatory nationalistic psychology, war as a necessary if not desirable thing under the circumstances, and war as a product of one's own nation's imperial ambitions. Like so much else in his work, Veblen's writings on war and national security point to sensitive aspects of the human condition—and the messenger is not honored for the largely unwelcome message.

Veblen was a heterodox economist, perhaps the greatest of all American dissidents in that fractious discipline, and our discussion of his views on war reveals his quite radical paradigm. Yet the foregoing also makes clear that on a number of very important matters Veblen was a mainstream economist possessed of very orthodox preconceptions, a consideration easily eclipsed by his overt heterodoxy. We are aware that for him these orthodox preconceptions were nested in a very unorthodox body of theory. Our point is simply that these mainstream beliefs were present in his total system of thought.

Veblen was essentially orthodox in these respects:

(1) He believed that the way to greater social welfare lay through the

production of more goods and services. This belief, shared by orthodox economists, underlies his distinction between making goods and making money. His stricture that firms practiced "industrial sabotage" by restricting output in pursuit of profits and his equation at one point (1917, 167) of "the economical use of the nation's resources" with "the largest and most serviceable output of goods and services" clearly rest on this orthodox assumption.[26] His radical conclusion that ordinary business practice is inconsistent with efficiency so defined conflicts with orthodox notions of Pareto efficiency and the rationality of profit maximization. But that is quite another matter, indicating that orthodox analysis is, at its foundations, more complex and pregnant than might be apprehended at first or second glance.

(2) Veblen was willing to use—one hesitates to say he believed in— the orthodox notion that what people received by way of income should bear some relationship to what they contributed to society. His criticism of social parasites and those who seek to get something for nothing, if it does not rest on a productivity notion, at least reflects a perception that the status quo income and wealth distributions depart considerably from the ideal relationship between mode of acquisition and pattern of final distribution.

(3) Veblen was very conventional in his cosmopolitan view of the world economy. Mainstream economists as a group, ever since the mid-eighteenth century, have been cosmopolitan, and Veblen was one of them in his unwillingness to give privileged analytical or policy status to his own nation or its peoples (which of course did not prevent him from taking sides in World War I). For him cosmopolitanism was a habit of thought in accordance with the developing state of the industrial arts. Because modern technology was "impersonal and cosmopolitan," "the effectual working of the modern industrial system" required "an order of things in which the nation has no place or value" (1917, 170; 1934, 389).

(4) Veblen basically accepted the conventional economic arguments in favor of free trade. Even though he had serious reservations about the price system and the power structure to which it gave effect, he was an unusually consistent free-trader, notwithstanding the fact that the arguments for domestic and foreign free trade are substantially identical. (We recognize that his arguments about the price system center much less on the price system per se and more on individual psychology and collective power structure. The point is that those factors enter into international as well as domestic trade.) He denigrates "mercantilist"

---

26. This leaves unanswered the question of which goods and services are "serviceable" and in what quantities; Veblen clearly did not consider all goods to be valuable from a social point of view.

trade policies. He affirms that free trade contributes to efficiency and economic growth and that attempts to achieve economic self-sufficiency impair a nation's industrial efficiency, in part by distorting the decisions of what to produce with the nation's resources (see, e.g., 1915, 171–75). The modern state of the industrial arts is such that it works to the most productive effect through free trade. Finally, as we noted above, Veblen saw free trade as indispensable to lasting peace.

So much for Veblen's iconoclastic orthodoxy.

We have spoken of his prescience with regard to matters of war and peace. We are not referring to an ability on his part to predict wars or other future outcomes in the area of international relations. If one looks for correct predictions of this sort in Veblen's writings, one easily finds them—mainly because, as we noted before, his view of the complexity of the forces at work in the process of social development led him to describe several possible scenarios that might arise out of a given situation, with the result that whatever did actually occur stood a good chance of corresponding to the outcome of one of the possible cases he sketched. However, it often seems that when a historical outcome has corresponded to a possible outcome described by Veblen, the key processes identified in his hypothetical scenario appear to have been among the important forces at work in generating the actual historical outcome. This is the prescience to which we refer.

For example, World War II continued the historic pattern of dynastic adventures and ambitions and the cooperation therein of the common man. The Treaty of Versailles and the reparations after World War I set in motion forces leading to future conflict, including the rehabilitation of Germany as an intensively nationalistic state bent on dominion. Veblen's concern with the actual and potential formidability of the Japanese war machine and the role of Japan as an aggressor and a threat to World peace, and more importantly his stated reasons for that concern, appear valid in the light of subsequent developments, as does his expectation that willingness of the Japanese people to make personal sacrifices for the sake of national glory (economic or military) would decline with the rise of pecuniary values imported from the West.

This brings us to a wider consideration of the post–World War II situation in light of Veblen's analysis. This article was written during the summer of 1990, by curious coincidence at the time when German reunification was in process, and when it was becoming increasingly apparent that one important consequence of the East-West division of powers following the war had been the division and disempowerment of Germany. The process leading towards reunification has produced concerns and anxieties over the future of a reunited Germany, especially in the light of 1870, 1914, 1939, and 1941. A question Veblen posed with regard to Germany—How long would it take the German people to overcome their habitual predatory behavior?—is the question of the day. Have the forty-five years since the end of World War II been enough? Has the experience of (West) Germany as a modern commercial democratic state constituted a suitable educational process?[27]

The foregoing questions suggest others. Are the postwar German and Japanese "miracles" indicative that those peoples and their leaders have matured, in Veblen's sense, into peaceable peoples willing to live and let live? Did enforced disempowerment coupled with economic success effectively sublimate and redirect earlier strong predatory tendencies, as Taussig might have suggested? Or does the strategic manipulation of industry and trade in the quest for and the achievement of commercial mastery merely keep alive a keen predatory temperament, an invidious national pride, and a condescending attitude toward "inferior" foreigners, until an opportunity arises for these sentiments to vent themselves in armed hostility? It would seem that many of the questions implicit in ongoing discussions of the prospects of a lasting peace in a post–Cold War era are similar to the questions that occupied Veblen's attention in his day. That being the case, a better understanding of Veblen's ideas might give us a clearer comprehension of the forces at work around us and their bearing on our hopes for a peaceful future.

The authors would like to acknowledge the helpful comments of Rick Tilman.

References

Barber, William J. 1991. British and American Economists and Attempts to Comprehend the Nature of War, 1910–1920. *HOPE,* this issue.

Dorfman, Joseph. 1934. *Thorstein Veblen and His America.* New York: Viking.

Hadley, Arthur T. 1897. *Economics.* New York: G. P. Putnam.

Meyer, Michael. 1990. The Myth of German Unity. *Newsweek,* 9 July, 30.

Samuels, Warren J. 1990. The Self-Referentiability of Thorstein Veblen's Theory of the Preconceptions of Economic Science. *Journal of Economic Issues* 26 (September): 695–718.

Spengler, Joseph J. 1948. The Problem of Order in Economic Affairs. *Southern Economic Journal* 15 (July): 1–29.

———. 1956. Evolutionism in American Economics, 1800–1946. In *Evolutionary Thought in America,* edited by Stow Persons, 202–67. New York: George Braziller.

Taussig, Frank William. 1929. *Principles of Economics.* Vol. 2. 3d ed., rev. New York: Macmillan.

27. And what of East Germany? An essay entitled "The Myth of German Unity" in a recent issue of *Newsweek* elaborates on the Veblenesque thesis that "the German question has . . . been reincarnated in a new form. The problem? The Federal Republic is prosperous, tolerant, and solidly democratic. The German Democratic Republic is impoverished, intolerant, and undemocratic—a product of oppression on the one hand and ideological conditioning on the other" (Meyer 1990).

————. 1930. *Inventors and Money-Makers*. New York: Macmillan.

Veblen, Thorstein. 1899. *The Theory of the Leisure Class*. New York: Viking.

————. 1904. *The Theory of Business Enterprise*. New York: Scribner's.

————. 1915. *Imperial Germany and the Industrial Revolution*. New York: Huebsch.

————. 1917. *An Inquiry into the Nature of Peace and the Terms of Its Perpetuation*. New York: Macmillan. Reprinted, New York: Kelley, 1964.

————. 1934. *Essays in Our Changing Order*. Edited by Leon Ardzrooni. New York: Viking.

Pareto on Conflict
Resolution and National Security

Vincent J. Tarascio

The term "national security" has different meanings depending on particular circumstances. In the case of Western industrial economies *currently* characterized by stable political institutions and economic prosperity, national security becomes a matter of foreign policy and objectives. However, in the case of many Third World countries where these characteristics are often lacking domestically, national security becomes a matter of both internal as well as external considerations. In general, domestic and foreign considerations are interrelated regarding the matter of national security; and for this reason Pareto linked the "social prosperity" of a nation to its political stability, economic prosperity, and national defense.

This paper examines Pareto's sociological writing regarding the nature and causes of the social prosperity of nations. It is thus necessary to review parts of his sociological and political theories which form the basis for his discussions. After outlining Pareto's theories in a general manner, I present his analysis of World War I as a case study of their application.

Pareto's Theory of Residues

Pareto's sociology represented, for him, a synthesis of the specialized studies dealing with human societies—economic, political, sociological, psychological, and so on. His approach was essentially historical. By examining historical "facts," from ancient Greece to modern Europe, he attempted to distill the "constant" elements from the apparently diverse forms in which they occurred throughout history. These "constant" elements he called "residues." He discerned among the historical materials at his disposal six general classes of residues, each containing several subclasses. These can be outlined briefly, keeping in mind that Pareto devoted an entire volume to them:[1]

Class I: Combinations. This residue represents individuals' propen-

---

1. For a detailed discussion of Pareto's theory of residues see Pareto 1935, vol. 2.

sities to seek new combinations from existing facts or observations. It manifests itself in diverse types of activities such as astrology and astronomy, numerology and mathematics, and so on. Very often it constitutes innovative activity. Concrete examples of those endowed with this class of residues are speculators, industrial entrepreneurs, innovative military strategists, religious prophets, and revolutionary leaders (political, intellectual, scientific).

Class II: Group persistencies. These are the conservative elements in society. Concrete examples are rentiers, landowners, peasants, and, more generally, those who support prevailing institutions and resist changing values. Modern manifestations would be those doing "normal science" in a Kuhnian sense, bureaucrats, religious fundamentalists, and political reactionaries. Class I and II residues are theories of personalities. In his discussions of Class I and II residues Pareto avoids the psychological problem of explaining the development of these personality types. Instead he takes them as empirically given on the basis of his observations, referring to observed behavior as manifestations of psychological states whose origins are unknown. What is important is that under certain conditions, which will be discussed later, conflict is often the conflict between individuals possessing different (Class I and II) residues.

Class III: Need of expressing sentiments by external acts. The best example of this is the "do something" mentality. Riots, wildcat strikes, demonstrations, religious revivals, and spontaneous acts of violence are examples of the need of individuals to express their emotions or beliefs in a physical manner.

Class IV: Sociality. This residue accounts for the fact that human beings have been "social creatures" throughout recorded history. Manifestations are need for uniformity, pity and cruelty, self-sacrifice for the good of others, social ranking, asceticism. Concrete frivolous examples are fads, fashions, bandwagons, and, more generally, peer-group pressures. More important are willingness to sacrifice self-interest for the public good, and submission to authority (parental, governmental, or employer). This residue is the cement that holds human societies together.

Class V: Integrity of the individual and his appurtenances. This residue reflects the role accorded the individual in human societies in spite of Class IV residues. Private property, self-preservation, criminal justice, and equality of individuals are some examples of manifestation of this residue.

The Class IV and V residues are not individual psychological characteristics, as in Classes I and II, but social characteristics of human societies. For example, traditional societies tend to be characterized by strong Class IV residues, whereas modern industrial societies tend to accord more recognition to individual rights and personal freedom, reflecting stronger Class V residues. Class IV and V residues can be viewed as polar cases, whereas in reality examples may be found which cover the entire range between these extremes.

Class VI: Sex. Pareto is interested in the social ramifications of this residue: more generally, these are taboos against pleasures of the flesh extended to consumption of foods and drinks.

The importance of "residues" in Pareto's sociology is that they transcend time and space. These are the historical "constants" or the uniformities which, for him, together characterize a particular society in time, distinguish between different societies in space and time, and account for the evolution of a particular society over time. In short his theory of residues made it possible for him to make comparative analyses of what appeared to be dissimilar societies.

Although Pareto's theory of residues provides a basis for comparison, such a characterization would be more or less taxonomical and therefore mechanical and arid. What he needed and what is needed here is a *process,* namely a political process. This is especially important for my purposes, since the problem of national security involves governments.

Pareto's Political Theory

Society is divided into two classes of individuals: elite and nonelite. The former class consists of leaders in every form of human activity; the remaining individuals comprise the latter class. The norms used to judge performance, and hence bestow leadership recognition, vary among activities. There are leaders in respected activities as well as leaders among thieves. In general, or for society at large, the norms obtaining in society more or less determine the conditions under which individuals will achieve leadership recognition. If social change brings about changes in norms which are disadvantageous to the existing elites, they will be replaced. The elites undergo transformation and, unlike thoroughbred horses, they do not reproduce themselves, according to Pareto. History is the graveyard of elites buried by social, political, and economic change.

The elites are divided into two groups, governing and nongoverning, for the purpose of political analysis. What emerges is a social stratification based on elites and nonelites and a political stratification consisting of governing and nongoverning elites.

Circulation between the governing and nongoverning elites has varied historically. The governing elites may be closed or open, in varying degrees, to accessions by the nongoverning elites. Sparta and Venice are examples of closed governing classes; modern Western democracies are examples of open ones. "Circulation of the elites" refers to a process in which new members are brought into the group of governing elites and existing members drop out—in other words, political mobility.

For Pareto the form of government is not important. In this way the political inventions of mankind—republics, empires, monarchies, democracies, and so on—which are catalogued throughout history take on a *functional* meaning according to the method by which consent is obtained by the governing elite and the extent to which force is used.

We now have all the relevant pieces of Pareto's theories (residues and circulation of elites) to turn to the matter of national security.[2]

Domestic Security

As pointed out above, national security involves both internal and external considerations. This section treats internal security within the context of Pareto's theories and also provides a background for discussion regarding international considerations.

In the section on residues we saw that Class IV residues of sociality account for the fact that human beings are social creatures and that this type of residues is the cement that binds humans together. It also imposes upon individuals a strong sense of uniformity which could be stifling to progress:

> Societies in general subsist because alive and vigorous in the majority of their constituent members are sentiments corresponding to residues of sociality (Class IV). But there are also individuals in human societies in whom some at least of those sentiments are weak or indeed actually missing. That fact has two interesting consequences which stand in apparent contradiction, one of them threatening the dissolution of a society, the other making for its progress in civilization. (Pareto 1935, § 2170, pp. 1510–11)

According to Pareto, an ideal state lies somewhere between these two extremes, namely, where Class IV residues are weak enough to permit some degree of individuality (Class V residues) but not so weak as to cause social dissolution. Class IV and V residues define the social characteristics of the community.

Turning next to the individual residues, Class I and II, we have an analogous distinction. Individuals strong in Class I residues are oriented towards change, whereas those strong in Class II are more oriented

---

2. The sections of this paper dealing with Pareto's theory of residues and his political theory follow Tarascio 1983, 122–25. For present purposes Class III and VI residues are not important, and they are not centrally included in discussion here. They were only mentioned earlier in order to provide the reader with Pareto's general theory of residues, which consists of six classes.

	IV	V
I	a	b
II	c	d

Figure 1.

towards the preservation of existing traditions and institutions. A society dominated by Class I residues tends to be "unstable," reflecting rapid changes and a state of ferment, whereas those strong in Class II residues tend to be more "stable." These four residues can be viewed as combinations in tabular form (see figure 1). Quadrants *a* and *b* are both characterized by innovative personalities, the difference being that in *a* innovation takes place within a *social* context, whereas in *b* it is individualistic and more competitive. Quadrant *c* represents a society characterized by conservative forces operating in an environment of strong social uniformity; quadrant *d,* a conservative and individualistic society.

The next step is to introduce Pareto's theory of the elites, which accounts for the social and political stratification in society. In general, for Pareto, the nonelites, namely the vast majority in all societies, are and have always been characterized by our quadrant *c*: those who normally lead a quiet life, observe norms, submit to authority, believe in and support prevailing religious and political institutions, are patriotic, and are capable of great sacrifice during national emergencies. They follow their leaders (political, religious, fashion, etc.) and are susceptible to ideologies and xenophobia.

What is important for our purposes is that the political or governing elites are found in either *a* or *c*. Governing elites in both these quadrants are socially oriented, since politics involve interpersonal interaction, but either innovative or conservative as reflected in their style of operation. The style of governments depends on the composition of Class I and II residues. If the governing elite is dominated by individuals strong in Class I residues, it tends to be adaptive, responsive, and more adept at compromise. The use of force is avoided, and disputes are often resolved by pecuniary means or by granting certain privileges to undermine discontent. Such governments stress expediency and therefore take a short-run view of circumstances.

Governments strong in Class II residues tend to be less adaptive to changing circumstances, more authoritarian, and ready to use force to deal with discontent. Traditions are preserved, and social innovation is suspect. Goals tend to be future-oriented rather than immediate, and citizens are expected to subordinate their individual interests to those of the community and "future."

Even though the majority of the population may be characterized as belonging in quadrant *c,* it does not mean that the population is homogeneous. For instance, although religious, these individuals may support different theologies, including secular theologies. In general, according to Pareto, populations are heterogeneous, and this is why economic, social, and political conflicts arise even though members of the population may be culturally similar. In such circumstances the role of government is to resolve conflicts, and as long as various groups are willing to submit to the authority of government in its role, solutions will be found through prevailing legal institutions.

If the leaders of a group refuse to accept the decision of a government and are disposed to political strife against the government, the response of government will depend on whether it is characterized by Class I or Class II residues (Pareto 1935, §§ 2274–77, pp. 1622–24). A government dominated by Class I residues will often attempt to assimilate the dissident leaders into the governing class and thus deprive the group of its leadership, or it may offer concessions (often monetary) to the leaders on behalf of the group.[3] Or, more generally, circulation of the elite (political mobility) serves as an escape valve and allows for an orderly change in the composition of the governing elite (broadly defined to include both elected and nonelected politically powerful individuals) (§ 2253, p. 1573). If the leadership of the dissident group is noncompromising and is bent on overthrowing the government—that is, it is strong in Class II residues—then the government has no choice but to use force if it is to remain in power. If it avoids force at all costs, it will fall.[4]

A government strong in Class II residues will meet threat of force with force. If it is successful it will prevail, but the problem underlying the unrest remains. Rather than assimilate the opposition leadership, it will banish the leaders of the opposition or may even imprison or execute them, but in doing so it deprives the country of its most spirited and talented elements (nongoverning elites).

Pareto observed a trend during his time, which continues today among modern Western governments: the tendency to rely less and less on the use of force as an instrument of power and more and more on the political (market and nonmarket) redistribution of income, since they

---

3. The problem with this response is that once other groups learn the "rules of the game," the government is beleaguered by civil "demonstrations" of all sorts.
4. Mussolini's march on Rome, which toppled the government, is such an example.

view their relationship with the governed as a client-patron one. According to Pareto, force has given way to the expensive art of government (1935, § 2305, p. 1638). Manifestations are budgetary deficits, inflation, and reduction in military expenditures relative to "social" expenditures. More and more governments are relying on economic prosperity to create the revenues needed to meet increasing expenditures:

> Modern governments commonly spend in a given period more than their revenues would allow, covering the differences by contracting overt or secret debts. That enables them to have the benefits of the money now and shoulder the burden of payment off upon the future. The future becomes more and more remote, the more rapidly economic prosperity increases; for in virtue of that increase, . . . [revenue] increases without any increases in taxes themselves and future state surpluses are expected, in part at least, to make up for past deficits. Our governments have gradually become accustomed to that state of things, . . . and they regularly discount future surpluses to pay for present expenditures. (§ 2306, pp. 1638–39)

According to Pareto, difficulties come in periods of economic depression and would become far worse if a depression were protracted. In such a case, he argued, the social order is such that no government can remain unaffected.

The necessity that a government avoid economic depression stems from the economic nature of modern government's political power. This development—holding the government responsible for economic conditions which may be beyond its ability to deal with effectively—is a new one, deriving from the client-patron relationship through which governments seek and maintain power. A government unable to live up to such expectations is in jeopardy.

In contrast, many governments in Third World countries are still dominated by Class II residues. The brutality with which they suppress opposition, their willingness to remain "closed" in spite of civil unrest, and huge military budgets are all a reflection of Class II characteristics.

In summary, economic prosperity, political stability, and national defense are all essential to the social prosperity of nation-states. The problems are the same, but the solutions are different depending on whether Class I or Class II residues prevail. From this perspective the style of government is more important than the form, and the polar cases mentioned in the theoretical parts of the discussion are problematical. For Pareto, a government characterized by a proper combination of both Class I and Class II residues among its members will be flexible and adaptive regarding domestic problems, but not so compromising as to undermine its power through fraud and corruption and special-interest politics, while at the same time principled enough not to succumb to every demand made upon it and willing to use force when necessary. Although for Pareto this balance of Class I and II residues was necessary to achieve and maintain prosperity, he argued that the recorded history of Western civilization was the history of a movement from one extreme to the other, from Class II to I to II and so on, but with individual nations at different stages of their historical evolution at any given time.

International Security

The discussion above can be extended to include international relations. A government dominated by Class I residues is less willing to use force in defense of national interests. Instead it uses pecuniary means to settle international disputes. It cements relations through the force of "aid." Thus its instruments of power are pecuniary rather than military: "Wars became essentially economic. Efforts are made to avoid conflicts with the powerful and the sword is rattled only before the weak. Wars are regarded as speculations. A country is often unwittingly edged towards war by nursings of economic conflicts which, it is expected, will never get out of control and turn into armed conflicts" (Pareto 1935, § 2179, p. 1512). On the other hand, a government strong in Class II residues will tend to use force as an instrument of power, not only domestically, as mentioned earlier, but also internationally. Expenditures are channeled more into military rather than domestic uses.

For Pareto, wars among countries whose governments are strong in Class I residues are often unintended consequences of their other activities.

> When we say that at the present time [1913] our speculators are laying the foundations for a war by continuously increasing public expenditures, we in no sense mean that they are doing that deliberately—quite the contrary! They are continually increasing public expenditures and fanning economic conflicts not in order to bring on a war, but in order to make a direct profit in each little case. There is another cause of greater importance—their appeal to sentiments of patriotism in the masses at large, as a device for governing. . . . Some day the war they have made way for but not wanted may break out; and then it will be a consequence of the past activities of the speculators, but not of any intent they have had either at that time or ever. (1935, § 2254, p. 1577)[5]

5. The term "speculators" as used by Pareto refers to the economic equivalent to Class I residues. Examples are business and financial interests influential in forging government policy.

In cases where international disputes involve nations whose governments have different residues the problem is quite different. A country whose government is strong in Class I residues will seek to avoid war in a case where it perceives its adversary as a near equal in military power, whereas it will rattle its sword at those it perceives to be militarily weaker. But where the opposing country's government is strong in Class II residues, it may be less willing to negotiate a settlement and rather risk war to resolve the dispute.

We are now in a position to turn to concrete cases—Pareto's assessment of World War I and why Germany lost that war.

World War I

Pareto's sociology was written before World War I, but because of the war its publication was delayed until 1918. Following the war Pareto wrote a book titled *Fatti e theorie* (1920) wherein he applied the principles developed in his sociology for analyzing, among other things, the war. He begins his analysis with the following observations:

> The defeat of the Central Powers is a phenomenon of great significance. In the first phase of the war, Germany's armies were successful; its military capacity contrasted sharply with the inadequate military preparations of the Entente plutocracies and Italy's utter unreadiness for war. But this phase was followed by another which eventually terminated in the total victory of Germany's enemies. There are many reasons for this outcome, and clearly one of them lies in the enormous disproportion of manpower and financial resources between the two sides—a factor of overriding importance given the new character of modern warfare. Another factor in Germany's defeat is the mastery at sea of England and later of the United States. But we must go further than this and investigate how this distribution of forces came about. ([1920], 1966, 287)

Pareto begins by arguing that the events which led to Germany's wars with Austria in 1866 and France in 1870–71 were different than those which led to the 1914–18 war. Although Germany's internal preparations were similar in all three cases, the international provisions for the third war were markedly different. In 1865 the diplomatic moves on the political chessboard of Europe were arranged with farsighted care by an expert and outstandingly shrewd player—Bismarck. No move was made without contemplating its consequences carefully beforehand. But in the case of World War I Germany was diplomatically unprepared, and its fate was totally entrusted to the military forces of "a player who had for every problem only one simple solution: the terror he assumed he must arouse, and who moved his pieces heedlessly without giving the

least thought to the indirect or eventual consequences of his moves"
([1920] 1966, 288). Pareto then documents his thesis with a detailed
comparative study of the diplomatic histories of the period. Several
paragraphs deserve quotation in full, as they illustrate the flavor of his
writing regarding Germany's diplomatic blunders prior to and during
World War I:

> Bismarck went to Biarritz; Bethmann-Hollweg neither went him-
> self to London nor sent a special mission. He seemed to be unaware
> of the existence of Italy. These omissions cannot be attributed to
> ignorance of England's power or of the possible consequences of
> Italian intervention. Indeed, not to make a long story of it, it is
> enough to record, in regard to England, Bethmann-Hollweg's stu-
> pefied anguish when the British ambassador gave him notice that
> the invasion of Belgium constituted a *casus belli*. Some indication
> of Italy's place in official German thinking is given by Marshal
> Konrad von Hoetzendorf in an interview published in *Correspon-
> denz Bureau,* July 16, 1919: "The intervention of Italy was the
> cause of the disaster. Had this not occurred, the Central Powers
> would certainly have won the war. All along we were hoping that
> Italy would remain faithful to the Triple Alliance."
>
> But really, prudence and wisdom are hard to seek in a policy
> which did nothing to ensure this desired fidelity of Italy to the Triple
> Alliance. And what conclusion does von Hoetzendorf draw from all
> this? Does he subscribe to the prudent view that it was necessary to
> come to terms with Italy and that, to win the high prize of victory,
> some rather considerable sacrifices had to be made? Not at all. His
> rash and ill-considered conclusion is that it was necessary first of all
> to make war on Italy. He says: "It was impossible to have freedom
> of action against Serbia without first subduing Italy. To this end it
> had been proposed that there should be a campaign against Italy in
> 1906, and after this, in 1908 and 1913, a war with Serbia." The
> worthy marshal fashions the future to his own liking. It never
> crosses his mind that these wars, so nonchalantly projected by him,
> were capable of having repercussions throughout Europe. . . .
>
> When war broke out with Russia and France, and with England
> very soon joining in, Germany's rulers at last began to realise the
> importance of a possible intervention by Italy. Had the neglect of
> such an important factor as Italian intervention been due to simple
> error, then they surely ought to have taken urgent steps to correct
> the mistake, employing all appropriate means. Now, though it is
> true they did seek to amend their blunder, they did so in a woefully
> makeshift fashion, quite unequal to the seriousness of the situation.
> Von Bülow was sent to Rome, but there he performed like the
> heavy father in a melodrama. He returned to Germany empty-

handed. His government could not be bothered with such triv-
ialities as are implicit in the old maxim: those who will an end must
also will the means. ([1920] 1966, 288–89)

Pareto then turns to the German government's diplomatic blunders,
which eventually led to the United States' entry into the war and turned
the tide against it.

The point of Pareto's discussion is to illustrate that Bismarck was able
to achieve great things in the Germany of his era because of an ideal
combination of Class I and Class II residues in the governing elite.
Bismarck worked in concert with Wilhelm I, the former being endowed
with Class I residues and the latter with Class II residues. Bismarck's
diplomatic and governing genius was supported by Wilhelm's iron fist.
In contrast, according to Pareto, the "mystical" Wilhelm II, dominated
by Class II residues, had no countervailing influences in government,
having gotten rid of Bismarck "because he would not tolerate chancel-
lors who used their heads as instruments for intelligent calculation"
([1920] 1966, 292).

Thus Pareto concludes:

> In the way Germany's rulers acted before and after the declara-
> tion of war, are there not clear indications of the same kind of
> sentiments as are exhibited by religious believers? Faith in "Ger-
> many's destiny," in its military strength and in the power of its
> "organisation," the dogma of "vital interests"—all this clouded the
> vision of its rulers. To employ the terminology used in the *Treatise,*
> we can say that in Germany's rulers Class II residues (persistence
> of aggregates) were potent, while among the rulers of the Entente
> nations, with the exception of Russia, Class I residues (instinct of
> combination) predominated. Russia's rulers, with their dreams of
> the illimitable power of Holy Russia and with their emperor under
> the sway of Rasputin, were heavily endowed, like Germany's, with
> Class II residues. And as in Germany, so in Russia it was this which
> dragged the nation and its rulers to ruin: a fate they could have
> easily avoided if only Russia had maintained its former alliance
> with Germany. ([1920] 1966, 292)

What is most remarkable, but understandable in the light of his analysis,
Pareto showed that the post mortems of World War I by Germany's
leaders displayed a total lack of comprehension of why they lost the
war.[6]

6. And later, it might be added, neither did Hitler grasp the reasons—who, after all,
was a product of that period and exhibited the same Class II residues in his mystical
rantings about the "destiny" of the Third Reich and a political movement which was
nothing less than a secular religion.

Summary and Conclusion

Pareto's approach to the matter of national security is much broader in scope than the usual discussions on the subject. For him the "social prosperity" of nation-states depends on economic prosperity, political stability, and national defense. All these aspects are important and interrelated. In addition national security has both an internal as well as the more familiar external dimension. The form of government may be important from the point of view of moral or political philosophy, but practically the *style* of government is what matters in relationships within and between nation-states. The style of government depends on the composition of residents in the governing class (defined broadly enough to include elites both within the government and politically influential elites outside of government). According to Pareto, nations whose governments exhibit a combination of Class I and Class II residues are best equipped to maintain "social prosperity." The polar cases of residues dominant in either Class I or Class II have resulted in a loss of "social prosperity" and eventual decline, either internally through economic decline and political instability or internationally through disastrous wars.

From a practical viewpoint, what might be said of Pareto's discussion regarding national security? It provides a method of differentiation of political regimes, and relevant strategies, based on a general and systematic analysis not found anywhere else. This is not to argue that his analysis is the only relevant approach. But it deserves some consideration given the insights it provides.

References

Pareto, Vilfredo. 1935. *The Mind and Society.* Edited and translated by A. Livingston. 4 vols. New York: Harcourt, Brace.

———. 1966. *Sociological Writings.* Selected and introduced by S. E. Finer. Translated by Derick Mirfin. New York: Praeger.

Tarascio, Vincent H., 1983. Pareto's *Trattato. Eastern Economic Journal* 9 (April–June): 119–31.

From the Economics of Welfare to the Economics of Warfare (and Back) in the Thought of A. C. Pigou

William J. Barber

"To the Political Economy we have read hitherto there is needed a companion volume, The Political Economy of War." A. C. Pigou (1877–1959) wrote these words in 1921 when assigning to himself the task of producing such a study. He then held that the "Great War" had presented a fundamental challenge to economic analysts: to explore "the anatomy and physiology" of a "strained and stressed economy." This phenomenon was quite different from the "cool rhythm of a settled order," and it needed to be understood on its own terms.[1]

In two respects Pigou might seem an unlikely candidate for this analytic undertaking. He made no secret of his personal repugnance to war. In 1914 he was still age-eligible for military service. On conscientious grounds he chose not to participate in any activity in which he might be called upon to take human life. This did not mean that he excused himself from exposure to personal danger. During vacation periods at the University of Cambridge he saw service in France as an ambulance driver in a unit organized by the Society of Friends. This experience amply confirmed his distaste for the business of warfare, and it left him with psychic scars that proved to be permanent.

Pigou's standing to comment on the economics of war might be questioned for another reason. Many of his professional contemporaries had an "insider's" view of the management of a mobilized economy between 1914 and 1918. Pigou had only slight acquaintance with the work of the bureaucrat-administrator in a post at the Board of Trade toward the end of the war. This episode had been both brief and unproductive. In E. A. G. Robinson's account of it, Pigou "showed little aptitude for the type of work in which others of his Cambridge colleagues and pupils were making names for themselves."[2]

How then can one understand Pigou's attraction to the economics of war? (He was, after all, one of the few economic theorists of stature in

1. Pigou 1921, 2.
2. Robinson 1971, 816.

the twentieth century to produce a book-length treatise on the subject.) It would appear that he was motivated by both practical and intellectual concerns. At the practical level, more thorough comprehension of the "anatomy and physiology" of a mobilized economy could contribute to the nation's security in the event of a future war. This was an unattractive prospect to contemplate, but it should not be consigned to the realm of the impossible. He was not convinced that appeals for the dispassionate exercise of reason would ultimately generate peace. In his reading of matters, nations (and subgroups within them) had irrational urges to dominate one another, and this was inherently friction-producing. Nor did he share the confidence of a Norman Angell that war could never be a paying proposition for the victor. Indemnities might be extracted which could benefit the recipient—though Pigou doubted that there would be net advantage to the winner once the costs of acquiring tribute had been properly calculated.[3]

Analysis of war thus had a claim for a continuing place on the economist's agenda. Pigou remained hopeful that "wise policy"—guided by insights supplied by economists—could reduce the threats to peace. He looked to the League of Nations to press countries to reduce barriers to international trade, and he called for international agreements to proscribe privileged concessions to international investors. He was concerned about the potential capacity of munitions makers (who had an obvious stake in enlarging the market for their product) to make mischief, and he sought ways to curb their influence. But it was still the better part of wisdom to recognize that the world remained a dangerous place. Pigou seconded Adam Smith's dictum that "opulence is no defense." Military preparedness—even though it was costly and imposed unfortunate distortions on normal economic activity—was still necessary. He likened this precaution to a national insurance policy. By the same token, analysis of the problems associated with management of a mobilized economy could pay dividends should a country again be obliged to adapt to such strains.

Though there was adequate practical justification for investigations of

3. "It is not, indeed, as was sometimes urged before 1914, in the nature of things impossible for a victorious nation to make an economic profit by exacting a war indemnity. An indemnity is equivalent to the wiping out of a foreign debt or to the receipt of a foreign loan on which no interest need be paid" (1921, 18). Nor did Pigou support the argument Keynes had advanced in *The Economic Consequences of the Peace* about the damage the recipient would suffer from the inflow of reparations. Pigou made no explicit mention of this book, but he attacked its thesis obliquely. In his view, "to assert in a general way that a nation which receives an indemnity must suffer a net economic injury from it is to uphold an apparent paradox. It will generally gain, just as an individual will gain if somebody gives him a present." He did add the qualification that "incidental damage" could occur in the "process of adjustment" if the indemnity were "received all at once in a form unwisely chosen" (1921, 18).

the political economy of war, Pigou also found intriguing theoretical puzzles in this subject matter. He had inherited the formal apparatus of Marshall's brand of neoclassicism, but he sought to extend it to a range of questions which his master had not asked. For Pigou analytic attention should not be concentrated on the specification of equilibrium conditions worked out in a market context. One could not presuppose that markets would always generate socially optimal results. It was thus important to broaden the scope of inquiry. With respect to the production process, the theorist should explore possible cases of divergence between social and private costs and benefits. Similarly, with respect to the distribution of income, Pigou insisted that the status quo should not necessarily be accepted as the best of all possible worlds. Economists should properly ask whether or not the aggregate satisfactions of the community could be increased by a transfer of income from the richer to the poorer. Pigou's reformulation of the neoclassical program thus invited a rethinking of the role of the state. One of the tasks of the theorist was to articulate the conditions under which intervention would be justified and to prescribe the forms which that intervention should properly take. These themes were explored at great length in the work for which Pigou is best known: *The Economics of Welfare,* the first of four editions of which appeared in 1920. With the publication of *Wealth and Welfare* in 1912, he had already set out this perspective on economic analysis.

Given Pigou's preoccupation with the issue of state intervention, his engagement with the political economy of war was fully in character. Circumstances of war obviously necessitated intervention on a massive scale. Moreover, they required radical shifts in the allocation of resources which the signals of a market could not be expected to direct satisfactorily. But if visible hands then replaced invisible ones, how should their actions be guided? This question presented a formidable challenge to economic analysts. The answers supplied could have significant bearing both on the successful conduct of a war itself and on the subsequent transition from the economics of "stress" to the "cool rhythms" of ordinary times.

War and the Reorientation of National Priorities

In circumstances of peace, the goal of economic activity was to maximize the nation's economic welfare (which was understood as the aggregate of community satisfactions). War mandated a different stipulation of the fundamental objective. The goal then became one of maximizing the "war fund"—a term Pigou introduced to describe the resources at the disposal of the state to pursue military victory. What then determined the size of the "war fund"? On the one hand, the volume of resources potentially available to the state could be swollen if the nation's output could be expanded to supernormal levels. In principle this might be accomplished if labor-force participation rates rose above the peacetime norm—i.e., with new recruits from women, as well as from the young and the old. Similarly, many of those already employed might be induced to lengthen their working week. Abnormal additions to labor input—combined with more intensive utilization of plant—could thus generate incremental output which could be placed at the disposal of the state.

Increases in aggregate output, however, could go only a small part of the way toward satisfying the requirements of the "war fund." Major reallocations of the national dividend would also be in order, and they would necessarily take the form of reductions in private claims on current production. In short, spending in real terms for private consumption and investment would have to be shrunk. Some depletion in private assets would probably also have to be accepted: the usual outlays to offset depreciation of physical capital would have to be postponed, and part of the nation's portfolio of assets held abroad might have to be liquidated.

Apart from war, none of these steps would be desirable. They clearly imposed heavy burdens on the community. Most of the "real economic cost" of war would be felt immediately: sacrifices in the form of reduced satisfactions from consumption and from leisure were both real and present. But part of the "real economic cost" would be shifted to the future: curtailment in normal spending to augment the capital stock and to renew the existing one would reduce production possibilities in the years ahead. An important distinction needed to be drawn, however, between the "economic cost" and the "total cost" of war. In Pigou's analysis of an economy in peacetime, economic welfare—defined as satisfactions which could be captured under the "measuring rod of money"—did not provide a statement of the total welfare of the community. Analogous reasoning, when extended to war, meant that the measurable economic costs fell far short of its total costs. In 1916 Pigou put this point emphatically when writing that the economic cost was "trivial and insignificant" in comparison to the cost "in values outside the economic sphere—the shattering of human promise, the accumulated suffering in wounds and disease of many who have gone to fight, the accumulated degradation in thought and feeling of many who have remained at home."[4]

4. Pigou 1916, 9.

*The Role of Intervention
in Maximizing the War Fund*

Formulating the overriding imperative for success in economic mobilization was a relatively straightforward matter. But how best could this objective be reached? This question raised issues that were both more complex and more interesting.

In principle the price signals of the marketplace could accomplish the necessary reallocations. The state would be the preemptive bidder for the resources it required, and private consumers and producers could compete against one another for what was left. At the theoretical level Pigou accepted that inflationary mechanisms could be set loose which would ultimately force the private sector to surrender claims on real resources. But he regarded this approach to feeding the "war fund" as unacceptable. A significantly inflated price level was to be resisted—primarily on the grounds that the current burdens of the war would be borne disproportionately by the low-income groups.

More particularly, the normal function of interest rates in rationing competing claims for loanable funds should be placed in abeyance. In circumstances of war governments could be expected to borrow on a considerable scale. This activity, other things being equal, would normally put upward pressure on interest rates. Pigou maintained that this outcome should be resisted. His reasoning on this matter was not based solely on the added problems in debt-servicing that higher interest rates would entail. Market-determined interest rates might also compromise the war effort itself. Pigou spoke to the latter point as follows: "One country dares not offer loans at a much higher rate than its opponents in war, for, if it does, public opinion in neutral countries may suspect its financial strength, and neutral governments are more likely to take sides against it."[5]

For yet another reason, normal market forces could not be relied upon to guide effectively the reallocations mandated by the exigencies of war. As Pigou saw matters, market adjustments were necessarily "gradual." This meant that labor and capital, when responding to price signals, would not move with the speed required by the urgencies of the moment.

> Friction, the general tendency to procrastination, imperfect knowledge of present facts and future prospects, all will hold them back. Many manufacturers, for example, of things not wanted for war, thinking, as they are sure to do, that the war will be short, will hesitate to adapt their works and train their work-people to new

5. Pigou 1921, 87.

tasks; they will keep them to the manufacture of their former products, with the idea of holding these in stock until peace returns. Yet again, work-people who used to make non-government things, on being thrown out of employment by the contraction of demand, will tend to stay where they are, instead of moving into other employments which are booming, in the hope of a rapid return to normal conditions. Finally, when the effective manufacture of government things requires special training in new processes to be given to work-people or special plants to be set up, private enterprise, even if it is tempted to provide these things at all,—which, in view of its knowledge that the war may end before they have yielded their profit, is doubtful—is sure to provide them slowly.[6]

When tested by the pressures of war, markets would thus fail to serve the national interest. The state would have no alternative to direct intervention in controlling key sectors of the economy. In some instances it would be desirable for the government to engage in commandeering. This did not imply confiscation: resource owners would be compensated at negotiated prices. But it meant that government would control the supplies of essential goods and services at their source. Thus Pigou spoke approvingly of the British government's activities during the Great War to take over the whole of the wool and wheat crops, along with all available timber supplies. By the same token the government was correct to commandeer the railway system, the bulk of the merchant marine, the engineering industries, the coal mines, and the flour mills. The problem of converting the base of the economy to a war footing was thus addressed in timely fashion. Government was the preemptive claimant of goods and services it needed; residual supplies could then be made available for private purchase at prices determined by the state. This procedure had two important recommendations: it kept prices far lower than they would have been under free market conditions; and it improved income distribution by suppressing profiteering. Without this intervention, Pigou believed, private sellers could have "demanded terrifyingly high prices" which would "have meant an enormous addition to the money expenses of the war, and this would have involved probably a further expansion of credit and currency, and certainly, a great increase in the national debt."[7]

Though these arrangements insured that government procurement enjoyed priority, they needed to be reinforced by other forms of intervention. For most commodities, the residual supply available to private

6. Pigou 1921, 69.
7. Pigou 1921, 68.

purchasers was likely to fall short of market-clearing quantities. How then should the conflicting claims of the private and the public sectors be adjudicated? With respect to private demand for investment purposes, much of the desired effect could be accomplished through a system of licenses to control allocation of scarce materials.

Adaptation of consumer demand to an environment of shortage introduced issues of greater complexity. Pigou suggested that propaganda be used to instruct citizens on their patriotic duty to economize as consumers, but he doubted that this technique would be fully effective. Theoretically, consumer spending on particular items in short supply might be choked off by levying indirect taxes. This possibility naturally suggested itself to an economist who frequently recommended the use of taxes to correct market "failures" in peacetime. In wartime, however, the matter should be viewed differently: duties which would raise the price of essential consumer goods should be avoided on grounds that they imposed differentially burdensome hardship on the poor. Techniques of rationing and price controls should instead be introduced—and it was crucial that they go hand in hand. Rationing without price control would discriminate against the poor because the richer would outbid them. Price control without rationing would be objectionable for analogous reasons. With the regulated price established below the market equilibrium, the actual distribution of goods—in the absence of ration entitlements—would depend on "a mixture of accident, ability to arrive first at a place of sale and the possession or otherwise of power to influence shopkeepers. It is probable that rich people will, in practice, have an advantage over poor people, because, since they are more valuable customers, shopkeepers may be more anxious to oblige them."[8]

What principles then should guide the allocation of ration entitlements? Pigou considered, but rejected, a system based on equality of sacrifice. This would imply that all members of the community reduced their consumption by the same proportion. Such a scheme would be objectionable because it would "involve some cut in the purchases even of the very poorest people, and would leave to rich people very much larger rations than were allowed to the poor." In Pigou's judgment, rationing should be organized on a different principle: the fundamental aim should be *"minimum aggregate sacrifice"* (emphasis his). In this

---

8. Pigou 1921, 139. While Pigou recognized that the usual consequence of imposing price ceilings would be to restrain production below the normal equilibrium quantity, he noted a possible exception: "When something is being produced by a monopolist, who is charging for it more than the supply price of the quantity he is selling, such price limitation, by preventing him from seeking his gain by high prices, may force him to seek it through large sales, and so may actually stimulate production" (129).

fashion the peacetime goal of "maximum aggregate satisfaction" was reformulated to the circumstances of war.[9]

War and Public Finances

Pigou was sufficiently orthodox in his views on budgetary policy to hold that governments should finance all of their current operations through taxation and, in ordinary times, should normally restrict borrowing to capital projects which would be remunerative. The extraordinary circumstances of war mandated that the usual rules be suspended. Ideally, war outlays—which, by their nature, were nonremunerative—should be met out of current tax revenues. Particularly if a war were prolonged, this ideal would be unattainable. Tax rates high enough to produce a balanced budget would mean that citizens would "seriously lessen their current exertions," and this would lead to "a serious depletion of that real income of services and goods from which alone the real war fund can be drawn."[10]

It was thus unavoidable that the government would be obliged to borrow. Pigou rejected the device of compulsion to force the public to provide funds to the state, characterizing compulsory lending as a "risky experiment."[11] As noted earlier, he also opposed increases in interest rates to spur voluntary lending. Two possible techniques for placing governmental debt were thus excluded. How then could the Treasury make its issues attractive to potential subscribers? Pigou offered a twofold answer to this question. In the first place, the government should "appeal to a wide range of tastes" by adapting the "form" of its issues "without any improvement in the actual terms offered." In short, it should provide a rich menu of portfolio options: war savings certificates (subject to lump-sum repayment with accrued interest within a fairly short time span); long-dated war loans; Treasury bills for the money market, etc.[12] More important to the success of loan finances in wartime were "direct negative methods" for placement of debt. These amounted to blocking a number of alternative ways in which the public might choose to allocate funds. The program of price control and rationing would check spending on consumer goods, and licensing of scarce materials would limit spending for capital goods. These measures, in combination with restrictions on capital export, would make the public more liquid and enhance prospects for successful war loan flotation. They would not, however, guarantee success. In the event of a shortfall in public subscriptions, the government would be compelled to borrow

9. Pigou 1921, 140.
10. Pigou 1921, 85.
11. Pigou 1921, 86.
12. Pigou 1921, 87.

from the banks, and this was "inherently bad" because of the inflationary pressures it would generate.[13]

The most serious problem associated with heavy reliance on borrowing as a source of war finance was its ultimate impact on income distribution. Pigou was convinced that the debt servicing it entailed would be regressive. Holders of government debt were to be found primarily in the upper income groups, whereas the population as a whole would be taxed to cover the interest payments. Hence the net result of these transactions would advantage the rich and disadvantage the poor. Characteristically, Pigou maintained that this outcome would be unfortunate. And, he argued, it need not happen. With the arrival of peace, the overhang of war debt could be wiped out at a single stroke!

In Britain capital obligations of the government had swollen roughly tenfold between 1914 and 1918.[14] Pigou was an ardent advocate of a capital levy to extinguish this war-accumulated debt. This would obviously be an extraordinary form of intervention, but it was intended to address problems created by extraordinary circumstances. Clearly a capital levy would have to be perceived as a once-and-for-all operation: otherwise it would seriously damage capital accumulation in the future. Why then should anyone recommend this potentially dangerous course? For Pigou the attractiveness of a capital levy reflected his preoccupation with an income distribution more favorable to the poor. An exaction based on the ownership of capital would self-evidently fall on the higher income groups, and the regressivity of debt servicing from regular taxation would be avoided. At the same time, a levy that wiped out the war debt would reduce future tax requirements: revenues would no longer be needed to pay interest to debt holders. Pigou argued that the subsequent reduction in annual taxation from "a level that is dangerously high, would promote work and saving and, through them, national productivity in a very important degree."[15] His rhetoric on this point has more than passing kinship with the "supply-side" arguments later deployed in the United States as "Reaganomics." Pigou's argument, however, was inspired by a concern to tilt income distribution in the direction of the lower-income groups.

There was, however, yet another reason why Pigou urged the elimination of the war debt. He anticipated that Britain would need to experience some deflation in the early postwar period if it were to be internationally competitive when gold convertibility was resumed. (Writing in 1921, he expressed no doubts about the desirability of rebuilding the gold standard or about the desirability of Britain's return to the prewar

13. Pigou 1921, 110.
14. Pigou 1920, 8.
15. Pigou 1920, 17.

exchange rate against the dollar.) In an environment in which the general price level fell, the burden of debt in real terms would become more weighty. These considerations reinforced the case for a capital levy.

A capital levy in Britain after World War I, Pigou insisted, was feasible because of one crucial fact: for all practical purposes, the war debt was internally held and was thus something that Britons "owed to themselves."[16] A capital levy meant that purchasing power would be withdrawn "from one set of people (the payers of the levy) and handed over to another set of people (holders of the war loan) inside the same country." Some critics, he noted, had expressed fears that these internal transfers would derange industrial life, but this view rested on a "misconception." True, some payers of the levy would have to sell assets to meet their obligations. But former holders of war debt who had now been paid out would be liquid and in search of assets to buy. Thus, Pigou maintained, there was "no reason to fear anything like a general slump in values."[17] He did, however, recognize that there were technical problems in administering a capital levy equitably: e.g., accurate appraisals of the value of assets would be difficult, and techniques would have to be devised to assess the value of human capital acquired by professionals, which, in common with physical capital, should be subject to the levy. These were bothersome matters of detail, but they were not insurmountable.

Lessons of War and the Management of an Economy in Peacetime

Many economists regarded the experience of economic mobilization during the First World War as a professional eye-opener. This was notably the case in the United States. Indeed, in the early 1920s, a body of American doctrine was formulated around the proposition that the management of the war economy had generated previously undiscovered truth about ways to improve economic performance in normal times. In particular it was claimed that great gains in efficiency could be accomplished through deliberate coordination. Thus it was argued that industrial associations should be encouraged to generate and share information to eliminate waste.

Pigou was not a party to this line of thinking. In his view of the economic universe the political economy of peace and the political economy of war were not subject to the same rules and should be sharply differentiated. He did not deny that gains had been achieved during the

16. Pigou was well aware that the British government had also borrowed abroad during the war, particularly from the United States. He calculated that these liabilities were offset by loans Britain had extended to other governments. External financial transactions were thus treated as self-canceling.

17. Pigou 1920, 46, 47.

war through "a sharing of information about methods and processes, in place of the wasteful secrecy of normal competitive production." It would be agreeable to preserve those gains. In peacetime, however, caution about such coordination was appropriate. If separate concerns continued such practices, "there may easily grow out of them powerful quasi-monopolistic organisations, able, if they choose, to mulct the public heavily."[18]

Nor would it be appropriate to conclude that some of the wartime innovations associated with the role of government could be success-fully replicated in peacetime. During a war government might well be prepared to underwrite highly risky ventures: it was a well-established fact that "experiments in new types of destructive apparatus" had been authorized "regardless of cost." But no conclusions applicable to nor-mal conditions could be drawn from this. Clear distinctions separated the standard behavior patterns of private and public enterprises, even though the general truths required some qualifications during war. In Pigou's reading, "the hope of gain operates more strongly on private enterprise than on public authority, the fear of loss operates more strongly on the public authority. . . . Public authorities are, in general, less willing than private concerns to take risks, or to put it technically, to provide the factor uncertainty-bearing."[19]

Nor could efficiencies associated with government's standard setting in its wartime procurement serve as a model for peacetime practice. Pigou acknowledged that standardization in specifications in govern-ment orders had met "an urgent need for immediate large output at a minimum cost." Moreover, he noted that "the experience of the Great War, in which military equipment and munitions had necessarily to be of uniform patterns, brought out more clearly than before the enormous scope for direct economies." Under governmental authority standard-ization had also been applied in the production of ships and boots.[20] But this did not translate into a formula for the way ordinary production should be organized. In normal circumstances economic welfare would be greater when consumers had much wider scope for choice. In addi-tion pressures toward standardization in peacetime would tend to be socially dangerous to the extent that they "lessen[ed] the inducement to manufacturers to devise and try new things." Put in Pigou's terms, "the marginal social net product of effort devoted towards standardising processes falls short of the marginal private net product, in so far as it indirectly checks inventions and improvements and so lessens produc-tive powers in the future."[21]

18. Pigou 1921, 237.
19. Pigou 1962, 398.
20. Pigou 1962, 208.
21. Pigou 1962, 209.

In short, Pigou concluded that "war experience can afford very little real guidance" to one's understanding of an economy at peace. The economics of welfare and the economics of warfare deserved to be in separate volumes. The tools of marginal analysis, of course, could be applied in each. But it was still fundamental to recognize the vital differences between them with respect to the appropriate roles for visible and invisible hands. There was still a thread of continuity in Pigou's conception of the way these problems should be approached. Whether the economy was undergoing the "stresses" of war or experiencing the "cool rhythms" of normal times, one of the benchmarks of its performance was the degree to which the interests of those at the weak end of the income distribution were defended.

A Concluding Note

Pigou first published *The Political Economy of War* in 1921. In late 1939 he prepared a reissue, which appeared in 1940. In its analytic essentials the substantive argument of the revised edition was a repeat of the original. The major significant change was the deletion of chapters dealing with the economic "aftermath": the problems of transition from war to peace. In an epilogue to the revised edition Pigou explained this editorial emendation as follows:

> We are at the start of a journey whose end we cannot foresee. Yet once again the young and gallant, our children and our friends, go down into the pit that others have digged for them. Yet once again men of greater age, we that, if it might be, would so gladly give for theirs our withered lives, we cumber the earth in vain. We wait and watch and—those who can—we pray. As an economist I have not the power, nor, as a man, the heart, to strain through a night so black to a dawn I shall not see.[22]

References

Pigou, A. C. 1916. *The Economy and Finance of War.* London: J. M. Dent.
———. 1920. *A Capital Levy and a Levy on War Wealth.* Oxford: Oxford University Press.
———. 1921. *The Political Economy of War.* London: Macmillan.
———. 1940. *The Political Economy of War.* New and rev. ed. London: Macmillan.
———. 1962. *The Economics of Welfare.* 4th ed. London: Macmillan.
Robinson, E. A. G. 1971. [Memorial essay for Pigou.] *Dictionary of National Biography, 1951–60.* Edited by E. T. Williams and Helen Palmer. Oxford: Oxford University Press.

22. Pigou 1940, 169.

League of Nations Economists and the Ideal of Peaceful Change in the Decade of the 'Thirties

Neil de Marchi, with the collaboration of Peter Dohlman

1

In June and July 1933 a World Economic Conference was held in London to seek ways of correcting the prevailing monetary dislocation and the worst effects of the collapse of world trade that had occurred after 1929. It was one in a long series of similar conferences, many under the auspices of the League of Nations, the first of which, called the Brussels Financial Conference, had been held shortly after the cessation of hostilities between the Allies and the Axis powers late in 1918.

Like most of the preceding conferences the 1933 conference was premised on the notion that enlightened self-interest could be made to prevail among rational men. Rationality here meant the perception and acceptance of the classical liberal ideal of a free multilateral trading system, based on division of labor and facilitated by a world currency. The scale and efficiency advantages of such a world system were implicitly assumed to outweigh the possible attractions of nationalistic policies. But this ideal neglected more elements of concern to national governments than it attended to. It had nothing to say about the massive unemployment that had begun to afflict certain mature economies even prior to the collapse of trade. It was silent on the issue of increased vulnerability to shifts of confidence of a system in which foreign loans had come to be used to provide the means for importing and to carry stocks of commodities in "oversupply," silent too on the destabilizing possibilities of such shifts inherent in the growing practice among central bankers of holding foreign currency reserves as well as gold. There was little understanding—because the ideal did not require it—of possible conflicts for any single nation between a policy of reflation and the external constraint implied by commitment to gold. Nor of how structural changes, disparate national aspirations, or the debt and reparations burdens from the Great War could be reconciled with a system that put price and monetary stability ahead of other considerations.

The World Economic Conference of 1933 was sabotaged by an unanticipated devaluation by the United States but would have failed anyway because of unbridgeable differences over whether an increase in commodity prices was a necessary preliminary to the reestablishment of exchange stability (Pasvolsky 1933) and because the French, who wanted a coordinated policy of reflation, were unable to make it worth the while of Britain and the United States to commit to such a policy (Eichengreen 1989b). In another sense, however, the conference may have marked a turning point. In the years immediately following there is evident, in certain circles, a process of growing mental disengagement from the notion that a return to the pre-1914 world order was either possible or desirable. This expressed itself in two forms. One was a more sophisticated understanding of world trade and payments flows as a finely balanced network of interdependencies. This replaced simple hydraulic models of more or less automatic price level (and specie flow) adjustment as the normal response to external disequilibria. There also began to emerge a sense that the world was a system in motion, with impulses to recession transmitted between nations in identifiable (and hence, in principle, controllable) ways. This was a striking departure from the limited conception of policy as being properly directed (only) to the removal of interferences with the international division of labor and the free flow of productive factors.

Nor was it just a matter of recessions and their transmission replacing interferences with free "trade" as the locus of policy discussions. There began to crystallize, somewhat more slowly, a conception of "economic order" that included norms, rules, and frameworks for discussion and decision making on a multinational level—this to supply the deficiency of the liberal ideal, in which the legal, institutional, and "moral" context was simply taken for granted. This new thinking explicitly joined economics and national security in two ways.

(1) There was a straightforward link via recessions. Suppose that a major cause of human suffering is economic insecurity, linked especially to cyclical downturns. Suppose, further, that cycles could be brought under control. Then an equally major source of international tension would be removed. A proper understanding of the dynamics of cycles and their transmission would mean an ability to grasp and use an important means to keeping change, and the challenges it posed, peaceful.

(2) The second connection to peace and war also had to do with lessening political tensions, but the context was the perception, noted above, that the world had become a system of finely balanced trade and financial linkages. Barber (1991) has shown how, prior to 1914, this notion of growing interdependence was used to argue that war was unlikely. No nation could long afford the derangement of markets implied by war. In the late 1920s and early 1930s, however, opportunistic national responses to recession, and nationalistic policies grounded in

territorial claims and other unfulfilled aspirations, had combined with interdependence to cause a startling and costly downward spiral of world trade and output that in effect realized many of the same results as war. Nobody pretended that the causes of noncooperative behavior were economic alone, yet it was strongly suspected by economists that autarkic interventions involved losses for the perpetrators as well as for the world at large.[1] If that was true, perpetrators had to be acting out of ignorance, self-denial, or viciousness. On the view that ignorance at least could be alleviated, economists could perform a valuable service simply by modeling, in a quantitative way, the interlocking flows of world trade and finance. This has never been done; but were it to be accomplished, it could be seen and judged just how destructive all round an artificial constriction imposed at any point might be. And, assuming that unintended losses did indeed fall upon the perpetrating nations too, one might hope that by making plain the immense system-wide losses all but those governments bent on harming their own subjects or others would modify their behavior accordingly. In itself this would lead to a larger world output and perhaps some lessening of tensions stemming from differences as to how it should be shared.

Notice how very different are these connections from the ones identified by Barber (1991) in his story of how economists in the decade 1910–20 approached the threat, reality, and aftermath of war. For the most part swayed more by the latent harmony rather than the latent conflict paradigm, the economists in his narrative engaged in bold cost-benefit analyses of the rational likelihood of war, of the likely duration of war, and of the probable sustainability of reparations. By contrast, the shifts in thinking of the 1930s—at least those to which I have drawn attention—accepted that there were inherited and still unresolved conflicts, recognized that existing mechanisms for stabilization and dispute settlement were not working well, and saw only a relatively modest role for economic analysis. It was still an enormously optimistic role. Understanding cycles and their transmission; depicting in operational fashion the world network of trade and finance—these were no tasks for the timid. But the emphasis was different: clarifying these things would at

1. If actors find themselves in a situation like the "prisoner's dilemma," their self-interested moves will result in a suboptimal result for everyone. Eichengreen (1989b, 18), presumably alluding to prisoner's-dilemma-type situations, where the point is strictly true, notes that uncooperative behavior may issue in suboptimal equilibria, and he cites Keynes as a contemporary economist who detected a loss for all concerned in the France–United States struggle, each to secure a larger share of the world's gold, in the late 1920s. Most writers in the period saw clearly the loss of output from noncooperative behavior in the trade and monetary spheres but simply assumed that the nations initiating restrictive action suffered along with everyone else. This assumption was not necessarily correct (see section 4 below).

best diminish some of the causes of political tension in a world where latent conflict seemed to have taken over from latent harmony. Moreover, the nature of the analysis was very distinctly different. From the methodological individualism of rational agents whose balancings of costs and benefits at the margin translate (somehow) into national perspectives, we have passed into the realm of world "orders," impersonal mechanisms (though they may be controlled), and macroeconomic phenomena such as slumps which are analyzed directly.

In the narrative which follows I focus on the mental disengagement and shifts in thinking just outlined. I do so by referring directly to work which illustrates the new approaches and without attempting to identify the full extent of such thinking. It is possible that the shifts I have just described began prior to 1933, and likely that they can be traced in a quite diverse literature, from international relations to structural-functional social analysis. I attempt no more than to give a glimpse of one specific forum for their development and expression, albeit one which from an economist's point of view must be judged quite central. With a few exceptions we shall be concerned with the work of the League of Nations Economic Intelligence Service. The Service operated within the Economic, Financial and Transit Department of the League. Department director Dr. Alexander Loveday brought together in this Service a changing group of economists who individually were as creative as any of their contemporaries and who collectively in important ways shaped international discussion on trade and monetary order and on economic policy in the three decades after 1935: Gottfried Haberler, Jan Tinbergen, James Meade, Tjalling Koopmans, J. J. Polak, J. M. Fleming, Ragnar Nurkse, J. B. Condliffe, and Folke Hilgerdt.[2]

---

2. This is a strong assertion, which I cannot claim to have investigated in all its ramifications. I think it applies, nonetheless, to both the academic and the policy environments, in respect of those discussions which required notions (1) of system, equilibrium, and interdependence/coordination at the international level (thus, e.g., what is a "fundamental disequilibrium" in the balance of payments? what is the mechanism by which cycles are propagated? what is the arterial structure of trade and financial flows?) and (2) of "appropriateness" in policy intervention at the national level (relating to targets and instruments, internal versus external balance, and so on). Measured by influential publications or participation in significant policy-making forums, the economists with League of Nations affiliations figure very prominently. Taking just publications, for illustration, Haberler's works on trade theory and policy and on the cycle are classics. But recall also Nurkse's *International Currency Experience* (1944), Meade's two-volume *Theory of International Economic Policy* (1951), Tinbergen's *On the Theory of Economic Policy* (1952) and *Economic Policy: Principles and Design* (1956), Fleming's "Domestic Financial Policies under Fixed and under Flexible Exchange Rates" (1962), Koopmans's work at Cowles during the 1940s on statistical inference and simultaneous equation estimation, and later on activity analysis, and—more directly within the policy sphere—Polak's numerous contributions at the International Monetary Fund to the quantitative analysis of

The Service benefited from a limited amount of outside funding in the form of grants from the Rockefeller Foundation. The Foundation also funded a much larger program of business-cycle research in Europe and helped support a subsidiary organization of the League based in Paris, the International Institute of Intellectual Cooperation (IIIC). Officers of the Rockefeller Foundation in 1933 proposed and the trustees approved a new thrust for the Foundation's involvement in the social sciences. This became a medium for fostering the shifts of thinking described above. Apart from its support for a large number of economic (especially business-cycle) institutes in Europe, of the IIIC, and of the business-cycle program of the League, the Rockefeller Foundation helped fund two international research efforts in the late 1930s intended to help delineate the old, and the new world economic system whose need was so sorely felt. Because of the financial and intellectual connections between the League and the Foundation it makes sense to discuss the changing thought on economics and national security in the 1930s as a sort of joint product.

Section 2 outlines the vision and role of the Rockefeller Foundation and the related work done by League of Nations economists. Section 3 offers an analysis of three approaches to the issue of world economic order and interdependence and how to achieve stability, drawing on the work of Alvin Hansen, Tinbergen, Polak, and Hilgerdt. Attention is focused on methods of analysis, ways of framing the issues, and the content of notions such as equilibrium, stabilization, and economic order. Contrasts are drawn between what I have referred to as new ways of thinking and the ideal of the old liberal order, using the gold standard system to exemplify the old order. Although individuals managed to strike out in new directions, for the bulk of economists it proved hard to escape the old timeless-equilibrium thinking embodied in static optimization. As a result, historical forces were left outside the typical economic analysis; neither could the right sort of attention be paid to the incentives making for cooperative behavior, even though this was essential to restoring the equilibrium of the system. These limitations of the old way of thinking are discussed in section 4.

---

international monetary problems. Polak's earlier work on the international transmission of cycles, Hilgerdt's world trade network (1942), and Condliffe's contribution to understanding the breakdown and possible reconstruction of world trade order are part of my subject matter below. These analyses and perspectives form the core of the theory of economic policy, the theory and application of quantitative policy modeling, and especially the theory of open-economy income determination up until about the mid- to late 1960s, when the monetary approach to the balance of payments emerged.

2

*Searching for the Mechanism of Harmony in
a Changing World*

In April 1933 the trustees of the Rockefeller Foundation approved economic stabilization as a program of concentration within the Foundation's overall support for the social sciences. The approval had been
sought by officers who argued that "in . . . recurrent periods of general
depression lie many of the most pressing problems of the present social
order."[3] No action was taken, pending the report of a Committee on
Appraisal and Plan; but in April 1935 it was determined to push ahead on
two fronts simultaneously: economic stabilization and social security.[4]
For reasons of space I neglect social security here; note, however, that
the officers responsible for shaping and administering the new program
were of the view that the means to sustain programs of social insurance
and relief depended ultimately on success in moderating economic
fluctuations. This linkage allowed the inference to be drawn that "the
primary task of society is to devise mechanisms that will harmonize
production and consumption and maintain the multiple operating factors in balance in a changing and dynamic world."[5]

The language used in specifying the economic stabilization part of the
new program is infused with the hope that economic researchers in this
area would perform like their counterparts in the harder sciences. In
Rockefeller Foundation internal memoranda business-cycle research is
distinguished from descriptive economic history in that it emphasizes
"the quantitative and measurable in its materials, and the statistical and
analytical in its methods."[6] True, the aim is "understanding" rather than
"prediction," since prediction is helpful only where human agency
cannot affect the outcome. Nevertheless the goal is to grasp the "forces
in operation." This is further explained to mean "factors having real
power to control other factors and to determine the general character of
the result." These, in addition, should be "capable of human control."[7]
Finding the underlying causes, it is acknowledged, will always be "the
work of individuals";[8] but being able to give a "reliable indication of our
momentary location in the business cycle," while not the same as

3. "Economic Security," Rockefeller Archive, General Records (GR) group 3, series
910, box 5, folder. 46.
4. "Economic Security" (above, n. 3), and "Economic Security Program," GR 3, ser.
910, box, 5, folder 44.
5. "Economic Security" (above, n. 3), emphasis mine.
6. "Economic Security" (above, n. 3).
7. "Economic Security" (above, n. 3).
8. "Economic Security Program" (above, n. 4).

knowing causes, "may well promote intelligent experiments in control."[9]

An Observatory to Chart the Path of the World Economy

In line with this conviction, the first task was seen as being to provide for
an improved statistical record. Efforts should be made too to extend the
geographic scope of the coverage. And, perhaps most important, there
should be "a central observatory": a coordinating center where national
data could be rendered comparable. Creating this central coordinating
agency quickly came to be viewed as "the next logical step" in the
development of the program.[10] Loveday's Economic Intelligence Service in Geneva seemed well suited to fulfilling this need, although the
League's credibility was being tested, following the Italian invasion of
Ethiopia, which had taken place early in October 1935. Moreover, it was
recognized that the League was not really in a position to discriminate
between national institutes or select and reject from among the materials they provided.[11] In any case, to avoid the appearance of using their
financial support to impose a choice, the officers of the Foundation
decided to set up a conference where prominent invited economists,
including representatives of the various European business cycle institutes, could address the issue for themselves.[12]

Eventually a conference was held at Annecy, in the French Haute
Savoie, in early July 1936, immediately following a meeting of economists organized by Loveday to discuss a draft of Haberler's *Prosperity
and Depression* and preceding the biennial meeting of the Standing
Committee of Business Cycle Institutes, which was scheduled to take
place in Vienna.[13] The timing was deliberate, to secure basic separation

9. "Nature of Foundation Program in Business Cycle Research," 20 September 1935,
GR 3, ser. 910, box 5, folder 44.
10. John Van Sickle to E. E. (Rufus) Day, director for the Social Sciences, 29 October
1935, GR 3, ser. 910, box 4, folder 29.
11. Van Sickle to Day, 29 October 1935 (above, n. 10); Van Sickle to Day, 11 November
1935, GR 3, ser. 910, box 4, folder 29.
12. Van Sickle to Day, 29 October 1935 (above, n. 10).
13. Apart from Rockefeller Foundation officers, the Annecy group included the following. (1) Representatives of various business cycle institutes: Oskar Anderson (Sofia),
Oskar Morgenstern (Vienna), Charles Rist (Paris), Léon Dupriez (Louvain), E. Lipinski
(Warsaw), Wesley Clair Mitchell (National Bureau of Economic Research, New York). (2)
University economists: J. M. Clark (Columbia), Haberler (League of Nations, but shortly
to leave for Harvard), Alvin Hansen (University of Minnesota), Winfield Reiffler (Institute
of Advanced Studies, Princeton), Bertil Ohlin (College of Commerce, Stockholm), Lionel
Robbins (London School of Economics), D. H. Robertson (Cambridge, and special
advisor to the League of Nations on business cycle research). (3) Representatives of the
League of Nations and other international organizations or private research centers:
Condliffe, Rosenborg, and Tinbergen (Netherlands Economic Institute, Rotterdam, but
shortly to move to Geneva) from the League of Nations; P. W. Martin (International Labor

of purposes and attendees yet allow for some overlap of personnel. The Annecy group approved the idea of central coordination, but no agreement was reached on its practical implementation, to the great disappointment of the Foundation's John Van Sickle, who had drawn up detailed plans for an International Institute of Economic Research, to be physically situated in the library of the headquarters of the League.[14] The stumbling block was a feeling among certain individuals and representatives of private institutes that creating a central body might be giving research into the hands of a new bureaucracy.[15] The Standing Committee of the Business Cycle Institutes subsequently agreed to pursue the idea of coordination within its own constituency, but the idea of a central "observatory" as such was laid to rest.

No Observatory, but a Surfeit of Research Proposals

As a possible alternative to the League the Foundation had entertained the Graduate Institute of International Studies, a private organization, also in Geneva, and headed by William E. Rappard. A third Genevan institution was the Geneva Research Center, directed by John B. Whitton. As it turned out, officers of the Rockefeller Foundation found themselves dealing with the Standing Committee, Loveday's Service, and both private institutes in Geneva, on a whole range of possible projects of an international comparative character. For the most concrete result of the Annecy initiative was not any definite move to centralize and improve the collection and comparability of statistics on the business cycle, but rather a plethora of ideas for collaborative research. Eventually, after consultative meetings of the Standing Committee, and a special conference of economists which met in Paris in February 1938, three projects were selected and presented to the Rockefeller Foundation as suitable for special funding, within the terms of its economic stabilization program: (1) a study, to be directed by W. Röpke of the Graduate Institute in Geneva, of structural changes since World War I, with the aim of distinguishing between changes due to "natural" causes and those attributable to government intervention; (2) a factual investigation by H. Laufenburger, director of the Institute of Social Sciences,

---

Office); W. E. Rappard, Ludwig von Mises, and Röpke (Istanbul, but shortly to leave for Geneva) from the Graduate Institute of International Studies. This list is, I believe, complete, except for one attendee, a Dr. Warren of Case Pomeroy and traveling with Reiffler, but whom I have not been able to identify further.

14. "International Coordination of Business Cycle Research," 15 November 1935, GR 1.1, ser. 700, box 2, folder 17; Van Sickle to Sydnor H. Walker, acting director of the Social Sciences Program, memo on "Standing Committee of Business Cycle Institutes," 13 September 1937, ser. 705S, box 4, folder 38.

15. Confidential note from Noel Hall (rapporteur at Annecy) to Van Sickle, n.d., GR 3, ser. 910, box 4, folder 31. Loveday also was unenthusiastic.

Strasbourg, of changes in the structure of money markets, banks, and credit in the same period; and (3) a review by J. B. Condliffe of new methods for controlling and organizing international trade since the late 1920s.[16]

Condliffe had been part of Loveday's Economic Intelligence Service, where he had written the annual *World Economic Survey,* a task assumed from 1938 by James Meade. Upon his resignation Condliffe had accepted a chair at the London School of Economics, but he was operating as director of the proposed study under the auspices of Whitton's Geneva Research Center. Since leaving the League in 1937 Condliffe had also become rapporteur of the International Studies Conference (ISC), an initiative of the International Institute of Intellectual Cooperation which brought together on a regular (two-year) basis various academics and others concerned with international affairs. ISC's conference theme for 1935–37 was "Peaceful Change," and for the next two-year period "Economic Policies and Peace," by which was meant "the possibility and method of the peaceful adjustment of international conflicts resulting from such causes as: colonial claims, population pressures, needs for raw materials and markets."[17] Condliffe was responsible for organizing the preparatory studies on these themes, for the ISC conference to be held in 1939.

Despite having given a fillip to the idea of international collaborative work through its Annecy conference, the Rockefeller Foundation was unenthusiastic about the proposals brought before it, though the reticence was more noticeable at headquarters in New York than in its Paris office. Van Sickle's disappointment was just one element in this. The very number, and the overlap, of research proposals that had developed over the two years following Annecy was another. Often these involved the same individuals and institutions in multiple appearances. Condliffe, wearing his several hats, and with his multiple institutional affiliations, was an embodiment of what some of the New York officers of the Rockefeller Foundation came to see as a sort of log-rolling phenomenon: interlocking, mutual support given by institutions and individuals to each other's proposals.[18] An even more basic problem was that there was no very clear relation between these proposals and the Foundation's original vision, to set up a central "observatory" for the study of world economic structure and change. This was true even of the three proposals selected and put forward by the Standing Committee of Busi-

16. "Conference of Economists, Paris, April 28–30 [1938]," GR 1.1, ser. 100, box 105, folder 949.

17. "Program, International Studies Conference," GR 1.1, ser. 100, box 106, folder 959.

18. Memoranda from Stacy May to Walker, 22 September 1938, and from Tracy B. Kittredge (of the Paris office) to Walker, 26 September 1938, GR 1.1, box 105, folder 950.

ness Cycle Institutes. For the "observatory" was to be just that. Van Sickle believed that analysis would always be the work of single, talented individuals, and the Foundation had sought to provide better "observations," not to fund new teams of would-be analysts.

Yet another cause for reticence on the part of the Foundation was that events seemed to be overtaking the researchers. As one internal memorandum put it, in concluding a review of the various proposals:

> meanwhile political events are crowding their way on the front pages to the consternation of all of us who have been raised in the tranquil tradition that certain patterns belong to history and that history is something that is behind one. Not only is it disconcerting to have history ahead, but political events seem to be shaping in a way that makes analysis of past economic procedures useful chiefly for purposes of post-mortem diagnosis.[19]

The same attitude seems to have been responsible, in part anyway, for the Foundation's refusing to fund a Brookings Institution proposal on restrictive commercial policy and its effects on trade. This proposal, which was not unlike Condliffe's, had been developed independently by Harold Moulton, head of Brookings, and Leo Pasvolsky, a Brookings staff economist and graduate (Ph.D., 1936) who was employed from 1937 and during the war as a special assistant to Secretary of State Cordell Hull. Moulton and Pasvolsky were convinced of the need for collaborative research on international economic policy, and Pasvolsky, with Rockefeller assistance, traveled widely in Europe in 1937 to explore the possibilities for joint work. While the response in Europe was positive, and Pasvolsky's visit gave impetus to the European effort already under way, Rockefeller balked at funding the Moulton-Pasvolsky proposal, after Van Sickle received advice from Herbert Feis, economic adviser to the State Department, to the effect that no inquiry which omitted noneconomic factors would be relevant, while the political situation made it unlikely that useful involvement by Italy and Germany could be expected.[20]

19. Stacy May to Sydnor Walker, 22 September 1938 (above, n. 18).

20. Craufurd Goodwin has in preparation a study ("The Brookings Institution and International Affairs") which will detail the views of Moulton and Pasvolsky. I am indebted to him for the information about Feis's advice to Van Sickle. That this advice may not have been the only reason for the Rockefeller Foundation's refusal is implied in a memorandum from Kittredge, reporting on a visit to Europe by Walter Stewart, a trustee. Kittredge states that Stewart had been under the impression that Pasvolsky was busy garnering European help towards "a scholarly report and explanation of the international economic program of Secretary Hull and the present administration. He [Stewart] explained that the Trustees, of course, were not particularly anxious to prepare the way for what might be considered election propaganda" (Kittredge to Sydnor Walker, 5 July 1938, Rockefeller Archive, GR 1.1, ser. 100, box 105, folder 950).

In the end the Rockefeller Foundation, somewhat reluctantly, gave $50,000 to the Graduate Research Center in Geneva towards the Condliffe study, a further $50,000 to ISC for its program on "Economic Policy and Peaceful Change," and a small ($7,500) grant-in-aid to Röpke.[21] The Laufenburger study, like the Moulton-Pasvolsky proposal, received no Foundation support.[22] As anticipated, war intervened before Röpke's and Condliffe's studies could be completed, although reports did appear in due course: Röpke's *International Economic Disintegration* (1942) and Condliffe's *Reconstruction of World Trade: A Survey of International Economic Relations* (1940).[23] I shall say something about Röpke's work in section 4, where Condliffe too reenters the story.

The League of Nations' Business Cycle Research Program

The Rockefeller Foundation was more successful (in terms of timely and usable results) with a five-year $125,000 general grant to the League for analytical research, made in 1933.[24] Under this grant a program of research into business cycles had been undertaken, in two stages. Stage 1 involved a theoretical investigation by Gottfried Haberler. This was to

---

21. Stacy May to Sydnor Walker, 22 September 1938 (above, n. 18).

22. I should not leave the impression that the Rockefeller Foundation was alone in involving itself in efforts to understand the changes and problems afflicting the world economy. Among others were the Carnegie Endowment for International Peace—central in Barber's narrative, above—and the International Chamber of Commerce (ICC). In 1935–36 these two organizations combined to produce a report focusing on the removal of trade barriers and the stabilization of monetary arrangements. This report, *International Economic Reconstruction* (Joint Committee 1936), incorporated studies by several prominent economists, including Robbins, Rist, Jacob Viner, T. E. Gregory, Andreas Predöhl, Mises, H. D. Henderson, and Ohlin. Rockefeller officers took care to get assurances that there was no conflict between their endeavors and those of Carnegie or ICC. These were forthcoming in terms suggesting that the latter two were concerned primarily with programs of diffusion rather than research, a self-characterization that seems consistent with the subtitle of the joint study, *An Economists' and Businessmen's Survey of the Main Problems of Today*. See Kittredge to Walker, 2 May and 5 July 1938, Rockefeller Archive, GR 1.1, ser. 100, box 105, folders 949, 950. Goodwin's work in preparation includes also a study of the Carnegie Endowment and contains a short section discussing the Carnegie-ICC proposals for a cooperative project in the mid-1930s. For background on the ICC see Ridgeway 1938.

23. Condliffe's *Reconstruction of World Trade* (1940) was a (personal) report based on studies prepared for the International Studies Conference in 1939 but seems close in content to the study he was supposed to undertake for the Geneva Research Center on new methods for controlling and organizing trade. I have not been able to identify a published volume reporting that separate inquiry.

24. The Foundation also made grants to the League of Nations for other purposes, including an appropriation of $50,000 in 1933 to the Fiscal Committee of the League, for studies of double taxation. A portion of this grant was subsequently allowed to be used for an investigation of the behavior of tax systems during the cycle, an investigation stimulated by and complementing the work on the cycle done under the general grant for analytical research. See interoffice memo summarizing Foundation grants to the League, 15 May 1939, and Loveday report on work done under grants for the period 31 August 1938 to 30 September 1939, Rockefeller Archive, GR 1.1, ser. 100, box 18, folder 152.

be a comparison of existing cycle theories, stressing areas of agreement but also pointing to areas of difference. In respect of the latter it was anticipated that empirical analysis might help in assessing the conflicting claims. The result was *Prosperity and Depression* (1937), revised almost immediately and reissued to take account of Keynes's *General Theory*. The second stage was to be the empirical analysis hinted at above. Jan Tinbergen was brought to Geneva in 1936 to attempt to establish quantitatively the roles of the various factors thought to cause cycles. Initially the Tinbergen project was thought of in terms of testing the several theories outlined by Haberler; but Tinbergen soon found that the verbally expressed theories were too vague and incomplete to use. What he therefore ended up doing was to construct and estimate the coefficients of a multi-equation model for one economy, the United States. Tinbergen worked on this from 1936 to 1938, assisted by Jacques Polak, who later came to be director of research at the International Monetary Fund. When Tinbergen returned to the Netherlands early in 1938 his investigation was continued, using British data, by Tjalling Koopmans, in collaboration with Meade and Nurkse. Tinbergen's initial work was published as *Statistical Testing of Business Cycle Theories,* vol. 1, *A Method and Its Application to Investment Activity* (1938), and vol. 2, *Business Cycles in the United States of America, 1919–32* (1939).

There was also an unanticipated third stage. Following Haberler's report, the Economic Committee of the League, impressed by the need to avoid a repetition of the disastrous years 1929–33, appointed a Special Delegation on Depressions, to advise governments on countercyclical measures.[25] The Delegation published two reports: part 1 in 1943, under the title *Transition from War to Peace Economy,* and Part 2 in 1945, entitled *Economic Stability in the Post-War World: The Conditions of Prosperity after the Transition from War to Peace.*

3

Having described the ways in which the Rockefeller Foundation initiative of 1933–35 came to be expressed in the following few years, I turn to an analysis of work related to the purposes of the Annecy gathering or pursued with direct Foundation assistance. My concern here is to identify ways in which different researchers conceived the world economic order. The question, whether stated or not, was this: Assuming there to be a world economic system or order, how is it to be expressed in model form and made use of for analysis and control?

    25. "Economic Intelligence Service, League of Nations," 19 June 1939, GR 1.1, ser. 100, box 18, folder 152.

Picturing the World Economy

In the literature spawned by League and Foundation involvement, two basic alternatives emerge.

(1) The world economic order (or system) is best thought of as an ideal or hypothetical world in which there is division of labor, free movement of factors and goods, and a system of world price levels tied to gold. Analysis of the world of the 1930s, it was implied, should proceed in terms of identifying deviations from the ideal. Hence the frequent focus in studies (including to some extent those by Röpke and Condliffe, and a lot of Pasvolsky's work) on trade interventions, cartels, moves away from gold, and so on.

Two variants of this notion of a world system must be distinguished. There was, firstly, the elusive (or at least not much analyzed) "system" of the gold standard world. Relatively sophisticated variants of this were developed during the 1930s, enabling certain structural changes to be incorporated alongside the purely static picture yielded by the "natural" or efficiency ideal of an international division of labor, positing given resources and wants. Let us look more closely at one such variant, by Alvin Hansen, whose ideas largely shaped the agenda items dealing with a world economic structure for the Rockefeller Foundation's Annecy conference.

Hansen applied a type of comparative statics. His theory, however, did not get beyond being a collection of partial relations among variables thought to be important. There was a markup equation for prices, for example, useful because it enabled the economist to isolate wage and productivity components, and a profit segment, hence possible structural and institutional influences on all three. The rise of trades unions, or social security legislation, for instance, was thought to have affected unit costs. Similarly, changes in the organization of production and, in particular, the increased importance of overhead costs and economies of scale, were thought to have affected productivity (positively) but also the vulnerability of profits to alterations in demand (negatively). Via the markup equation, and others, these causes and effects could be discussed in an operational manner, even while no overall model of the world system might emerge.

The second variant of the ideal allocational model of a world economic system supplied this deficiency while remaining operational. This version was the "World Trade Network" developed for the League of Nations by Folke Hilgerdt; a simple model of integrated trade (and implicitly financial) flows teased out of the available statistics.

I stress the word "operational" in alluding to both versions of the ideal or natural order for the reason that control was so central a concern. This was the era of operational-positivist ideals in philosophy of science, according to which unambiguous theoretical meaning was to be sought by focusing on procedures of measurement. With unambiguous empirical referents for theoretical concepts, theory assessment too would become feasible, and the world would be a step closer to reliable understanding. In the hands of the physicist Percy Bridgman these notions were part of an attempt to bridle the unconstrained innovativeness that seemed to have swept over theoretical physics, but more generally they were part of an effort to grasp how science had achieved its successes. The Rockefeller Foundation's faith in observation, the League's program of testing business-cycle theories, the universal desire to manage responses to cyclical downturns—all were expressions of an underlying hope that reliable explanations would issue in control. Of course there were theoretical analyses of multimarket, multifactor trade, notably Ohlin's *Interregional and International Trade* (1933); but these were nonoperational.

(2) The second notion of world economic order is due to Tinbergen. He introduced successfully an endogenous dynamic into the static "natural" order, thereby incorporating the fact of movement and of cycles in particular. The insight that cycles might be represented as endogenous came very early (Tinbergen 1928). It was several years before a policy model for a single economy could be worked out (1936 for the Netherlands); and some years more before a model showing the international transmission of cycles was ready (Polak 1937–39).

The models of Hilgerdt and of Tinbergen and Polak were operational expressions of the idea that the world economy was an integrated system. League efforts late in the 1930s and during the war to persuade the world to believe in multilateral coordination of policy in the new order to follow World War II were based squarely on that basic idea and its model articulations. Tinbergen's own first "simulation" of a dynamic process in economics, a sort of cobweb model with a one-period lag between price and supply, and Hilgerdt's trade "network" model are pictured later in this essay (see figures 1 and 2 below) to convey directly their clarity and their potential for evoking new conceptions of equilibrium and order.

The "Natural" Order of a Free-Trade World

The former of the alternatives just listed, the free-trade/division-of-labor ideal, is thoroughly familiar to economists. It is the Smithian-Paretian picture of a world specialized according to comparative advantage, maximizing output through efficient allocation but abstracting from issues such as the appropriateness of initial endowments, or of the inequalities between individuals or those caused by organizations, in the exchange process.

This ideal functions in two roles that are usually not distinguished. On the one hand we have here a method of analysis rather than a claim about how the world should be. The method is that of isolation and successive approximation (to more realistic conditions). Yet because the ideal has to do with efficiency, it functions along that single dimension also as a sort of goal. Assuming higher national incomes or per capita incomes to be desirable, other things being equal, rational policy might be said simply to involve the removal of the deviations from the ideal identified in the analysis. This application comes close to describing the League's operating philosophy in negotiating the removal of barriers to trade and migration, and the restoration of monetary stability—"allowing the maximum freedom of circulation of commodities . . . as a means towards enabling the citizens of each country to attain a standard of living higher than they could reach by relying on their own resources," as the Australian representative put it in a speech to the nineteenth session of the League Assembly.[26]

The method of isolation itself is so "natural" to economists that it is not surprising to find it being used widely in the literature within our field of concern. Thus Haberler's approach in drawing together some of the links between cycles and trade was "to start with the hypothesis of a spaceless closed economy embracing the whole world and to introduce circumstances which divide and disintegrate that economy" (1937, 406–7). And a report by the Rockefeller Foundation's John Van Sickle, of a 1937 outline by Röpke of his research project, noted that Röpke spoke of comparing the present division of resources with that which would exist if natural forces determining their location had had free play—in effect, as Van Sickle put it, the distribution that would be settled upon "if a world dictator had distributed productive effort with a view to maximizing world income."[27]

It is worth stressing that, natural though it might appear, the method as such has no substance and can only be turned into an application for policy purposes if what is postulated as part of the ideal corresponds roughly to some identifiable state of the world and this state is judged positively. Although economists in the 1930s for the most part distanced themselves from any naive longing for a return to the world order represented by the gold standard era, they could not escape the need for

26. 22 September 1938, GR 1.1, ser. 100, box 18, folder 151.
27. "European Projects in the Field of International Commercial Policy," [January 1938], GR 1.1, ser. 100, box 105, folder 950.

a reference point in their own applications of the method of isolation, and this reference was usually the real or imagined world of the gold standard.

Analyses during the 1930s of the gold standard "system" vary considerably in the importance they attach to the role of short-term capital flows as distinct from gold movements and to the underlying notion of an integrated "world" capital market with interest rates related by arbitrage possibilities. They give different weight to the roles of short- versus long-term capital movements; some stress the virtual absence of automaticity in the application of the supposed rules of the game, with London exercising considerable independence in manipulating interest rates, so that price levels and levels of activity at the "center" bear less of the adjustment to trade imbalances than the rules presupposed.[28] Yet whatever the orientation or the relative emphasis in the exposition of how the rules worked, there are certain unmistakable features that characterize the ideal gold-standard "world":

1. Trade follows "natural" channels, set by the requirements and consumption habits, on the one side, and the production, on the other, of countries differing in climate, resources, and economic structure. These channels establish a pattern of relative permanence.

2. Balance for each individual country requires that exports plus net invisible earnings and/or short-term credits equal imports. The means to achieve balance are immediate borrowings (or gold "flows") and, in the longer term, changes in competitiveness involving relative price levels. Domestic activity is led by trade.

3. Exchange rates are fixed and linked through gold.

The result of these conditions is an integrated entity, a world econ-

28. The range of interpretations of how the system worked and why it had gone wrong is considerable. It is striking, despite the differences, how common was the theme of a system that worked best when it was needed least—or, alternatively, of the need of cooperation and coordination to get back onto gold, while conditions were precisely those that made such cooperation unlikely. Section 4 below takes up the latter theme. Useful recent discussions of contemporary and later analyses, with an independent investigation of how the system worked, are in Eichengreen 1989a and 1989b. In relation to the first theme mentioned Eichengreen offers an interesting alternative perspective. He treats in this context shocks to confidence, such as occurred in 1890 and 1907, unrelated to trade or foreign lending, and points out that the system worked as well as it did because the international commitment to gold meant that foreign central banks could be relied upon to help the Bank of England in a crisis. The markets, knowing this, would respond as if help (gold stocks) were in fact sent, making actual transshipment unnecessary. The result was that the system was not only stable in the face of shocks to confidence but "cheap" (my term), in the sense that British gold reserves commensurate with foreign obligations were rendered unnecessary (Eichengreen 1989a, 29–31).

omy. As Hilgerdt's study for the League, *The Network of World Trade* (1942), put it: "The frictionless functioning of a world economy upon which all countries depend for their well-being implies the existence of a world market to which all countries are admitted on equal terms and in which there is a uniform valuation of currencies and commodities" (88). But this conceptual structure or world economy was just that, a theoretical entity. What the officers of the Rockefeller Foundation were hoping might be achieved at their Annecy conference in mid-1936 was a definition closer to statistically identifiable trends and realities. As John Van Sickle put it in his letter of invitation to Alvin Hansen: "We particularly want to know whether, in the opinion of the group, present efforts to explain structural and cyclical changes suffer from lack of an adequate background knowledge of world changes. Is the concept 'world economy' sufficiently real to warrant subjecting it to continuous study?"[29]

But as *The Network of World Trade* also pointed out, the implied structure was not much analyzed until it was so rudely disturbed in the 1930s (Hilgerdt 1942, 84). It might have added that the League itself was responsible for the first efforts to present comparable and aggregated statistical materials on which such analysis might rest, and these materials too only began to make their appearance in the 1920s. Not surprisingly, what we have before the mid-1930s is detailed partial studies— e.g., Viner on Canada's balance of payments (1919); Bullock, Williams, and Tucker on the United States' balance of payments (1919); Brookings studies by Pasvolsky and Moulton on German, Russian, and French debt problems (1923, 1924, 1925)—and general discussions which focus on elements of what makes for or disturbs equilibrium, but without showing the structure or system itself.

One such general discussion is Alvin Hansen's *Economic Stabilization in an Unbalanced World* (1932). This is of special interest because (as noted above) Hansen ended up being responsible for structuring the agenda items dealing with a world economy for the Annecy conference, and his agenda reflects his earlier published ideas.[30]

---

29. Van Sickle to Hansen, 13 March 1936, GR 3, ser. 910, box 4, folder 29.

30. Initially Van Sickle had asked Oskar Anderson to prepare a draft agenda. This draft was deemed not to capture sufficiently well the Foundation's vision and intentions with the conference, and Hansen, quite late in the day, was invited to submit an alternative. This was grafted onto Anderson's, but Anderson declined to take credit for items that were not his. The final conference agenda, which bears no name, was closer to Hansen's than to Anderson's on the basic issues of "what is the world economy?" and "what are the forces shaping it?" See Rockefeller Archive, GR 3, ser. 910, box 4, folders 29–31: Van Sickle to Anderson, 20 April 1936; Hansen to Van Sickle, 28 April; Van Sickle to Hansen, 4 May; "Revised Agenda for Business Cycle Conference," 18 May; and Conference Agenda. The following discussion draws on Hansen's version of an agenda as well as on *Economic Stabilization*.

Incorporating Structural Changes

Hansen, like many others, was disturbed by what were commonly called "structural changes" which had imposed themselves on the nineteenth-century division of labor. Concern was expressed about population pressures; about changes in the direction and control of capital flows (especially the growing power of creditor nations such as the United States); about altered patterns of production, including the re-agrarianization of industrial areas and the industrialization of areas previously specialized in raw-materials production; about the alterations in cost structures and productivity relations brought about through the diffusion of technology; and about the growing importance of large-scale operations and the lumpiness of investment.

For the most part these changes were regarded, in the theoretical manner of the day, as autonomous, stemming from (unexplained) differential growth and technological developments—"the dynamics of larger historical change," in Barber's apt phrase (1991). But the adjustments they required, and of course the processes themselves, were modified in various ways by policies. Either way, relative price levels, goods flows, payments mechanisms, and so on were impinged upon so as to "unstructure" the world economy. And some of them—particularly the capital flows, which could be and in some cases had been reversed (see below), and the sensitivity of large-scale enterprises to changes in demand—rendered the system more vulnerable to shock. It was important therefore to identify cause-and-effect connections, so that at least the channels for control would be clear. That, basically, was Hansen's contribution.

Hansen viewed disequilibrium as violent shifts in the "normal" relationship between items contained in the balance of payments, causing gaps that must be filled by abnormal gold and capital movements. He makes reference to equilibrium cost/price relations between nations, and to a sustainable interest component in the balance of payments (as a way to capture the element of long-term capital flows). The focus is thus still on gold-standard variables; but he manages to combine them with operational counterparts to structural (and policy) changes of the sort I have indicated. The important cause-and-effect connections to which Hansen wanted to draw attention stand out more clearly if we reexpress his verbal analysis in algebraic terms.

The markup relation may be defined as

$$L/O \cdot w(1 + \lambda)_i = P_i, \tag{1}$$

where L/O is labor per unit of output, w is the money wage rage, λ is a coefficient between zero and one, and P is unit price—all for a particular good i, and for just one country.

"Terms of trade" may be defined as

$$\alpha = P_X/P_M, \tag{2}$$

where P_X is the domestic price level of exportables and P_M is the price of importables (both Ps being indexes). Note that Hansen does not specify (even implicitly) the functions showing how exports and imports are determined. The link between the nominal exchange rate and the "terms of trade," which we need to create a real exchange rate or measure of competitiveness, is also left unstated. As it stands, definitional relation (2) simply underscores the fact—noted under (1)—that although the discussion is ostensibly about international relations, it is couched wholly in terms of a single country.[31]

The equilibrium condition is

$$X/Y = (D_f^*/Y)(R - g), \tag{3}$$

where X/Y is the trade balance as a percentage of GNP, D_f^*/Y is the desired ratio of foreign debt to GNP, R is the real interest rate, and g is the real growth rate. This equilibrium condition is not quite Hansen's. He wrote in terms of a sustainable interest component in the balance of payments, in a world with long-term capital flows. But desired (or sustainable) foreign debt as a ratio of GNP, and the resulting balance-of-trade/GNP ratio necessary to meet this target, sufficiently approximate his thought.[32]

With these simple relations Hansen had identified the entities, and their connection to each other, to enable one to specify possible causes of disequilibrating movements that would be felt across nations (see table 1).

The Network Model

As has been pointed out already, Hansen's work leaves us without any operational notion of an integrated structure: the links between nations are present but are detectable only in the structure of a single nation's balance of payments. Hilgerdt went much further in modeling explicitly the flows that link nations. His network is a pragmatic entity, derived through trial and error. It shows a certain order of trade dependence

31. Since P_x and P_m are both domestic indexes, no exchange rate is necessary here. But as soon as P_x is thought of as a domestic currency price, and P_m as a foreign currency price, the terms of trade expression becomes $\alpha = (P_x/P_m) \cdot E$, where E is foreign currency units per unit of domestic currency. Haim Barkai, in a masterful essay (1989), shows how disastrous was the failure to attend to the microeconomic factors (for example, productivity) underlying the nominal exchange rate in the British debate about returning to gold in the 1920s.

32. This condition is derived and discussed in de Marchi 1990 and, more fully, in Howard 1989.

Table 1. Causes of Disequilibrating Movements across Nations (derived from Hansen)

Cause	Parameter or Variable Affected
Technological change disparity	$L / O, g$
Growth (hence demand) disparity	$X, \alpha (\rightarrow X)$
Trade union action, social legislation	$w (\rightarrow P_X)$
Monopoly (domestic)	λ
Fiscal manipulation	P_X, Y
Dumping	$\alpha (\rightarrow X)$
Monetary (bank policy) manipulation	R, E

between regions and to some extent defines puzzles that can be explained only by explicit reference to financial flows. It is static, but successive networks were devised for different years to enable change to be studied. To use it successfully one typically needs to refer also to his underlying and more detailed tables showing the balances of payments of individual countries or areas. Nonetheless it helps shed light on indirect linkages, and these are crucial to showing how sensitive is the whole set of flows to stoppage or constriction at any single point.

To illustrate both points, in the network for 1928 (see figure 1) Continental Europe had an import surplus with other continents several times larger than the export surplus it ran with non-Continental Europe (Hilgerdt 1942, 81). This suggests that balancing transfers of interest and dividends to creditor nations were taking place on a grand scale; or that capital imports helped sustain import surpluses; or that freight and insurance earnings artificially inflated import costs. As it turns out, elements of all three explanatory factors were present. Germany dominated the European group. It ran import surpluses with most countries in other continents but trade surpluses with most countries of Europe, including Belgium and the Netherlands. These last were important creditor and shipping nations, and their trade deficits with Germany were a channel for the transfers due to them from other parts of the world (Germany in effect relending to them the credit it received from its non-European trading partners). Belgium and the Netherlands in turn ran surpluses with the United Kingdom, indicating a channel for transfers from Germany via the Lowlands to the non-Continental Europe group (which meant mainly the United Kingdom) (81). In addition Germany was the recipient of large U.S. loans, which enabled it to increase net imports from the countries of the Recent Settlements category (and they

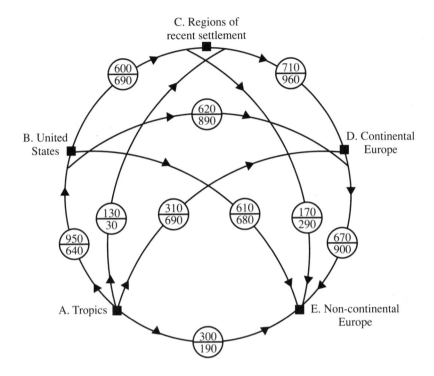

Figure 1. The system of multilateral trade, as reflected by the orientation of balances of merchandise trade in 1928.

Source: *The Network of World Trade*, Geneva: League of Nations, 1942, p. 78.

Note: The balances, derived from Figure 1, are given in millions of dollars (according to the parity in force in 1928). Both import and export balances are shown: the smaller of the two figures in each circle represents the export balance of the group from which the arrows emerge, and the larger figure the import balance of the group to which the arrows point. The difference between the amounts in question is due largely to the inclusion in imports of transport cost between the frontiers of the exporting and importing countries.

in turn from the United States (79, 81). That this complex set of interdependencies was vulnerable to shocks can be seen from what followed when the volume of new foreign loans issued in the United States fell by 50 percent during 1928, and French funds placed abroad on call or at short notice began to be withdrawn in the same year. The reduced flow of capital from the United States caused Canada to lose gold, and the Argentine peso was depreciated. Meanwhile, with the stabilization of the French franc in June 1928 there began a reversal of French capital flight, causing countries with short-term obligations to France to cut imports, contributing thereby to the fall in commodity prices that presaged the general depression (93–94).

There is something mechanical about this sort of use of the network. But as a way of displaying the possible channels of interdependence, and for highlighting the nicety of the balance of the whole, the model itself, though based on simple accounting identities, was vastly superior to what Hansen's and other modified gold-standard analyses had to offer.

Endogenous Cycles and Their Transmission

Tinbergen and Polak's work may be regarded as an attempt to model in a more causally explicit and quantifiable way an international transmission mechanism for cycles of nonmonetary origin. In a sense, therefore, it complemented without directly competing with Hilgerdt's network approach. The idea behind it was that modern industrial economies, and in particular the United States, are subject to ups and downs related perhaps initially to changes in market conditions but which get translated into cycles because of informational problems, lumpiness in investments, and lags. If governments respond with policies meant to preserve domestic activity but without being aware of either the causes or the consequences of their actions, cumulative movements towards recession are likely. Informed and coordinated responses are thus needed, and these depend on an understanding of the world economic system and its internal linkages.

Tinbergen's (1928) insight that there might be an endogenous mechanism involved in the cycle was extended in two directions. The first involved empirical support for the notion of repeated cycles. His early attempts at describing an endogenous dynamic focused on hypothetical interactions, illustrated by the damped cycles pictured in figure 2. But he subsequently found ample evidence of repeated cycles in a German study of hog production and in Dutch shipbuilding.[33] In shipbuilding, demand for tonnage (T) varied with the international cycle, but supply endogenized this movement: *investment* in shipbuilding (ΔT) could be modeled as varying inversely with lagged changes in total tonnage. By 1936 he had developed for the Dutch economy a multiequation model in terms of which one might trace the impact of selected anticyclical (anti-recession) policies (devaluation, wage-rate change, public works, and so on). For present purposes we may note two special features of this model. One was that the Dutch economy, being small and open, was for the most part merely the passive absorber of shocks imposed from the

33. I am indebted for details of the evolution of Tinbergen's work in the period 1927–35 to Marcel Boumans of the University of Amsterdam, who is preparing a Ph.D. dissertation on Tinbergen. I also owe him special thanks for having brought to my attention Tinbergen's 1928 article on the theory of exchange. A detailed discussion of the meaning of endogenous dynamic in Tinbergen's early work can be found in Boumans 1991.

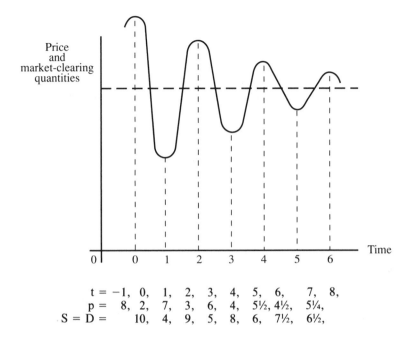

$$
\begin{array}{rllllllll}
t = & -1, & 0, & 1, & 2, & 3, & 4, & 5, & 6, & 7, & 8, \\
p = & & 8, & 2, & 7, & 3, & 6, & 4, & 5\tfrac{1}{2}, & 4\tfrac{1}{2}, & 5\tfrac{1}{4}, \\
S = D = & & & 10, & 4, & 9, & 5, & 8, & 6, & 7\tfrac{1}{2}, & 6\tfrac{1}{2},
\end{array}
$$

Figure 2. Tinbergen's "simulation" of a periodic movement in price and quantity induced by a fixed lag. Assume a (fixed) one-period lag in the response of supply to price; assume also that markets clear (demand equals supply in the period of offer). Price, demand and supply relationships take the following form:

Price:	0	1	2	3	4	5	6	7	8	9	10
Demand:	16	12	10	9	8	7	5	4	3	2	1
Supply:	0	2	4	5	6	7	8	9	10	11	11

Thus if p_{t-1} is 8, supply, after the postulated lag, will be 10, which amount will be taken off the market at a price of 2. The new price will induce a (lagged) supply of 4, for which the market-clearing price will be 7. Next period's supply will then be 9, and the market-clearing price will be 3; and so on. The movements of price and of (equal) supply-and-demand quantities are captured in the following schematic time path.

outside. Tinbergen was convinced that the originator of those shocks was the United States, where presumably something like an endogenous mechanism was at work. This partly explains the decision in his work for the League to focus on the United States case.

The second notable feature was that Tinbergen chose to reduce the many equations in his model down to one, which he then used, together with the estimates of coefficients already derived, to trace the effects of possible policies in the manner just noted. The reduction to a single equation could go in many directions; the one he chose was an equation in nonearned income, or profits, interest, speculative gains, etc. This focus is evident in the same 1928 article, "Observations on the Theory of Exchange," where he first indicated the possibility of an endogenous dynamic. At that time he was interested in discovering how far the simple Edgeworth-Pareto models of exchange seemed applicable to modern conditions. What struck him was that as soon as one introduces exchange for purposes other than immediate use, the close link between valuation and personal utility functions disappears. Intermediate exchanges, and exchanges involving mediators and organizations, may take place for profit; but it is no longer obvious how we can use the theory based on individual utility functions to generate results for entities whose "utility" functions seem to be of a different order (not personal; not related to use value). He quickly seized upon the fact that we can specify what profit-maximizing means only with a knowledge of prices but that the prices themselves, in most situations, are the outcome of strategic interaction between the parties involved, under conditions where the information shared by the parties is quite imperfect. Along with many of his contemporaries Tinbergen saw as being of increasing importance union-employer struggles; cartel- and trust-formation; and impersonal, large-scale industrial operations, which were both sensitive to market conditions for their own products and capable of affecting the market conditions for the products (and jobs) of others.

These reflections issued in three decisions affecting the way Tinbergen modeled. (1) He decided that existing competitive-exchange models were inadequate for discussing most of the business of modern societies. (2) He therefore moved away from determinate equilibrium modeling and opted instead for a more empirical and descriptive analysis of interactive and strategic processes. (3) Finally, he chose to focus on profit (or nonlabor) income as a key variable.[34] Profit in competitive equilibrium is zero; but in the real modern world, nonwage incomes, which involve strategic behavior and expectations and hence lags-in-reverse (production decisions taken in anticipation of demand), become both a generator and a mirroring device for the endogenous cycle. In these respects Tinbergen not only added the cycle to the older models of competitive allocation but did so in such a way as to make possible analyses of structural change and important institutional features of modern economies. And he modeled so as to allow policy simulations. Thus his work, though it was independently developed in the early

34. For this, and the argument in the following sentence of the text, see Tinbergen 1937, esp. 24–26, 48–51.

years, fully fit, and of course served, the emerging consensus in favor of coordinated policies to promote stability in a dynamic and changing world.

Tinbergen's model for the Dutch economy has been discussed in detail by Mary Morgan (1990, ch. 4). I therefore devote no further attention to it here. But the extension by Polak, "International Propagation of Business Cycles" (1937–39), needs to be discussed, if only briefly, to make the connection between the model for understanding and empirically tracing the course of the cycle in a "recipient" country and the enlarged model involving both propagator and recipient countries. Polak's work was conceptually uncomplicated. Using Dutch metaphors he pictured economic activity at home as reflecting the height of the wave of the cycle abroad, and the dike-structure (or exchange rate) as determining how much of the wave is allowed to pass through into domestic prices and thereby affect competition and production (79). One would expect to observe a positive correlation between the cycle at home and abroad, and a negative correlation between the cycle at home and the price of the home currency in terms of currencies abroad. Using proxies for the "world cycle" and for the domestic exchange rate "against the world," devised from data for eight countries covering the period 1925–36, Polak both found the anticipated signs and was able to confirm that the values of his estimated coefficients were close to the "true" values. This last involved various independent checks, including one applying Tinbergen's model for the Dutch economy, which was deemed to provide the desired explicit (and "true") causal structure rather than being just a set of empirical correlations. Polak also argued that the propagator in the whole set of relations was the United States. Here, then, was a quantified and credible (or at least carefully reasoned) set of relationships, ready-made for the international policy coordinator.

4

Truly "Enlightened" Behavior Where Cooperation Is not Guaranteed

Two connections were noted at the outset between League economists' work and the larger questions of peace and war. Both, as stated, ignored the issue of coordination (or the need for awareness of interdependence). The omission on my part was deliberate, to allow me to draw attention to a curious question-begging element in the literature of the period. The need for coordination was a fairly constant theme. The rationale was also clearly stated on many occasions: lack of coordination in the way nations had responded to the depression had produced collective losses; coordination presumably would avoid these. It was simply assumed that losses and gains for all meant losses and gains for each. The Australian chairman of the League's Committee of Co-ordination, in a speech to the nineteenth session of the Assembly from which I have already quoted, appealed implicitly to this logic: "we are still all suffering to-day [1938] from the contraction of markets due to the recovery measures adopted in the years following 1929 . . . a *really enlightened* self-interest requires that in framing commercial policies the interests of other countries must be taken into account."[35]

The League's own Delegation on Economic Depressions tried to put a figure on the cost of the defensive recovery measures that had been adopted: more than 25 million industrial workers unemployed in 1932, for a loss equal to two and one-half times U.S. national output in the boom year of 1929 (League 1943, 21–22). And a 1938 report of the League's Second Committee on Economic and Financial Questions neatly identified a major reason why coordination had proved so elu-sive: "many countries would prefer to-day to adopt policies designed to improve purchasing power when depressions occurred . . . were it not for the adverse effects on their balances of payments."[36] But taking such statements together, the argument one gets is simply that lack of coordi-nation has demonstrably negative social effects; coordinated action might prevent these; if all share in the gains, each nation's self-interest then implies action of a sort that a coordinator could approve. But there is also an unstated premise needed. The argument holds, provided such action is indeed followed by everyone. Even assuming that what is experienced by all is felt by each, in the absence of the last-mentioned condition the argument curls in upon itself, and truly self-interested behavior could once again turn out to be policy taken in isolation and for local ends.

The difficulty here of course is exactly the one identified by Keynes as causing the paradox of thrift. But where coordination among individual citizens might not be spontaneously forthcoming, a government could step in. In the international sphere there was no government able to impose policy, only voluntary assemblies such as the League, which could exhort but could not—not effectively anyway, to judge by the unimpressive attempt at sanctions against Italy—enforce. And actually the difficulty has a still sharper edge to it, as can be seen if we construe the situation in which nations found themselves in 1929 as a sort of

35. 22 September 1938 (above, n. 26).
36. Report to the Assembly, Second Committee for Economic and Financial Ques-tions, 26 September 1938, A.64, 1938, II.B, p. 3.

prisoner's-dilemma game. A crucial aspect of such situations is that the parties (players) do not make binding agreements beforehand. Technically this makes it a noncooperative game. As is well known, the best—risk-minimizing—strategy for each party is to defect. Mutual cooperation holds higher rewards for all parties, but since this cannot be agreed upon or credibly promised by all concerned in advance, defecting at least saves one from a still worse outcome, the result associated with cooperating while the others defect (CD). This was precisely the risk identified by the League's Second Committee report of 1938.

If in the absence of a guarantee that cooperation would be widely practiced a "really enlightened" nation should respond to downturn by acting so as to avoid the CD result, the basic problem was the lack of a guarantee. The balance of payments loss mentioned by the Second Committee was simply the measure of that particular payoff to cooperation. But this distinction was only vaguely sensed in the literature of the 1930s. The repeated exhortation to behave as would be appropriate only if everyone else was behaving well completely missed the point just made: that it may be better for single nations to pursue their own interests than to act as if coordination were present when it is not. This was a serious weakness in the case for acting in the general interest. There were others too, more specific. One of these involved the question whether a single nation might not turn the distribution of the gains from trade in its favor—not so much by depressing import prices, since commodity prices anyway were already so low, but by seeking a temporary advantage through competitive devaluation. The contemporary reading of things, reflected in the statements quoted above, was that this merely spread the depression. Eichengreen and Sachs (1985), on the other hand, have suggested that, in tandem with expansionary monetary policies, devaluations in fact may have helped the initiating countries.

Of course it was widely recognized that there was a problem of trust bedeviling efforts to climb back onto the free-trade/gold-standard platform; my point is simply that the problem of trust, or cooperation, was addressed very largely in terms of exhortation to do better, without any very clear notion of whether the incentives to do better were working in the same or a different direction than the exhortations. Economists working at or within the ambience of the League were better placed than most to be aware of the difficulties of securing trust on a wide scale. Even they, however, failed to do much more than point out how central trust was to coordination.

The best analysis along these lines was Röpke's study of the disintegration of the world economy. He suggested that the old integrated market system had functioned only because it existed in a context of codes of behavior, institutions, and psychomoral forces which were real and respected, even if largely unwritten (1942, 21, 68–69). Indeed the competitive market system was not neutral, "but a highly sensitive artefact of occidental civilization" (68). Hence to the extent that the old system still functioned it was living on its psychomoral reserves.

Timeless Equilibrium versus "The Dynamics of Larger Historical Change"

The more dominant line was the one I have been stressing: that economic self-interest and the social good are one, a conjunction secured by the force of efficiency, which is promoted by specialization and free exchange. On this view the economist's role is to hammer home the notion that rationality requires attending to these underlying economic truths and constraints. Bertil Ohlin well expresses this perspective, in a report prepared for the joint Carnegie Endowment–International Chamber of Commerce study of 1935–36, *International Economic Reconstruction* (see Ohlin 1936). Ohlin tried to find a place in his analysis for the fact that "there are nations which regard military power and other non-economic goals as more important for the economic policy than a high social standard." Surely it was these noneconomic goals that caused the problems, for international trust and goodwill and also for the economist. Or was it? Even such nations, Ohlin was happy to be able to demonstrate, cannot gainsay economic logic. A high national income makes for better education and hence for more efficient soldiers; and it clearly enhances the ability to finance armaments. Hence "far-reaching [autarky] may result in a reduction of military power. . . . It therefore becomes obvious that even for countries which do not regard a high standard of living as the principal aim to be pursued, it is necessary to analyse the conditions under which the maximum national income can be obtained" (23). And when this is done, and it is realized that "war means the destruction of much capital and the disorganisation of the public finances," then "what is certain is that, *in the long run,* there can be no greater danger to rapid economic progress than war" (24, emphasis mine).

If one puts Ohlin's argument alongside the equally rational economic arguments of Hitler, as brilliantly set forth by Lawrence Birken in his contribution to this collection, what strikes one is the total absence of a historical dynamic in Ohlin's analysis. If there are hints of war but it is not certain that war will come, or when, decisions about whether and when to increase armaments production or army strength become very complex. There is no guarantee that one will get it right with a knowledge of the larger historical causes; but it is virtually sure that an analysis of the conditions under which the maximum national income can be obtained will help very little towards deciding correctly. Despite verbal nods in the direction of a dynamic there is in the allocational ideal no past or future or any movement through time; everything developmental is reduced to remarks about "the long run," which, however, turns out to be merely a device for encapsulating the discussion firmly within the metaphor of a static balance. Hansen labored under the same constraint: wishing to address problems of structural change, he ended up indicating merely the sort of adjustments needed in the solution values of the static balance equations.

Tinbergen pointed up the difference with characteristic directness: "The nature of the central problem in dynamic economics is different from that in static economics. In the latter it is: what is the (constant) value of any variable if the system is in equilibrium? In the former it is: what is the course in time of each variable?" (1940, 82). But he was one of only a small number interested in the latter problem. At the same time, those who sensed the limitations of its typically static character did not claim more for economic analysis than that understanding the positive contribution to national income of a well-functioning monetary and trade system might lessen international tensions (see, e.g., Condliffe 1938, 6–7). Ohlin, of course, understood all that; yet his words claimed more, and in doing so while having no theory about the larger historical forces making for cooperation or conflict he made the economist's contribution seem like an offer of a well-honed chisel to someone whose problem is to drive a nail.

One more contentious comment along these lines. Birken (1991) suggests that "Hitler's ideology was permeated by the classical notion of progress." We need to make a distinction, however, between "progress" in eighteenth-century and in nineteenth-century classical economics. Nineteenth-century classical economics was concerned with system equilibrium as a balancing of forces; but unlike its eighteenth-century progenitors it incorporated time: the system had origins, and it was going somewhere (Wise 1989–90). The economic ideal of the 1930s, with its allusions to natural allocations, normalcy, maxima (optimum conditions), and timeless stability, looks more like a revival of the eighteenth century than of the nineteenth (cf. esp. Wise 1989–90, part 1, passim; part 2, 395–97).

Loveday: Understanding Depressions, and Codes for Combating Them

Loveday, sitting atop a lively hive of researchers, some of them brilliantly creative but, like Ohlin, also influenced by contemporary currents of thinking among economists, could not but take on some of the same basically eighteenth-century conceptual apparatus. He was also

alive to realities. In his own writing we find therefore the same unresolved tension we see in the work of the economists: an acknowledgment of the importance of distinctly modern political and national-
economic assertions, and of the modern problem of how to generate
trust in an interdependent but skeptical world; but an engine of analysis
deriving, for the most part, from the earliest years of the Industrial
Revolution. We also find a very down-to-earth acceptance of the fact
that the existing mechanisms for settling differences and fostering mutual trust had not resolved any of the forces making for conflict. Those
forces, he had to admit, had in effect been ignored in the repeated
idealistic proposals regarding commercial policy put forward at international conferences.[37]

Loveday's special contribution was to raise the matter of understanding depressions and securing coordinated responses to them almost to
the status of a holy mission. He had a faith to match, and a willingness to
overlook temporary setbacks in the confidence that the ends he sought
formed part of a sure convergence of enlightened opinion. He gave a
public lecture in 1937 (part of the Sir Halley Stewart Lectures for that
year) entitled "Problems of Economic Insecurity," in which he argued
that the reactions of governments to events after 1928 were entirely
predictable but that these experiments in self-protection were only a
phase. The increased likelihood of depressions was a world problem
that could not be solved nationally; with understanding, therefore, the
phase of national experiments must pass. Moreover, if the scientific
endeavor to understand the causes and course of depressions did succeed, "we may look with much greater confidence not only to the
economic but to the political future. It is uncertainty, misgiving, doubt,
lack of understanding, ignorance, that lead to discord and jealousy and
war" (Loveday 1938, 34).

Nor was this extraordinary confidence disturbed by the outbreak of
hostilities in Europe. On 30 September 1939, three weeks after the
general declaration of war on Germany by Great Britain and France, we
find Loveday looking beyond the period of conflict and reporting to the
Rockefeller Foundation that the Economic Service would be studying
intensively the structural changes which took place between 1914 and
1923, and the causes of the depression of 1921, with a view to understanding "the readjustment of society from war to peace conditions and
more especially . . . the ways in which a post-armistice depression may
be averted or diminished." For the war would pass (just like the national
experiments to cope with the depression), and afterwards "the problem

---

37. Loveday, "Memorandum on the League of Nations' Economic Intelligence
Work," 3 November 1939, GR 1.1, ser. 100, box 18, folder 152.

of economic depressions will be [no] less acute . . . than it was before."[38] Loveday's vision in 1939 in fact almost replicates that of the officers of the Rockefeller Foundation, who in 1933 had set up the funding for the League to pursue a program of business-cycle research. Tracy Kittredge, of the Paris office of the Foundation, reported a conversation with Loveday on these matters in which Loveday "stated that the fate of democratic and liberal societies might be determined by the success or failure in mitigating the consequences of economic depressions, and thus providing at least a minimum of social security for the masses," as the totalitarian states had done, though at the cost of suppressing "the remnants of political, social and economic liberty."[39]

Since, on Loveday's reading of history, depression typically follows war, the rationale for Tinbergen and Polak's sort of modeling could be represented as, if anything, strengthened by the arrival of war. On the other hand, the flaw in the case for coordinated effort—its failure to attend to incentives to cooperate, with roots in the failure to think of the forces of change as anything but disturbing influences upon a static and basically stable equilibrium—became a mammoth rift. Loveday the realist saw this clearly and virtually wrote off the interwar period as a lost era.

> In 1918 we looked back upon 1913 and assumed that if the damage caused in the four years of war was repaired the world economic mechanism would begin to function again more or less in the manner in which it had functioned, and it was thought satisfactorily, in 1913.
>
> Now the pre-war year is 1939, the end of a decade of quasi-permanent emergency. No one wants to restore the system of 1939. It broke down in war with all its questions unsolved. . . . there was no operative economic organisation, no unity of system and no unity of view.

The war, on this view, was a cathartic: "We may expect that peace will bring with it a greater will to act largely and a greater prospect of peace."[40]

In this conviction Loveday set to work on the postwar world economic order. The League's Delegation on Economic Depressions met in Princeton during the war and reported in two stages, as noted above (see

38. "Report for the Period August 30th, 1938, to September 1st, 1939, on Work Done under Rockefeller Appropriations nos. RF. 33023, RF. 37116 and RF. 33004, and under the Arrangement Regarding Statistical Study Tours," GR 1.1, ser. 100, box 18, folder 152.

39. "Program and Plans of Economic Organization, League of Nations," 16 January 1939, GR 1.1, ser. 100, box 18, folder 152.

40. Memorandum on League Intelligence Work, 3 November 1939, GR 1.1, ser. 100, box 18, folder 152, pp. 6–8.

League 1943, 1945). Loveday and his staff provided the basis for the text
of the reports and did background studies. Part 2 of the report was a
detailed analysis of the nature, mechanism, and spread of depressions,
and of coordinated means to combat them. This was a statement of the
problem and of a plan for dealing with it. But part 1, in an introduction
that seems to bear the stamp of Loveday's thinking, stressed the importance of having a statement of objectives *before* a statement of the plan.
The exaggerated nationalism of the interwar years, it was suggested,
reflected political insecurity but also the lack of objectives and a plan.
Economic cooperation presupposes that political security is firmly established; but that being done, the case for the relative primacy of
objectives becomes apparent: if there is prior agreement on objectives,
then should the plan come to be obstructed "by lack of co-operation
or"—a new element, this—"the danger of lack of co-operation," it may
be necessary to demand, on the basis of the agreed objectives, that the
uncooperative nations give up some of their sovereign freedom to act in
ways adversely affecting other nations (1943, 7, 13). The various objectives listed include such economic liberties as free access to markets,
the right to work, and a guaranteed minimum standard of living. Difficult, and sometimes conflicting objectives, it was admitted, but objectives for which there was now a good deal of acceptance among the
nations of the world (1943, 15).

Even from this brief summary it is plain that a definite sequence to
attaining world economic order was being proposed by the League's
Delegation: step 1, a guarantee of political security; step 2, agreement
on universal economic rights (for which the climate was now right,
following the collapse of a system based too heavily on national rights);
step 3, implementation of programs, such as coordinated antidepression
policies, together with rules governing behavior. The Delegation's focus
on universally agreed rights and on rules is important. This was a
formula for solving the intractable problem of cooperation, trust, or
commitment, against which appeals to economic rationality alone had
proved feeble. The language parallels that of the pertinent draft articles for the organization of the United Nations, as proposed at Dumbarton Oaks. The General Assembly was to have the power to initiate
studies and make recommendations "for the purpose of promoting cooperation in political, economic and social fields and of adjusting situations likely to impair the general welfare," the authority of the Assembly to "facilitate solutions" being vested in an Economic and Social
Council (UN Articles, cited in League 1945, 286–87).

This parallel in the formula for order is not surprising. At the State
Department Leo Pasvolsky had in 1942 become director of research for
an Advisory Committee on Post-war Foreign Policy, and in 1943 he was
made head of International Organization and Security Affairs, charged

with drafting the United Nations Charter. Present at Bretton Woods, Dumbarton Oaks, and San Francisco, he was also chairman of the Co-ordination Committee of the United Nations Conference at San Francisco. We know that Pasvolsky and Moulton, his old collaborator at Brookings, were agreed on the sort of postwar system that was needed, and that Moulton was convinced that it had to be proof against tinkering to achieve national ends. Moulton, it is also important to note, had pursued his own program of wartime research at Brookings into the most desirable structure of the postwar economic system, aided by a team of consultants led by Condliffe, who had moved in the meantime from London to the University of California, Los Angeles.[41] Condliffe's views had been stated plainly, remained consistent over many years, and were virtually indistinguishable from Loveday's: agreement to co-operate internationally, the key to a free trade environment, must be based on prior political understanding and a regulated code of behavior (1938, 55; 1947, 19–20).

If the interwar era was one of failure and the 1930s a lost decade, as Loveday suggested, what had been done wrongly? There was an implied judgment directed at politicians and nations for their self-interested interventions, but targeted also were economists. They had mostly been unable to escape the mindset of timeless equilibrium states, and their economics could only accommodate structural change as adjustment to equilibrium solution values and see nonmaximizing social or even self-serving economic behavior as irrational deviation from the ideal. At the same time Loveday was immensely proud of those of his own research economists who had produced operational models by which the channels and mechanisms of interdependence and of wrecking nationalistic responses to depression could be traced for all to see. Hilgerdt's network was prominently featured in part 1 of the League's Delegation on Depressions Report, and Tinbergen and Polak's perspective on cycles infused part 2. The issue of how to secure cooperation, to which no good answer had been found in the 1930s, was thought to have been resolved partly through the painful lessons and cooperation enforced by war and was, as we have seen, embodied in postwar plans in the form of agreed objectives and a code of behavior. The code, nonetheless, was only partly the spontaneous emergence of a norm of cooperation, and it remained to be seen how effective the rules would be once the chastening effects of the war had worn off.[42]

41. This paragraph reports details shared with me by Craufurd Goodwin from the study he is preparing on the Brookings Institution and international affairs.
42. The troubled Uruguay round of trade negotiations may be one sign of a declining commitment to international cooperation. My discussion in section 4 has been influenced by Bianchi 1990.

Special thanks are due to Lisa Boccia for invaluable exploratory research in the literature
of the period, and to Jacques Polak, who directed my thinking in important ways at a
formative stage. Useful comments on draft versions were received from Craufurd Goodwin, Mary Morgan, and Haim Barkai. A succession of students at the University of
Amsterdam have contributed to my grasp of events in the interbellum: Pepín Cabo, who
examined the Loveday Papers at Nuffield College, Oxford, and—with Esther-Mirjam
Sent—examined materials relating especially to Tinbergen in the League of Nations
Archive in Geneva; Ron Both, who delved extensively into Röpke's work; and Joost de
Ridder and Reinout van Asbeck, who investigated the interwar statistical record on
production, trade, employment, migration, and capital flows. My thanks and appreciation
to them all. Tom Rosenbaum, of the Rockefeller Archive, helped me uncover relevant
materials over a three-year period involving repeated visits. Peter Dohlman has been both
an able research assistant and a sounding board. The essay has benefited enormously from
his involvement.

References

Barber, William J. 1991. British and American Economists and Attempts to
Comprehend the Nature of War, 1910–20. *HOPE,* this issue.

Barkai, Haim. 1989. Productivity Patterns, Exchange Rates and the English
Stabilization Debate of the '20s. Mimeo.

Bianchi, Marina. 1990. How to Learn Sociality: True and False Solutions to
Mandeville's Problem. Mimeo. University of Rome.

Birken, Lawrence. 1991. The Political Economy of Adolf Hitler: Power, Plenty,
and Ideology. *HOPE,* this issue.

Boumans, Marcel. 1991. Paul Ehrenfest and Jan Tinbergen: A Case of Limited
Physics Transfer. Mimeo. University of Amsterdam.

Bullock, C. J., J. H. Williams, and R. S. Tucker. 1919. The Balance of Trade in
the United States. *Review of Economics and Statistics* 1:215–66.

Condliffe, J. B. 1938. *Markets and the Problem of Peaceful Change.* International Studies Conference, International Institute of Intellectual Cooperation. Paris: League of Nations.

———. 1940. *The Reconstruction of World Trade: A Survey of International
Economic Relations.* New York: Norton.

———. 1947. *Obstacles to Multilateral Trade.* National Planning Association
(NPA) Planning Pamphlets, no. 59. Washington, D.C.: NPA.

de Marchi, Neil. 1990. Deficits, Debt and the Dollar. *ABN Economic Review,*
April, 3–6.

Eichengreen, Barry. 1989a. The Gold Standard since Alec Ford. National Bureau of Economic Research Working Paper no. 3122.

———. 1989b. International Monetary Instability between the Wars: Structural
Flaws or Misguided Policies? National Bureau of Economic Research Working Paper no. 3124.

Eichengreen, Barry, and Jeffrey Sachs. 1985. Exchange Rates and Economic
Recovery in the 1930s. *Journal of Economic History* 45:925–46.

Fleming, J. M. 1962. Domestic Financial Policies under Fixed and under Flexible Exchange Rates. *IMF Staff Papers* 9:369–80.

Haberler, Gottfried von. 1937. *Prosperity and Depression.* Geneva: League of
Nations.

Hansen, Alvin. 1932. *Economic Stabilization in an Unbalanced World.* New
York: Harcourt Brace.

Hilgerdt, Folke. 1942. *The Network of World Trade.* Geneva: League of Nations.

Howard, David H. 1989. Implications of the U.S. Current Account Deficit. *Journal of Economic Perspectives* 3:153–65.

Joint Committee, Carnegie Endowment/International Chamber of Commerce (ICC). 1936. *International Economic Reconstruction: An Economists' and Businessmen's Survey of the Main Problems of Today.* Paris: ICC.

League of Nations. 1943. *The Transition from War to Peace Economy.* Report of the Delegation on Economic Depressions, part 1. Geneva.

———. 1945. *Economic Stability in the Post-War World: The Conditions of Prosperity after the Transition from War to Peace.* Report of the Delegation on Economic Depressions, part 2. Geneva.

Loveday, A. 1938. Problems of Economic Insecurity. In *The World's Economic Future,* Sir James Halley Stewart Lectures for 1937, 17–42. London: Allen & Unwin.

Meade, J. E. 1951. *The Theory of International Economic Policy.* 2 vols. Oxford: Oxford University Press.

Morgan, Mary S. 1990. *The History of Econometric Ideas.* Cambridge: Cambridge University Press.

Nurkse, Ragnar. 1944. *International Currency Experience: Lessons of the Inter-War Period.* Geneva: League of Nations.

Ohlin, Bertil. 1933. *Interregional and International Trade.* Cambridge: Harvard University Press.

———. 1936. Introductory Report on the Problem of International Economic Reconstruction. In *International Economic Reconstruction* (Joint Committee 1936), 17–156.

Pasvolsky, Leo. 1933. *Current Monetary Issues.* Washington, D.C.: Brookings Institution.

Pasvolsky, Leo, and H. G. Moulton. 1923. *Germany's Capacity to Pay.* Washington, D.C.: Brookings Institution.

———. 1924. *Russian Debts and Russian Reconstruction.* Washington, D.C.: Brookings Institution.

———. 1925. *The French Debt Problem.* Washington, D.C.: Brookings Institution.

Polak, J. J. 1937–39. International Propagation of Business Cycles. *Review of Economic Studies* 5–6:79–99.

Ridgeway, George L. 1938. *Merchants of Peace: Twenty Years of Business Diplomacy through the International Chamber of Commerce, 1919–38.* New York: Columbia University Press.

Röpke, Wilhelm. 1942. *International Economic Disintegration.* London: William Hodge.

Tinbergen, J. 1928. Opmerkingen over Ruilteorie [Observations on the Theory of Exchange]. *De Socialistische Gids* 13:431–45, 539–48.

———. 1936. Kan hier te lande, al dan niet na Overheidsingrijpen, een verbetering van de binnenlandse conjunctuur intreden, ook zonder verbetering van onze exportpositie? In *Prae-advies voor de Vereeniging voor de Staathuishoudkunde en de Statistik.* The Hague: Nijhoff.

———. 1937. *An Econometric Approach to Business Cycles.* Paris: Herman.

———. 1938. *Statistical Testing of Business Cycle Theories.* Vol. 1, *A Method and Its Application to Investment Activity.* Geneva: League of Nations.

———. 1939. *Statistical Testing of Business Cycle Theories.* Vol. 2, *Business Cycles in the United States of America, 1919–32.* Geneva: League of Nations.

———. 1940. Econometric Business Cycle Research. *Review of Economic Studies* 7:73–90.

———. 1952. *On the Theory of Economic Policy.* Amsterdam: North-Holland.
———. 1956. *Economic Policy: Principles and Design.* Amsterdam: North-Holland.
Viner, Jacob. 1919. *Canada's Balance of Payments.* Cambridge: Harvard University Press.
Wise, Norton (with the collaboration of Crosbie Smith). 1989–90. Work and Waste: Political Economy and Natural Philosophy in Nineteenth Century Britain. [In three parts.] *History of Science* 27:263–301, 391–449, 28:221–61.

The Political Economy of
Adolf Hitler: Power, Plenty, and Ideology

Lawrence Birken

If few scholars would grant Adolf Hitler even a footnote in the history of economic ideas, it may be in part because that history has been over-idealized. It is easy to argue that the "German catastrophe" was an aberration, a tragic misstep in the glorious march toward freedom and knowledge. Surely, the fragmentary half-baked notions of a Hitler appear to have little place in the sober chronicles of economic science. Moreover, even specialists who recognize that Hitler actually possessed a coherent world view would be the first to deny that it was an economic one. If we are unsure whether Hitlerism meant a return to a preeconomic feudalism or a flight into a posteconomic totalitarianism, we are certain that it was the antithesis of the economic (and thus civilized) vision that has otherwise shaped the modern world. Unfortunately, a deeper analysis of Hitler's ideas must cast doubt on this certainty. This analysis reveals not only that Hitlerism possessed the elements of a political economy but that it was just these elements which gave a logical basis to Hitler's two primary aims: the conquest of living space, and the elimination of the Jews.[1]

The central place of political economy in Hitlerism is in part obscured by Hitler himself. Again and again, he claimed to have come to destroy the primacy of "Jewish" economics and reassert the old "Aryan" primacy of politics. As early as 1919 he opposed the dissolution of society into individualism and internationalism by the spread of money, denouncing it as a "racial tuberculosis of the nation."[2] In *Mein Kampf* he further argued against the primacy of economics in the Bismarckian and Wilhelmine epoch, seeing in it the roots of Germany's failure in the First World War. Germany failed, he believed, because it rejected military conquest for "economic conquest," only to have to resort to war anyway, and from a weakened position.[3] Thus Eberhard Jäckel concludes

---

1. For conventional discussions of National Socialist economic ideology see Schumpeter 1954, 1154–56; Pribram 1983, 387–91.
2. See Hitler's first letter against the Jews, 1919, in Hitler 1974, 213–16.
3. Hitler 1971, 143ff.

that for Hitler, "economic policy was . . . only an instrument, a means to the end of providing the state with freedom of action."[4] Most other commentators agree, taking Hitler at his word that the National Socialist *Weltanschauung* demoted economics to a subordinate role. At most, a few writers have conceded that if Hitler did not have an economic theory, he at least possessed a "substitute for an economic theory."[5] It is of course correct that Hitler had neither the education nor the inclination to express his ideas about economics in professional terms. This does not mean, however, that he did not share with political economists many of the fundamental assumptions that had helped shape the modern world. Hitlerism is in fact the doctrine of a brilliant if ruthless ideologue, who could not help but reproduce the materialism and scienticism of the world around him even if it was a world he wanted to transcend. It is with this recognition that we need to examine anew the fundamental economic ideas in Hitler's writings.

One clue to the character of these writings is the unexpected stress they place on individualism.[6] Thus the creatively productive individual stands at the very center of the Hitlerian world view. All invention, Hitler tells us, is the product of real, individual geniuses of high *personality value*. Thus value is ultimately derived from the human labor embodied in actual individuals, and not from sterile capital in itself. Nature selects such individuals according to the *aristocratic principle,* so that the capitalist's wealth is not so much justified on the basis of his legal ownership of the means of production as on the basis of his superior inventiveness.[7] For Hitler the ultimate goal of a people is to apply those material laws which will enable the multiplication of personality values and thus the proliferation of inventions necessary to raise the material and cultural level to a higher and higher state. Nor is there any end to this process, which will enable the best of humanity, "having achieved possession of this earth," to "have a free path for activity in domains which will lie partly above it and partly outside it." This is the vision of unlimited expansion that Hitler promised his followers.[8]

But what are the material laws which will secure this expansion? Hitler saw personality value, embodied in great minds and judged on the basis of their creative productivity, as a function of *race value*. Thus the value of races could be estimated according to their capacity to bring forth personality values and thus a high cultural-technological level. But if race value is necessary in order to produce personality value, it does not automatically do so. Thus in his long-suppressed *Secret Book* Hitler

4. Jäckel 1981, 78.
5. See Carroll 1968, 95.
6. For a discussion of the individualism in Hitler's ideology see Dumont 1986, 149–79.
7. Hitler 1971, 352, 442–51.
8. Hitler 1971, 383–84.

noted that "on the basis of its general race value a people can certainly entertain a justified hope that it can bring real minds into existence," but only if that people does not "restrict such brains in their activity" by diluting them in a sea of mediocrities. Only a leader-state, dedicated to selecting the best minds from among a people and giving them freedom of action, can permit that people to transform its race value into the personality values necessary to raise the level of overall wealth and culture. Thus, even at this point, it is the state and not the economy that is a means to a higher end.[9]

But how is the race value of a people itself enhanced? For Hitler, race value may be diluted or strengthened first of all according to the relationship between the two factors of production, land and labor. Since labor tends to outgrow the land which supports it, the race value of a people will depend on the resolution of this disparity. First, Hitler noted, a people might limit births. But such a limitation frustrates that natural law which would have the most creative and productive individuals win out *after* they are born. Since birth control randomly limits the birth of individuals irrespective of their future contribution, it acts against the tendency of the highest personality values to raise triumphantly the present standard of living and future race value of a people. Thus Hitler concluded that birth control must at the least lower the race value of the people which practices it in comparison to those peoples who do not.[10]

Second, Hitler considered emigration as a solution to the unfavorable land-to-labor ratio of a people—only to dismiss it immediately. Only the highest personality values of a people would be likely to have the courage and inventiveness to strike out on their own, thus robbing that people of its best minds and any chance for future viability.[11] A third solution he advances is that of "internal colonization" by means of the technological intensification of agriculture. Creative minds being cultivated by a wise policy of outlawing birth control and emigration, what is to prevent such minds from using their inventiveness to raise the productivity of the soil? It is significant that Hitler was very careful in answering this question. The bias toward technology implicit in his ideology prevented him from dismissing internal colonization all at once. On the contrary, he recognized that the "history of human cultivation of the soil is one of permanent progress, permanent improvement and therefore of increasing yields." While there might be an absolute limit "somewhere," the real limit seems to be a *relative* one, since

9. See Hitler 1961, 31ff.; 1971, 443.
10. Hitler 1971, 131–33; 1961, 17–18. See also Carroll 1968, 96ff., and Jäckel 1981, 34–35, for discussions of the different options to redress the land/labor imbalance.
11. Hitler 1961, 18.

countries with comparatively fewer people could apply equally advanced technology to the soil and still have that much more room to grow, both in terms of standard of living and in terms of population. Long before the more densely settled people begin to reach the "absolute" limit, they will reach a "relative" limit in which they will begin to sink below the generally accepted standard of living established by the more sparsely settled people. But for an advanced people for whom past luxuries have become present necessities, this relative limit will appear as an absolute limit. Such a people will then be prematurely forced into limiting their population by birth control and emigration, thus diluting their race value, personality values, and ultimate strength at a time when their more sparsely settled neighbors are still growing.[12]

Eventually a people may drift toward a fourth solution based on foreign trade by producing nonagricultural commodities in return for food. In this case such a people's numbers could grow far beyond their territory's capacity to support them. But, Hitler argued, international trade is itself highly competitive. As population expands in all the major states, more and more industrial goods will be dumped on the market in exchange for food, so that their value will also fall to the vanishing point. Increasing competition for customers would thus lead the most highly advanced peoples toward eventual war.[13]

Thus Hitler found his way to the inevitable fifth solution: a territorial as opposed to a commercial war. A successful people, endowed with high race value and a leader-state which can transform those race values into personality values, must ultimately seek to expand its territorial base. The conquest of greater space will make possible a still greater population, thus increasing the potential for a higher race value, better personality value, more inventiveness, and an overall richer culture. This in turn increases the potential for further expansion, thus starting the cycle all over again, until a single people expands over the entire globe, extinguishing all other "inferior" peoples in the process, and raises human life to the highest conceivable level. Conversely, an unsuccessful people will become overpopulated, limit births, dilute its race value, dissipate its personality values, lose its inventiveness, become increasingly weaker in relation to its neighbors, and thus give up territory to them. This in turn increases the potential for further contraction, until such a people is extinguished from the earth.[14]

In all this, surprisingly, the state is the means and not the end. The end is nothing else but economics, in the sense that economics concerns itself not only with the static provisioning of a people but that people's

12. Hitler 1961, 18–19, 95ff.; 1971, 133ff.
13. Hitler 1971, 142ff.; 1961, 20–24.
14. See Jäckel 1981, 95–96, for what he calls "Hitler's dialectics of history."

dynamic capacity to expand its productive and thus its cultural forces. In this context even war is judged only in terms of how it serves this transcendent end. A good war is a short struggle or *Blitzkrieg,* since a short struggle selects for the most clever and inventive soldiers; a bad war is a long struggle, since a long struggle selects for the shirkers and the most cowardly soldiers. A short war thus enhances race value, while a long war is as effective as birth control and emigration in destroying it.[15]

Hitler applied this economy of life and death to all humanity. In particular, though, he presented two extreme cases, whose adaptations to nature are portrayed as diametrically opposite. For Hitler, the Aryan embodied the idea of "creative work" in the most idealized sense. It was the Aryan, he maintained, who developed the forces of production and built up the state out of those forces. As the population of Aryan peoples expanded, they instinctively applied the laws of nature to regulate themselves. This allowed them to bring forth great personalities who in turn further raised the cultural and technological level necessary for expansion. The Aryan thus appears as the light unto the world and the idealization of a positive humanity based on work. In absolute contrast is the Jew, who, Hitler maintained, utterly lacks a "correct interpretation of the concept of work." From a Hitlerian standpoint, which awards race value on the basis of creativity, the Jews appear to have zero race value. According to the peculiar anti-Semitics theories Hitler appropriated from "folkish" circles, the Jews either never possessed or in the dim past lost the capacity for work intrinsic to other peoples. Unable to exploit a specific territory directly by creative work, they should have disappeared from the face of the earth according to the natural law delineated above. But somehow, the argument went, they were able to find a way to short-circuit nature and escape the cycle of creative work by injecting themselves into the social body of productive peoples everywhere. Thus the Jews occupy no single territory but exist in all territories, where they maintain an "unnatural" existence. From the folkish standpoint that Hitler elaborated, they are a ghost people, an impossibility that artificially and vampiristically lives off the natural economies of living states. Utterly devoid of race value and personality values, the Jews exhibit no creativity except the creativity to devise ways to live off the creativity of others. Thus they developed ideologies to conceal their real nature and to make it easier for them to gain control of the productive forces of the people they exploit. Ultimately, though, this parasitism must destroy the nations from which it draws its strength by sapping their productive forces. In the end, without any victims on

15. See Hitler 1961, 10.

which to feed, the parasite must also die, so that the triumph of the Jews will result in their destruction, along with the rest of the world. Thus, "if . . . the Jew is victorious over the other people of the world, his crown will be the funeral wreath of humanity and the planet will, as it did thousands of years ago, move through the ether devoid of men."[16]

The two great goals that Hitler pursued as a politician, expansion and extermination, can of course be logically deduced from the ideology delineated above. In a sense he merely applied a set of general principles to the "German Question." As soon as he came to power he set in motion principles of a leader-state which would create a new elite of personality values drawn from the most efficient, ruthless, and original members of the *Volk*. He further sought to enhance race value by encouraging the expansion of the Aryan and the extinction of the Jew within the framework of territorial growth. This of course constituted nothing less than a repudiation of the Bismarckian commerce-oriented state, whose policy resembled in certain ways that of present-day Germany. The Hitler regime thus stands out from previous as well as later German regimes, not because it had no economic theory but because it had a different kind of economic theory. From the perspective of *that* theory, trade was merely an unnatural palliation of the land-labor problem which must eventually lead to war anyway. Yet the Bismarckian state decided on its economic policy for ultimately *political* reasons. Since Bismarck's main purpose was to preserve the Prussian state within the framework of a more competitive Europe, he had to make Prussia large enough that it was viable but not so large that its Prussian (and thus Protestant and dynastic) character would be drowned in a sea of Germans. So Bismarck aimed for the establishment of a *lesser* German Reich whose truncated size and limited territorial ambitions had to be supplemented by a commercial policy.[17] Despite Hitler's emotional tributes to the Prussian tradition as a means of coopting the military, his world view constituted a devastating critique of that tradition and the Bismarckian Reich which sought to preserve it. From the standpoint of Hitlerism, the old Bismarckian state had "artificially" preserved Prussian hegemony by limiting the territory of the Reich and thus increasing its dependence on an unnatural commercial policy. Despite his rhetoric, Hitler's ire was not directed at the primacy of economics as such, but at the primacy of an *unnatural* economic life dictated by archaic political traditions. It was in fact precisely because it did take a stand against the remnants of traditionalism in German life that National Socialism could consider itself a revolutionary philosophy. Yet, conversely, National Socialism also took what it considered to be a conservative stand

16. Hitler 1971, 65, 284–300; 1961, 211–13.
17. For an excellent discussion of Hitler's geopolitics see Calleo 1980, 85–121.

against the coming internationalism and hypercommercialism of the Soviet Union and the United States.

Against the once and future internationalism which he dismissed as "economic," Hitler upheld a *natural* economics based on the notion of self-contained or *autarkic* regional economies. This idea was ultimately sustained by his belief that a true people must possess its own productive forces within a specific territory. Autarky presupposes a natural balance between that territory and the people it supports. But the very dynamism of the Hitlerian system precludes an absolute conception of autarky in which a people is in perpetual equilibrium with its land. Rather, land and labor, population and productive forces, are never completely in equilibrium, so that peoples are ever expanding or contracting in power. Strong states merely move from a smaller to a larger autarky, while weak states move from a larger to a smaller autarky. It is precisely because further expansion requires present economic imbalance that a high standard of living could actually weaken a people by making them too self-satisfied, without giving up the ultimate goal of securing a higher standard of living. Conversely, military values may necessitate a short-term sacrifice of a people's well-being, but only to secure that well-being in the long run. Thus what seem like antieconomic statements in Hitler's writings from a static perspective, become proeconomic statements from a dynamic perspective.[18]

Hitler was of course not a trained economist but a half-educated man of exceptional brilliance, shrewdness, and ruthlessness. He cast himself in the role of the founder of a new doctrine that transcended the disciplines of the academic world and spoke directly to the masses. He also claimed to fight not only for Germany but for the whole world. Despite this megalomania which makes him seem "unbalanced," he was far from ignorant about the basic ideas which had dominated modern Western history. Like many semieducated Europeans he was a creature of the nineteenth century and the classical thought which structured it. Thus even if he was no economist, the place of economics in his thought must be reassessed. Much of his repudiation of economic thought and other cultural manifestations of post-Enlightenment modernity was mere posturing. His neomedievalism, for example, was very much a sop for the class of aristocratic Junkers whom he secretly despised, while his pseudo-Keynesianism was fundamentally a matter of practicality in dealing with the workers; from the beginning he knew that he had to nationalize the masses by ending the depression if he was to stay in power, just as he knew that he had to satisfy the military. But at heart, he was neither a mercantilist nor a Keynesian, neither a medievalist nor a

18. Hitler 1971, 151–52.

marginalist. Rather, as the above analysis of his ideas suggests, his assumptions about humanity fit all too well into the classical-physiocratic style of economic thought.

Firstly, like the classics and other thinkers of the Enlightenment long before Darwin, Hitler began with the assumption of self-interested individuals. More surprising, but also quite classical, is his derivation of productivity and invention from the efforts of individual personalities. As Louis Dumont notes, with Hitlerism we are confronted with the fact that a supposedly totalistic ideology puts extreme stress on the importance of individual persons.[19]

Secondly, and again like the classics, Hitler subordinated individual competition to a higher or natural law, which enabled him to justify that competition. This natural law preserves a quasi-religious character in the Hitlerian *Weltanschauung* by subjugating individual sentiment and perception to a higher purpose which mercilessly resolves competition into collective harmony. Thus Hitler cast himself in the role of the philosopher-king whose duty is to enforce the objective laws of nature irrespective of individual suffering and pain. It was precisely in preserving the distinction between natural and unnatural, to which he subordinated the individual, that Hitler also preserved the Enlightenment compromise between modernity and religion against the hyperexistentialist nihilism of twentieth-century thought.

Thirdly, Hitler's ideology was permeated by the classical notion of progress. Again and again, he claimed that by following the laws of nature a people can raise itself to the level of a "higher" humanity. Cruelty, warfare, and even extermination can be justified on this basis. This of course is as much a classical as it is a "Darwinian" notion; or rather, it takes a superficial knowledge of the "struggle for existence" and subjugates it to a pre-Darwinian if postcreationist teleology in which progress in *this* world replaces salvation in the next. Hitlerism thus appears as a kind of "folkish" transformation of the Marxist version of classical thought, which offers a secular substitute for salvation.

Like Marx, Hitler conceived of progress in highly materialistic, technological terms. To be sure, his vision of progress emphasizes its aesthetic at the expense of its ethical dimensions. But he did follow Marx in linking progress to a theory of growth. Like classical thought in general, Hitler's ideas are dynamic more than static. Thus space is necessary to make war to secure more space to make war to secure more space— until the entire world is covered by a single people of the highest race value and thus the highest personality values, who can lift humanity beyond and above the earth. What we have here is the old quasi-

19. See Dumont 1986.

messianic classical idea of unlimited growth, implicit in the Marxist rejection of *absolute* scarcity and marginalism. It is true that both Marx and Hitler possessed a concept of *relative* or *temporary* scarcity which is vital in providing a motivation for the dialectic of history. For Marx this temporary scarcity was imposed by class oppression; for Hitler, by the competition for space. But just as the triumph of the proletariat will free up the limitless productive forces of humanity, so the triumph of the Aryan will enable humanity to transcend the narrow limits of earthly space itself.

Fourthly, Hitler placed the classical distinction between productive and unproductive activity at the very center of his *Weltanschauung*. The hagiography of labor and the demonology of laziness were no mere propaganda points but fundamental axioms that set the whole system of valuation in motion. The distinction between creative work and parasitism became the means for distinguishing between life and death itself; the former for the industrious Aryan, the latter not only for the parasitic Jew but for the Gypsy as well, along with anyone else too sick or handicapped to earn his keep. Yet this horror was deeply rooted in the classical conception of economic life, where it was bound up with the assumption of growth; if economies could expand or contract, that which contributed to their expansion was productive and that which contributed to their contraction was unproductive. The productive/unproductive distinction thus became a universal constant in eighteenth- and nineteenth-century political economy, even if precisely *what* was productive and unproductive varied from savant to savant. Marx merely adopted the distinction to his particular interpretation by stigmatizing all capital, whether financial or industrial, as unproductive. In contrast, the Hitlerian ideology sought to unite German capital and labor on a territorial base by stigmatizing only financial capital, since it had no specific location but flowed from region to region. A revolutionary distinction which had arisen as a means of stigmatizing unearned aristocratic wealth was thus transformed into a reactionary defense against an increasingly international economy. What remained was the ideology of labor, which conferred life on those who worked and death on those who did not.[20]

Fifthly, Hitler was also following the larger classical tradition in giving economic life a fundamentally regional foundation. From its inception classical thought was concerned with the provisioning of the middle-sized state. It constructed its ideology on the basis of the Enlightenment

20. For the way in which the worship of labor replaces that of God in classical political economy see Baudrillard 1975, 33–41; for some insights into productivist themes in National Socialism see Zimmerman 1990, passim.

assumption that the world was composed of a set of discrete modes of production, each occupying a specific territorial base. Even Marxism, despite its commitment to internationalism, saw the earth in terms of a number of competing productive modes scattered over its surface. Bound up with this was the classical tendency to see "real" production as a physical process occupying a definite space. Hitler did not have to restore but merely preserve on a popular level this "territorial" conception of the economy, a conception which contains an implicit bias against extreme individualism on the one hand and extreme universalism on the other, since both appear too indefinite and abstract. Territory thus became the ultimate criterion for "real" or natural economic life. But this connection between economy and territory was itself predicated on that Enlightenment essentialism which opens up a distinction between the real and the unreal, the natural and the unnatural, the productive and the unproductive. Quasi-theological and even ethical, this distinction provides a moral basis for distinguishing those forms of life that were regarded as tolerable from those that were not. Thus Hitler preserved into the increasingly relativistic—but also tolerant—culture of Western Europe an outmoded secular religion complete with a warrant for genocide.

In short, Hitler's contention that his world view was the antithesis of "economics" must be qualified severely. In fact a kind of political economy stood at the very core of that world view. Thus he did not restore the primacy of the state after all but, quite the contrary, subordinated politics, warfare, and the state to a dynamic of aggressive technological and cultural expansion. In doing this he also asserted himself against the last remnants of aristocratic civility at the same time that he opposed the emerging relativism and marginalism of a developing consumer culture. But commentators have missed this because they have taken "economics" to be synonymous with neoclassical economics, thus interpreting Hitler's classical tendencies as a reimposition of politics. This is a shame, because the full implications of the Hitlerian *Weltanschauung* can only be understood by recognizing its "classical" dynamism, a dynamism which made it an ideology of the long run and thus a kind of secular religion. For Hitler, politics, whether in war or peace, constituted nothing more than a set of tactical "blitzes" necessary to achieve the long-run mission of his movement. Thus warfare had to take the form of the *Blitzkrieg,* which was the embodiment of cynicism itself. Indeed an understanding of the dynamism implicit in Hitlerism finally explains how it could simultaneously be so cynical about short-run goals and so fanatically committed to long-term obsessions.

To link Hitlerism to classicism seems more perverse than ironic. But historical analysis should be a process of self-recognition and demystification. The affinities between Hitler and the Enlightenment should not lead us to rehabilitate the former but to scrutinize the latter more thoroughly. However beneficial the aspirations of the classics, their overidealization of natural law, productivism, and essentialism also contained the seeds of a radical evil.[21]

References

Baudrillard, Jean. 1975. *The Mirror of Production*. New York: Telos Press.

Calleo, David. 1980. *The German Problem Reconsidered: Germany and the World Order, 1870 to the Present*. Cambridge: Cambridge University Press.

Carroll, Berenice. 1968. *Design for Total War: Arms and Economics in the Third Reich*. The Hague and Paris: Mouton.

Dumont, Louis. 1986. *Essays on Individualism: Modern Ideology in Anthropological Perspective*. Chicago: University of Chicago Press.

Hitler, Adolf. 1961. *Hitler's Secret Book*. Translated by S. Attanasio. New York: Grove Press.

———. 1971. *Mein Kampf*. Translated by Ralph Manheim. Boston: Houghton Mifflin.

———. 1974. *Hitler's Letters and Notes*. Edited by Werner Maser. New York: Harper & Row.

Jäckel, Eberhard. 1981. *Hitler's World View: A Blueprint for Power*. Cambridge: Harvard University Press.

Pribram, Karl. 1983. *A History of Economic Reasoning*. Baltimore: The Johns Hopkins University Press.

Schumpeter, Joseph A. 1954. *History of Economic Analysis*. New York: Oxford University Press.

Zimmerman, Michael. 1990. *Heidegger's Confrontation with Modernity: Technology, Politics, Art*. Indianapolis: Indiana University Press.

21. Since this essay concentrates on political economy, it excludes a direct discussion of Hitler's biological and racial ideas. Nevertheless the question does arise as to how those ideas can be reconciled to my assertion that Hitlerism has classical assumptions. Note, however, that the classics assumed a prepolitical sexual and biological order of inequality which was given to the economic realm. In this context race and sex can be understood from Hitler's perspective as biological "givens" or endowments, which are either enhanced or diluted by political-economic policy.

Marxist and Soviet Defense Economics, 1848–1927

Christopher Mark Davis

In the nineteenth century Marx and Engels founded and partially elaborated a theory of the historical development of society that was based on the concepts of materialist determinants of phenomena, conflicting economic classes, and the inevitability of successive transitions from one type of economic system (mode of production) to a superior one, in terms of productive forces, that would culminate in the victory of communism. Their ideas were influenced by their observations and experiences in a period of robust but unstable growth of European capitalist economies in states that for the most part were governed by undemocratic political regimes, insurrections by nationalist and revolutionary forces (e.g., uprisings throughout Europe in 1848, the Paris commune in 1871), repression of liberal or radical movements by police and military units of authoritarian states, and numerous major wars (e.g., the Crimean War in 1853, the U.S. Civil War in 1860–65, the Franco-Prussian War in 1870). Given their theoretical orientations, personal commitments to revolutionary movements, and politicoeconomic environment, Marx and Engels devoted considerable attention to wars, the military, and defense economics. However, their analyses of defense topics were not fully integrated into their theoretical studies of economics and politics, and for obvious reasons they did not consider a number of issues that were of importance in later years.

From the death of Engels in 1895 (Marx died in 1883) until the Bolshevik revolution in Russia in 1917 Marxists such as Lenin, Hilferding, Luxemburg, and Bukharin made further contributions to the literature on defense economics. Their analyses were influenced by new theories of imperialism, the state, and the vanguard party as well as by the experiences of the 1905 revolution in Russia and World War I. However, as a result of their oppositional roles in society, lack of experience with defense-sector management, and ideological biases their studies of defense problems and policies were critical (e.g., antimilitary), limited in coverage, and abstract.

This situation changed after the Bolsheviks under the leadership of

Lenin wrested control of the state in Russia through armed insurrections in 1917. For the first time a Marxist party had responsibility for the detailed management of a large defense establishment in a threatening security environment. Over the next decade the military experiences of the Soviet Union included the dismantling of the tsarist armed forces, creation of a small volunteer Red Army, civil war, rapid development of a mass army through conscription, total mobilization of the economy in support of the military effort, rapid demobilization after victory, transition of the Red Army from a standing to a mixed regular-territorial militia force, and reform of the military. In the same period the economy shifted from the state-dominated tsarist market economy to a chaotic revolutionary economy (1917–18) to the centralized barter economy of War Communism (1918–21) to the regulated socialist market economy of the New Economic Policy (1921–27). These systemic and policy changes produced interesting interactions between the defense sector and the economy and challenges in the defense field for both the Bolshevik political leadership and economists.

This historical summary suggests that any survey of early Marxist and Soviet defense economics should consider several questions. Was there consistency in the defense economic issues studied by Marxists and in the conclusions from their analyses? Did the theoretical foundations provided by the prerevolution contributions of Marxist analysts assist the Bolsheviks in dealing with the real problems of defense and shape state policies? What impacts did the novel conditions in Russia and the experiences of the Bolshevik state have on assessments and decision making in the defense economic field? Did Soviet analysts carry out much original research on defense economics in the period 1917–27? In an attempt to answer these questions this essay reviews writings on the same topics by analysts in three periods: Marx and Engels (1848–95); Lenin, Hilferding, Luxemburg, and Bukharin before the Bolshevik revolution (1905–17); and Soviet specialists during 1917–27.[1]

Several qualifications should be made concerning this review of the

1. The main issues are identified in Kennedy 1983: (1) the relationship between economic classes, the state, and the military; (2) the role of the defense sector in the economic system; (3) the linkage between economic and military power; (4) economic development, technology, and the military; (5) economic considerations in choosing the form of military organization; (6) the influence of security requirements on the choice of economic organization and policies; (7) defense and macroeconomic processes such as consumption and investment; (8) the impact on the economy of the peacetime defense burden; (9) defense expenditure and budgeting; (10) organization of military supplies (logistics); (11) defense industry; (12) economic factors in military science and doctrine; (13) arms races, militarism, and disarmament; (14) mobilization of the economy for war; (15) security considerations in formulating foreign economic policies; (16) economic causes of war; and (17) economic consequences of war.

literature. First, early Marxist and Soviet writings on defense economics were scattered across a variety of articles and books and can only be given coherence in presentation by imposing an ex post framework. This is attempted below with the acknowledgment that an interpretative effort of this type is subjective and with the hope that it will stimulate more thorough studies in the future. Second, in the past a number of Soviet and Western scholars have examined Marxist-Leninist writings related to aspects of defense economics.[2] Many disputes have arisen concerning interpretations of the classic texts, but given the time scale under study in this article and the large volume of literature under review it is only possible to identify, not resolve, controversies concerning Marxist analyses of military-related economic matters. Third, the actual economic history of the Soviet defense sector during 1917–27 has been covered in another paper (Davis 1990b).

Marx and Engels on Defense Economics (1848–95)

By the end of the 1840s Marx and Engels had developed a materialist explanation of history, identified the proletariat as the revolutionary class in the epoch of capitalism, formed the first communist party, and issued calls for armed struggle by workers. The events in Europe in 1848–49 focused their attention on the role of insurrections, armies, and war in class struggles. For example, in the period March–May 1849 Engels wrote eighty articles on war and military issues in the newspaper *Neue Rheinische Zeitung*.[3] In subsequent years he and (to a lesser extent) Marx continued to produce works on defense topics.[4]

As a result of the continuity of their interest in military affairs, holistic analytical approach, materialist interpretation of phenomena, and prodigious written output Marx and Engels discussed many issues in the field of defense economics. But no coherent study of defense economics was made, and economic and military studies usually were poorly integrated despite the proclaimed features of the Marxist theoretical approach. For example, most of the journalistic and scholarly writings on military affairs by Engels (who had the nickname "The General") were devoted to technical and tactical issues and neglected economic factors. In contrast, Marx excluded defense topics to a surprising extent from

2. Among the past reviews of Soviet defense economics are Latnikov 1976, Pozharov 1981, Semmel 1981, Lider 1981, and Chechinski 1985.

3. These articles are contained in *Karl Marx/Frederick Engels Collected Works*, vol. 9 (London: Lawrence & Wishart, 1978).

4. The major works include Marx's "Class Struggles in France: 1848 to 1850" (1850) and Engels's "Conditions and Prospects of a War of the Holy Alliance against France in 1852" (1851), "Army" (1858a), "The Prussian Military Question and the German Workers' Party" (1865), and *Anti-Dühring* (1878).

his major economic works. In *Capital* there are three minor comments of military relevance in volume 1, one in volume 2, and two in volume 3.[5] In consequence a coherent exposition of early Marxist defense economics can only be achieved by reorganizing writings in the period 1848–95.

One of the fundamental concepts developed by Marx and Engels was that history evolved through the struggle of economic classes and related shifts in the dominant mode of production. They believed that this process was interrelated with military developments in at least two ways. First, the emergence of new classes and more sophisticated production techniques made it possible for societies to enhance military capabilities. Second, armies could intervene in class conflicts and either accelerate or retard historical processes.

In their writings they argued that the decline of feudalism resulted in a diminution of the power of the aristocracy, the emancipation of the peasantry, and the emergence of the bourgeoisie as a new class. These changes in the class structure and the related development of productive forces of capitalism enabled the state to maintain larger armies than in the past. Engels calculated that the average size of the military, measured as a share of the population, increased from about 2 to 3 percent in feudal conditions to 5 to 6 percent in capitalist societies ([1851] 1978, 554). In order to maintain a larger military it was necessary to shift from a professional army to one based on universal conscription and to expand the officer corps. The latter policy provided new opportunities for the sons of the bourgeoisie that undermined the military caste of the aristocracy and contributed to the democratization of the armed forces. Regular soldiers initially were recruited from the peasantry and urban lower classes. But as capitalism developed it generated an important new class, the proletariat, which exerted an increasing influence on the military.

The expanded modern army could be utilized by the state in a repressive manner, but in the longer term it undermined the feudal order, acted as a constraint on the ability of reactionary forces to carry out a coup d'état, and facilitated capitalist development (Engels [1865] 1985, 60). Eventually "the monopoly of capital becomes a fetter on the mode of production," and the class struggle between the bourgeoisie and proletariat becomes more acute (Marx [1867] 1970, 763). When this occurs, the military skills of the workers acquired through universal service will prove to be useful, because the revolution is likely to be accompanied by a civil war fought with modern means (Engels [1851] 1978, 556). Follow-

5. Defense-related issues *Capital* are in Marx [1867] 1970, 433, 751, 773; [1885] 1986, 144; [1894] 1981, 152, 703.

ing victory in the revolution and the emancipation of the proletariat, productive forces will expand at a faster pace, thus enabling communist societies to maintain larger, more mobile armies.

Another contribution of Marx and Engels was their economic interpretation of the relationship between the state and the military.[6] They believed that the state was a socially necessary institution that developed over time to take care of various tasks, such as defense of the nation, that could not be handled by individuals or specific classes (Engels 1878). The state was an element of the superstructure and tended to be an instrument of the dominant class. Its activities and effectiveness in the military and other areas were strongly influenced by economic factors.

In feudalism the state had close links with the aristocracy, which made frequent use of the army to maintain the system by military force. In *Capital* Marx argues that in the transition from feudalism to capitalism state coercion can be interpreted as an economic force.[7] Under competitive capitalism there was the clearest separation between economic and political institutions. Although the state served the bourgeoisie, the capitalist mode of production usually relied on economic, rather than physical, force to expropriate surplus value. In exceptional circumstances of acute class conflict (e.g., Paris in 1848 and 1871) the bourgeois state would use the military to suppress workers' strikes and insurrections (Marx 1850, 1852). It also was possible in a situation of divisions within the bourgeoisie for the state to acquire greater independence and impose a military dictatorship, such as in France under Louis Napoleon.

Over time the proletarianization of the army, discussed above, would undermine the effectiveness of the military as a repressive instrument of the bourgeoisie. But Marx and Engels expected that the workers would have to destroy the state and its residual forces at the time of the revolution.[8] The succeeding state would be a dictatorship of the pro-

6. Draper 1977 provides a review of their ideas on the state.
7. "The different momenta of primitive accumulation distribute themselves now, more or less in chronological order. . . . In England at the end of the 17th century, they arrive at a systematical combination, embracing the colonies, the national debt, the modern mode of taxation, and the protectionist system. These methods depend in part on brute force, e.g., the colonial system. But they all employ the power of the State, the concentrated and organised force of society, to hasten, hothouse fashion, the process of transformation of the feudal mode of production into the capitalist mode, and to shorten the transition. Force is the midwife of every old society pregnant with a new one. It is itself an economic power" (Marx [1867] 1970, 751).
8. "Do not pass from one hand to the other the bureaucratic-military machine, as it has existed up to now, but destroy it, and especially in such preliminary circumstances as any actual popular revolution on the continent" (Marx [1871] 1982, 177).

letariat which would make use of its armed forces to protect the revolutionary nation from foreign and domestic enemies (Engels 1878).

In their works Marx and Engels did not either clearly define the defense sector or fully assess its multiple roles in the different economic systems (modes of production) of its six main institutions: central defense bureaucracy, armed forces, military supply, defense industry, military research and development, and military foreign trade.[9] In their discussions of the central defense bureaucracy there are numerous mentions of the activities of top military officers in developing tactics, leading troops, and interfering in civilian political processes, but little analysis of the economic functions and interactions of the elite of the military-industrial complex: politicians, defense industrialists, and leaders of the armed forces.

Marx and Engels considered the military to be a component of the nonproductive sphere of the economy, since it was not producing commodities that generated surplus value but rather was a consumer of income generated elsewhere.[10] Despite this they believed that the military was an economic actor of significance and repeatedly discussed its importance as a consumer of industrial products and raw material and as a stimulus to technological innovation. Occasionally they mentioned the contributions of the armed forces to economic development in the civilian sphere (e.g., building roads and bridges). On a more abstract level, Marx wrote to Engels that

> the history of the army all the more clearly confirms the correctness of our view about the link between productive forces and social relations. In general, the army plays an important role in economic development. For example, wages fully developed first of all in ancient armies. . . . Here also machines were used for the first time on a large scale. . . . In armies the division of labor within one branch of production was first carried out. ([1857] 1982, 103)

In a subsequent letter to Engels he observed that "our theory about the determination of the organization of labor by the means of production is

9. In Davis 1990a the Soviet defense sector is defined to consist of these same six institutions. They produce goods and services and engage in economic interactions with each other and civilian establishments. Engels discusses the defense sector as a whole in his article "Army" ([1858a] 1982, 125–26).

10. In the chapter "Productive and Unproductive Labour" (Marx [posthumous] 1951) there are several comments on the military as a component of the nonproductive sphere of the economy. Marx quotes with approval the judgment of Adam Smith that "the labour of some of the most respectable orders in the society is, like that of menial servants, unproductive of any value. . . . The sovereign, for example, with all the officers both of justice and war who serve under him, the whole of the army and navy, are unproductive labourers. They are the servants of the public, and are maintained by a part of the annual produce of the industry of other people" (156).

nowhere so brilliantly supported as in the man-killing industry" ([1866] 1982, 162). He admitted that he did not have sufficient knowledge to elaborate this idea and suggested that Engels prepare a supplement on this topic for inclusion in the first volume of *Capital*. There is no record that this was ever done, but Engels applied the industry analogy to the armed forces years later in *Anti-Dühring:* "The modern warship is not only a product, but at the same time a specimen of modern large-scale industry, a floating factory—producing mainly, to be sure, a lavish waste of money" ([1878] 1970, 191).

Engels was interested in logistics and often examined the adverse or beneficial impacts on military effectiveness of existing supply and transportation systems in his writings on the armed forces and war (1858a, 1878). He believed that improvements in the organization of logistics were preconditions for the development of modern mass armies, which require more extensive means of transport, better communications, and greater supplies of ammunition during campaigns than did previous forces. For this reason he associated advanced military logistics networks with the capitalist mode of production.

Although Marx and Engels did not prepare any specific studies of defense industries, they were well aware of their importance for military institutions. In his histories of the army, artillery, and navy (1858a, 1858b, 1858c) Engels argued that innovations and improvements of weapons and military-related technologies in defense industries provided the foundation for the military superiority of advanced states. For this reason the armies of the bourgeoisie, supported by capitalist manufacturing, were considerably superior to those of the feudal era.

Marx and Engels examined the relationship between economic power (an aggregate measure of human resources, capital stock, and raw materials) and military capabilities repeatedly and at length.[11] They believed that throughout history the growth of productive forces in general and developments in technology in particular were responsible for the performance of armies. This point is made most clearly in the chapters on "the force theory" in *Anti-Dühring:*

> the triumph of force is based on the production of arms, and this in turn on production in general—therefore on "economic power," on the "economic order," on the material means which force has at its disposal. . . . Nothing is more dependent on economic preconditions than precisely the army and navy. Their armaments, composition, organization, tactics and strategy depend above all on

11. For a recent interpretation of their teachings on the importance for the military of economic power see Pozharov 1981.

the stage reached at the time in production and communications. ([1878] 1970, 184–85)[12]

In their opinion economically advanced states not only were able to produce and distribute arms and munitions more effectively than backward nations but also could mobilize their industry and population in support of wars to greater degrees.[13] In various articles Engels argued that the relatively developed economies of Britain and the United States provided decisive support to their armies and navies whereas the backwardness of the Russian economy ensured that it could not sustain great-power status.[14]

Engels identified the technological dimension of economic power as especially important for the armed forces. In his studies of armies he provided many examples where technological progress in artillery and firearms had led to advances in military capabilities (1858a, 1858b). Nonmilitary technologies (e.g., railroads, steam propulsion of ships, and telegraphs) influenced the outcomes of conflicts as well.[15] Naval warfare, he believed, had been changed radically by technological innovations in guns, steam engines, and armor plating.[16] Another relevant subject mentioned in the early Marxist literature is that of civilian spinoffs from progress in defense technologies.[17] Despite his interest in

12. A related comment is that "the whole organisation and method of fighting of armies, and along with these victory or defeat, proved to be dependent on material, that is, economic conditions; on the human material, and the armaments material, and therefore on the quality and quantity of the population and on technical development" (189).

13. Engels 1851 discusses the differential mobilization capabilities of nations at length. For example: "Like mobility, the mass character of means of attack is necessarily the result of a higher stage of civilisation, and, in particular, the modern proportion of the armed mass of the total population is incompatible with any state of society inferior to that of the emancipated bourgeoisie" ([1851] 1978, 553).

14. For example: "All these calculations prove, incidentally, that a lasting subjection of Western Europe to Russia is quite impossible and becomes more impossible every day" ([1851] 1978, 554).

15. The link between the mobility of modern armies and the technologies of railroads and telegraph is discussed in Engels 1851. In a later article, "The Campaign in Italy" he wrote: "The second factor that has changed warfare significantly since the time of Napoleon is steam. It was only by means of railways and steamships that the French were able to throw such masses of troops into Piedmont in the five days between the delivery of the Austrians' ultimatum and their actual invasion that any Austrian attack on the Piedmontese position was doomed to failure" ([1859] 1980, 347).

16. Developments in naval technology through the 1850s are discussed in Engels 1858c and in subsequent works. For example, in 1862 he wrote an article on the development of ironclads by the North and South in the American Civil War. Smirnov (1987, 18) provides a recent assessment of the economic pressures which stimulated the construction by the South of the first ironclad, the *Merrimac,* and of the military impact of this technological innovation. My thanks to Oleg D. Baklanov for presenting me with a copy of Smirnov's book.

17. See Marx [1867] 1970, 433, for a discussion of the impact of the American Civil War on improvements in machinery of the British cotton industry.

military technology and often insightful analyses of past trends, Engels was fallible in predicting developments:

> The Franco-Prussian War marked a turning-point . . . the weapons used have reached such a stage of perfection that further progress which would have any revolutionising influence is no longer possible. Once armies have guns which can hit a battalion at any range at which it can be distinguished, and rifles which are equally effective for hitting individual men, and what is more loading them takes less time than aiming, then all further improvements are more or less unimportant for field warfare. ([1878] 1970, 188)

Marx and Engels considered economic factors to be crucial determinants not only of conflicts but also of military science and doctrine. In his articles that surveyed the histories of the army and the navy (1858a, 1858c) Engels argued that strategy and tactics were heavily influenced by developments in technology and industrial capacity. Elsewhere he discussed how the invention of the telegraph had made possible the strategic direction of modern mass armies and had resulted in an intensification of tempo of tactical operations. He asserted that in military art, as in industry, it was not possible to achieve new results by old means: "Every great general . . . either himself invents new material means or first discovers the correct use of new material means invented before him. . . . Napoleon's epoch-making achievement lies in the fact that he found the sole correct tactical and strategic application for the more colossal army masses made possible by the revolution" ([1851] 1978, 556). He believed that transition from feudalism to capitalism transformed military science and that the same would be true in the future.[18]

A variety of other defense economic topics were discussed occasionally by Marx and Engels. In a number of writings they mentioned decisions to increase military budgets, financial constraints on the development of armed forces, and the fiscal consequences of high defense spending (budget deficits, increased taxes, loans, national debt). In *Anti-Dühring* Engels was critical of the spirit of militarism in the Europe of the 1870s and its associated arms races that generated heavy defense burdens on the economies of the major powers.[19] In this literature one

18. "The emancipation of the proletariat, too, will have its particular military expression, it will give rise to a specific, new method of warfare. . . . But just as in the proletarian revolution the question for industry is not one of abolishing steam machines but of multiplying them, so for warfare it is a question not of diminishing but of intensifying the mass character and mobility of armies. Increased productive forces were the precondition for the Napoleonic warfare; new productive forces must likewise be the precondition for every new perfection in warfare" ([1851] 1978, 554).

19. "The army has become the main purpose of the state, and an end in itself; the

also can find works on economic aspects of disarmament, such as Marx's "The French Disarmament" (1859) and Engels's "Can Europe Disarm?" (1893).

Although Marx and Engels wrote many articles about past and present wars, they did not advance an economic explanation for these conflicts. This is somewhat surprising in light of their materialist approach. They did, however, write extensively about the economic consequences of war. These included the destruction of productive forces, acceleration of technological progress, growth in national debt, and revolution leading to a new mode of production.[20]

Marxist Defense Economics, 1905–17

From the death of Engels to the 1917 Bolshevik revolution significant changes in the politicoeconomic environment influenced Marxist studies: continuing rapid growth of advanced market economies, the division of the Russian social democratic movement into Bolshevik and Menshevik factions, the 1905 revolution in Russia and its suppression, the intensification of competition between European powers for colonies and of the arms races between major powers, the catastrophic experience of the First World War, and the February 1917 revolution in Russia. In response to these phenomena traditional theory was supplemented by ideas such as the vanguard role of the revolutionary party, finance capital, the enhanced role of the modern state, and imperialism. These developments generated new research agendas and shifted the focus of analyses of Marxists writing on defense economics away from areas explored in the past. For example, the socialists of this time devoted far more attention than did Marx and Engels to the economic causes of militarism and war.

One of the contributors to Marxist defense economics in this period was V. I. Lenin, the head of the Bolshevik party. He wrote about topics

---

peoples are only there in addition in order to provide and feed the soldiers. Militarism dominates and is swallowing Europe. But this militarism also carries in itself the seed of its own destruction. Competition of the individual states with each other forces them, on the one hand, to spend more money each year on the army and navy, artillery, etc., thus more and more hastening financial catastrophe; and on the other hand to take universal compulsory military service more and more seriously, thus in the long term making the whole people . . . able at a given moment to make its will prevail in opposition to the commanding military lords. . . . At this point the armies of princes become transformed into armies of the people; the machine refuses to work, and militarism collapses by the dialectic of its own evolution" ([1878] 1970, 189).

20. For example, in *Capital* Marx wrote the following: "On the other hand, the American Civil War brought in its train a colossal national debt, and, with it, pressure of taxes, the rise of the vilest financial aristocracy, the squandering of a huge part of the public land on speculative companies for the exploitation of railways, mines &c., in brief, the most rapid centralisation of capital. The great republic has, therefore, ceased to be the promised land for emigrant labourers" ([1867] 1970, 773).

such as the relationship between economic and military power, military organization, logistics, militarism, and the causes and consequences of wars.[21] His ideas are of special interest because of his subsequent role as leader of Soviet Russia, which gave him a unique opportunity to link his theories to practice.

The early works of Lenin concerning defense economics analyzed the Russo-Japanese War of 1904–5 and the 1905 revolution. He argued that "never before has the military organisation of a country had such a close bearing on its entire economic and cultural system" ([1905c] 1962, 52). The tsarist military had performed disastrously because of the failings of the corrupt autocracy, backwardness in class structure, and underdeveloped economy of Russia.[22] He believed, like Engels, that modern warfare required high-quality manpower but that the Russians had a parasitic military bureaucracy, incompetent commanders, uneducated officers, and ignorant peasant soldiers. His class analysis indicated that Japan had a progressive bourgeoisie whereas Russia had a reactionary one and therefore that Russian revolutionaries should view favorably the victory of the former over the latter ([1905c] 1962, 52; [1905d] 1962, 268).

In his comments on the linkage of economic and military power Lenin pointed out the backwardness of productive forces in Russia relative not only to Europe but also to Japan. Russia was unable to produce competitive modern weapons using its own resources and had an ineffectual logistics system. These were systemic problems that could not be remedied by purchases of technology abroad financed by loans from the European bourgeoisie.[23]

At this time Lenin offered only unsophisticated explanations of the economic causes of war. He seemed to believe that the wars of the tsarist state were inevitable results of "adventurism" and were "fought to further dynastic interests, to satisfy the appetite of a band of freebooters, or to attain the objects of the knights of capitalist profit" ([1905e] 1962, 485; [1905f] 1962, 565). His discussion of the economic consequences of the Russian defeat was more thorough. First, it had

21. See Marx, Engels, and Lenin 1982 for selections of Lenin's writings on the military and war, and Zinoviev 1931 for an interpretation of them.

22. His general conclusion was that "tsarism has proved to be a hindrance to the organisation of up-to-date efficient warfare, that very business to which tsarism dedicated itself so wholeheartedly, of which it was so proud, and for which it offered such colossal sacrifices" (Lenin [1905c] 1962, 51).

23. "Events have corroborated the opinion of those foreigners who laughed upon seeing hundreds of millions squandered on the purchase and building of splendid warships, and who declared that those expenditures were useless if no one knew how to manipulate such modern vessels, if there were no people with the necessary technical knowledge to utilise the latest achievements of military engineering" (Lenin [1905c] 1962, 51–52).

resulted in the massive loss of human life (potentially productive labor) and the squandering of the huge sums allocated to equip and support the army and navy units that fought in the Far East.[24] Second, it had undermined Russia's credit rating and thereby made it more difficult and costly to obtain necessary loans from European bankers ([1905b] 1962, 41; [1905d] 1962, 267, 272). Third, it had discredited the tsarist autocracy, raised the consciousness of the population concerning the deficiencies of capitalism, heightened class tension, and increased the probability of revolution ([1905a] 1962, 26, 28; [1905c] 1962, 48, 50, 53; [1905e] 1962, 483). Finally, it signified that "advancing, progressive Asia has dealt backward and reactionary Europe an irreparable blow" that would undermine the whole capitalist system and accelerate the "social revolution of the proletariat" ([1905c] 1962, 47–48).

In the subsequent years leading up to the world war Lenin's writings of relevance to defense economics concerned growing tensions between the major economic powers, conflicts between colonies and their metropolitan centers, militarism, and arms races. With respect to the first topic, his early analyses reflected developments in the theory of imperialism by others (see below) but tended to be narrow and empirical in nature. He did pay attention to the situation in the colonies of European nations and considered that the various strikes, uprisings by nationalist movements, and struggles between the big powers over territory were providing "inflammable material" that could be ignited into war by some spark ([1908] 1963, 191). He considered that the militarism and arms races in Europe at that time had an economic foundation: "Modern militarism is . . . the 'vital expression' of capitalism—as a military force used by the capitalist states in their external conflicts . . . and as a weapon in the hands of the ruling classes for suppressing every kind of movement, economic and political, of the proletariat" (192). He also believed that the related armaments buildups in Britain, Germany, and France were supported by the capitalist elite and the states that served them because of the high profits generated by military programs ([1913] 1982, 272–73). He claimed that the tensions and arms races would produce wars in the near future that could not be averted by diplomatic means since they were systemic in character. He argued against "patriotism" and "bourgeois chauvinism" and for antimilitarist tactics that would promote social revolution in the aftermath of war.

---

24. Lenin [1905a] 1962, 28; [1905b] 1962, 41; [1905c] 1962, 48–49). "Hundreds of millions of rubles were spent on hastily dispatching the Baltic fleet. . . . The great armada—as huge and unwieldy, as absurd, helpless, and monstrous as the whole Russian Empire—put to sea, expending a fortune in coal and maintenance, making itself the laughing-stock of Europe. . . . According to the most conservative estimates this armada cost nearly 300,000,000 rubles, besides 100,000,000 rubles on the expedition. Altogether 400,000,000 rubles were thrown away on this last war gamble of the tsarist autocracy" ([1905e] 1962, 482).

One major advance in Marxist theory in the prewar period that provided a foundation for explanations of militarism and wars was the elaboration of the theory of imperialism by Hilferding and Luxemburg. Hilferding presented his ideas in the book *Finance Capital* (1910). He argued that after the death of Marx capitalism had reached a new stage that was characterized domestically by the decline of competition and of the power of individual capitalists, concentration of industry into monopolies, domination by financial institutions such as banks, and the strengthening of the state. The modern capitalist government attempted to maintain high rates of monopoly profits by adopting protectionist trade policies (e.g., imposition of high tariffs on imports). But these efforts were insufficient due to internal contradictions of monopoly capitalism. Thus increasingly aggressive attempts were made to export capital, form international cartels, and divide up the less-developed world into colonies that would guarantee supplies of raw materials and markets for industrial goods. Hilferding argued that in the new era armed forces were needed to support imperialist policies in the face of competition by other nations: "finance capital demands unlimited power politics, and this would be the case even if military and naval expenditures did not directly assure the most powerful capitalist groups of important markets, which provide in most cases monopolistic profits" ([1910] 1981, 335). In such an environment of militarism and expansionism the chance of military conflicts between states increased. However, Hilferding believed, such wars were not inevitable because of resistance by the increasingly powerful proletariat and the disaffected middle strata of the capitalist class.[25]

Luxemburg's main research goal in her 1913 book *The Accumulation of Capital* was to explain the reasons for the need of the capitalist economy to expand through the exploitation of noncapitalist markets (e.g., the peasant economy). In initial phases of development capitalist nations exhausted the possibilities of financing accumulation through the extraction of surplus value from domestic markets. They then shifted their attention to underexploited external markets and entered the phase of imperialism, the economic roots of which "must be deduced from the laws of capital accumulation" (Luxemburg [1915] 1972, 61). She argued that militarism was characteristic of imperialism and that the tensions it generated probably would lead to war.[26]

25. He further argued (370) that the struggle against the ruling class would be facilitated by the creation of the strong state and the concentration of industry. The conquest of the former by revolutionary forces would mean that abrupt expropriation of productive forces would be unnecessary. Eventually "the dictatorship of the magnates of capital will finally be transformed into the dictatorship of the proletariat."

26. "Militarism fulfils a quite definite function in the history of capital, accompanying as it does every historical phase of accumulation . . . militarism is a weapon in the competitive struggle between capitalist countries for areas of non-capitalist civilisation"

One of her innovations was the description of the domestic economic roles of militarism: "In addition, militarism has yet another important function. From the purely economic point of view, it is a pre-eminent means for the realisation of surplus value; it is in itself a province of accumulation" (Luxemburg [1913] 1951, 454). She argued that the defense effort had four impacts on the capitalist economy. First, the indirect taxes collected to finance the defense budget transferred purchasing power of the working class to the state, reduced the consumption of the means of subsistence, and improved the efficiency of exploitation of the proletariat. This occurred because such taxation only reduced variable capital (v), not constant capital (c) or surplus value (s), and therefore it "decreases the cost of producing surplus value" ([1913] 1951, 463). Second, military taxation enhances accumulation by forcing the peasantry to participate more in the commodity economy through the sale of their agricultural goods and subsequent purchases by them of capitalist products (465–66). Third, state expenditures on weapons and equipment create new markets and opportunities for "creating and realising surplus value."[27] Finally, she foreshadowed future arguments by Marxists that the monopoly capitalist system employs arms spending as an instrument of economic control:

> In the form of government contracts for army supplies the scattered purchasing power of the consumers is concentrated in large quantities and, free of the vagaries and subjective fluctuations of personal consumption, it achieves an almost automatic regularity and rhythmic growth . . . production for militarism represents a province whose regular and progressive expansion seems primarily determined by capital itself. (466)

The outbreak of World War I in August 1914 focused the attention of Lenin and the other Bolsheviks on its causes, nature, and consequences. They argued that the war was an inevitable outgrowth of the mode of production characterized by finance capital and imperialism.[28] According to Lenin, the true goals of the bourgeoisie in this imperialist war were to obtain markets, loot countries, suppress revolution, and

---

([1913] 1951, 454). "The more capitalist countries participate in this hunting for accumulation areas, the rarer the non-capitalist places still open to the expansion of capital become and the tougher the competition; its raids turn into a chain of economic and political catastrophes: world crises, wars, revolution" ([1915] 1972, 60).

27. "Now we see how the taxes extorted from the workers can afford capital a new opportunity for accumulation when they are used for armament manufacture. . . . By lowering the normal standard of living for the working class, it ensures both that capital should be able to maintain a regular army, the organ of capitalist rule, and that it may tap an impressive field for further accumulation" (464).

28. The causes of World War I are discussed in Lenin [1914b] 1964, 27; [1915a] 1964, 159; [1915c] 1964, 301.

slaughter workers.[29] The war was intensifying tensions and contradictions in the capitalist nations and would provide new opportunities for revolution. But it also had created a crisis in the socialist movement and the collapse of the Second International because a number of important parties, especially the German one, had adopted policies of "petty-bourgeois opportunism" and "social-chauvinism" by supporting their nations' war efforts (Lenin [1914a] 1964, 16; [1915c] 1964, 306–7). He considered that the correct legal and underground tactics of revolutionary socialist parties were to combat both bourgeois chauvinism and pacifism, refuse to support any war credits, support colonial struggles for self-determination, fight for the defeat of one's own government, and attempt to convert the imperialist war into a civil war.[30] He argued that the latter actions were interrelated: "A revolution in wartime means civil war; the conversion of a war between governments into a civil war is, on the one hand, facilitated by military reverses ('defeats') of governments; on the other hand, one cannot actually strive for such a conversion without thereby facilitating defeat" ([1915b] 1964, 276).

The intellectual foundation for the Bolshevik analysis of the World War and for the unpatriotic concepts in its revolutionary program was provided by the theory of imperialism developed by Nikolai Bukharin and Lenin during the war. In his *Imperialism and World Economy* (1915) Bukharin accepted many of the basic ideas of Hilferding concerning imperialism (e.g., concentration of capital, sharp competition between national economic units) but presented new or contradictory arguments about economic aspects of the state, the armed forces, militarism, and war. He argued that in the monopoly capital mode of production the state acquires and plays a decisive role in the economy ([1915] 1976, 123–24). The state champions its national capitalist trusts in the struggle with competitors, and the outcome of negotiations between states over commercial treaties, loans, or control of territories is "reduced in the final analysis to the relations between their military forces":

> If state power is generally growing in significance, the growth of its military organisation, the army and the navy, is particularly striking. The struggle between state capitalist trusts is decided in the first place by the relation between their military forces, for the

29. Lenin identified the objectives of the war as follows: "A struggle for markets and for freedom to loot foreign countries, a striving to suppress the revolutionary movement of the proletariat and democracy in the individual countries, a desire to deceive, disunite, and slaughter the proletarians of all countries by setting the wage slaves of one nation against those of another so as to benefit the bourgeoisie—these are the only real content and significance of the war" ([1914a] 1964, 15). See also the related statements in Lenin [1914b] 1964, 27; [1915c] 1964, 301–4.

30. Lenin [1914a] 1964, 18; [1914b] 1964, 31, 33, 34; [1915a] 1964, 162–63; [915c] 1964, 313–17.

military power of the country is the last resort of the struggling "national" groups of capitalists. The immensely growing state budget devotes an ever larger share to "defense purposes," as militarisation is euphemistically termed. (124–25)

National defense industries were protected by the state from foreign competition and expanded their production, because "armaments are an indispensable attribute of state power" (127). The state financed the operations of the economically vital military-industrial establishment through taxation that imposed most of its costs on the working class and elements of the bourgeoisie.

In his discussion of arms races Bukharin observed that within any country "the rule of finance capital implies both imperialism and militarism" but that "every expansion of the military power of one state stimulates all the others" ([1915] 1976, 126–27). In the case of the feverish arms buildups that preceded the First World War he thought it was necessary to identify the deeper causal factors. He was critical of antimilitarists who argued that the armaments industries (e.g., Krupp in Germany) and mobilizations were responsible for militarism and wars:

not the existence of arms is the prime cause and the moving force in wars (although wars are obviously impossible without arms) but, on the contrary, the inevitableness of economic conflicts conditions the existence of arms. This is why in our times, when economic conflicts have reached an unusual degree of intensity, we are witnessing a mad orgy of armaments. (127)

He considered that it was absurd to assume that "peaceful rivalry" and disarmament were possible in the era of finance capital.

In contrast to Hilferding, Bukharin believed (with the benefit of hindsight) that "every capitalist expansion leads sooner or later to a bloody climax" and that in the period of imperialism "a series of wars is unavoidable" ([1915] 1976, 139, 142). He predicted that after the world war was over there would be a further concentration of capital and a reemergence of irreconcilable conflicts that would be solved by warfare on a more massive scale: "even were all of Europe to unite, it would not yet signify 'disarmament.' It would signify an unheard of rise of militarism because the problem to be solved would be a colossal struggle between Europe on the one hand, America and Asia on the other" (139–40).

Bukharin examined the economic consequences of wars in his chapter "War and Economic Evolution." One obvious result was "the destruction of the material means of production and of the living labour power." He expected that World War I would produce several important changes in the structure of state capitalist economies: further centralization of capital, greater state control, redistribution of productive

forces from civilian to defense industry, promotion of economic autarky, and strengthening of the position of finance capital (e.g., banking
trusts). Estimates of the cost of the world war were reviewed, and the
future implications for fiscal policy (e.g., financing large national debts,
the need for high tax rates) and for the world economic power balance
were discussed.[31]

Lenin wrote the introduction to Bukharin's 1915 book and soon made
his own contribution with *Imperialism, the Highest Stage of Capitalism*
(1917). He accepted Bukharin's main theses and attempted to support
them through analysis of historical trends and the institutional features
of contemporary capitalist economies.[32] He criticized Hilferding for
paying insufficient attention to "the tendency to stagnation and decay"
and the intensification of the contradictions of monopoly capital and for
neglecting the systemic nature of wars (Lenin [1917a] 1977, 240, 259).
He argued that "imperialism is, in general, a striving towards violence
and reaction" and that "imperialist wars are absolutely inevitable under
such an economic system" (172, 234).

Another book written by Lenin in 1917, *The State and Revolution,* is
of interest not only because it contains some concepts of relevance to
Marxist defense economics but also because it influenced the policies of
the Bolshevik government after the revolution. Many of Lenin's ideas in
the book about the history and functions of the state were similar to
those of predecessors (such as Marx, Engels, Hilferding, and Bukharin)
and are therefore not reviewed here. Instead attention is focused on the
relationship between the state and the military and on the concept of the
dictatorship of the proletariat.

Lenin believed that in the abstract the state was an instrument of force
used by the ruling class for the exploitation of oppressed classes. Its
power "consists of special bodies of armed men having prisons, etc., at
their command" ([1917b] 1977, 268). In the finance-capital period the
state had become more important, and the bureaucracy and the standing
army were its most characteristic institutions (282). The world war had

31. Bukharin pointed out that "the war has placed the United States in an unprecedented, exclusive position . . . the continuation of the war, the payments for war orders
and loans, later the immense demand for capital in the post-war period . . . will increase
the financial importance of the United States still more. It will hasten the accumulation of
American capital; it will widen its sphere of influence in the rest of America, and will
rapidly make the United States a prime factor in the world struggle for markets" ([1915]
1976, 145–46).

32. In his explanation of the imperialist urge Lenin placed greater emphasis than his
predecessors on the desire to obtain guaranteed sources of inputs: "The more capitalism
is developed, the more strongly the shortage of raw materials is felt, the more intense the
competition and the hunt for sources of raw materials throughout the whole world, the
more desperate the struggle for the acquisition of colonies" ([1917a] 1977, 228). See also
his related statement on p. 258.

accelerated the transformation of the mode of production into one of state-monopoly capitalism and had made the bourgeois state more of an obstacle to revolutionary forces.[33] For this reason Lenin observed that whereas "all previous revolutions [had] perfected the state machine," in a proletarian revolution "it must be broken, smashed": "The words, 'to smash the bureaucratic-military machine' briefly express the principal lesson of Marxism regarding the tasks of the proletariat during a revolution in relation to the state" (288).

Lenin did not, however, believe that the state would wither away immediately after the revolution; there would be resistance by the deposed class within the country and the forces of the bourgeoisie in other capitalist nations. Instead the revolutionary forces needed to establish a "dictatorship of the proletariat" for the transitional period of conflict.[34] The proletarian state would rely for its coercive power on a "self-acting armed organisation of the population" that was made up of armed workers, most of whom had received military training because of universal conscription ([1917b] 1977, 269).[35] The revolutionary army would include elements of the old military organization that had sided with the working class, such as the sailors on the battleship *Potemkin* in 1905 and Bolshevik party members who had served in the Imperial Russian Army during World War I.

The ideas of Lenin and policies of the Bolshevik party acquired greater significance during 1917 because of spontaneous mass uprisings of the population in Russia in February that resulted in the abdication of the tsar, the formation of a provisional government, and the emergence of Soviets in most major cities. The new government rapidly promulgated a set of liberal democratic reforms, but in the end they proved to be ineffectual because of the growing disruption in the economy and political unrest.[36] Its popularity was further eroded by the decision, supported by all major parties except the Bolsheviks, to remain in the

33. "Imperialism . . . has clearly shown an extraordinary strengthening of the 'state machine' and an unprecedented growth in its bureaucratic and military apparatus in connection with the intensification of repressive measures against the proletariat both in the monarchical and in the freest, republican countries" (284).

34. "The theory of class struggle, applied by Marx to the question of the state and the socialist revolution, leads as a matter of course to the recognition of the political rule of the proletariat, of its dictatorship, i.e., of undivided power directly backed by the armed force of the people. The overthrow of the bourgeoisie can be achieved only by the proletariat becoming the ruling class, capable of crushing the inevitable and desperate resistance of the bourgeoisie, and of organising all the working and exploited people for the new economic system" ([1917b] 1977, 279).

35. In an earlier article he wrote: "The revolutionary army is needed because great historical issues can be resolved only by force, and, in modern struggle, the organisation of force means military organisation" ([1905f] 1962, 563).

36. Among these measures were amnesty of political prisoners, replacement of police with a people's militia, abolition of discrimination against national minorities, introduction of an eight-hour work day, and the promise of democratic elections.

world war despite the growing disintegration of the Imperial Army and its continuing defeats in combat with the Germans.[37]

In the first months after the revolution the Bolshevik party had a limited influence on the activities of the Soviets. But in April 1917 Lenin returned to Russia from exile, assumed direct leadership of the Bolshevik party, and unveiled an attractive revolutionary program which rejected most government policies and offered simple solutions to complex problems (e.g., immediate withdrawal from the war, redistribution of land to the peasants). Support for the Bolsheviks grew in key urban areas as military, economic, and political conditions worsened. The Bolshevik party developed plans for an insurrection and formed units of Red Guards and a Military Revolutionary Committee with Trotsky as chairman. Their coup was successfully carried out on 7 November 1917, enabling the Bolsheviks to gain control of the weak Russian state.

Soviet Defense Economics, 1917–27

After the revolution the Bolshevik government was confronted by the problems of retaining political power and transforming the backward Russian capitalist economy into a socialist one in the face of fierce domestic and external opposition. In dealing with these challenges in the years 1917–27 the military and supporting defense sector institutions of the Bolshevik state played important roles, as did analyses and policies in the defense economics realm. This section surveys Soviet defense economics during this decade, which can be subdivided into three distinct periods according to economic and military developments: revolution and withdrawal from the world war (1917–18); civil war and war communism (1918–21); and the New Economic Policy and military reform (1921–27). The following review of Soviet literature includes not only the contributions of Bolshevik figures, such as Lenin and Bukharin, but also studies of defense economics by military specialists in the defense establishment and by non-Marxist scholars.[38]

Revolution and the Creation of the Red Army, November 1917–May 1918

In the initial seven months after the revolution the Bolshevik regime encountered severe problems in the political and economic realms.[39]

---

37. Background information about the situation in Russia at this time can be found in Gatrell 1986, Nove 1989, and Conte 1990.

38. There had been a considerable amount of non-Marxist research on defense economics in Russia prior to 1917. According to Svyatlovskii (1926) these early works included the following titles (translated): M. Gazenkampf, *The War Economy in Our and Foreign Armies in Peacetime and War* (1880); A. Gulevich, *War and the National Economy* (1898); and S. Prokopovich, *War and the National Economy* (1917).

39. A review of economic and political developments of relevance in this period can be

210 Christopher Mark Davis

There were serious external threats to the new regime as well, primarily from Germany.[40] Given the unstable environment, no significant theoretical studies of defense economics were produced in this period. However, substantial efforts were made to solve vital practical problems, such as the withdrawal from the world war and the Treaty of Brest Litovsk, the demobilization of the Imperial Army and conversion of defense industry, and the organization of the Red Army.

The Bolsheviks were strongly opposed to the world war as a result of the Marxist theoretical analysis of imperialism discussed above. They also recognized that Russia did not have the economic power or the popular political will to sustain the war effort against Germany. One of the first actions of the Bolshevik state, on 8 November, was to issue its "Decree on Peace."[41] A German-Soviet armistice was signed in December, and peace negotiations commenced with Trotsky, commissar for foreign affairs, representing Soviet Russia. The Germans recognized the manifold weaknesses of the Bolshevik state and made exorbitant demands for territory and for the disarmament of the Russian military. This provoked a heated debate in the Bolshevik party. Lenin argued for peace at any price in order to ensure the survival of the Bolshevik state and enable it to have a breathing space in order to build up its economic and military strength. The majority of his colleagues, including Trotsky, favored rejection of the treaty in the mistaken expectation that the Germans would not resume their offensive and that revolutions soon would break out in other European countries. Trotsky therefore returned to the negotiations, declined the German terms, and announced the policy of "neither peace nor war," which had some economic content:

> In expectation of the approaching hour when the working classes of all countries seize power . . . we are withdrawing our army and our people from the war. Our soldier, the tiller of the land, should go back to his land to till it this spring, the land which the revolution has taken from the landlord and given to the peasant. Our soldier,

---

found in Davis 1990b. More detailed studies are presented in Davies 1958, Zaleski 1971, and Nove 1989.

40. At the time of the revolution Russia was still at war with the Central Powers, and the demoralized Imperial Army was collapsing. The danger of defeat was diminished temporarily by the new peace policy (see below) and the German-Soviet armistice. But this provoked the Allied Supreme War Council to take a decision to support anti-Bolshevik groups in favor of continuing the war against Germany (Erickson 1962; *Sovetskie* 1978; Benvenuti 1988).

41. The "Decree on Peace" proposed that all participants agree to an immediate three-month armistice and to settle within this period peace terms on the basis of no territorial gains or reparations and self-determination of nations. One hope behind this proposal was that the peace would provide an opportunity for workers and soldiers in the other European states to carry out their own revolutions (Hagen 1990).

the worker, should return to the factory bench to turn out not tools of destruction but tools of construction and to build, together with the tiller of the land, a new socialist economy.[42]

This rhetoric did not impress the German army, which resumed offensive operations in February 1918, decimated Soviet opposition, occupied large areas in the Ukraine and the Baltic region, and threatened to capture Petrograd. Eventually the Soviet government was issued an ultimatum to accept a revised treaty with less favorable terms within two days. After further heated debate the humiliating Treaty of Brest Litovsk was accepted. In subsequent works Lenin stressed the importance of defense-economic considerations in determining his peace policy.[43]

The initial attitude of the Bolshevik regime toward the tsarist military-industrial complex was hostile, and their policies reflected Lenin's injunction to smash the state machine after the revolution. The Bolsheviks considered the large army to be their greatest domestic threat and recognized that military service was unpopular and that the workers and peasants serving in the armed forces could be employed more productively to rebuild the economy. Taking these factors into consideration, the government ordered a rapid demobilization of the army that commenced in November and was completed by March 1918.[44] Problems quickly arose as soldiers left their units in mass with their arms and without waiting for orders. The rail system was overwhelmed by the demands of the demobilized soldiers, and the economy could not absorb the sudden influx of labor. Naturally the sudden dispersal of troops severely weakened the capability of Russia to resist German attacks. In early 1918 the Bolshevik military leadership unsuccessfully attempted to slow the demobilization.

As for the Russian defense industry, the government launched a conversion program that "proposed the cutting back of the preparation

42. The excerpts from Trotsky's speech are published in Deutscher 1965, 380.

43. Lenin's justifications for the peace treaty are summarized in the following quotations: "All our efforts must be exerted to the very utmost to make use of the respite given us by the combination of circumstances so that we can heal the very severe wound inflicted by the war upon the entire social organism of Russia and bring about an economic revival, without which a real increase in our country's defence potential is inconceivable" ([1918a] 1977, 398–99); "until the world socialist revolution breaks out, until it embraces several countries and is strong enough to overcome international imperialism, it is the direct duty of the socialists who have conquered in one country (especially a backward one) not to accept battle" ([1918b] 1977, 430).

44. The dismantling of the Imperial Army was supervised by the Commission for the Demobilization of the Army and the Navy. All aspects of the demobilization process, including economic ones, were discussed at the All-Army Congress on Demobilization of the Army which was held in Petrograd from 28 December 1917 to 16 January 1918 (*Sovetskie* 1978, 17; Hagen 1990, 17–20).

of military items, the shift to the production of items of a peaceful nature."[45] The changes in government policies and the worsening economic environment resulted in a significant deterioration in the situation of defense-industry enterprises.[46] Their output fell substantially, and some factories went bankrupt.

The collapse of the Imperial Army in a situation of growing external and internal military threats focused the attention of the Bolshevik leadership on the issue of the organization of the revolutionary army of the dictatorship of the proletariat. Many Bolsheviks were strongly opposed on principle to a standing army and thought that a workers' militia, such as the Red Guards, would be most appropriate and consistent with the teachings of Marx and Engels. Others, citing Engels ([1851] 1978, 556) to the effect that future civil wars would be fought by modern armies with contemporary means, argued for a volunteer regular army. In the end the government authorized the creation of the Worker-Peasant Red Army in January 1918 (*Sovetskie* 1978; Benvenuti 1988; Hagen 1990). The Red Army was barely functioning by the time the Germans resumed their offensive, and it performed disastrously in initial combat operations.

After the regime obtained its breathing space by signing the Treaty of Brest Litovsk, greater attention was devoted to building up the military capabilities of the Soviet state, a task that involved considerable defense-economic work by the People's Commissariat for Military Affairs (Narkomvoen) under the leadership of Trotsky. The high command was reorganized, and the size of the Red Army grew to 300,000 men (Erickson 1962). Its logistics support was improved and placed under the control of Narkomvoen, which created an advisory Military-Economic Council (*Sovetskie* 1978, 25). Defense-industry enterprises were grouped together and placed under the management of the Department of the Metal-Working Industry of the Supreme Council of the

45. Rozenfel'd and Klimenko 1961, 161–62. For a detailed discussion see Kovalenko 1970, ch. 2. The conversion process continued into the spring of 1918: "Following the conclusion by Soviet Russia of the Brest peace and the transition to peaceful construction in the country a sharp cut-back of military production commenced. Plants, factories, workshops and construction enterprises were shifted over to the production of civilian goods, decisions were taken to dissolve railroad troops and automotive detachments" (*Razvitie* 1989, 15).

46. Rozenfel'd and Klimenko describe the situation as follows: "There was a large amount of unfinished production that had been ordered for military-naval purposes, but at that time there were in reality no customers. Nor were there customers for civilian items. This resulted in extreme indeterminacy in the work of factories: the demobilization of machine-building and metal-working enterprises was decreed, but in fact did not take place" (1961, 162). Within factories the introduction of workers' control and undermining of management weakened labor discipline, disorganized production, and lowered labor productivity. Enterprises experienced serious difficulties in obtaining inputs of fuels, metals, and spare parts (*Sovetskie* 1978, 25).

National Economy (VSNKh) (Rozenfel'd and Klimenko 1961; Kova-lenko 1970). However, in this period the priority of the defense sector remained relatively low, which meant that insufficient resources were allocated to its institutions to enable them to improve their performance significantly.

Civil War and War Communism, May 1918–March 1921

By May 1918 a civil war had broken out in Russia. It grew in intensity and on several occasions threatened the survival of the Soviet state. The most severe internal dangers to the Soviet regimes came from the attacks of various White armies.[47] The military situation of the Bolsheviks was made worse by armed interventions at various times of most other major foreign powers: Germany, Turkey, Japan, Britain, France, Canada, the United States, and Poland. These occupation forces imposed trade embargoes and supported the various anti-Bolshevik movements.

The continuing precariousness of the Soviet regime, the intensity of the civil war, and the large-scale military interventions by leading capitalist powers resulted in a militarization of Bolshevik ideology. It justified dictatorship by a party elite, tight censorship, the policies of "Red Terror," and the maintenance of a moneyless economy based on barter and rationing. The Bolsheviks developed an undifferentiated hostility toward Western nations and believed that the growing crisis of capitalism would spawn workers' revolutions in the near future.

During the civil war the Bolsheviks acknowledged the challenges presented to the proletarian state by a number of defense economic problems and devoted considerable effort to their solution: the choice of the optimal economic system and macroeconomic policies to mobilize and utilize the scarce resources of a backward economy in order to best serve the military; the identification and resolution of obstacles to the performance of defense-sector institutions at the microeconomic level; the judgment of whether war communism provided a suitable model for the socialist economy in peacetime; and the assessment of the consequences of war for the economy.

There was a significant increase in theoretical and practical work in the defense-economic area. In the first instance this was carried out by higher Bolshevik party bodies and was reflected in official party debates and documents (Berman 1927). Party theoreticians such as Bukharin and Preobrazhenskii made more scholarly contributions. Within the

47. The main assaults by White Armies occurred in the summer of 1918 (General Deniken, the Czechoslovakian Legion, the Don Cossacks, and General Miller), spring–summer 1919 (Admiral Kolchak, General Deniken, General Wrangel), and summer 1920 (General Wrangel). For discussions of the civil war see Erickson 1962, *Sovetskie* 1978, and Benvenuti 1988.

214 Christopher Mark Davis

state apparatus investigations of defense economic issues were made by permanent organizations such as the Council of Worker and Peasant Defense and VSNKh and by temporary ones such as the Commission on Demobilization. Additional detailed studies relating to procurement, mobilization, and logistics were prepared by departments of Narkomvoen and the central military staffs.

The thinking of the Bolshevik leadership about the causes, nature, and consequences of the civil war was influenced by prerevolution Marxist analysis. They therefore recognized the fundamental importance of the link between economic and military power. In the case of Soviet Russia the economy was technologically backward relative to the West and in chaos due to enemy occupation of traditional sources of fuels and raw materials, the breakdown in price and trade systems, shortages of all goods, declines in industrial production and marketed agricultural output, and a worsening food situation in cities (Davies 1958; Nove 1989). In order to defend the state from internal and external enemies, with severely limited resources, it was necessary to gain firm central control of economic processes by introducing the policies of war communism, which included giving defense institutions highest priority in resource allocation.[48]

In the war-communism period extraordinary emphasis was placed on the development of defense-sector institutions and the rapid solution, irrespective of cost, of any problems that adversely affected their performance. This effort was directed by the Council of Worker and Peasant Defense (later called the Council of Labor and Defense), headed by Lenin, which was established in November 1918 to command the whole war effort and to control interactions between defense and civilian sectors of the economy. It was assisted by military departments of VSNKh and Narkomvoen, the Revolutionary Military Council of the Republic (Revvoensovet) headed by Trotsky, and the Main Staff of the Red Army.

Party thinking about the nature and size of the armed forces changed radically upon the outbreak of the civil war. The Red Army was transformed from a small volunteer force dominated by party activists and workers into a mass army based on universal conscription (mainly of peasants) with many commanders who were ex–Imperial Army officers. From May 1918 to December 1920 the Red Army grew in size from 300,000 to 5.3 million. Over time its military leadership, organiza-

48. The features of the war-communism economic system during 1918–20 were central state control, nationalization and militarization of enterprises, food dictatorship and forcible requisitioning of grain from the peasantry, central, mandatory direction of labor, imposition of firm labor discipline through material rewards, terror, and ideology, and central rationing of consumer and producer goods (Zaleski 1971, ch. 2; Malle 1985; Nove 1989).

tion, strategy, and tactics improved. In part this was due to Trotsky's policy of minimizing the influence on military decision-making of political commissars and Bolshevik party cells (Erickson 1962; Benvenuti 1988; Hagen 1990).

Although the Red Army proved to be an effective, if not always efficient, instrument of the state, there were repeated criticisms of it by left-wing Bolsheviks. At the Eighth Congress of the Bolshevik Party in March 1919 a Military Opposition emerged that complained about the Red Army's use of "military specialists," privileges for commanders, neglect of party members and commissars, diluted proletarian character, militarist spirit and organization as a standing army. These critics argued for rapid demobilization after victory in the civil war, the transformation of the army into a socialist militia, and reallocation of defense-sector resources to benefit the deprived civilian economy (Berman 1927; Benvenuti 1988, ch. 5). Similar criticisms and demands were made at the Ninth Congress in the spring of 1920 and the Ninth Conference in September 1920.

Logistics was another important topic for defense economists. The challenges confronting the military supply network grew considerably as a result of the expansion of the Red Army, the increased intensity of combat, and geographical extension of supply lines in support of offensives. During the civil war the supply network expanded, its management structure was rationalized, and its performance improved.[49]

Political leaders and defense managers paid urgent attention to the Soviet defense industry. At the start of civil war its enterprises had limited capacity and were operating in difficult conditions due to the earlier demobilization and conversion programs. Over the next several years it was reorganized, expanded, and militarized.[50] Defense enterprises were awarded "shock" status, which guaranteed them special access to supplies, exemption of workers from the draft, and above-average rations for employees. During the civil war the defense industry operated as a high-priority sector in a shortage economy.[51] Its output

49. The organizations with initial responsibility for supply tasks were the All-Russian Main Staff (established May 1918), the Narkomvoen Main Administration for Supply of the Red Army (created June 1918), and the VSNKh Department of Military Purchases (created October 1918). In November 1918 the Council of People's Commissars (Sovnarkom) created the Extraordinary Commission for the Production of Items of Military Equipment, which "coordinated the work of all enterprises engaged in military production and was responsible for the accounting, distribution, and control of output and the expenditure of material resources" (*Razvitie* 1989, 28). The Council of Labor and Defense had overall responsibility for military supply.

50. Discussions of the Soviet defense industry during the civil war can be found in Rozenfel'd and Klimenko 1961, ch. 13; Kovalenko 1970, chs. 3–4; and Malle 1985, ch. 9.

51. The functioning of the high-priority defense sector in the Soviet shortage economy is analyzed in Davis 1990a.

rose, and the technological sophistication of some of its products improved despite the difficult circumstances.

Theoretical justification for the organization and policies of war communism in general and of defense-economic policies in particular was provided in two important books published in this period: Bukharin and Preobrazhenskii's *The ABC of Communism* (1919) and Bukharin's *Economics of the Transformation Period* (1920).[52] The authors argued that an imperialist war accentuates the anarchy of production and class conflict in a capitalist country to such an extent that a proletarian revolution is inevitable. This in turn results in a civil war, establishment of a dictatorship of the proletariat, and a deterioration in production relations in the economy. There are "costs of the revolution" due to "a diminution of the process of reproduction and a decline of productive powers."[53] But this process of decline is reversed after the victory of the revolutionary forces, when a socialist economy is established. In the transition from the old to the new system the state plays a vital role, and its "force is the midwife." Bukharin argued that "the greater this 'extra-economic' power, which in reality represents an 'economic exponent,' the smaller are the 'expenses' of the transition period (of course, all conditions otherwise being equal), the shorter is this transition period, the faster appears a social equilibrium on a new base, and the quicker the curve of productive powers begins to rise" ([1920] 1971, 150–51). However, after the world victory of the proletariat is achieved, the use of coercive measures will cease, and the state will wither away (172).

In the transformation period the primary task of the state is to win the civil war with the help of a proletarian army with strict self-imposed discipline.[54] The economy needs to be reoriented to support the armed forces and to adopt a "model of proletarian-militarized production" (Bukharin [1920] 1971, 127). Although this method of war organization is effective in accomplishing military objectives, it is wasteful in eco-

52. These were outgrowths from Bukharin's prerevolution writings (reviewed above), so there was considerable continuity in the analysis of the interconnections between finance capital, militarism, imperialism, and the world war. Their novel arguments concerned the inevitability of revolution and civil war, the nature of the socialist state (dictatorship of the proletariat), and the organization of the economy for war in the transition period.

53. According to Bukharin ([1920] 1971, 107–9) the costs of this revolution fall into four categories: the "physical annihilation of elements of production"; "disqualification of elements of production" (i.e., depreciation of machinery, exhaustion of workers, exclusion of bourgeois elements); "decay of the connection between elements of production" (i.e., breakdown of authority and discipline); and "the regrouping of productive powers in terms of unproductive consumption" (i.e., diversion of resources to support the socialist army in the civil war).

54. See Bukharin and Preobrazhenskii [1919] 1970 on "the programme of the communists in relation to army organization." They argue that even under socialism the military is unproductive in economic terms because it is "maintained at the cost of the goods produced by the workers and peasants" (394).

nomic terms: "the process of reproduction assumes with the war a 'deformed,' regressive, negative character, namely: with every successive production cycle the real base of reproduction grows narrower . . . this process can be designated as expanded negative reproduction" (44–46).[55] The civil war would exhaust the economy but makes possible a reorganization of productive relations that would facilitate a technological revolution and the movement to a communist society of material abundance. After this occurs, "the armies and the fleets will die out" (172).

Bukharin's theorizing about the economic consequences of war was supplemented by empirical studies of the costs of both World War I and the civil war in Russia.[56] It was recognized that during the civil war the conflict and the war effort had caused destruction of productive assets, diversion of resources to unproductive purposes, a severe drop in the output of civilian industry and agriculture, disastrously low living standards, famine, and epidemics of infectious disease. Despite these problems, the Bolshevik leadership remained committed to the war-communist economic model even after victory in the civil war had been achieved, and expressed its intention to extend to the civilian sector organizational forms and techniques that had worked effectively in the military and defense industry.[57] However, by early 1921 the exhausted population had reached the limit of its tolerance of the sacrifices required by war communism. Unrest grew among the peasants in the countryside, and workers in urban areas engaged in strikes and riots. The final blow to the militarized economic system was the revolt by the sailors at Kronstadt in February 1921.

New Economic Policy and Demilitarization, March 1921–December 1927

At the Tenth Party Congress in March 1921 the Bolshevik party responded to the growing crisis in the country by adopting the reform strategy of the New Economic Policy.[58] These market-oriented arrange-

55. Bukharin ([1920] 1971, 45–46). This quotation refers to the war effort in the capitalist system. But he later makes clear that the concept of "expanded negative reproduction" applies as well to the socialist economy in the transition period (109).

56. For example, see the sections "The Disastrous Legacy of the Imperialist War" and "The Forms of the Civil War and Its Cost" in Bukharin and Preobrazhensky 1919.

57. Malle 1985 and Benvenuti 1988 provide thorough analyses of debates over the appropriateness of militarizing labor and civilian sectors of the economy after the civil war.

58. The New Economic Policy is outlined in Lenin 1921. Its main elements were replacement of the requisitioning of food by the tax in kind on the peasants, privatization of small-scale industry and retail trade, revival of markets and the price system, and reintroduction of a stable currency. But the government maintained control of key industries and economic policy levers. See discussions in Davies 1958, Zaleski 1971, and Nove 1989.

ments and policies were maintained throughout 1921–27 and were successful in reviving the economy and returning industrial output to prewar levels. This economic reform was not accompanied by liberalization in the political sphere. In fact, as Stalin consolidated his control of the party apparatus during the 1920s, democracy was reduced even within the Bolshevik party. In ideology there was a retreat from the extreme positions characteristic of the war-communism period, best expressed in *The ABC of Communism,* but the Bolsheviks retained the core of Marxist-Leninist class analysis (hostility towards capitalism, belief in the dictatorship of the proletariat), objectives (world revolution), and expectations. They recognized that after the successful conclusion of the civil war the imperialist nations were unlikely to intervene in the near future. Instead the immediate threat to the state was internal: a mass revolt by workers and peasants disgruntled by the political repression and low standard of living.

In light of these shifts in economic policy, ideology, and actual threats the Bolsheviks decided to reorient their national security strategy in accordance with the new thinking, which involved placing greater stress on threat reduction measures (diplomacy, propaganda, espionage, arms control) and less on military power. The economic relationship between the defense sector and civilian branches was redefined. The high priority and resource allocations of the former were reduced to lessen the burden on the latter. New defense doctrines and policies were adopted with the objectives of improving the quality of the military to enable it to fight effectively against sophisticated Western armies in the future.[59]

The reforms affected all defense institutions. In the central defense bureaucracy the main developments were the removal of Trotsky as commissar for military affairs and chairman of the Revvoensovet in January 1925 and his replacement by Frunze, the appointment of Tukhachevskii as chief of the Red Army Staff, and the reform of the high command in July 1926.[60] The Red Army was cut in size from 5.3 million in December 1920 to 562,000 in December 1924. By 1925 it was a mixed regular-territorial army, with forty-six of its seventy-seven infantry divisions functioning as low-cost territorial units (*Sovetskie* 1978). The scale of the military supply network was reduced, it lost many of its powers over the civilian economy, and it was reorganized extensively (*Razvitie* 1989). As a result of the shifts in macroeconomic priorities and policies the defense industry's military output was drastically cut and its en-

59. Developments in and debates over Soviet military doctrine are examined in Svechin 1926, Berkhin 1958, Erickson 1962, Latnikov 1976, Chechinski 1985, Benvenuti 1988, and Lobov 1989.
60. The military reforms of the 1920s are discussed in Berkhin 1958, Erickson 1962, Vashchenko and Runov 1989, and Lipitskii 1990.

terprises were converted to produce civilian goods (Rozenfel'd and Klimenko 1961). Attempts were made to modernize the core defense industries, using German and other Western technology, so that they would be able to produce sophisticated weapons in the future.[61]

Soviet defense economics flourished in this period in response to the demands by the party and the military for a rethinking of traditional policies, the establishment of related teaching programs and research institutions, and the opening up of Soviet intellectual life to outside influences (Chechinski 1985). Defense-economic issues were discussed at all the major Bolshevik party congresses and conferences in this period (Berman 1927). Interesting literature was produced by party theoreticians, military officers on staffs, defense industrialists, and academics. A significant number of books by Soviet authors on defense-economic issues were published, including N. A. Danilov's *Influence of the Great World War on the Economy of Russia* (1922), P. P. Lebedev's *State Defense* (1925), P. Karatygin's *Main Foundations for the Mobilization of Industry for the Needs of War* (1925), A. Svechin's *Strategy* (1926), and E. Svyatlovskii's *Economics of War* (1926). Articles on defense economics appeared occasionally in the major economic journals and often in the ten military ones. For example, the journal *Voina i Revolyutsiya* had a regular section entitled "Military Economics and Mobilization" that contained two or three articles per issue, and *Voina i Tekhnika* had sections for "Defense Industry" and "The Military Economy."[62] Advances in this field were assisted by the publication of Russian versions of major Western works such as: N. Angell's *The Versailles Peace and Economic Chaos in Europe* (1921), J. M. Keynes's *Economic Consequences of the Versailles Peace Treaty* (1922), N. I. Deitsch's *Foundations of the Military Economy* (1922), V. Neubold's *How Europe Armed for War (1871–1914)* (1923), and A. Pigou's *Political Economy and War* (1924).[63]

A separate article would be required to review in detail Soviet defense economics in the 1920s because of its large volume, the diversity of issues covered, and the intensity of debate. In any event other Soviet and Western scholars, most notably Latnikov (1976) and Chechinski (1985), already have presented useful preliminary surveys. Taking these

61. As a result of the secret clauses of the Treaty of Rapallo the Soviet Union received substantial German help with the modernization of its defense industry. See Sutton 1968, ch. 15, "German-Russian Military Cooperation and Technology"; Erickson 1962, ch. 6.

62. Among the defense-economics articles in *Voina i Revolyutsiya* in 1925 were "Management of Railroads and Military Authorities," "The War of Materials," "Unity of Perspective and Plannability," "Fuel and War," and "Foundations of the Mobilization of Industry in the USSR."

63. These translations of foreign works on defense economics were selected from the list of references in Svyatlovskii 1926, which also provides information about more comprehensive Soviet bibliographies on this topic.

factors into account, discussion here is restricted to some general, concluding comments on its main features and relationship with previous Marxist and Soviet writings.

During the 1920s the ideological foundation of Soviet defense economics changed in accordance with the shifts in the general line, and works varied in the attention they paid to ideology. There was less discussion of class tensions within the USSR, the dictatorship of the proletariat, the need for class purity in the armed forces, and the role of the state and its military in combating domestic enemies. The Bolsheviks remained highly critical of monopoly capital, militarism, and imperialism as the causes of war and were convinced that the imperialist nations eventually would attack the USSR. But they accepted that the collapse of capitalism, additional workers' revolutions, or a major war were unlikely in the near future. The differing treatment of ideology can be seen by comparing Lebedev (1925), who places great emphasis on Marxist-Leninist analysis, with Svyatlovskii (1926), who devotes minimal attention to such issues. Many of the articles on defense economics in the military journals ignored ideology.

Major studies were made of the relationship between economic and military power at the macro and micro levels. This was the primary topic of Svyatlovskii (1926), who presented detailed analyses of defense-economy interconnections in sections of his book headed "Military Power and the State Economy" and "World Economic Factors of Military Power." Lebedev (1925) and Svechin (1926) also examined these issues. In connection with this there was considerable debate over the form of economic organization best suited to supporting the defense effort and the appropriate economic strategy to ensure a strong defense sector in the future. Some analysts were critical of the cutbacks in the armed forces and defense industry and wanted more resources devoted to defense in the current period, whereas others argued that it was necessary to divert scarce resources to civilian industry to enable it to expand and modernize and thus be able to produce better weapons at a later date (Chechinski 1985).

There was adequate coverage of defense expenditure topics. For example, Svyatlovskii (1926) offered chapters entitled "The Military Budget and Its Place in the General Budget" and "The Covering of Military Expenditures (the Financing of War)," and Lebedev (1925) had a section on finance. There was discussion in professional and popular articles of the need to reduce the defense burden on the Soviet economy and of economic considerations in selecting the appropriate organization for the armed forces, with many arguing for the development of territorial units as a low-cost alternative to regular ones.

Numerous articles were written by military specialists on economic aspects of specific defense-sector institutions. Some were devoted to the work of central defense planning and management organs in the civil war and peacetime.[64] Others studied economic aspects of the armed forces, such as economizing on resource utilization and scientific organization of labor. Military logistics issues were examined in depth in the journals *Voina i Tekhnika* and *Tekhnika i Snabzhenie Krasnoi Armii* and in various monographs. Defense-industry organization, performance, and mobilization were examined in journal articles and in books such as Lebedev's (1925), Svechin's (1926) and Svyatlovskii's (1926). Unlike in the period of war communism, when the USSR was subjected to a blockade, the defense-economics literature of the 1920s contained studies about arms sales and the transfer of military-related technology from the West to Soviet defense institutions (see, e.g., the section in Svyatlovskii 1926 headed "Foreign Economic Relations as a Factor of the Development of War and Military Power").

Another topic examined was that of economic factors in military science and doctrine.[65] Soviet scholars in this period also carefully examined the economic consequences of war. Nearly two hundred pages of Svyatlovskii's book (1926) are devoted to the study of the impact of war on labor, living standards, agriculture, industry, trade, public finance, and the overall economic system.

In conclusion, throughout the Soviet period defense decision-making was primarily determined by pragmatic reactions to actual events, problems, and pressures. However, Marxist defense-economic theory appeared to influence Bolshevik thinking at crucial times. In particular, policies during the civil war reflected the ideas of Marx, Engels, and Lenin on class conflict, dictatorship of the proletariat, the use of military force and terror, the character of the revolutionary army, and the linkage between economic and military power.

By the mid-1920s the discipline of defense economics was well developed in the USSR, and most important topics were investigated in a scholarly manner. Publications in the period of the New Economic Policy were, on the whole, more empirical and less ideological than those produced during war communism. Nevertheless, to the extent that Soviet works contained an ideological element, they expressed Marxist-Leninist conceptions of the economy and the military. As this

64. Vol'pe 1925 presents a detailed study of the work of the Extraordinary Representative Council of Worker and Peasant Defense Concerned with the Supply of the Red Army and Red Navy (Chusosnabarm) in the coordination of defense industry and the military supply network.

65. The original works include Lebedev 1925, Svechin 1926, and others not examined in this review, by Frunze, Vatsetis, Tukhachevskii, and Shaposhnikov. This literature has been surveyed in Latnikov 1976 and Chechinski 1985.

review has indicated, though, the writings of Marx, Engels, and Lenin were sufficiently incomplete in coverage and inconsistent that virtually any argument that was politically feasible in the USSR could be supported with citations from the classics.

Research for this paper was supported by grants from the Pew Charitable Trusts through projects at the Hoover Institution for War, Revolution and Peace and at Duke University, and from the Ford Foundation through projects at Birmingham on "The Economics of the Soviet Defense Sector" and "Soviet Defense and Conventional Arms Control Policies: 1985–2000." I thank Henry S. Rowen for including me in the Hoover Institution project; Craufurd Goodwin and Jim Leitzel of Duke for inviting me to present the first draft of this paper at their August 1990 conference on "The Interaction Between Economics and National Security: History and Prospects" and for encouraging me to prepare a revised version for publication; Oleg D. Baklanov of the Central Committee CPSU for discussing with me past and present issues of Soviet defense economics during a visit to Moscow in November 1990; and Ron Smith of Birkbeck College, an old friend from Cambridge University, for his comments and suggestions concerning Marxist defense economics. This essay is dedicated to my late father-in-law, Marcus Cunliffe (1922–90), who was a founder of American studies in Britain and a noted military historian.

References

Benvenuti, F. 1988. *The Bolsheviks and the Red Army, 1918–1922.* Cambridge: Cambridge University Press.

Berkhin, I. V. 1958. *Voennaya Reforma v SSSR (1924–1925).* Moscow: Voennoe Izdatel'stvo.

Berman, Ya. L. 1927. *VKP(b) i Voennoe Delo v Rezolyutsiyakh S'ezdov i Konferentsii Vsesoyuznoi Kommunisticheskoi Partii (Bol'shevikov).* Leningrad: Izd. Voenno-Politicheskoi Akademii RKKA im Tolmacheva.

Bukharin, N. I. [1915] 1976. *Imperialism and World Economy.* London: Merlin Press.

———. [1920] 1971. *Economics of the Transformation Period.* New York: Bergman.

Bukharin, N. I., and E. A. Preobrazhensky. [1919] 1970. *The ABC of Communism.* Harmondsworth: Penguin.

Chechinski, M. 1985. The Economics of Defense in the USSR. *Survey* 29, no. 1.

Conte, F., et al. 1990. *Les grandes dates de la Russie et de l'U.R.S.S.* Paris: Larousse.

Davies, R. W. 1958. *The Development of the Soviet Budgetary System.* Cambridge: Cambridge University Press.

Davis, C. 1990a. The High-Priority Military Sector in a Shortage Economy. In *The Impoverished Superpower: Perestroika and the Burden of Soviet Military Spending,* edited by H. Rowen and C. Wolf, Jr. San Francisco: Institute for Contemporary Studies.

———. 1990b. Interactions between National Security and Economics in the USSR during a Period of Radical Systemic Changes: 1917–1925. Paper presented at the Conference on the Interaction between Economics and National Security: History and Prospects, Duke University, 10–12 August 1990.

Deutscher, I. 1965. *The Prophet Armed: Trotsky, 1879–1921.* New York: Vintage Books.

Draper, H. 1977. *Karl Marx's Theory of Revolution*. London: Monthly Review Press.

Engels, F. [1851] 1978. Conditions and Prospects of a War of the Holy Alliance against France in 1852. In *Karl Marx/Frederick Engels: Collected Works*, vol. 10. London: Lawrence & Wishart.

———. [1858a] 1982. Army. In *Marx/Engels: Collected Works*, vol. 18.

———. [1858b] 1982. Artillery. In *Marx/Engels: Collected Works*, vol. 18.

———. [1858c] 1982. Navy. In *Marx/Engels: Collected Works*, vol. 18.

———. [1859] 1980. The Campaign in Italy. In *Marx/Engels: Collected Works*, vol. 16.

———. [1865] 1985. The Prussian Military Question and the German Workers' Party. In *Marx/Engels: Collected Works*, vol. 20.

———. [1878] 1970. *Anti-Dühring*. New York: International Publishers.

———. [1893] 1982. Mozhet li evropa razoruzhit'sya? In Marx, Engels, and Lenin 1982.

Erickson, J. 1962. *The Soviet High Command: A Military-Political History, 1918–1941*. London: Macmillan.

Gatrell, P. 1986. *The Tsarist Economy, 1850–1917*. London: B. T. Batsford.

Hagen, M. von. 1990. *Soldiers in the Proletarian Dictatorship: The Red Army and the Soviet Socialist State, 1917–1930*. London: Cornell University Press.

Hilferding, R. [1910] 1981. *Finance Capital*. London: Routledge & Kegan Paul.

Kennedy, G. 1983. *Defense Economics*. London: Duckworth.

Kovalenko, D. A. 1970. *Oboronnaya Promyshlennost' Sovetskoi Rossii v 1918–1920 gg*. Moscow: Nauka.

Latnikov, V. 1976. Razvitie sovetskoi voenno-ekonomicheskoi mysli v 20-e gody. *Voenno-Istoricheskii Zhurnal*, no. 1.

Lebedev, P. P. 1925. *Gosudarstvennaya Oborona*. Moscow and Leningrad: Voennoe Izdatel'stvo.

Lenin, V. I. [1905a] 1962. The Autocracy and the Proletariat. In *V. I. Lenin: Collected Works*, vol. 8. London: Lawrence & Wishart.

———. [1905b] 1962. The New Russian Loan. In *Collected Works*, vol. 8.

———. [1905c] 1962. The Fall of Port Arthur. In *Collected Works*, vol. 8.

———. [1905d] 1962. European Capital and the Autocracy. In *Collected Works*, vol. 8.

———. [1905e] 1962. Debacle. In *Collected Works*, vol. 8.

———. [1905f] 1962. The Revolutionary Army and the Revolutionary Government. In *Collected Works*, vol. 8.

———. [1908] 1963. Bellicose Militarism and the Anti-militarist Tactics of Social-Democracy. In *Collected Works*, vol. 15.

———. [1913] 1982. Vooruzheniya i kapitalism. In Marx, Engels, and Lenin 1982.

———. [1914a] 1964. The Tasks of Revolutionary Social-Democracy in the European War. In *Collected Works*, vol. 21.

———. [1914b] 1964. The War and Russian Social-Democracy. In *Collected Works*, vol. 21.

———. [1915a] 1964. The Conference of the R.S.D.L.P. Groups Abroad. In *Collected Works*, vol. 21.

———. [1915b] 1964. The Defeat of One's Own Government in the Imperialist War. In *Collected Works*, vol. 21.

———. [1915c] 1964. Socialism and War: The Attitude of the R.S.D.L.P. towards the War. In *Collected Works*, vol. 21.

————. [1917a] 1977. *Imperialism, the Highest Stage of Capitalism.* In Lenin 1977.

————. [1917b] 1977. *The State and Revolution.* In Lenin 1977.

————. [1918a] 1977. The Immediate Tasks of the Soviet Government. In Lenin 1977.

————. [1918b] 1977. Left-Wing Childishness and the Petty-Bourgeois Mentality. In Lenin 1977.

————. [1921] 1966. The New Economic Policy and the Tasks of the Political Education Departments. In *Collected Works,* vol. 33.

————. 1977. *Lenin: Selected Works.* Moscow: Progress Publishers.

Lider, J. 1981. *Military Force: An Analysis of Marxist-Leninist Concepts.* London: Gower.

Lipitskii, S. 1990. Voennaya reforma 1924–1925 godov. *Kommunist,* no. 4.

Lobov, V. N. 1989. Aktual'nye voprosy razvitiya teorii sovetskoi voennoi strategii 20-x–serediny 30-x godov. *Voenno-Istoricheskii Zhurnal,* no. 2.

Luxemburg, R. [1913] 1951. *The Accumulation of Capital.* London: Routledge & Kegan Paul.

————. [1915] 1972. *The Accumulation of Capital: An Anti-Critique.* In Tarbuck 1972.

Malle, S. 1985. *The Economic Organization of War Communism, 1918–1921.* Cambridge: Cambridge University Press.

Marx, K. [1850] 1978. The Class Struggles in France: 1848 to 1850. In *Karl Marx/Frederick Engels: Collected Works,* vol. 10. London: Lawrence & Wishart.

————. [1852] 1979. The Eighteenth Brumaire of Louis Bonaparte. In *Marx/Engels: Collected Works,* vol. 11.

————. [1857] 1982. K. Marks iz pis'ma F. Engel'su 25 Sentyabrya 1857 g. In Marks, Engels, and Lenin 1982.

————. [1859] 1980. The French Disarmament. In *Marx/Engels: Collected Works,* vol. 16.

————. [1866] 1982. K. Marks iz pis'ma F. Engel'su 7 Iyulya 1866 g. In Marx, Engels, and Lenin 1982.

————. [1867] 1970. *Capital,* vol. 1. London: Lawrence & Wishart.

————. [1871] 1982. K. Marks iz pis'ma L. Kugel'manu 12 Aprelya 1871 g. In Marx, Engels, and Lenin 1982.

————. [1885] 1986. *Capital,* vol. 2. London: Lawrence & Wishart.

————. [1894] 1981. *Capital,* vol. 3. Harmondsworth: Penguin.

————. [posthumous] 1951. *Theories of Surplus Value.* London: Lawrence & Wishart.

Marx, K., F. Engels, and V. I. Lenin. 1982. *K. Marks, F. Engels, V. I. Lenin o Voine i Armii: Sbornik Proizvedenii.* Moscow: Voennoe Izdatel'stvo.

Nove, A. 1989. *An Economic History of the U.S.S.R.* Harmondsworth: Penguin.

Pozharov, A. I. 1981. *Ekonomicheskie Osnovy Oboronnogo Mogushchestva Sotsialisticheskogo Godudarstva.* Moscow: Voennoe Izdatel'stvo.

Razvitie Tyla Sovetskikh Vooruzhennykh Sil (1918–1988). 1989. Moscow: Voenizdat.

Rozenfel'd, S. Ya., and K. I. Klimenko. 1961. *Istoriya Mashinostroeniya SSSR.* Moscow: Izd. Akademii Nauk SSSR.

Semmel, B. 1981. *Marxism and the Science of War.* Oxford: Oxford University Press.

Smirnov, G. 1987. *Korabli i Srazheniya.* Moscow: Dyetskaya Literatura.

Sovetskie Vooruzhennye Sily: Istoriya Stroitel'stva. 1978. Moscow: Voennoe Izdatel'stvo.

Sutton, A. C. 1968. *Western Technology and Soviet Economic Development 1917 to 1930.* Stanford: Hoover Institution.

Svechin, A. 1926. *Strategiya.* Moscow: Voennoe Izdatel'stvo.

Svyatlovskii, E. 1926. *Ekonomika Voiny.* Moscow: Izdatel'stvo "Voennyy Vestnik."

Tarbuck, K. J., ed. 1972. *Imperialism and the Accumulation of Capital.* London: Allen Lane/The Penguin Press.

Vashchenko, P. F., and V. A. Runov. 1989. Voennaya reforma v SSSR. *Voenno-Istoricheskii Zhurnal,* no. 12.

Vol'pe, A. 1925. Chusosnabarm. *Voina i Revolyutsiya* 1, no. 5.

Zaleski, E. 1971. *Planning for Economic Growth in the Soviet Union, 1918–1932.* Chapel Hill: University of North Carolina Press.

Zinoviev, G. 1931. *Uchenie Marksa i Lenina o Voine.* Moscow and Leningrad: Gossotsekonizdat.

When Games Grow Deadly Serious: The Military Influence on the Evolution of Game Theory

Philip Mirowski

I have prefaced this paper with a photocopy of the short story "Game" by Donald Barthelme, not because I am trying to innovate some new bastard genre of academic paper, but rather because it captures in a concise way what game theory meant to someone living in the United States in the early 1960s.* When it appeared in the 30 July 1965 *New Yorker,* "games" had taken on a new, sinister connotation due to the work of John von Neumann and Oskar Morgenstern.[1] A word that had previously referred to the carefree frolic of children and the relaxed social activities of adults had now acquired overtones of a standoff, the equipollence of aggression and mutual dependence, the self-paralysis of reason, the rough-and-tumble of the (theoretical) marketplace, and last but not least, the nuclear arms race. Barthelme, the unparalleled master of the late twentieth-century short story, captures each one of these meanings in his little absurd fable without ever once signaling his familiarity with the mathematical theory of games. Morgenstern must have appreciated the subtlety, since he kept a copy of this short story in his files.[2] It should be possible to ask how this curious turn of events came to be and, more particularly, how it was that what may initially seem to be only an abstract mathematical doctrine could come to assume such an oppressive burden of cultural baggage. To anticipate our conclusions, the connections between the military and game theory were numerous and pervasive in the first two decades of its existence, extending into the very mathematics itself.

---

*Barthelme's story is now reproduced directly following this essay.—*The Editor.*

1. The Barthelme story was reprinted in his collection *Unspeakable Practices, Unnatural Acts* (1969). The first edition of von Neumann and Morgenstern's *Theory of Games and Economic Behavior* appeared in 1944; all citations here are from the third edition (1964).

2. Oskar Morgenstern Papers (OMP), Duke University Manuscript Department, Perkins Library, box 15.

Can Mathematics Be Subject to
Social Influences?

While the ubiquity of social influence upon the structure and content of various branches of science has grown to be a commonplace in recent years (Barnes and Edge 1982; Bloor 1976; Brown 1989), it does seem to be the case that most mathematicians still think of themselves as Platonists: that is, that to whatever extent that physics and biological theories are impugned and overthrown by subsequent developments, mathematics is forever, because it exists in some aetherial realm free of human taint, waiting to be discovered.[3] Opposed to this orthodoxy are arrayed a small band of philosophers and sociologists who take their cue from Ludwig Wittgenstein, who asserted in his *Remarks on the Foundations of Mathematics* that "the mathematician is an inventor, not a discoverer" (1978, 99).

Despite some notable attempts to flesh out this maverick doctrine (e.g., Bloor 1973, 1978; Wilder 1981; Tiles 1984, ch. 3), success in this endeavor does seem more palpable in the areas of applied or "mixed" mathematics than in the purest realms of abstraction. Profound work on the construction of probability and statistics has been produced (see MacKenzie 1981; Porter 1986; Daston 1988), on the mathematics of classical mechanics (Grattan-Guiness 1984; Rowe and McCleary 1989), approaches to non-Euclidean and projective geometries (Richards 1988), and the construction of programs to check other computer programs (de Millo, Lipton, and Perlis in Tymoczko 1986). This paper should be situated within this latter tradition, in the sense that game theory is a prime example of a twentieth-century vintage of "mixed mathematics," taking its mandate and content largely from problems thrown up in extramathematical areas of human endeavor. Yet as in the previously cited cases, part of the "social constructivist" thesis arises from an awareness that the apparent arena of application is rarely sufficient to encompass the shape and content of the outcome. For instance, the notion that probability theory is not a simple empirical extrapolation from the observation of gambling is an important thesis (Daston 1988); simple observation of the *puissance* of machines was not at all sufficient to explain classical mechanics (Grattan-Guiness 1984); and simple observation of the economy cannot explain the rise of neoclassical economic theory (Mirowski 1989a).[4]

---

3. Even some of the protagonists in our drama worry about the strength of their Platonist convictions. See, for instance, the interview of David Blackwell by Morris DeGroot (in Duren 1988–89, 3:608): *DeGroot:* "One's political views or social views seem to be pretty much independent of the technical problems we work on." *Blackwell:* "Yes. Although it's hard to see how they could *not* have an influence, isn't it? I guess my life seems all of a piece to me yet it's hard to see where the connections are."

4. Indeed much of my recent work (from Mirowski 1986 to Mirowski 1991) has as its

A critical preliminary in the social-constructivist program for mathematics is to sketch out a score for the orchestration of cognitive influences as a preliminary to historical explanation. Here is where the pervasive overtones of military metaphors seem to drown out any other strains of the history of game theory. In the first two decades of its existence, to discuss game theory was to discuss "strategy," and from there attitudes towards militarism and the arms race rapidly took over. Some laid the blame for the escalation of nuclear weaponry directly at the door of game theory; other, cooler heads claimed that game theory was symptomatic of an apologetic bias in favor of the military-industrial complex; still others asserted it was an expression of abstract rationality ideally attuned to the technological character of the Cold War. But in no instance have I found a text willing to make the case that the military connection actually shaped the content of game theory. Yet it is this social-constructivist thesis which would most closely parallel the project of the authors cited in the previous paragraph; and I would venture to suggest it would be the thesis most likely to disconcert the Platonists in the audience, not to mention those economists who harbor the conviction that game theory is primarily an economic construct.

The idea that the military milieu and, more specifically, defense funding of research and development, has influenced the course and content of such hard sciences as physics has been gaining ground in recent times (Noble 1985; Hacking 1986; Schweber 1988; MacKenzie and Spinardi 1988). The best historical study at the micro level has been Paul Forman's (1987) examination of the impact of military imperatives upon quantum electronics and the evolution of the laser, where, among other interesting bits of history, one learns that the seemingly benign blessing of fiber optics was originally developed with the intent to circumvent the massive electromagnetic pulse attendant upon the explosion of a nuclear weapon.

Looking at the numbers, the existence of a potential bias to scientific research becomes all the more plausible: military research and development as a proportion of all federal research and development in the United States shot up from 25 percent in 1935 to roughly 90 percent in 1943, and, more importantly, remained at that level well into the 1950s (Forman 1987, 153). This explosion of federal funding came on the heels of the Great Depression, when the prospects for a mathematical or physical career were bleak. "From its opening in March 1943, Los Alamos absorbed physicists like a sponge" (Kevles 1978, 329), and the mathematicians also were blotted up by the Applied Mathematics

---

common denominator an argument that all mathematical discourse in economics is underdetermined by the economic "data."

Group (Rees in Duren 1988–89; Owens in Rowe and McCleary, 1989). But more importantly, once absorbed, the mathematicians and the physicists were loath to be wrung out again; and in the immediate postwar battle over the shape of federal funding of research, a civilian-dominated paradigm lost out to an extension of the military model, particularly under the auspices of the Office of Naval Research (ONR) and the Atomic Energy Commission. To take one example at random, the proportion of *total* sponsored research at MIT derived from ONR alone was 52 percent in fiscal year 1947, 53 percent in 1949, and 48 percent in 1950.[5] As Daniel Kevles summarized it in his survey *The Physicists:*

> In 1945 liberals like [Senator] Kilgore may have wanted a federal program balanced between civilian and military needs, between big business and small business, between the leading and the less developed universities, between the welfare of science and the welfare of the nation. By the early 1950s the outcome was quite different: a program for the physical sciences dominated outside of atomic energy by the military, its dispensations concentrated geographically in the major universities, its primary energies devoted to the chief challenges of national defense and fundamental physics. While the Cold War had made such an outcome possible, the result was produced not by design but by a combination of demands and defaults, including the demands and defaults of a new political power group, the nation's physical scientists. (1978, 365)

With only minor qualifications the same situation reigned in mathematics in that era; it was particularly the case for the protagonists in our present drama. As Richard Bellman writes in his guileless autobiography: "I was horrified to see the genteel poverty in which many faculty people lived. Here were people who had devoted over twenty years to training and they made less than a checker in a supermarket. I promised myself I would never live like that" (1984, 147). Bellman's solution was to consult for RAND and work on—guess what?—game theory.

In this environment there was one mathematician of great genius who not merely flourished, but came into his own true calling as a political animal: John von Neumann. He was but one of many émigré mathematicians and physicists to make their way to the land of opportunity in the Depression decade; he arrived in 1930. By 1955 he was one of the most powerful scientific men in the United States (Heims 1980, 275). But let him describe his own status in his own words as of 1946:

---

5. Taken from F. Leroy Foster, "Sponsored Research at MIT," unpublished manuscript, MIT archives.

I have been connected with Government work on military matters for nearly ten years: As a consultant of Ballistics Research Laboratory of the Army Ordinance Department since 1937, as a member of its scientific advisory committee since 1940; I have been a member of various divisions of the National Defense Research Committee since 1941; I have been a consultant of the Navy Bureau of Ordinance since 1942. I have been connected with the Manhattan District [*sic*] since 1943 as a consultant of the Los Alamos Laboratory, and I spent a considerable part of 1943–45 there. (von Neumann, 1963, 499)

If there were any more of an "insider" than von Neumann in the military establishment of that era, it could only be in the shadowy paranoid dreams of a Thomas Pynchon. Moreover, this activity fell right in the period of the genesis of the *Theory of Games and Economic Behavior* and its early promulgation. But there remains the nagging question: how could this have substantially shaped the *mathematics?*

In most instances objections to the social-constructivist thesis assume that the scientific object of investigation exists independent of human will or endeavor: the gas laser or the gene has an integrity which it would preserve in a universe void of *Homo sapiens*. I think that this notion becomes rather strained in the case of mathematics; it is hard to see how the calculus or the coefficient of correlation come etched in the face of Nature. Nevertheless, in the specific case of game theory we may even avoid this level of objection for a simple reason: there is no such thing as a unified mathematical object called "game theory." I have begun to attempt to make this case (see Mirowski 1986b) and view the present essay as a further historical elaboration upon the theme. But in order to understand the narrative that follows it may be helpful to restate it in the most abstract terms. I believe that underlying most of the key components of the mathematics of games were various attempts to define a notion of "rationality" which would encompass most or all previous connotations of that sadly abused word, and thus realize the dream of Leibniz, who hoped all controversies would one day be settled by the exhortation, "Gentlemen, let us calculate!"[6]

One may take two attitudes towards this quest, both of which lead to the conclusion that it is a will-o'-the-wisp. The first is that a context-independent structure of rationality does not exist, and therefore these mathematicians are merely constructing local and temporary character-

6. The comparison is not mine, but Morgenstern's. Once Kurt Gödel mentioned some similarities between game theory and Leibniz on a *mathesis universalis* to Morgenstern (OMP, diaries, 17 September 1944), it became one of Morgenstern's hobbyhorses. He mentions it in a number of places, such as his article in the December 1961 *Aerospace Engineering* and his entry on game theory for the *Encyclopedia of the Social Sciences*.

izations of what a small coterie of people in a certain cultural context might be willing to call "rational behavior." This merely restates the "recipe formulated by Girschick and his colleagues at RAND: First guess the solution of a game, and then prove it" (Thomas in Mensch 1966, 254). The second is that the entire program is governed by a sequence of historical accidents, which I have described in some detail (Mirowski 1989a). In this narrative human rationality, and particularly economic rationality, has been repeatedly patterned upon the West's own understanding of the physical world, and in particular upon its theories of motion. When motion meant returning to your "natural place," rationality meant staying in your natural place. When motion meant the passing about of a conserved substance between bodies, rationality meant the exchange of equivalents between traders. When motion was subsumed under the physics of extrema of energy, rationality was subsumed under the extrema of its analogue, utility. Thus rationality has been little more than a projection of our culture's notions of order in the natural world onto its self-images of social life.

The place of game theory in this sequence of projections has been rather a curious one. I suggest that it too was prompted by a change in images of the natural world in the 1930s, mainly revolving around experiences with quantum mechanics and simultaneous critiques of determinism and causality.[7] But the original inspiration for the new construction of rationality did not hold for very long, mainly because the new concepts of "optimization," "solution," and "equilibrium" had opened up a Pandora's box of conundrums about the nature of communication, interpretation, and the very meaning of rules and context. In trying to free itself from the mechanical determinism of the nineteenth century, the game-theoretic program found itself proliferating solution concepts and alternative game specifications that led to wildly counterintuitive and divergent conclusions.[8] Rationality, given its free rein, rapidly made mock of any single definition of rationality; and that is why there is no such thing as "game theory." As Martin Shubik once put it, "Fundamentally, there is no single theory of games. When we talk about a theory of games, we are usually referring to a theory of the solution of a game" (in Mensch 1966, 396). Of course, there are various proposed solution-concepts and techniques one associates with this program; there are even paradigm textbooks and syllabi; but any honest

7. This case is made in much greater detail in my forthcoming paper "What Were von Neumann and Morgenstern Trying to Accomplish?" (Mirowski in press).

8. A good example of this loss of direction was a talk given by Howard Raiffa at the Duke Conference on the History of Game Theory on 5 October 1990. Raiffa reported that he was disheartened by his experience in 1949 of finding that his own proposed solution-concepts for 2×2 bimatrix non–zero-sum games were not generally chosen in situations of simulated play; nor were they chosen by other game theorists when playing the game.

practitioner must admit that we are no closer to a *mathesis universalis* than in Leibniz's day. The only thing that has created the impression of a unified mathematical discipline is the credibility of the arbitrary sequence of groups who have taken up the program and made it their own. That is why a social-constructivist history of game theory is not only possible; it is the only plausible candidate.

But What Precisely Is Game Theory, Anyway?

Just as a short-story writer is a different creature from a professional mathematician, and therefore Donald Barthelme's portrait of game theory hardly resembles that of, say, Robert Aumann, so too will the portrait of a historian of science (my assumed persona) differ from each. This divergence will begin at the very beginning, the very construction of the frame of reference and the definition of the object in question. Let us for the sake of comparison start with two definitions of game theory. I will reject definition 1 and juxtapose it to one more consonant with the present inquiry, definition 2:

1. "Game Theory is a mathematical theory which deals with conflict situations. A conflict situation is a situation in which two or more individuals interact and thereby jointly determine the outcome. . . . It is assumed that these preferences can be described by a von Neumann–Morgenstern utility function, hence, that each player is characterized by a numerical function whose expected value he tries to maximize. Game theory is a normative theory: it aims to prescribe what each player in a game should do in order to promote his interests" (van Damme 1987, 1).
2. "the problem [of game theory] is that of pursuing analysis sufficiently far so as to single out strategic choices which will either bring about the preferred outcomes or are 'likely' to bring them about. . . . Game theory is properly a branch of mathematics" (Rapoport 1970, 49).

The first definition is recognizably that of an orthodox economist engaged in modern game-theoretic research. From this perspective game theory has been a progressive generalization of the original concerns of the Walrasian neoclassicals, a rigorous elaboration of the insight that "conflict" may be found where before there was only the passive (zombie-like?) acquiescence in the mysterious coordination wrought by the market. This is a saga of the smooth development of game theory, from the first glimmers of the idea of a "strategy" and the minimax "solution" by Emile Borel in 1921 (Frechet 1953); through the triumphant proof of the existence of a minimax solution for all zero-sum games by von Neumann in 1928; through the codification and axiomatization of the theory by von Neumann and Morgenstern in 1944.

Although the next part of the narrative might be a bit more contentious, given that no canonical history exists, our orthodox economist would probably choose to flesh out the implied organic progress by citing the work of Nash (1951) on solutions for non–zero-sum games and its economic applications from 1975 onwards. In the meantime the "core" of the cooperative game was defined in 1959 and shown to converge to Walrasian equilibrium by Debreu and Scarf in 1963, thus explaining how the Walrasian program was a special case of the broader game-theoretic framework. (Some at the time interpreted the formal subsumption as just the reverse; but it would not matter for our orthodox narrative.) New advances gained momentum in the 1980s, with games spreading to politics and evolutionary biology, and essentially coming to define the subfields of industrial organization and law and economics and coming to pervade the new model "macroeconomics." "Refinements" of equilibrium concepts proceed apace, and in all precincts game theory looms as the formalist *nouvelle vague*.

Nevertheless this narrative has a suppressed dark side. All is not well in the House of Game Theory—in every dreamhome a heartache—and signs of pathology can no longer be ignored. For instance, Nobel Prize winners have taken to disparaging comments at their acceptance ceremonies (Simon 1982, 486–87) as well as less auspicious circumstances (Arrow in Feiwel 1987b, 215; Samuelson 1986, 492; Sonnenschein in Feiwel 1987b, 334). Von Neumann–Morgenstern utility has failed nearly every conceivable test to which it has been subjected (Machina 1989; Thaler 1987). The applications of game theory to subfields of economics have been deemed minuscule by respected theorists: "Candidly put: anything that one might imagine as sensible can turn out to be the answer" (Fisher 1989, 116). And as for the formalization of "conflict" so praised by our first definition, it may be worthwhile to quote a newer generation of game theorist at length:

> (i) Nash (or correlated) equilibrium is an inadequate and at times incoherent formalization of the notion of rational strategic behavior. (ii) The concept of a Bayesian game offers a much more limited opportunity for extending the scope of noncooperative game theory than is often assumed. (iii) An adequate, unified theory of microeconomic interaction based solely on strategic and informational concerns of the type that constitute the focus of noncooperative game theory is, for the time being, not within reach. (Gul 1989, 1)

I think there is no other rational conclusion than to infer that if game theory were what van Damme thinks it is, then it is on its last legs. But it is not; and therefore it is imperative to understand what precisely it is that is going on under this rubric.

In line with the second definition, game theory is first and foremost a mathematical tradition motivated by some very specific extramathematical questions, much as calculus was provoked by some very specific concerns in celestial and rational mechanics. Initially in the 1920s, I believe, the object was mainly to formalize some very basic games (in the original sense of playful folk amusements, such as "scissors, paper, stone") in the same spirit that Pascal and the Chevalier de Mére were attempting to decide the best manner to deduct simple wagers at the dawn of probability theory (Hacking 1975). Although it is of some interest for our subsequent narrative that Borel explicitly suggested that the analysis might equally be applicable to "the art of war or of economic and financial speculation" (Frechet 1953, 100), little attempt was made to follow up on these alternative sources of inspiration.[9] Indeed, as has been argued by Leonard (1990), prior to the 1944 volume by von Neumann and Morgenstern there was no serious context in which "game theory" could be considered a coherent mathematical inquiry, and therefore it simply did not exist. In other words, no one cared if "scissors, paper, stone" could be expressed in mathematical formalisms.

Looking for a Home

By 1940, however, the problem situation had changed dramatically. Von Neumann had done nothing on either games or his expanding economy model since 1928, but he had been extremely busy and productive in the areas of analysis and combinatorics, where "analysis" followed in the tradition of Hilbert and Weyl as based in foundations of linear algebra and topology (Dieudonné 1976). In 1932 he published his *Mathematische Grundlagen,* which discussed the question of indeterminism versus causality in quantum mechanics, concluding that no introduction of hidden variables could restore the classical world picture. As perhaps the premier inheritor of the Hilbert program of formalism in the foundations of mathematics, he was severely shaken by Gödel's 1931 paper which demonstrated that if arithmetic is consistent, its consistency could not be established by any metamathematical reasoning which encompassed the structure of arithmetic (Nagel and Newman 1958; Kline 1980). In reaction to this deconstruction of the eternal verities of the nineteenth century von Neumann increasingly turned to what one might call "artificial intelligence" in order to sweep away the ruins of

9. The analogy between Borel and Pascal is more serious than it might first appear. Borel makes a literary allusion to Pascal's distinction (found in his *Pensées*) between "l'esprit de géométrie" and "l'esprit de finesse" (Pascal 1962, 256–58); the significance of this allusion is that it signals Borel's awareness of the fragility of the aspirations of a theory of games, something to which von Neumann was largely immune.

nineteenth-century platitudes and replace them with more direct models of human thought which could survive the great skepticism regarding formalization (Ulam 1976, 241–42). One can observe this in his concern over the issue of the lack of separation of the observer and the experiment in quantum mechanics; in his fascination with the Turing machine understood as an ideal machine capable of imitating any other Turing machine; and in his work on automata and computers, leading ultimately to his late work on direct models of the human brain. In that later work he suggested that the brain "is a sort of frequency-modulated system of signalling; intensities are translated into frequencies . . . the message-system used in the nervous system, is of an essentially statistical character" (von Neumann 1958, 77–79). This might frighten those enamored of a model of the brain as a clockwork mechanism, but not someone conversant with the latest findings in quantum mechanics. In other words, von Neumann had become increasingly doubtful about conventional images of "rationality."

Hence when he met a fellow Austro-Hungarian émigré in February 1939 at tea at Princeton in the company of Niels Bohr, and the fellow started to suggest that the problem in quantum mechanics of the disturbance of the experiment by the observer had a parallel in economic life—the disturbance of the macroeconomy by the expectations of the participants—and moreover, he harbored a conviction that von Neumann's 1928 paper was just the ticket to formalize the problem, the great mathematician could not help but be intrigued (Morgenstern 1976, 807–8). At first Oskar Morgenstern proposed to write a summary article on von Neumann's game theory, but he was so inept at the mathematics, yet was so endearingly in awe of the subject and the man, that von Neumann subsequently deigned to collaborate upon what was envisioned to be a rather long journal article—and ended up being *The Theory of Games and Economic Behavior*.

The rather curious circumstances of its composition and its subsequent reception are central to a social-constructivist narrative of the structure of what became "game theory." Clearly Morgenstern thought of it first and foremost as a theory of economic rationality; it was he, for instance, who insisted upon denominating the payoffs in "utility" to pacify the orthodox economics profession; the subsequent axiomatization of "von Neumann–Morgenstern utility" was an afterthought, a two-finger exercise for a mathematician like von Neumann. But for von Neumann the elaboration of the theory of games had more of the character of an exploration of a generic type of formal rationality, one more in tune with twentieth-century physics and less redolent of the nineteenth-century maximization over an inert objective. This is the source of the numerous remarks about procedures in the physical sciences in the book (von Neumann and Morgenstern 1964, 3, 32, 45) as well as von Neumann's aside to Morgenstern concerning Paul Samuelson's *Foundations:* "one would think the book contemporary of the time immediately following Newton."[10] I believe that if the following passage left out the phrase "in a social economy," it would be an exact representation of von Neumann's views in this matter:

> we wish to find the mathematically complete principles which define "rational behavior" for the participants in a social economy, and to derive from them the general characteristics of that behavior. And while the principles ought to be perfectly general— i.e., valid in all situations—we may be satisfied if we can find solutions, for the moment, only in some characteristic special cases." (von Neumann and Morgenstern 1964, 31)

For von Neumann, his 1928 proof of the existence of a minimax "solution" for all zero-sum games, if one allowed for the existence of "mixed" or randomized strategies, expanded to become the very epitome of the abstract rationality which was his goal. He came to see the introduction of stochastic considerations as something more than it was in 1928, namely, a way to ensure the existence of a saddlepoint in games where the payoff structure did not immediately provide one. It became a representation of the stochastic nature of thought itself, an acknowledgment of the contingency which he had demonstrated in the physical world with his axiomatization of quantum mechanics. The analogy was present in the very mathematics, since both the quantum mechanics and the minimax theorem relied upon the newfangled devices of matrix quadratic forms and stochastic vectors.

The problem, at this juncture, was how to convey the radical departure in thinking about rationality, and to figure out whom it would interest. After all, who could fathom this strange *potage* of mathematical sophistication, philosophical speculation, stochastic foundations, and strategic considerations? At the end of his life von Neumann took to addressing the biological community directly, as well as the fledgling community of computer specialists, but in 1943 that was not a plausible option. Philosophers didn't have a clue as to what was going on. Mathematicians really didn't regard it as a new departure in mathematics, since mostly it cribbed together a few tools from combinatorics, topology, and linear algebra. Hence the avid Morgenstern seemed a godsend by proposing an alternative audience, namely, the economists. While

10. OMP, box 8, notebook entry dated 15 December 1972. Claims about the "schizophrenic" character of the *Theory of Games* made below are documented in Mirowski (in press).

von Neumann's opinion of the economics community was not high, it did initially appear to hold out the promise of applied problems which has always been so fertile for the development and elaboration of novelty in mathematics.

And at first the response of the economics community did seem enthusiastic. There are very few books in twentieth-century economics which have rated full-length article reviews in all the major journals hot on the heels of publication; the *Theory of Games* received such treatment. Reviews ranged from the absolutely laudatory in the *Journal of Political Economy* (Marshak 1946), the *Nordisk Tidsskrift* (Leunbach 1948), and the *Economic Journal* (Stone 1948) to cautious but enthusiastic (Hurwicz 1945) to cautiously skeptical (Kaysen 1947). But it rapidly became apparent that the reviewers were most excited about the "wrong" things, from von Neumann's perspective: they seemed captivated by the side issues concerning "measurable" utility and risk, as well as the more distant resemblances to the Cournot duopoly model, and tended to skirt the more profound reconceptualization of the nature of rationality. Hurwicz (1945, 924) went so far as to scold the authors for naughtily "attacking (rather indiscriminately) the analytical techniques at present used by economic theorists," which might "give aid and comfort to the opponents of rigorous thinking in economics or increase their complacency."[11]

Of the entire gamut of economists in 1945, the most likely collection of potential enthusiasts for game theory should have been found at the Cowles Commission, then located at the University of Chicago. There a dazzling array of mathematical talent had been gathered precisely in order to infuse economics with a double shot of rigor, not to mention to forge a rapprochement between the deterministic structure of Walrasian general equilibrium and the seemingly stochastic character of most economic variables (Mirowski 1989c). Among such a gathering the ruminations of a mathematical lion like von Neumann had to be reckoned with, and initially Jacob Marschak and Leonid Hurwicz set out to grapple with the beast.[12] In a development which was repeated elsewhere in the profession, Marschak got sidetracked into the whole issue

11. The identity of this fifth column of fuzzies can only be understood within the context of the battle going on between the Cowles Commission and the National Bureau of Economic Research in the late 1930s and early 1940s. On this incident see Mirowski 1989b.

12. See Marschak's report to the Rockefeller Foundation, dated 17 June 1946, in the Rockefeller Archives: "[Cowles's work is] typical of our effort to express economic hypotheses in the clearest possible and empirically manageable way; and to make maximum possible use of the theory of rational behavior without unduly forcing it upon irrational facts. The same desire underlies the work of Hurwicz and Marschak on evaluating von Neumann's new theory of economic behavior." Note well that Morgenstern's name is not included.

of measurable utility under risk; later in life he would concoct his own neoclassical "theory of teams" in preference to the more elaborate structures of game theory. Hurwicz left Cowles for the University of Iowa in September 1946 and did nothing more on game theory. Indeed the Cowles Discussion Paper Series numbers 101 to 151, which date from April 1947 to April 1950, contain not one paper on game theory.

It would appear that the original plan to create a context for "game theory" in the economists' camp failed, at least in the period 1945–55.[13] The metaphor linking the economy to "games" was regarded as a rhetorical trope unbefitting the dignity of a science like economics; and in the era before "artificial intelligence" was a household word, there was appreciable resistance to the idea that even poker might be adequately described by the theory.[14] If anything, the doubts about "games" (as opposed to the axiomatized utility theory, etc.) grew a bit more shrill in the second half of the decade, with the minimax solution concept itself coming under increasingly accurate fire (Neisser 1952; Ellsberg 1956). The sources of this indifference verging upon overt hostility are not our concern in this venue, although one can easily see that they ranged from fear about its corrosive effect upon the central tenets of Walrasian general equilibrium to anxiety over the possible indeterminacy of multiple solutions and dependence upon intricately specified rule structures. What does matter here is that it was soon apparent (and sooner for von Neumann than for Morgenstern) that the economists were not the fertile

13. Some of the hostile reactions may be gleaned from the Morgenstern diaries. For instance, Morgenstern presented the new theory to a seminar at Princeton, and reported in an entry dated 2 May 1944: "Lutz was hostile and ironic. It appears that he perceives the disagreement the most because he has vested interests in theory. This will be the reaction of most theoreticians." After a visit to Harvard, he wrote on 8 June 1945: "None of them has read *The Theory of Games* and no one has said anything besides Haberler, who has not read any further. But they will not be able to ignore it because the mathematicians and physicists there, as elsewhere, ought to be very enthusiastic about it." After a subsequent visit to Harvard, when he gave a seminar on game theory, he recorded on 4 March 1946: "The economists are partially hostile and partially fascinated because the physicists so strongly and masterfully rule over it." On 20 December 1947: "Röpke even said later that game theory was Viennese coffeehouse gossip." And on 13 June 1947, after a lecture on game theory at the Perroux Institute, he wrote: "Allais opposed: we had *not* disproved there was a social maximum for free competition[!] . . . Nobody has even seen the book. The copy I sent to Perroux has not yet arrived." After a talk at Chicago on game theory, the entry for 1 January 1948 reads: "It is clear from what he says that Schumpeter has never read the book." After a talk at Rotterdam on 30 October 1950: "They had heard of game theory, but Tinbergen, Frisch, etc. wanted to know nothing about it because it disturbs them." And finally, the entry for 8 October 1947: "[Johnny] says [Samuelson] has murky ideas about stability. He is no mathematician and one should not ascribe the analysis to him. And even in 30 years he won't absorb game theory." Not a bad prediction on Johnny's part.

14. "Metropolis once described what a triumph it was to win ten dollars [at poker] from John von Neumann, author of a famous treatise on game theory. He then brought his book for five dollars and pasted the other five on the inside cover as a symbol of his victory" (Ulam 1976, 169–70).

loam in which to cultivate game theory; it would be a good idea to look for yet another pasture to till. For someone in von Neumann's position, an alternative immediately suggested itself: there existed, after all, the other metaphor for a game which had been present since the beginning, that of *war*.

I think it is fair to say that the *Theory of Games* was not written with this target group in mind. For instance, in a letter to Arden Bucholz late in his life, Morgenstern denied that a reading of Clausewitz had anything to do with the composition of the book, although he admits that World War II was much on their minds in that period. Morgenstern's diaries from that period are full of references to war news, but the connection is never made to the work they were then busily composing.[15] However, that is not to say that lines of communication were not kept open to the military even at the earliest stages of composition. For instance, when it came to publishing an arcane mathematical manuscript filled with difficult typesetting in wartime conditions of stringency, which the authors had rather self-indulgently let swell to more than 650 pages, Princeton University Press understandably balked. But these were not your ordinary authors, and a discreet word to J. D. Rockefeller, who at that time happened to be Chief of Naval Operations, produced a subsidy more than sufficient to guarantee publication.[16]

When the reception from economists began to look less than promising, von Neumann started to use his ever-expanding military influence to encourage the creation of a coterie of mathematically inclined "strategists" to take up the cudgels for game theory, apparently without including Morgenstern in his plans. There were three separate centers of this incipient movement; in rough order of chronological appearance they could be found in the Applied Mathematics Panel (AMP) during World War II, and in particular the subset known as the Statistical Research Group at Columbia University (Rees in Duren 1988–89; Owens in Rowe and McCleary 1989); RAND, at first a subsidiary of Douglas Aircraft but rapidly spun off as a free-standing think tank closely connected to the Air Force (Kaplan 1983); and finally the Office of Naval Research (Old 1961; Nanus 1959).

The Applied Mathematics Panel during World War II was distributed

15. Morgenstern to Bucholz, 17 June 1974, OMP, box 15; Morgenstern diaries, OMP, box 4. Actually Bucholz gets the comparison wrong. Clausewitz was part of the German Romantic era, rejecting the abstractions of reason in favor of imagination, the analytical in favor of the historical, repudiating the Enlightenment. Hence Clausewitz rejected the comparison of war to chess, since war was an activity where genius could rise above all rules into the realm of free, unsystematic thinking. Von Neumann was actually closer to the earlier tradition of Grotius and Pufendorf, who attempted to subject war to the rule of reason and law.
16. J. D. Rockefeller to Morgenstern, 16 September 1943, OMP, box 15.

geographically across the country, but von Neumann's proximity to New York City undoubtedly accounts for the fact that the lion's share of recruits came from the sections at Columbia, NYU, and Brown. Mina Rees was an important administrator of this project, and later was even more important as head of the mathematical research program at ONR as a favorable funding source for game-theoretic research (Rees in Duren 1988–89, 275). New York tended to collect refugees from the war, and three such displaced persons who found themselves in the employ of AMP were early recruits to the game-theoretic cause. Olaf Helmer, a German refugee with Ph.D.s in mathematics and logic, worked on operations research during the war and went to RAND soon thereafter, bringing with him a new-found enthusiasm for the theory of games. Abraham Wald, a Romanian Jew brought to the United States by Morgenstern, was the earliest mathematician to develop an application of game theory outside those suggested by von Neumann, namely, the reconceptualization of statistical estimation as a game against Nature in his *Sequential Analysis* (1947). Meyer Girschick, a mathematical statistician and third AMP refugee, also went to RAND in 1947. Other important AMP employees were John David Williams, Herbert Solomon, Ed Hewitt, and Ed Paxson, all of whom conceived their enthusiasm for the novel mathematical doctrine in this period.

In 1944, looking beyond to the postwar period, von Neumann's close friend Theodore von Karman, a Hungarian refugee, began work on a multivolume report for the Army Air Force Scientific Advisory Board which called for the creation of a nucleus of scientists funded by the military; this became the blueprint for what became Air Force Project RAND. During the fall of 1945 arrangements with Douglas Aircraft were finalized, and in March 1946 the first contract was signed. In the organization that General Curtis LeMay was later to stigmatize as "Research and *No* Development," civilian engineers, mathematicians, and economists were brought together to apply their speculative skills to military problems; the most obvious candidates were those who had been already working in some war research capacity. John David Williams was the fifth person hired at RAND; he in turn brought in Helmer, Paxson, and Girschick, essentially guaranteeing that math at RAND meant game theory. Girschick in turn brought in Blackwell (Duren 1988–89, 590); and Bellman was recruited from Los Alamos, probably at the instigation of von Neumann, who was himself enlisted as part-time consultant in 1947. The fledgling RAND game theory group was rounded out by the addition of Melvin Dresher in July 1947 from the War Assets Administration. Dresher, like so many other key players in our drama, had a Ph.D. in mathematics with some background in physics and was a Central European refugee (from Poland). This element of displacement was important for the creation of a certain camaraderie in a group disparaged by both the mathematics and economics communities in the times ahead.

The third phase of the development of an alternative game-theoretic community came with the dominance of ONR with respect to government research funding in the immediate postwar period. ONR's favor was weighted towards previous members of AMP, such as the statistician Herbert Solomon, who began the statistics department at Stanford, recruiting Girschick there from RAND, only to subsequently become an ONR official himself. At Columbia, Solomon arranged ONR support for Howard Raiffa and Duncan Luce to produce their highly influential *Games and Decisions* (Gani 1986, 17). The Navy also belatedly began to fund Morgenstern's own shop at Princeton directly under the instigation of von Neumann,[17] ultimately providing support for such graduate students as Lloyd Shapley (soon to go to RAND), John Nash, and Martin Shubik. Although this funding nominally came with no strings attached, all of these individuals (Morgenstern included) were drawn increasingly into mathematical models of military questions such as "deterrence" and optimal siting of missile installations. The Princeton/ONR connection also seems to have been a major stimulant to the building of computers explicitly dedicated to the solution of games for the military, by as early as 1951 (Morgenstern 1954, 505).

While there is no "smoking gun," in the guise of a memo stating von Neumann's intentions, the concentration of individuals who were willing to believe that game theory had something serious to offer to military planning and strategic behavior was too correlated with von Neumann's activities to be accidental. Once set in motion and encouraged by the lush support of these military sources in the immediate postwar period, these individuals constituted an entirely novel "discipline," called variously "organizational research," "dynamic programming," or the less euphemistic "strategic theory," all of which boiled down to more or less the same thing: they were mathematicians outside of math departments doing game theory.

But just as there are no *intrinsic* capacities of game theory which render it ideal for application to economic questions (since we have argued that there is no single coherent doctrine which constitutes "game theory"), there is likewise nothing which renders it ideal for military

17. In the Morgenstern diaries the entry for 22 July 1942 mentions in passing that "Johnny has taken an important position in the Navy." Then, on 29 March 1948, Johnny recommends that OM be awarded a contract by the Navy, "where there is an unclear project on economic comparisons." This initiated extensive relations between Morgenstern and the military, primarily through ONR and WSEG, although he did later have some trouble with his security clearance in 1950. See the entries of the OM diaries for 20 November 1949 and 5 May and 2 December 1950.

application. This newly created collection of individuals had to concoct this "need" out of whole cloth, particularly since the military, even more than the economics profession, was intent upon quick and tangible results. Because the "strategic community" were the only really qualified mathematicians trying to develop game theory into a body of rigorous doctrine, the military conception of "strategy" held dominant sway over the early elaboration of game theory.

Solving for Rational Terror

So how, precisely, did this unholy alliance between the mathematicians and the military actually affect the mathematics? I shall try to organize the answer under four large headings.

The Image of Conflict

First and foremost, the military connection created and reinforced the conviction that somehow game theory was about formalizing "conflict," and this in turn led to the misleading classification of all games into the categories of "cooperative" and "noncooperative." This refrain is first found in the early popularizations of game theory by the strategic community (McDonald 1949; McKinsey 1952, 1), solidifies in the work of Nash (1951), and persists down to the present in such definitions as that of van Damme (1987), quoted above. But nothing in the original mathematics either endorses or encourages such a conviction. Von Neumann's notion of a solution transcended classical optimization in that it recognized that payoffs may depend upon the choices of others which the player may not control, but a moment's reflection will reveal that mutual interdependence is not isomorphic to "conflict" in the usual connotation of that word. Indeed, to juxtapose "conflict" with a "game" reveals a linguistic ambivalence: do we mean the macho sparring of friendly contestants, or do we mean an all-out attempt to destroy and devastate the opponent? In the former instance we are still in the ambit of the von Neumann–Morgenstern organon, since the rules for the game are given and respected for the duration of the joust; but in the case of decimation we have left the formalism, since, "When one is losing, [the player] is under strong pressure to enlarge the game—change the rules" (Mensch 1966, 264).

But the enforced stress on conflict due to the clientele of the strategic community had two effects, partially contradictory, on game theory. On the one hand it severely limited what might count as the "solution" of a game formalism: this is the subject under our next heading below. But on the other hand it persistently caused the strategic community to retreat from claiming to describe real war, and towards situations where players were able to order their conflict "rationally." One can observe this in the move from formalizing submarine evasive maneuvers, optimal attack on a hidden object, fighter-bomber duels, and the like in the late 1940s towards the fascination with nuclear "deterrence" of the 1950s and 1960s. The problem for the strategic community was that "real warfare does not rigorously satisfy any of the rules of game theory" (Mensch 1966, 366; Haywood 1951, 4–5). Few objectives are well defined in wartime; the strategy set is seldom known in any detail or exhaustiveness; payoffs are vague and themselves contingent upon larger historical forces only approximately appreciated in retrospect. The marriage of the Bomb and game theory was thus a match made in heaven, since it was a kind of war without war, a rivalry without actual conflict.

Hence the first impact of the military on game theory was the construction of a very unusual interpretation of "conflict" and its reification in the mathematics. While strategists followed the lead of von Neumann and Morgenstern in designating the payoffs as being denominated in "utility," no one asked whether "conflict" was not already present in the utility functions themselves, in the sense that all interaction was already incorporated into the "values" of the various options. Indeed, just as the phenomenon of gaining pleasure from the act of betting undermines the neoclassical theory of risk, the possibility of gaining "utility" from harming the opponent and breaking the rules undermines the game-theoretic conception of self-seeking behavior. This indeterminacy when it comes to the meaning of conflict shows up in the subsequent history as a tergiversation over what precisely distinguishes a "cooperative" from a "noncooperative" game. It cannot be that platitudinous phrase "lack of communication," since—as we shall see below—it is communication which renders any notion of mechanical rationality nugatory. One sophisticated practitioner (Shubik 1982, 217) instead claims it is a kind of indifference to the desires of other players, but that just reveals the extent to which any real conflict escapes the game theorist.

The Minimax Solution

Secondly, the alliance with the military had the effect of reifying the minimax solution as purportedly the acme, the quintessence, the "fundamental theorem," or the ultimate solution concept in game theory (Dresher 1961, 79). Since, as I have already argued, there is no such thing as a flawless solution-concept, the effect of military support was to postpone the day when the minimax concept was downgraded to just one of many possible solution-concepts; and when that day finally came, alternative purported noncooperative solution-concepts such as the Nash equilibrium were generated *before* other "cooperative" concepts directly because of the military imperative. Hence the very concept of a solution to a game, really the hinge upon which all the mathematics pivots, was initially dictated within the mathematical community by the military connection.

The minimax was, of course, von Neumann's own chosen solution-concept, mainly because of its similarity to the mathematics he had already developed in the quantum mechanics context.[18] However, in the joint book with Morgenstern, it is interesting to see how the minimax is justified. Skillful play is implicitly defined as choosing a strategy which will ensure a value of the game greater than or equal to some constant (1964, 107); then in the two-person zero-sum context it is pointed out that the interests of the players are precisely opposed: what Adam wants to maximize, Eve wants to minimize (98). From there we are whisked to the proof that the existence of a saddlepoint means that both players' minimax strategies coincide; the argument is clinched with the assertion that "in a zero-sum two-person game the rationality [i.e., the minimax strategy] of the opponent can be assumed, because the irrationality of his opponent can never harm a player" (128).

Von Neumann and Morgenstern managed to preserve the minimax solution in an n-person framework by dividing the problem into two phases, the first being choice over the combinatorial possibilities of the formation of coalitions with their attached "values," and the second being the reduction of the game to the coalition's playing "everyone else" as in a two-person framework. But this did not disguise that their entire reasoning was predicated upon the zero-sum assumption: namely, that whatever the players did, they could not alter the global magnitude of the payoff by their actions. This was nothing other than the presumption of a conservation principle, and the justification of such principles is the central problem of the Western theory of economic value (Mirowski 1989a). However, von Neumann and Morgenstern were unable to endow the assumption with any economic legitimation, treating it merely as one convenient simplification which would be abandoned with the subsequent development of game theory. This stance created a problem, since the very rationality of the minimax solution depended upon it.

This is where the military connection became important. The strate-

18. That is not to say it did not also appeal to an aspect of his own personality. Ulam (1976, 232) described "Johnny's" obsequiousness around military types as follows: "I believe it was due more generally to his admiration for people who had power. . . . I think he had a hidden admiration for people or organizations that could be tough or ruthless. He appreciated or even envied those who at a meeting could act or present their views in a way to influence not only others' thoughts, but concrete decision-making. He himself was not a very strong or active debater in committee meetings, yielding to those who insisted more forcefully. On the whole he preferred to avoid controversy." Those who understand the minimax see it fits his yearnings to a tee.

gic community had no qualms about the two-person restriction, since they thought in Manichaean terms of Blue versus Red, capitalists versus communists, USA versus USSR. But they also had no difficulty with the zero-sum restriction. In deployment or dogfight models, they believed, winning or losing was a simple offsetting payoff structure: one observes this in the large class of Colonel Blotto games, or in fighter duels (Mensch 1966, 258; Dresher 1961, 68; Haywood 1951, 9). Moreover, the application of games to the face-off of atomic weapons only reinforced the two-person zero-sum mindset, including the all-important stipulation that the game could not be repeated (O'Neill 1989, 149; 1990, 22; Isaacs 1975, 6). Since it was only under these conditions that the minimax had a prayer of being considered some sort of expression of "rationality," the adoption of game theory by the strategic community had the consequence of making minimax look like an embodiment of generic or technocratic rationality long after it had ceased to be plausible as a solution-concept.

The critique of the minimax solution, when it finally came, assumed two formats: one, meliorist and nonthreatening to the fundamental structure of the strategic community, was mainly associated with Thomas Schelling's *Strategy of Conflict* (1960); the other, much more harsh and pyrrhic, came from Daniel Ellsberg (1956).[19] Schelling correctly pointed out that both the prescription of mixed or "randomized" strategies and the minimax solution exist to avoid any possibility of interpretation of the other player's moves or intentions or, indeed, any meeting of minds at all.

> In purely zero-sum problems, like search and evasion, there is an exclusive premium on secrecy and the denial of intelligence to the enemy; in non–zero-sum situations there is often a premium on revelation, on convincing a potential enemy of the truth, or providing credible information. In zero sum situations the enemy's confusion is our goal and his misunderstandings a bonus; in non–zero-sum situations our interest is often to avoid misunderstanding. (in Mensch 1966, 472)

The reason Schelling's critique was meliorist was that he invariably made it appear as if the mere extension of games to non–zero-sum

19. After wading through most of the early game theory literature I cannot resist registering my impression that the most consistently brilliant writings on game theory were by Ellsberg. Yet his articles never appear in the anthologies of game theory, and game theorists never mention his profound critique of the minimax solution. Although few were more deeply involved with strategic planning than he (Kaplan 1983, 277), I cannot help but suspect that the dramatic reversal in his career in the affair of the Pentagon Papers is foreshadowed in his unwillingness to accept the trite conventional wisdom prevalent in the strategic community of the 1950s.

situations would take care of this difficulty; but such an inference was patently false. Von Neumann and Morgenstern repeatedly insisted that theirs was an incorrigibly "static" theory precisely because the minimax solution loses all justification in repeated play (1964, 44, 147, 189n.); and the main reason why this is so is that repeated play opens up the possibility that one could benefit from paying attention to the past strategies of the opponent. Hence the bogey of *interpretation* would enter into the image of rationality in this case, just as it would in the non–zero-sum case; and both vitiate the whole minimax stance of treating the opponent as a black box. Once this Pandora's Box is opened, it will never be closed again: witness the subsequent degeneration of game theory into a myriad of incommensurate solution-concepts once the bogey was let loose in the mathematics. The strategic community could purvey a tough-minded scientific rationality only so long as they kept the box firmly shut—which is precisely what they did.

It was Ellsberg (1956) who went further, questioning the presumption that minimax embodied "rationality" in the narrow case of the two-person zero-sum game. His critique was prosecuted at three levels. In the first, he foreshadowed the entire critique of von Neumann–Morgenstern utility as ignoring such empirical regularities as the prevalence of framing and what was later called the "Ellsberg Paradox" (Thaler 1987; Gärdenfors and Sahlin 1988). In the second, he pointed out that a minimax player passes up the opportunity to take advantage of any nonminimax behavior in the opponent. "Their conception of 'harm' [of an 'irrational' opponent] seems to exclude any element of 'opportunity cost,' 'regret,' any notion of the pain incurred by passing up a real chance of great gains or in discovering, afterwards, that one could have done much better than he did (by risking slightly worse)" (Ellsberg 1956, 917). In other words, this whole issue of protection against being "found out" by the hostile opponent was a bit of a red herring, and a peculiarly paranoid position to take when the game is restricted to a single play. Finally, driving the last nail in the coffin of the minimax, Ellsberg then demonstrated that the minimax strategy was not stable under small perturbation of the opponent's minimax strategy in a repeated game; and since there was no legitimate dynamic solution-concept, the minimax strategy hardly ever represented a generic "rationality." He capped the argument with an exquisite rhetorical touch, asking "when did 'rational' become synonymous with 'defensive'?" And he characterized minimax as "the psychology of a timid man pressed into a duel" (922–23).[20]

With a deft touch Ellsberg called into question the whole alliance

20. See note 18 above on von Neumann's own personality.

between the military and the game-theory community; but it is my impression that in contrast to Schelling, he made hardly a dent in the demeanor of that community. Instead attention was focused on further attempts to leach the mathematics of all taint of issues of interpretation, creativity, and social factors. The primary instance of this bent is the famous Nash equilibrium, which attempted the reduction of all potential situations of negotiation to ones where negotiation was absent, or unnecessary (Rapoport 1964, 68, 73). As Nash himself admitted (1951, 286), his novel solution-concept was merely "a generalization of the concept of the solution of a two-person zero-sum game." Yet that was precisely what the military applications required, and not what the logic of the critique demanded.

Getting Rid of the Context

The third way that the military connection influenced the evolution of the mathematics is that it postponed (perhaps until 1990?) the realization that game theory is not a normative theory, in that it does not define rational play of even something so "simple" as chess (Rapoport 1964, 75). Had the mathematical tradition developed in the absence of pressures to preserve certain inadequate notions of solutions, and had the mathematics been taken up by a community with higher standards of self-criticism, I believe the outlandish claims of game theorists and their acolytes (Kreps 1990) would have been nipped in the bud long ago.

One can begin this counterfactual scenario with some meditation upon the very idea of a "payoff" (Wolff 1970). The neoclassical economists would have remained wedded to their notion of preferences as a conservative vector field until hell froze over (Mirowski 1989a); but no other mathematical community would have had such an intellectual investment in that concept as not to have realized that much of the mathematical structure of game theory was a direct consequence of the presumed shape of payoffs. Thomas Schelling saw vaguely that something like this was the case but characteristically did not carry the insight out to its disturbing conclusions: "the greatest contribution of game theory to social science in the end is simply the pay-off matrix itself that, like a truth table or a conservation principle or an equation, provides a way of organizing and structuring problems so that they can be analyzed fruitfully" (in Mensch 1966, 480).

The significance of this insight is that most of the structure of the math problem is freighted in under the cover of secondary or auxiliary assumptions about invariance, additivity, transferability, transitivity, and foreknowledge. What was a hallmark of the strategic community was the particularly cavalier way they approached these issues. In fighter duels opponents either won or lost, so why worry about the nature of the payoffs? The situation in strategic studies only got worse from there: should the payoffs of battles be kill-ratios? Or perhaps be the money cost of the resources gained and lost? Atomic weapons only exacerbated the gruesome farce: astronomical numbers of deaths were thrown about with no basis in any tangible knowledge. If anyone would object (as did the members of the Peace Studies group at the University of Michigan), one could always retreat to "utility," as if the economists had any better handle on the problem. The strategic community could not mount a serious rebuttal to the critique, since their primary role was to uphold the appearance of technical, calm, measured rationality in the face of bottomless nuclear horror.[21] Atomic wars had to be planned deductively, come hell or high water, because there were no historical precedents upon which to base an alternative hermeneutic account (O'Neill 1990, 31). Game theory fit these requirements, and therefore quibbles about the structure of the payoffs had to be regarded as mere auxiliary assumptions rather than the core of the argument.

This cavalier attitude about the mathematical structure of the payoffs extended to a similar attitude towards the format of the initial specification of the game. Von Neumann and Morgenstern had claimed early in their book (1964, 85) that the expression of a game in "extensive" form—i.e., specifying in detail the sequence of moves, the knowledge of each player at each stage, and so forth—was "strictly equivalent" to its specification in "normal" form—i.e., a list of the outcomes of all possible combinations of strategies. (Whenever mathematicians attempt to call something "normal," beware!) This was at best a half-truth, since it occurred in the part of their book devoted to static one-shot two-person zero-sum games. In any situation that diverges from that rather restricted class of games, who knows what, and when, is of the utmost importance in divining strategy, and of course immediately reintroduces the bogey of the importance of interpretation. It was the alliance of game theory with the military community, in conjunction with the disinterest in the mathematical structure of the payoffs, discussed above, that resulted in a general attitude that normal form was practically equivalent to extensive form in the theory of games.

Consequently the flawed claims that game theory represented some species of generic rationality were masked by the practice of always writing games in normal form for mathematical purposes. The bracing tonic of the extensive form is to have it brought home with alacrity how

21. The only skeptical evaluation of this desire for a technocratic rationality I have found among the military was the warning of Haywood (1951, 67): "There have been hopes that a mathematical theory employed in conjunction with a qualitative concept of worth will tend to eliminate bias and emotional influences from our decisions. These hopes appear largely unfounded."

small changes in interpretation will alter what is thought to be optimal. For instance, extensive form often raises the possibility that any given game might be regarded as only a part of a much larger or extended game: Did losing the battle of Pearl Harbor help America to win World War II? Did losing World War II help Japan to win the subsequent peace? And so on *ad infinitum*. A game only looks well-specified if one arbitrarily expresses its boundaries in such a way that the process seems to have little bearing upon the results.

The way the strategic community tended to use game theory did bother some people. In one instance particularly relevant for orthodox economics, it seems these practices of the strategic community helped Kenneth Arrow get his Nobel Prize.

> When we were at RAND together, Helmer remarked that there was something that bothered him about game theory or about its applications. We wanted to talk about the US, the USSR and Western Europe as players, but they are not like people, in what sense do they have utility functions? . . . "Oh!" I said, "that is nothing, Abram Bergson has written on that type of thing." "Oh," he said, "would you write an exposition of this?" Well, that was the thing that led to the social choice book. (Arrow in Feiwel 1987b, 193)

What is relevant to our present theme is that Arrow's impossibility theorem did not alter the way game theory was done at RAND. Nor did it puncture the pretense that it embodied some sort of generic rationality.

The Deconstruction of the Progenitors' Original Intent

The final impact of the military upon game theory was the way it tended to undermine the original project of von Neumann and Morgenstern, namely, that of formalizing the meaning of rationality in situations of social interdependence. One must admit that the seeds of the contradictions were already implicit in their volume: for instance (1964, 32), isn't it a travesty committed upon the word "rational" to insist that decisions be made by flipping a coin or some other randomizing device? But the military connection only exacerbated the difficulty. The military needed a "science" which could produce results in a mechanical fashion; perhaps all strategy might become mechanized, programmed into a bank of computers, guaranteeing the optimal battle. The last thing they wanted was a bunch of philosophers sitting around using formalisms to explore the various connotations of human rationality.[22] Yet it was that mechanistic nineteenth-century notion of rationality which Morgenstern, and to a lesser extent von Neumann, wished to escape.

---

22. This, in my humble opinion, is the only real use of game theory, insofar as it exists as a mathematical project.

The strategic community persistently misrepresented what game theory could ever hope to do. For example: "The significance of game theory as a decision tool is that it eliminates guessing an opponent's intentions . . . [it] indicates just how complicated the real world problem is—and from this we can infer that most intuitive decisions presently made are non-optimal" (Moglewer in Mensch 1966, 234). On the contrary, under the tutelage of RAND, guessing was degraded from art to cryptoscience, and optimality was leached of all rational content. Or take Schelling (in Mensch 1966, 476): "If game theory can discover the existence of prisoner-dilemma situations it is not a 'limitation' of the theory that it recognizes as 'rational' an inefficient pair of choices. It is a limitation of the situation." It seems an inversion of the project of von Neumann and Morgenstern to blame any dissonance in our images of rationality upon the (objective?) situation rather than the actions of the theorist in attempting to formalize the meaning of the "rational."

Norbert Wiener, a prominent mathematician, called this perversion by its rightful name, the Golem. He asserted, correctly, that the von Neumann–Morgenstern formalism did not describe how experts played chess; because of their limitations, they did not exhaustively scan the universe of strategies but rather used rules of thumb in conjunction with subtle cues gleaned from the opponent as to how they should play. Their "bounded rationality" was itself rational, however, because a perfect strategist à la von Neumann and Morgenstern would fall prey to all sorts of paradoxes of self-reflexivity in the hopeless quest for optimality (Wiener 1960, 1356). The irony of the situation was that Gödel's theorem was one of the events which prodded von Neumann out of his belief in the old-fashioned rationality; and yet it was Gödel's theorem which also was the strongest argument against the quest for a perfect solution in game theory (Binmore 1987–88).

The military, and hence the strategic community, would have none of this. Their image of game theory was one of the purest instrumentality, of the lab-coated expert "thinking about the unthinkable." In the end all that happened was that game theory was but a pawn in a larger game, that of the rivalry between the armed services to control the Bomb (Kaplan 1983), and the even larger game, that of superpower politics.

The author would like to thank Pam Cook for the translations from the German, Steve Heims, Roy Weintraub, and Silvan Schweber for their help, and Neil de Marchi and Craufurd Goodwin for facilitating examination of the Oskar Morgenstern papers.

References

Aumann, Robert. 1985. What Is Game Theory Trying to Accomplish? In *Frontiers of Economics,* edited by K. Arrow and S. Honkapohja. Oxford: Basil Blackwell.

Barnes, Barry, and David Edge, eds. 1982. *Science in Context*. Cambirdge: MIT Press.

Barthelme, Donald. 1969.*Unspeakable Practices, Unnatural Acts*. New York: Bantam.

Bellman, Richard. 1984. *Eye of the Hurricane*. Singapore: World Scientific.

Bianchi, Marina, and Hervé Moulin. Forthcoming. Strategic Interaction in Economics. In *Transitions in Research Programs,* edited by M. Blaug. London: Edward Elgar.

Binmore, Ken. 1987–88. Modeling Rational Players. [In two parts.] *Economics and Philosophy* 3:179–214, 4:9–55.

Bloor, David. 1973. Wittgenstein and Mannheim on the Sociology of Mathematics. *Studies in the History and Philosophy of Science* 4:173–91.

———. 1976. *Knowledge and Social Imagery*. London: Routledge & Kegan Paul.

———. 1978. Polyhedra and the Abominations of Leviticus. *British Journal for the History of Science* 11:245–72.

Brennan, D. 1965. Strategy and Conscience. *Bulletin of the Atomic Scientists* 21 (December): 25–30.

Brown, James Robert. 1989. *The Rational and the Social*. London: Routledge & Kegan Paul.

Craver, Earlene. 1986. The Emigration of the Austrian Economists. *HOPE* 18:1–32.

Cross, John. 1961. On Professor Schelling's Strategy of Conflict. *Naval Research Logistics Quarterly* 8:421–26.

Daston, Lorraine. 1988. *Classical Probability in the Enlightenment*. Princeton: Princeton University Press.

Dieudonné, Jean. 1976. Johann von Neumann. *Dictionary of Scientific Biography*. New York: Scribners.

Dresher, Melvin. 1950. Methods of Solution in Game Theory. *Econometrica* 18:179–81.

———. 1961. *Games of Strategy*. Englewood Cliffs, N.J.: Prentice-Hall.

Dresher, Melvin, et al. 1949. *Mathematical Theory of Zero-Sum Two-Person Games with a Finite Number or a Continuum of Strategies*. Santa Monica: RAND.

Duren, Peter, ed. 1988–89. *A Century of Mathematics in America*. Parts 1 and 3. Providence: American Mathematics Society.

Ellsberg, Daniel. 1956. The Theory of the Reluctant Duellist. *American Economic Review* 46: 909–23.

Feiwel, George, ed. 1987a. *Arrow and the Foundations of Economic Policy*. New York: New York University Press.

———. 1987b. *Arrow and the Ascent of Modern Economic Theory*. New York: New York University Press.

Fisher, Franklin. 1989. Games Economists Play: A Noncooperative View. *RAND Journal of Economics* 20:113–24.

Forman, Paul. 1987. Behind Quantum Electronics: National Security as a Basis for Physical Research in the U.S. *Historical Studies in the Physical Sciences* 18:149–229.

Frechet, Maurice. 1953. Emile Borel, Initiator of the Theory of Psychological Games. *Econometrica* 21:95–127.

Gani, J., ed. 1986. *The Craft of Probabilistic Modelling*. New York: Springer.

Gärdenfors, Peter, and Nils-Eric Sahlin. 1988. *Decision, Probability and Utility*. Cambridge: Cambridge University Press.

Grattan-Guiness, Ivor. 1984. Work for the Workers. *Annals of Science* 41:1–33.

Green, Philip. 1966. *Deadly Logic*. New York: Schocken.

Gul, Faruk. 1989. Rational Strategic Behavior and the Notion of Equilibrium. Paper presented at the meetings of the American Economic Association, Atlanta, December.

Hacking, Ian. 1975. *The Emergence of Probability*. New York: Cambridge University Press.

———. 1986. Weapons Research and the Form of Scientific Knowledge. In *Nuclear Weapons, Deterrence and Disarmament,* edited by D. Copp. Boulder, Col.: Westview.

Haywood, Oliver. 1951. *The Military Doctrine of Decision and the von Neumann Theory of Games*. Santa Monica: RAND RM-258.

Heims, Steve. 1980. *John von Neumann and Norbert Wiener*. Cambridge: MIT Press.

Hurwicz, Leonid. 1945. The Theory of Economic Behavior. *American Economic Review* 35:909–25.

Isaacs, Rufus. 1975. The Past and Some Bits of the Future. In *The Theory and Application of Differential Games,* edited by J. Grote. Boston: Reidel.

Kaplan, Fred. 1983. *The Wizards of Armageddon*. New York: Simon & Schuster.

Kaplansky, I. 1945. A Contribution to von Neumann's Theory of Games. *Annals of Mathematics* 46: 474–79.

Kaysen, Carl. 1947. A Revolution in Economic Theory? *Review of Economic Studies* 14:1–15.

Kevles, Daniel. 1978. *The Physicists*. New York: Knopf.

Kline, Morris. 1980. *Mathematics: The Loss of Certainty*. New York: Oxford University Press.

Koo, Anthony. 1959. Recurrent Objections to the Minimax Strategy. *Review of Economics and Statistics* 41:36–43.

Kreps, David. 1990. *A Course in Microeconomic Theory*. Princeton: Princeton University Press.

Leonard, Robert. 1990. Creating a Context for Game Theory. Available from the author, Economics Department, Duke University.

Leunbach, G. 1948. Theory of Games and Economic Behavior. *Nordisk Tidsskrift fur Teknisk Okonomi*.

McDonald, J. 1949. A Theory of Strategy. *Fortune* 39:100–110.

Machina, Mark. 1989. Dynamic Consistency and Non-Expected Utility Models of Choice. *Journal of Economic Literature* 27:1622–68.

MacKenzie, Donald. 1981. *Statistics in Britain: 1865–1930*. Edinburgh: Edinburgh University Press.

MacKenzie, Donald, and Graham Spinardi. 1988. The Shaping of Nuclear Weapon System Technology. *Social Studies of Science* 18:419–64, 581–624.

McKinsey, J. 1952. *Introduction to the Theory of Games*. New York: McGraw-Hill.

Marschak, Jacob. 1946. Von Neumann and Morgenstern's New Approach to Static Economics. *Journal of Political Economy* 54:97–115.

Mensch, A., ed. 1966. *Theory of Games*. New York: American Elsevier.

Mendelsohn, E., et al., eds. 1988. *Science, Technology and the Military*. Boston: Kluwer.

Mirowski, Philip. 1986a. Mathematical Formalism and Economic Explanation. In *The Reconstruction of Economic Theory,* edited by P. Mirowski. Boston: Kluwer.

————. 1986b. Institutions as Solution Concepts in a Game Theoretic Context. In *The Reconstruction of Economic Theory,* edited by P. Mirowski. Boston: Kluwer.

————. 1989a. *More Heat than Light.* New York: Cambridge University Press.

————. 1989b. The Measurement without Theory Controversy. *Economies et sociétés,* no. 11:65–87.

————. 1989c. The Probabilistic Counter-revolution. *Oxford Economic Papers* 41:217–35.

————. 1991. The How, the When and the Why of Mathematical Expression in Economics. *Journal of Economic Perspectives* 5:145–57.

————. In press. What Were von Neumann and Morgenstern Trying to Accomplish? *HOPE,* Special Issue, 24.

Morgenstern, Oskar. 1949. Economics and the Theory of Games. *Kyklos* 3:294–308.

————. 1976. Collaborating with von Neumann. *Journal of Economic Literature* 14:805–16.

————, ed. 1954. *Economic Activity Analysis.* New York: Wiley.

Nagle, E., and J. Newman. 1958. *Gödel's Proof.* New York: New York University Press.

Nanus, Burton. 1959. Evolution of the Office of Naval Research. M.Sc. thesis, MIT School of Industrial Management.

Nash, John. 1951. Non-Cooperative Games. *Annals of Mathematics* 54:286–95.

————. 1953. Two-Person Cooperative Games. *Econometrica* 21:128.

Neisser, Hans. 1952. The Strategy of Expecting the Worst. *Social Research* 19:346–363.

Noble, David. 1985. Command Performance. In *Military Enterprise and Technical Change,* edited by Merritt Roe Smith. Cambridge: MIT Press.

O'Neill, Barry. 1989. Game Theory and the Study of Deterrence of War. In *Perspectives in Deterrence,* edited by Paul Stern et al. New York: Oxford University Press.

————. 1990. A Survey of Game Theoretic Models of Peace and War. In *Handbook of Game Theory,* edited by R. Aumann. Amsterdam: North Holland.

Pascal, Blaise. 1962. *Pensées.* Paris: Seuil.

Pfeiffer, John. 1949. The Office of Naval Research. *Scientific American* 180:11–15.

Porter, Theodore. 1986. *The Rise of Statistical Thinking 1820–1900.* Princeton: Princeton University Press.

Princeton University Logistics Research Project. 1953. Report of an Informal Conference on the Theory of N-Person Games. Mimeo.

Rapoport, Anatol. 1964. *Strategy and Conscience.* New York: Schocken.

————. 1970. *N-Person Game Theory.* Ann Arbor: University of Michigan Press.

Richards, Joan. 1988. *Mathematical Visions.* New York: Academic Press.

Rhodes, Richard. 1986. *The Making of the Atomic Bomb.* New York: Simon & Schuster.

Rowe, David, and John McCleary, eds. 1989. *The History of Modern Mathematics.* Vol. 2. New York: Academic Press.

Samuelson, Paul. 1986. *Collected Papers.* Vol. 5. Cambridge: MIT Press.

Schelling, Thomas. 1960. *The Strategy of Conflict.* Oxford: Oxford University Press.

Schweber, Silvan. 1988. The Mutual Embrace of Science and the Military. In Mendelsohn et al. 1988, 1–45.

Shubik, Martin. 1981. Perfect or Robust Noncooperative Equilibrium: The Search for the Philosopher's Stone? In *Essays in Game Theory*. Mannheim: BI.

———. 1982. *Game Theory in the Social Sciences*. Cambridge: MIT Press.

Simon, Herbert. 1982. *Models of Bounded Rationality*. Cambridge: MIT Press.

Steinhaus, H. [1925] 1960. Definitions for a Theory of Games and Pursuit. Translated by E. Rzymovski. *Naval Research Logistics Quarterly* 7:105–8.

Stone, Richard. 1948. The Theory of Games. *Economic Journal* 58:185–201.

Thaler, Richard. 1987. The Psychology of Choice and the Assumptions of Economics. In *Laboratory Experimentation in Economics,* edited by Alvin Roth. New York: Cambridge University Press.

Tiles, Mary. 1984. *Bachelard: Science and Objectivity*. Cambridge: Cambridge University Press.

Tucker, A., and R. Luce. 1959. *Contributions to the Theory of Games*. Vol. 4. Princeton: Princeton University Press.

Tymoczko, Thomas, ed. 1986. *New Directions in the Philosophy of Mathematics*. Boston: Birkhauser.

Ulam, Stanislaw. 1976. *Adventures of a Mathematician*. New York: Scribners.

van Damme, Eric. 1987. *Stability and Perfection of Nash Equilibria*. Berlin: Springer.

von Neumann, John. 1958. *The Computer and the Brain*. New Haven: Yale University Press.

———. 1963. *Collected Works*. 7 vols. Oxford: Pergamon Press.

von Neumann, John, and Oskar Morgenstern. [1944] 1964. *Theory of Games and Economic Behavior*. 3d ed. New York: Wiley.

Wald, Abraham. 1945. Generalization of a Theorem by von Neumann Concerning Zero-Sum Two-Person Games. *Annals of Mathematics* 46:265–80.

———. 1947. *Sequential Analysis*. New York: Wiley.

Wiener, Norbert. 1960. Some Moral and Technological Consequences of Automation. *Science* 131 (6 May):1355–58.

Wilder, Raymond. 1981. *The Cultural Basis of Mathematics*. Oxford: Pergamon Press.

Wittgenstein, Ludwig. 1978. *Remarks on the Foundations of Mathematics*. Cambridge: MIT Press.

Wolff, Robert Paul. 1970. Maximization of Expected Utility as a Criterion of Rationality in Military Strategy and Foreign Policy. *Social Theory and Practice* 1:99–111.

Game

Donald Barthelme

Shotwell keeps the jacks and the rubber ball in his attaché case and will not allow me to play with them. He plays with them, alone, sitting on the floor near the console hour after hour, chanting "onesies, twosies, threesies, foursies" in a precise, well-modulated voice, not so loud as to be annoying, not so soft as to allow me to forget. I point out to Shotwell that two can derive more enjoyment from playing jacks than one, but he is not interested. I have asked repeatedly to be allowed to play by myself, but he simply shakes his head. "Why?" I ask. "They're mine," he says. And when he has finished, when he has sated himself, back they go into the attaché case.

It is unfair but there is nothing I can do about it. I am aching to get my hands on them.

Shotwell and I watch the console. Shotwell and I live under the ground and watch the console. If certain events take place upon the console, we are to insert our keys in the appropriate locks and turn our keys. Shotwell has a key and I have a key. If we turn our keys simultaneously the bird flies, certain switches are activated and the bird flies. But the bird never flies. In one hundred thirty-three days the bird has not flown. Meanwhile Shotwell and I watch each other. We each wear a .45 and if Shotwell behaves strangely I am supposed to shoot him. If I behave strangely Shotwell is supposed to shoot me. We watch the console and think about shooting each other and think about the bird. Shotwell's behavior with the jacks is strange. Is it strange? I do not know. Perhaps he is merely a selfish bastard, perhaps his character is flawed, perhaps his childhood was twisted. I do not know.

Each of us wears a .45 and each of us is supposed to shoot the other if the other is behaving strangely. How strangely is strangely? I do not know. In addition to the .45 I have a .38 which Shotwell does not know about concealed in my attaché case, and Shotwell has a .25 calibre

Reprinted by permission from *Unspeakable Practices, Unnatural Acts* (New York: Bantam Books, 1969).

257

Beretta which I do not know about strapped to his right calf. Sometimes instead of watching the console I pointedly watch Shotwell's .45, but this is simply a ruse, simply a maneuver, in reality I am watching his hand when it dangles in the vicinity of his right calf. If he decides I am behaving strangely he will shoot me not with the .45 but with the Beretta. Similarly Shotwell pretends to watch my .45 but he is really watching my hand resting idly atop my attaché case, my hand resting idly atop my attaché case, my hand. My hand resting idly atop my attaché case.

In the beginning I took care to behave normally. So did Shotwell. Our behavior was painfully normal. Norms of politeness, consideration, speech, and personal habits were scrupulously observed. But then it became apparent that an error had been made, that our relief was not going to arrive. Owing to an oversight. Owing to an oversight we have been here for one hundred thirty-three days. When it became clear that an error had been made, that we were not to be relieved, the norms were relaxed. Definitions of normality were redrawn in the agreement of January 1, called by us, The Agreement. Uniform regulations were relaxed, and mealtimes are no longer rigorously scheduled. We eat when we are hungry and sleep when we are tired. Considerations of rank and precedence were temporarily put aside, a handsome concession on the part of Shotwell, who is a captain, whereas I am only a first lieutenant. One of us watches the console at all times rather than two of us watching the console at all times, except when we are both on our feet. One of us watches the console at all times and if the bird flies then that one wakes the other and we turn our keys in the locks simultaneously and the bird flies. Our system involves a delay of perhaps twelve seconds but I do not care because I am not well, and Shotwell does not care because he is not himself. After the agreement was signed Shotwell produced the jacks and the rubber ball from his attaché case, and I began to write a series of descriptions of forms occurring in nature, such as a shell, a leaf, a stone, an animal. On the walls.

Shotwell plays jacks and I write descriptions of natural forms on the walls.

Shotwell is enrolled in a USAFI course which leads to a master's degree in business administration from the University of Wisconsin (although we are not in Wisconsin, we are in Utah, Montana or Idaho). When we went down it was in either Utah, Montana or Idaho, I don't remember. We have been here for one hundred thirty-three days owing to an oversight. The pale green reinforced concrete walls sweat and the air conditioning zips on and off erratically and Shotwell reads *Introduction to Marketing* by Lassiter and Munk, making notes with a blue ballpoint pen. Shotwell is not himself but I do not know it, he presents a calm aspect and reads *Introduction to Marketing* and makes his exemplary notes with a blue ballpoint pen, meanwhile controlling the .38 in my attaché case with one-third of his attention. I am not well.

We have been here one hundred thirty-three days owing to an oversight. Although now we are not sure what is oversight, what is plan. Perhaps the plan is for us to stay here permanently, or if not permanently at least for a year, for three hundred sixty-five days. Or if not for a year for some number of days known to them and not known to us, such as two hundred days. Or perhaps they are observing our behavior in some way, sensors of some kind, perhaps our behavior determines the number of days. It may be that they are pleased with us, with our behavior, not in every detail but in sum. Perhaps the whole thing is very successful, perhaps the whole thing is an experiment and the experiment is very successful. I do not know. But I suspect that the only way they can persuade sun-loving creatures into their pale green sweating reinforced concrete rooms under the ground is to say that the system is twelve hours on, twelve hours off. And then lock us below for some number of days known to them and not known to us. We eat well although the frozen enchiladas are damp when defrosted and the frozen devil's food cake is sour and untasty. We sleep uneasily and acrimoniously. I hear Shotwell shouting in his sleep, objecting, denouncing, cursing sometimes, weeping sometimes, in his sleep. When Shotwell sleeps I try to pick the lock on his attaché case, so as to get at the jacks. Thus far I have been unsuccessful. Nor has Shotwell been successful in picking the locks on my attaché case so as to get at the .38. I have seen the marks on the shiny surface. I laughed, in the latrine, pale green walls sweating and the air conditioning whispering, in the latrine.

I write descriptions of natural forms on the walls, scratching them on the tile surface with a diamond. The diamond is a two and one-half carat solitaire I had in my attaché case when we went down. It was for Lucy. The south wall of the room containing the console is already covered. I have described a shell, a leaf, a stone, animals, a baseball bat. I am aware that the baseball bat is not a natural form. Yet I described it. "The baseball bat," I said, "is typically made of wood. It is typically one meter in length or a little longer, fat at one end, tapering to afford a comfortable grip at the other. The end with the handhold typically offers a slight rim, or lip, at the nether extremity, to prevent slippage." My description of the baseball bat ran to 4500 words, all scratched with a diamond on the south wall. Does Shotwell read what I have written? I do not know. I am aware that Shotwell regards my writing-behavior as a little strange. Yet it is no stranger than his jacks-behavior, or the day he appeared in black bathing trunks with the .25 calibre Beretta strapped to his right calf and stood over the console, trying to span with his two arms outstretched the distance between the locks. He could not do it, I had already tried, standing over the console with my two arms outstretched, the distance is too great. I was moved to comment but did not comment, comment would have provoked countercomment, comment would have led God knows where. They had in their infinite patience, in their infinite foresight, in their infinite wisdom already imagined a man standing over the console with his two arms outstretched, trying to span with his two arms outstretched the distance between the locks.

Shotwell is not himself. He has made certain overtures. The burden of his message is not clear. It has something to do with the keys, with the locks. Shotwell is a strange person. He appears to be less affected by our situation than I. He goes about his business stolidly, watching the console, studying *Introduction to Marketing,* bouncing his rubber ball on the floor in a steady, rhythmical, conscientious manner. He appears to be less affected by our situation than I am. He is stolid. He says nothing. But he has made certain overtures, certain overtures have been made. I am not sure that I understand them. They have something to do with the keys, with the locks. Shotwell has something in mind. Stolidly he shucks the shiny silver paper from the frozen enchiladas, stolidly he stuffs them into the electric oven. But he has something in mind. But there must be a quid pro quo. I insist on a quid pro quo. I have something in mind.

I am not well. I do not know our target. They do not tell us for which city the bird is targeted. I do not know. That is planning. That is not my responsibility. My responsibility is to watch the console and when certain events take place upon the console, turn my key in the lock. Shotwell bounces the rubber ball on the floor in a steady, stolid, rhythmical manner. I am aching to get my hands on the ball, on the jacks. We have been here one hundred thirty-three days owing to an oversight. I write on the walls. Shotwell chants "onesies, twosies, threesies, foursies" in a precise, well-modulated voice. Now he cups the jacks and the rubber ball in his hands and rattles them suggestively. I do not know for which city the bird is targeted. Shotwell is not himself.

Sometimes I cannot sleep. Sometimes Shotwell cannot sleep. Sometimes when Shotwell cradles me in his arms and rocks me to sleep, singing Brahms' "Guten abend, gut Nacht," or I cradle Shotwell in my arms and rock him to sleep, singing, I understand what it is Shotwell wishes me to do. At such moments we are very close. But only if he will give me the jacks. That is fair. There is something he wants me to do with my key, while he does something with his key. But only if he will give me my turn. That is fair. I am not well.

War as a "Simple Economic Problem": The Rise of an Economics of Defense

Robert J. Leonard

This paper has a dual purpose. The first concern stems from the larger question which forms a catalyst for the present volume: why has the economics of defense not become as developed an academic subdiscipline as, say, health or education economics? After all, a curious disparity exists between the amount of public resources devoted to defense expenditure and the degree to which academic economists have devoted intellectual energy to understanding the phenomenon. The second concern is to offer a reconstruction of the institutional development of an applied economics of defense, beginning in World War II and culminating in the Pentagon reforms, of the 1960s, under Secretary of Defense Robert McNamara. Section 1 examines the early application of economics to conflict in the wartime research groups operating in the United States and England. The RAND Corporation, which was formed in 1946, is presented as a continuation of this line of work. Section 2 shows how economic thinking played an important role in RAND's subsequent evolution and eventually stimulated the budgetary reform known as the McNamara Revolution. Section 3 reflects on this reconstruction in an attempt to understand the paucity of academic concern.

1. *A Foot in the Door: World War II and the Establishment of RAND*

Scientists against Time

J. P. Baxter's (1946) account of the involvement of American scientists in World War II through the Office for Scientific Research and Development (OSRD) is long on the impact of physicists and chemists, and the importance of such places as the Radiation Laboratory at MIT, but quite neglectful of the wartime role of social science in general, and economics in particular. Indeed, reading his reconstruction, one might believe that the war was essentially won on the basis of physical ideas, the innovations of physicists and chemists, with the concepts of economic efficiency and marginal cost and benefit having no place in the heat of conflict.

261

Such a conclusion would be wrong. Economists, like virtually every other academic group, found themselves plunged into the national war mobilization, and though their output was less tangible than the physical hardware produced by scientists, they achieved a measure of success, reputation, and authority which was ultimately to propel them further in the strategic realm than anybody in 1940 would have dreamed possible. Their application of the economic paradigm to the relatively "small," localized problems of strategic bombing or aircraft armory created a voice for economists in the consideration of conflict, a voice which grew increasingly loud in the postwar period, by the 1960s booming resoundingly across the stage of national strategic design. The winning of access to this stage is our concern here. An understanding of it can be gained only by examining the place of economic ideas in World War II.[1]

The Birth of Operational Research

That the framework which allowed economics to influence strategy in the United States for at least two decades after World War II had its genesis in Britain, not America, may strike some as curious. However, the main impetus for the evolution of what was eventually to become systems analysis grew from the role in military advice given to scientists in England, beginning roughly in the 1930s (see Stockfisch 1987; Harrod 1959; Macdougall 1951; Great Britain 1963). In 1934 an ad hoc committee, chaired by H. T. Tizard, was set up by the British Air Ministry to investigate "how far recent advances in scientific and technical knowledge can be used to strengthen the present methods against hostile aircraft" (Stockfisch 1987, 5). From this came the development of radar by Robert Watson-Watt, and there followed a series of experiments designed to discover how the device could best be employed. The effort to make radar operational involved the close cooperation of scientists and the military: the former became privy to RAF knowledge and operations. This kind of interaction with civilian scientists quickly became common in many units in the RAF, the Admiralty, and the Army. By 1940 scientists were addressing problems of aircraft acquisition, antiaircraft gun location, and radar sighting. By 1942 the Admiralty had its own Department of Operational Research, headed by Dr. P. M. S. Blackett, and throughout 1942 and 1943 such expertise was extended to aiding Army forces in the Middle East, Italy, and India on land warfare.

---

1. Certainly economists were crucial to *financing* the war in the Treasury Department, Office of Price Administration, and War Production Board, but others, particularly in the Office of Strategic Services (OSS) and Statistical Research Groups (SRG) of Columbia and Princeton, were more concerned with *fighting* it (see Katz 1989; Leonard 1990). Here economics and economists proved vital to strategic planning and gained an influence which was to ensure a place for them in related research when the war was over.

The nexus described above seems to be a technological one, but in fact it permitted the influence of the neoclassical economic framework in framing and answering certain related questions. The best British example was that of the Statistics Branch (S-Branch), which from late 1939 supported the Oxford physicist F. A. Lindemann (later Lord Cherwell) in his role as scientific advisor to Churchill. Although ostensibly appointed for his scientific acumen, Lindemann in effect spent almost two-thirds of his time addressing what can best be characterized as economic questions (see (Macdougall 1951; Harrod 1959). For this purpose he surrounded himself with a group of university economists, including Roy Harrod, G. L. S. Shackle, and Donald Macdougall. They collected and analyzed extensive statistics on the wartime economy, predicting shortages and designing rationing schemes, and offered economic arguments to guide the transfer of national resources from civilian to military use, essentially acting as watchdog against the excessive "requirements" of the latter. Both Churchill and Lindemann, it seems, were particularly concerned with sustaining civilian morale and with having solid statistical arguments to back them up in mediating between the claims of various departments: "There was a classic occasion on which the Prof. [Lindemann] got the requirement for anti-aircraft shells defeated . . . by calculating how many thousands of shells would, according to this requirement, be needed to bring down each separate enemy bomber and showing that the resources required for their production would be many times as great as the damage that the enemy bombers could, on the most pessimistic assumption, inflict" (Harrod 1959, 200).

The general success of operational research in the branches of the British forces stimulated a strong interest on the part of the U.S. forces in Britain. By late 1942 General "Hap" Arnold, commander of the Army Air Forces, recommended that each air command have an operations research capability. Stockfisch (1987) suggests that "oneupmanship" played a role here: it was intolerable to the Americans that they should have to face their British counterparts without having their own scientists in tow. Regardless of the reason, the strengthened position of science in military operations paved the way for the involvement of American economists in Britain, and a core of them was soon installed in London. To understand how they got there, however, we must retrace our steps somewhat and examine what was happening in economic circles in the United States.

Economics and the OSS

In mid-1941, arguing that the gaps in American intelligence-gathering were leaving the United States dangerously ignorant on the eve of war, the swashbuckling "Wild Bill" Donovan had himself appointed Coordinator of Information by President Roosevelt (see Katz 1989). Donovan lost no time in constructing his own little empire, and within a year the COI had become the Office of Strategic Services, forerunner of today's CIA, with a staff of more than two thousand. In addition to Secret Intelligence and Special Operations sections, the OSS had a Research and Analysis Branch (R&A) to "transform raw intelligence data into concise, factual and rigorously objective analyses for the use of government agencies" (Katz 1989, 14).

A Board of Analysts administered R&A, recruited through the old-boy network by director J. P. Baxter (who was soon replaced by William Langer in 1942). This "college of cardinals" included, among others, the economists Ed Mason (Harvard) and Calvin Hoover (Duke).[2] These, in turn, used their university contacts to recruit economists, historians, sociologists, and anthropologists, who were distributed among Economic, Psychological (Political), and Geographical groups under the R&A umbrella. The organizers of this intelligence-gathering machine overlooked ideological differences they may have had with able young scholars, and room was readily found for Marxists Paul Sweezy and Paul Baran, and virtually all the critical-theory scholars of the exiled Frankfurt School, then at Columbia, including Max Horkheimer, Herbert Marcuse, and Franz Neumann. Among the fifty or so economists, headed by Mason, were Emile Despres, Charles Kindleberger, and Chandler Morse (all from the Federal Reserve), Moses Abramowitz, Sidney Alexander, Carl Kaysen, and Abram Bergson. In addition to the central office in Washington, D.C., R&A had outposts in London, Stockholm, Moscow, Honolulu, Algiers, Cairo, Istanbul, New Delhi, and Chungking. These all gathered, analyzed and interpreted data "in the field," passing it back to Washington or on to the Allies in Europe. As we shall see, the London outpost was later to become singularly important for the activity of economists.

With the invasion of Russia by Hitler in late June 1941, the Economics Division in Washington launched an analysis of the German economic and military position. Why had the Germans been forced to a halt five hundred miles inside the Soviet Union? And, given the freezing weather, what were the requirements for a continued offensive, and how did the rail system constrain the passage of physical supplies? The questions were posed and answered in a manner amenable to the tools of simple economic analysis. The emphasis was placed on potentially quantifiable entities, those which could be described by expected values

2. The complete board comprised Mason, Hoover, D. McKay (French history, Harvard), Ed Earle (military history, Institute for Advanced Study), and J. Hayden (political science, Michigan).

if not certain quantities. Furthermore, the staff showed a painstaking application to the gathering of detailed data, a feature which characterized most of the wartime work in this vein and, indeed, a decade later, the work of their counterparts at RAND. Chandler Morse sent out economists to collect information on issues related to the German position: technical information from railway officials on the efficiency of locomotives at subzero temperatures; daily forage requirements of horses used by the German infantry; volume and weight of dehydrated troop rations; ammunition expended at different levels of combat intensity; meteorological records to forecast weather conditions. Nor were correlations on a priori grounds always used in statistical forecasts: estimating German aircraft losses, for example (see Katz 1989, 109), was done using a spurious correlation between this and the mean of Russian admissions of Soviet losses and German claims of Russian losses! This labored attention to detail was to prove essential to the economics fraternity in their gaining authority in military circles and was also a source of empiricist pride in relation to their historicist and humanist colleagues. Interdisciplinary tension was a feature of life at R&A. As Kindleberger recalls,

> There was a methodological struggle between historians and economists. When it came to estimating Russian wheat production, for example, Russian historians claimed that the economists could hardly make a contribution if they did not know how to read Russian, which would give them access to crop reports and the like. The economists, on the other hand, claimed that with data on acreage, historical yields and weather they were in a better position statistically to estimate output and the wisps of evidence from the daily press were diversionary rather than helpful. (1980, 238)

This intolerance and at times belligerence towards the "blindness" of other disciplines was to become a recurring theme for the next twenty years in the involvement of economists in military affairs. As shown below, economists remained loath to cooperate significantly with others, such as historians or political scientists, and only those who adopted the tools of economic analysis commanded their professional respect.

Especially valuable in the work done abroad was the serial number analysis undertaken by a group headed by Sidney Alexander. Traipsing around the Tunisian desert, Alexander gathered serial numbers from captured and damaged enemy equipment and used them to reconstruct the sources and patterns of German tank production. Such information was particularly useful to R&A's London outpost, which in early 1943 began to assume particular importance. As mentioned above, the U.S. Army Air Corps had begun to make operational research a feature of its planning by late 1942. Now, several months later, there was rivalry on air strategy against Germany between the RAF Bomber Command and the U.S. Army Air Corps. The former, after the Battle of Britain, favored area-bombardment of Germany, in the belief that a larger number of civilian deaths would sap German morale. The latter, on the other hand, favored precision bombing of selected economic targets in order to reduce German ability to sustain the war. Accordingly, in the fall of 1942, Colonel R. Hughes, senior target planning officer for the U.S. Air Force, persuaded John Winant, U.S. ambassador to England, to bring in economists to guide on target selection. A group of the Washington R&A economists were transferred to the Enemy Objectives Unit (EOU) in the Economic Warfare Division at the U.S. embassy in London. The earliest arrivals, in late 1942, were Morse, Walt Rostow, and William Salant. Soon they were joined by Kindleberger, Kaysen, R. Rosa, and H. Barnett. Also present was Charles Hitch, who had been there in 1941–42 as staff economist at the Mission for Economic Affairs, had spent the previous year at the War Production Board in Washington, and was now returning with the OSS. Hitch had been at Oxford since 1934 and was particularly well placed to ease the path of a new group of Americans operating in England.

EOU had initial difficulties in gaining the ear of American Air Force people, who had until then relied on intelligence provided by the British Air Ministry. A difference of opinion, however, between EOU and its British counterpart, in which the former were proved correct, soon resolved this problem. Using aerial photographic interpretation, prisoner-of-war interrogations, and Polish intelligence, EOU concluded that the Folke Wolf plant had been moved from Bremen to Marienberg, Poland. The Air Ministry disagreed but were soon proved wrong. "From that time on, the Air Force was willing to listen to its most unmilitary economists" (Kindleberger 1980, 238). The growing importance of target selection, and hence of EOU, became clear when Alexander's serial number analysis revealed that German tank engine manufacturing was confined to two companies and that gearboxes were being made in only two plants (Katz 1989, 111).

In response to Colonel Hughes's request for aid in target selection, EOU in late 1942 and early 1943 completed a series of Aiming Point Reports containing microscopic detail on location, function, and layout of various industrial facilities. These impressed the Air Force, and there followed a further series of Target Potentiality Reports which showed how to maximize damage to the German war machine for a given effort in air attack. Kindleberger (1980) recalls how this was little other than the intuitive application of input-output analysis and capital theory. The former showed how removing one row of inputs, such as oil, would bring the economy to a halt; the latter suggested that account also be taken of the possibility that labor could be substituted for damaged capital. They reasoned in terms of "depth," the lag between production and its use on the German fighting front, and "cushion," those inventories and alternative supplies which could be substituted to sustain supplies to the front. This sort of analysis had a concreteness and immediacy which gained the attention of the Joint Chiefs of Staff and enhanced the authority of economists relative to their humanist colleagues.

The extent to which the bombing strategy advocated by EOU was effective in the defeat of Germany is a controversial issue on which the books have still not been closed. Their main opponent in this debate on appropriate strategy was Britain's Lord Solly Zuckerman, scientific adviser to the joint Allied Expeditionary Air Forces. With regard to securing the beachheads for the Normandy landings in mid-1944, Operation Overlord, Zuckerman favored bombing the French railway "marshalling yards" on the grounds that this would render the railroad system dysfunctional and useless for transporting German soldiers and supplies to the Atlantic front. Eight months previously Zuckerman had examined the preinvasion bomb damage in Italy between Sicily and Naples, where railroad marshalling-yard damage had been extensive. As a consequence he had developed great faith in the importance of railyards as bomb targets. EOU, on the other hand, favored a strategy of railway and road *bridge* interdiction to restrict German supply lines, on the a priori grounds that marshalling yards could be repaired within hours and that, furthermore, rail traffic had a civilian "cushion" of up to 85 percent. As might well be expected from a conflict of enormous scale, the historical evidence yielded by the leadup to the Normandy landings remains sufficiently unclear to vindicate either group: both line interdiction *and* yard bombing occurred, and differences as to their relative importance remain unresolved.[3] Similarly, in the strategic bombing of Germany itself, Zuckerman stuck to his marshalling-yards targets while EOU favored fighter aircraft and ballbearing plants, and synthetic oil facilities. To the latter's chagrin, Zuckerman's policy was officially adopted at first, but again the evidence yielded by war was less then clear: aircraft manufacturing plant was in fact bombed. The postwar Strategic Bombing Survey shows this to have had a limited effect on German fighter production; but, Kindleberger claims (1978, 40), it directed German pilots away from resisting the Allied landings on D-Day. Also, oil targets were officially adopted as the bombing proceeded, thus legitimating at least some of EOU's advice.

3. For the details of this debate on strategy, which continued long after the war ended, see Zuckerman 1978, Rostow 1981, and Kindleberger 1978, 1980.

While the contribution of R&A in Washington and London may never be assessed in a manner satisfactory to both sides of the debate, economists emerged with a confidence in the applicability of the economic paradigm to conflict. For some of them, war, like inflation, unemployment, or economic growth, was now just another difficulty to which the tools of economic analysis could be fruitfully applied: "War is a relatively simple economic problem. The objective function has only one argument—winning . . . and one constraint, to keep the domestic civilian economy moving" (Kindleberger 1980, 239).

The Statistical Research Group

If the R&A branch of the OSS facilitated the direct influence of economic reasoning on war strategy, the Statistical Research Groups of Columbia and Princeton also contributed to the creation of an authoritative voice for economists, though in a less direct manner. Administered by the National Defense Research Committee (NDRC), the Applied Mathematics Panel (AMP) coordinated the bulk of mathematical and statistical research directed towards the development and deployment of weapons (see Wallis 1980; Leonard 1990). AMP was run by Warren Weaver, director of natural sciences at the Rockefeller Foundation, assisted by Mina Rees of the Hunter College Mathematics department.

Much of the research in probability and statistics with weapons application was done by the Statistical Research Group at Columbia (SRG-C), run by Allen Wallis with Harold Hotelling as principal investigator, both of whom were economists as well as statisticians. As neighbors in their building on West 118th Street, New York, they had the Strategic Bombing Section of the Princeton SRG, run by John D. Williams, applying statistical methods to similar issues as EOU in London. The two groups interacted closely, focusing in particular on aerial conflict. Using the geometry and tactics of aerial combat, and the probability of hitting, they suggested the optimal placement of machine guns on fighter aircraft. Similar studies were made of antiaircraft weapons and aircraft turret sights. As with EOU, photographic interpretation played a role; for example, photographs of Japanese ships yielded information on their maneuverability which helped in the design of optimal lead angle of aircraft torpedo salvos.

The gathering assembled by Wallis and Hotelling was as mathematically capable a group as one could have desired. It included A. Wald, M. Friedman, G. Stigler, R. Bennett, M. Hastay, J. Wolfowitz, J. Savage, A. Girschick, and F. Mosteller. While their work was primarily in mathematical statistics, it was by no means insignificant for postwar developments that "7 of the 18 principals were primarily or secondarily economists." First, they influenced the subsequent work in game theory and decision theory, "both of which are essentially economic theories" (Wallis 1980, 329). Second, they sufficiently impressed their leaders—Weaver, Wallis, and Williams—that the latter actively sought the inclusion of economists in related postwar research. The institution that was ultimately destined to draw together the strands which linked economics and conflict would appear neither in London nor in Washington, but on a beach overlooking, somewhat ironically, the Pacific.

The Emergence of RAND

As the war drew to a close, it became clear that much of the civilian scientific advice which had proved decisive in securing military victory would disappear as scientists and engineers returned to academe. Nobody was more keen to retain a coterie of scientific advisors than General "Hap" Arnold, head of the Air Force. Science had served the military well during the war. SCR-584 radar, the M-9 director, and the proximity fuse, all developed under NDRC, had been crucial in turning the odds against the Germans after June 1944 (Baxter 1946, 36). Above all, the work of the Manhattan Project, with the bombing of Hiroshima and Nagasaki, had ended the war. Ambitious in his plans for the Air Force, Arnold saw the harnessing of scientific progress as a path by which he might secure superiority among the military branches.

Discussions in the latter half of 1945, between Arnold, some engineers from Douglas Aircraft Company, and various advisors who had been attached to the War Department, led to Arnold's committing $10 million of wartime funds to research.[4] Project RAND (Research and Development) was attached to the Douglas firm in Santa Monica and comprised a group of physicists, engineers, and mathematicians engaged in a "program of study and research on the broad subject of Aerospace Power with the object of recommending to the United States Air Force preferred methods, techniques, and instrumentalities for the development and employment of Aerospace Power" (Goldstein 1961, 3).[5] The project was given a remarkable degree of freedom, with the power to accept or reject Air Force suggestions, strong financial support without pressure for tangible results, and scope to pose questions and analyze problems as the staff saw fit. This was a reflection of the

---

4. The engineers in question were A. Raymond, chief engineer at Douglas, and his aide F. Collbohm. Both had advised Arnold in a particularly successful project on the B-29 bomber during the war. Smith (1966) claims that the RAND idea essentially came from the Douglas people, who were keen because wartime projects were being liquidated and staff reductions were likely. The key meeting took place 1 October 1945, at Hamilton Field outside San Francisco, attended by Arnold, Raymond, Collbohm, D. Douglas (senior), E. Bowles, and F. W. Conant.

5. Early suggestions during RAND's formative stage, of integrating the project with the work of the Army and Navy were quickly rejected (see Smith 1966).

confidence on Arnold's part in the value of scientific research directed towards conflict. To smooth RAND's path in its dealings with a less flexible Air Force materiel and procurement bureaucracy, Arnold installed Curtis LeMay as a liaison officer mediating between the two.[6]

The early characteristics of RAND—in particular its "self-conception" as revealed through its policy statement and the prevalence of physical-science and mathematics types on its staff—show little evidence of the impact that social science, and economics in particular, was to have on the institution. By the time it officially started, in May 1946, Project RAND had four employees in a walled off section at Douglas working on two projects with a distinctively "hardware" connotation. The first, presciently requested by LeMay, was "a study of the feasibility, design and military utility of an earth-circling satellite" (Goldstein 1961, 6); the second was a comparison of ramjets and rockets as strategic offensive weapons systems. As one veteran of those days put it, "In the beginning, the engineers were topdogs at RAND."[7] Within a year, however, as the institution started to expand, the authority that the economic paradigm had earned during the war began to resurface.

The process by which this occurred reflected exactly the network of alliances and influences that had grown around economics and economists in the wartime context discussed above: OSS in Washington and London, and SRG in New York. One of RAND's first employees, John D. Williams, had come from the New York SRG to Santa Monica to lead the work by mathematicians and budding game theorists in RAND's department for the "Evaluation of Military Worth." In late 1946 Williams successfully persuaded LeMay to allow him to begin recruiting social scientists, especially economists (see Smith 1966, ch. 2). This he undertook at the instigation of Allen Wallis, former head of the Columbia group discussed above, who was influential in postwar research and optimistic about what economists in this area might achieve. Williams's first recruit was Armen Alchian, formerly Wallis's student at Stanford and now assistant professor of economics at nearby UCLA. Alchian began as a part-time consultant, talking "with some difficulty" to the mathematicians and physicists then dominant at RAND.[8] The

6. LeMay was quite forceful in removing institutional obstacles that might have shackled RAND. Air Force materiel and procurement officers at Wright Field wanted RAND to fulfill only very specific orders for equipment development but were quickly overruled by LeMay. It is ironic that twenty years later LeMay would become one of the harshest critics of strategic thought associated with RAND and its alumni at the Pentagon.

7. Interview with J. Digby, 5 March 1990, Santa Monica.

8. By this time Project RAND had moved away from the Douglas Corporation and had relocated in a different part of Santa Monica. Alchian recalls not really knowing what he should discuss with the RAND staff, as he had little in common with them and no experience of this type.

drive to net social scientists continued, and in September 1947 Williams arranged a meeting in New York to which economists, sociologists, and others of that ilk were invited. The group was addressed by Warren Weaver, former head of the Applied Mathematics Panel, who explained the tentative, still fuzzy character of the RAND enterprise. Among those present was Charles Hitch, who had been an OSS economist in London working with Kindleberger, Morse, and the rest of the Enemy Objectives Unit. Hitch was appointed head of RAND's new Economics Division.

The lines of influence were short but clear: from OSS through Hitch and from SRG through Wallis and Williams. They all knew each other, and their work had been significant during the war. They could have had no conception, however, of the impact the group now in the making would subsequently have, nor of how far the application of simple economic principles would carry them. For the moment, Hitch simply had to gather a staff and give it, or let it find, its own direction.

2. Storming the Citadel: From Santa Monica to the Pentagon

At the time of Hitch's arrival in 1948, RAND was still a fledgling think tank with a large budget and much flexibility but little direction. Essentially it was a hodgepodge of physicists, engineers, mathematicians, and newly arrived social scientists, working on a range of issues from nuclear propulsion to two-person zero-sum game theory, all reflecting as much the academic interests of the staff as the military concerns of the Air Force. It had neither a clear self-conception nor an established public image but still leaned towards research of a technical, engineering kind. Had anybody at the time suggested that RAND's identity was soon to be molded by articulators of the economic method, the analysis of costs and benefits, rather than nuclear physicists or even aeronautics engineers, they might have been ridiculed. That, however, is exactly what happened. The affiliates Hitch assembled quickly made their presence felt among their colleagues—often in neither a diplomatic nor timorous manner—and, by the 1960s, RAND had become identified with *systems analysis,* a cost-benefit approach to conflict, refined and implemented by economists.

The Criterion Problem

With the help of Alchian, Hitch quickly recruited a collection of economists, mainly graduates or young professors from the more prestigious universities.[9] These included Stephen Enke, J. Kershaw, A. Marshall,

9. Alchian recalls that they had difficulty attracting Harvard graduates at the time, many of whom were interested in working in Washington on budgetary and macroeconomic problems (interview with Alchian, 5 March 1990, Los Angeles).

R. Nicholls, J. Hirshleifer, and D. Novick.[10] Hitch's managerial style—which is universally deemed important for RAND's subsequent history—was to maintain a low profile, giving his colleagues much leeway. With them they brought an emphasis on cost, central to the language of economic analysts but not necessarily to that of engineers, whose concerns were more technical. Coupled with the emphasis on cost was the stress on the need for adequate criteria in making choices about weaponry. This marked the beginning of the intellectual hegemony of economic thinking at RAND. With a belligerence similar to that formerly in evidence in R&A, Enke hammered home to audiences of engineers and physicists the need for adopting economic criteria when making engineering choices. The issues are best illustrated by an example (see Enke 1965, 417). By 1950 the U.S. Air Force faced a choice among several conceivable "next generation" strategic bombers. Some were turbo-props: slow, low-flying, and quite accurate in bombing but also relatively vulnerable. Others were turbojets: less accurate but fast, high-flying, and not as open to attack. What criterion should be applied in choosing which type of bomber should constitute the strategic force? Assuming the task is to destroy a particular target, is it the bomber of which the least number are required? The kind that will be subject to less loss of planes and hence crew? Or the one that will achieve a hit with the least number of costly nuclear bombs? The bomber chosen will differ depending on the criterion adopted, as will a host of ancillary choices such as penetration tactics, bombs required, and planes sacrificed. Engineers suggested all sorts of criteria: for example, minimizing the total weight of aircraft construction, assuming that weight and construction costs were positively correlated. Economists responded that *all* resource costs should be taken into account when making choices about weapons: maintenance costs for a bomber force were no less important than those incurred in acquiring it. Also, choices of particular *strategic* bombers implied choices about necessary support functions as well as sacrifices in other areas such as *tactical* force. The systemic and intertwined nature of military choices was presented as a gordian knot which could be either chopped at haphazardly, or systematically unraveled using economic rationale.[11]

While Enke was pounding the desk at RAND, the case for economic

---

10. Enke had recently been fired from UCLA. Hitch had met Kershaw in Brazil, where the former had spent the previous year visiting the University of São Paulo. Marshall and Nicholls were both Chicago graduates, and Novick, somewhat older, was a Roosevelt "brains truster" (Alchian, Digby interviews, 5 March 1990).

11. Addressing an audience of economists, Enke (1965, 420) happily points out that principles of efficient allocation were demonstrated to senior generals using Edgeworth-type box diagrams. Isoquants showed the number of strategic and tactical targets destroyed respectively, with aircraft and nuclear weapons on the axes.

thinking in defense analysis was also being made by his colleagues outside Santa Monica. Nobody did this more eloquently than Bernard Brodie, a student of Jacob Viner's at Chicago who became an influential strategic thinker at RAND.[12] In an article in *World Politics* Brodie illustrated and condemned the absence of any significant body of strategic thought: the "profession of arms . . . has yet to round out a five foot bookshelf of significant works on strategy" (1949, 476). Classical principles of strategy—such as "Don't divide the fleet!"—had become slogans, without any hints as to how or when they should be implemented in practice. These principles, inherited from the nineteenth century and earlier, were without any theoretical foundation and, in a nuclear age when war techniques were changing more rapidly than ever, had become dangerously anachronistic. The best hope for elaborating any theory of strategy, Brodie argued, lay in exploring its parallels with "the science of economics," which had "enjoyed the most systematic and intensive development among the social sciences" (475). Strategy was the development and utilization of the resources of the nation "for the end of maximizing the total effectiveness of the nation in war" (476), and its broader variant, security policy, would incorporate political, social, and economic considerations as well as military ones. Such a complex of functions could "hardly be the province primarily of the soldier" (477). The methods of economics, he argued, were necessary to give meaning to such widely used concepts as "balanced force": balance in one set of circumstances was imbalance in another; once this was realized, the concept of marginal utility became useful. Only in such terms could one discuss the optimal allocation of military forces in contingencies of various risk.[13]

Writing for an audience of operations researchers, Hitch too made similar arguments (1953). Operations research typically tackled local problems: for example, the adequate placing of escort gunboats in the Atlantic during the war, or the best way to arrange a unit of manufacturing assembly line. As such, of necessity, it focused on "low-level criteria," taking as given the broader context within which the problem was situated: in these examples, respectively, the achievement of victory in World War II, and maximizing profit for the firm as a whole. Ideally, however, local problems should be solved with an eye to the bigger problems of which they were a part. Thus the choice of criteria to be

12. From Yale's Institute of International Studies, Brodie went to the Air Force's Air Targets Division. There his philosophy of restraint with respect to the use of nuclear weapons quickly estranged him from his military peers, and he moved to RAND in 1950. See Herken 1985, 30–35.
13. Interestingly, Brodie (1949, 479 n. 13) also refers to von Neumann and Morgenstern's *Theory of Games and Economic Behavior* (1946), casting doubt, without stating reasons, on the applicability of their theory to military strategy.

satisfied was crucial, and these should recognize the existence of opportunity costs, possibly borne outside the confines of the immediate problem but nonetheless significant. Hitch harked back to a use of economic reasoning in operations research during World War II: the problem of deciding the optimal size of North Atlantic shipping convoys. In that case it had been decided that the ratio of German U-boat losses to domestic merchant ships lost was the correct objective function. Given the relationships between convoy size and these two losses, it was decided that raising the average convoy size would be desirable. Hitch pointed out that this choice of ratio as criterion had no basis in economic theory and that, even more importantly, the whole exercise ignored the reduced shipping efficiency of larger convoy size. For the sake of sustaining the flow of supplies to Normandy, it may well have been worth sustaining the loss of a few extra ships. Hitch's punchline was qualitatively no different from Enke's or Brodie's:

> The only discipline I know which has made any attempt to explore the characteristics of operations criteria, and the intimately related question of the relation between lower and higher level suboptimization, is economic theory. Some of its conclusions and insights have wide applicability to operations research . . . and indeed constitute the modest beginnings of a scientific analysis of the problem of selecting operations criteria. (1953, 93)

The a priori case for economic analysis in military decisions was being made unambiguously and unequivocally. All advocates were essentially making the same point and were implicitly echoing Kindleberger's view that "war is a relatively simple economic problem." The correct allocation of military resources could be achieved only by recognizing the "general equilibrium" nature of the problem. The protagonists were also implicitly challenging the authority of the military in what had traditionally been regarded as the latter's own arena. The full impact of this challenge, however, would not be felt for more than a decade, during which time economists had to "prove" themselves in military and policy circles. Such a task ultimately fell to one of Hitch's newer acolytes, Albert Wohlstetter, in a study which transformed RAND and proved pivotal in the intellectual history of economics and defense.

The Strategic Bases Study

In May 1951 the Air Force requested that RAND examine the future acquisition, construction, and use of overseas air bases. They envisaged significant building of new bases and sought guidance principally on questions of efficiency: minimizing the cost of a given number of facilities. For a while nobody at RAND showed interest, until Hitch persuaded Wohlstetter to take a look at the issue.[14] The latter had only recently come to RAND, with a background in mathematical logic and a prior career ranging from the National Bureau of Economic Research (NBER) through the War Production Board to his own construction business.[15] At RAND the Bases Study was his first significant project.

Through most of 1951 Wohlstetter worked with Harry Rowen, another economist, who also had an engineering background. One of their first documents, late that same year (see Wohlstetter and Rowen 1951), drew attention to the fact that foreign air bases were particularly vulnerable to surprise attack. Note that in raising this objection they were implicitly questioning the accepted strategic context in which the Air Force had requested the study: in Hitch's terms (1953 and above), they were moving from low- to higher-level criteria. Given this observation about vulnerability, they began considering strategic alternatives to advanced overseas bases. The three other options considered were (1) bombers based on intermediate overseas bases operating in wartime, (2) U.S.-based bombers operating intercontinentally, with air-refueling, and (3) U.S.-based bombers operating intercontinentally, with ground refueling at overseas bases. Taking into account vulnerability of equipment on the ground, distances from bases to targets, and points of entry to enemy defenses and making various assumptions about Soviet atomic capabilities and deployment, Wohlstetter and Rowen—by now working with two others—concluded that the third choice was strategically the best option under various scenarios. The choice of U.S. bases with foreign ground-refueling was considerably superior to the scheme of advanced overseas bases then deployed. In a full report produced in mid-1952 (*RAND R-266*), they suggested that not only was their proposal strategically securer, it would also save the defense budget practically $1 billion!

Wohlstetter and his supporters were convinced by their analysis, but they still faced the difficult task of persuading the Air Force, which was naturally reluctant to adopt drastic policy changes and insisted on going over everything with a fine-tooth comb.[16] Finally, however—Wohlstetter by this stage having confronted the Air Chief of Staff, Thomas White—the Air Force Council concurred with the need for a strategic

14. Discussion in this section draws on Smith 1964.
15. Wohlstetter claims that he went to RAND because he was tired of writing about abstractions and wanted to learn about "the empirical world." His wife, Roberta, was already with RAND's Social Science Division, and several other RAND staff, including J. C. C. McKinsey, A. Girschick, and O. Helmer, were also acquaintances of his (interview with Wohlstetter, 28 February 1990, Los Angeles).
16. An ad hoc committee of the Air Staff was created in early June 1953 to doublecheck the RAND study.

shift and concluded that the RAND findings, for the most part, should be adopted. In particular, vulnerability was to be recognized in all Air Staff planning: critical overseas bases were to be hardened against attack, and new overseas bases were to be designed for refueling. In short, RAND's systems analysis—the cost-benefit analysis of strategic posture—had caused a significant reorientation in Air Force thinking.[17] Civilian advisers had made an impression upon their military patrons in a manner qualitatively different from that done during the war. They had gone from responding to calls for advice on target selection to now claiming that the Air Force was, in fact, asking the wrong questions. As Wohlstetter wryly remarked, " 'Requirements' are not deliverances from heaven. [They] come down . . . from higher up, but not from On High" (1964a, 116). And further, the systems analysts had laid persuasive claim to having not just the "right" question but also the best achievable answer.

RAND's Reconstitution

The success of the Bases Study had implications for RAND. In Santa Monica the emergence of systems analysis, as applied in that study, resolved the uncertainty and lack of direction which had characterized RAND's earlier years. The Economics Division became one of RAND's most prominent units, and economists came to form almost one-fifth of the research staff (see Smith 1966, 63). While systems analysis called for interdisciplinary input, its intellectual foundation was cost-benefit analysis within the economic paradigm, and its successful application earned particular prestige for economists in the RAND hierarchy.

Just as economics rose in the intellectual pecking order, so other disciplines fell. In the late 1940s and early 1950s RAND had been the key institution in the development of game theory. Hopes for its application had been very high, and much effort went towards the elaboration of game-theoretic conflict models such as bomber-fighter duels and the construction of computerized war games for battle simulation (see Brewer and Shubik 1979). With confidence among RAND management and the Air Force that game theory would yield concrete strategic guidance (see Haywood 1951), mathematicians enjoyed the freedom to do abstract research.[18] The systems analysis typified by the Bases Study, however, was much closer to an elaborate "back of the envelope"

17. RAND's Jack Stockfisch suggests (correspondence, August 1990) that some debate still exists over the extent to which the Bases Study actually influenced Air Force policy. The account here is based largely on Smith 1964. Herken (1985, 93ff.) focuses on SAC commander Curtis LeMay's opposition to the idea of sheltering SAC bombers and his general incredulity towards the threat of a Soviet first strike. The actual changes as recounted by Smith, however, are not incompatible with Herken's account.
18. Interviews with Alchian, Digby, and Harris (5 March 1990, Los Angeles).

calculation than an exercise in complex modeling and computer simulation.[19] Wohlstetter, though never keen to portray systems analysis as something accessible to the unsophisticated, was quick to disparage the "new toolism" which favored complex techniques: "Mathematical models figure then as necessary but quite subordinate tools. . . . The tools that turn out to be useful for analysis here are likely to be more homely, but more productive" (1964a, 105).[20]

Consequently, as systems analysis ushered in a new era during which it became RAND's emblem, the environment there for academic research deteriorated.[21] The success of applied cost-benefit analysis implicitly cast shadows of doubt on areas, such as game theory, which the military had supported but found relatively unsuccessful. Hence the increased pressure from the Air Force for "mission-oriented research" and work with clearer military application.[22] The 1950s saw the exodus of many game theorists to universities where Office of Naval Research (ONR) support was now available, and RAND's mathematics department itself was dissolved in the mid-1960s. In 1968 the physics department resigned en masse to form their own private consultancy, a move which reflected the extent to which they had felt themselves marginalized as RAND evolved.[23]

The late 1950s and early 1960s also saw a considerable diversification in RAND's clientele: between 1959 and 1962 Project RAND, the original contract with the Air Force, declined from 95 percent to 68 percent of total support (Smith 1966, 131). Most significantly, RAND began to make contracts with agencies at the Office of the Secretary of Defense (OSD) level, an initiative which strained relationships with the Air Force: in effect they were now dealing with the Air Force's "boss." The most significant of these contracts was with the Office of the Comptroller in OSD in 1961, an agency then headed by none other than Charles Hitch himself.

McNamara's "Whiz Kids"

In the 1960s the influence of economics on defense policy reached a peak. The ideas of control and efficiency, central to systems analysis, soon outgrew the RAND–Air Force nexus. In one sense it was natural

19. That said, Wohlstetter spent great effort in accumulating data and a detailed knowledge of the workings of the Strategic Air Command, visiting bases to discover the degree of readiness of squadrons, etc., in a manner similar to Morse and Alexander in the OSS during the war.

20. Wohlstetter's repudiation of game theory as being central to systems analysis is inconsistent with the popular conception of its "insidious" role in strategic thinking. See especially Wohlstetter 1964b.

21. Interview with T. Harris, 5 March 1990, Los Angeles.

22. Interview with N. Dalkey, 27 February 1990, Los Angeles.

23. Interview with C. Wolf, 27 February 1990, Los Angeles.

that the systems analysts would find their way onto the larger stage: designing optimal strategic *air* posture was but one task in the overall project of providing adequate *total* defense; and, if nothing else, Hitch and Wohlstetter had continuously encouraged a general rather than partial equilibrium view of defense matters.

Naturally, however, systems analysis required a catalyst for its fusion with the federal defense policy process. Such an agent was Robert McNamara, defense secretary extraordinaire of the Kennedy-Johnson administration. An Air Force lieutenant-colonel, Harvard M.B.A., Harvard professor teaching statistical control methods, and, most recently, president of Ford Motor Company, McNamara was well disposed, intellectually, to the adoption of rational costing and efficient planning. The complete overhaul of the defense budget that he desired, however, would not be achieved if the main architects remained in an Air Force think tank. Consequently, by 1961, he had recruited three of RAND's key people—Hitch, Rowen, and Alain Enthoven—to the Pentagon, giving them the broad task of redesigning defense budgeting practices with the watchwords of "efficiency" and "control."[24]

Up to that point, criticisms of budgeting procedures were becoming particularly harsh, with the Rockefeller report on U.S. defense problems calling for a budget that "corresponds more closely to a coherent strategic doctrine" (Enthoven and Smith 1971, 11). The problem lay essentially in the fact that budgeting and planning were two distinct activities in the Pentagon. The former, done by the comptroller, projected only one year ahead and reflected needs in such functional categories as military personnel, operations and maintenance, procurement, etc. (see Hitch 1963, 5). Military planning, on the other hand, done by the Joint Chiefs of Staff (JCS), did project several years ahead, but in categories such as Strategic Retaliatory, Continental Air Defense, Antisubmarine Warfare, etc. Thus budgeting was done without direct reference to what it was designed to achieve: adequate defense of the nation. Furthermore, the individual Services—Army, Navy, and Air Force—tended to develop weapons acquisition priorities on a unilateral basis, with no consideration as to how they complimented other service activities in providing defense. "As a result, the Secretary of Defense each year found himself in a position where he had to make major decisions on forces and programs without adequate information. . . . Choices with important long-range resource implications were often forced to decision prematurely or without adequate consideration of all the major alternatives" (Hitch 1963, 5).

24. Wohlstetter too was invited, but he declined the offer. In the Department of Defense, Hitch became comptroller, Enthoven became assistant secretary for defense (PPBS), and Rowen became budget director.

A golden opportunity was thus available to put into practice all the prescriptions of system analysis, at the highest possible level: the consideration of the entire national defense function and the allocation of the defense budget among its various components. The procedure developed to cope with this task was the Planning, Programming, Budgeting System (PPBS), refined at RAND by Hitch and Novick (see Novick 1965). Complex in detail, but simple in purpose, this linked budgeting and planning phases, allowing the secretary of defense to evaluate individual service budget requests on the basis of their overall contribution to the nation's defense capability. It likewise allowed him to strive for a balance between the defense mission's key components, such as tactical air forces and land forces.

The PPBS exercise ruffled many military feathers:

> The process seems straightforward enough, but it hit the Pentagon with the force of a thunderclap. All the pet projects that had been for years in the private preserves of the service chiefs were suddenly dragged out into the white glare of McNamara's relentless scrutiny, subjected to the unremittingly logical analysis of the systems intellectuals, stripped of their lazy rhetoric to expose their underlying irrationalities, the confusions of purpose, the overlappings and the duplications, the lack of any integrating strategic and tactical overview. Hardest to take was the lack of respect for the old-line military wisdom. (Morris 1984, 27)

Among the projects axed on the recommendation of the Systems Analysis Office were the B-70 bomber and the Skybolt air-launched ballistic missile program, both pet projects of—of course—the Air Force. The first, it was claimed, was inferior to a ballistic missile system and the second inferior to non–air-launched systems such as Minuteman and Polaris.[25] Traditional interservice rivalry over weapon systems held no place in the search for efficiency, and Hitch, Rowen, and Enthoven were quite prepared to tread on military toes. As far as the Air Force were concerned, their RAND protégés had grown "too big for their boots": the ideas spawned at RAND were in a sense backfiring on LeMay, RAND's original protector and now Air Force Chief of Staff. On retirement he warned, "Today's armchair strategists . . . can do incredible harm. 'Experts' in a field where they have no experience, they propose strategies based upon hopes and fears rather than upon facts and seasoned judgements" (1968, x). His colleague Thomas White, who only a decade before had guided Wohlstetter's Bases Study recommendations through the Air Force, wrote: "I am profoundly apprehensive of the

---

25. For a detailed discussion of these cases see Enthoven and Smith 1971, 243–66.

pipe-smoking tree-full-of-owls type of so-called professional 'defense intellectuals' who have been brought into this nation's capital. I don't believe a lot of these often overconfident, sometimes arrogant young professors, mathematicians and other theorists have sufficient worldliness or motivation to stand up to the enemy we face" (1963, 10).

The adverse reaction they elicited was a measure of the controversial influence gained by Hitch's group. They had attained the highest reaches of decision-making in the defense policy area: their ideas were based upon economic notions of opportunity cost and the equimarginal principle, yet they informed completely what was to become known as the McNamara Revolution. The application of rational costing and budgeting was widely hailed and received a further boost when, in 1965, President Johnson ordered that PPBS be applied to the entire federal budgeting process. Also, defense budget design naturally rested on strategic considerations, a discourse sustained by Enthoven, Rowen, and, externally, Wohlstetter. From them came the ideas that variously dominated the strategic scene: preservation of "second strike" (i.e., retaliatory) capability through missile silo hardening, "flexible response" to achieve destruction of military but not civilian targets, and emphasis on building up conventional forces.

From fairly humble beginnings in the war, the application of simple economic principles carried a small group of economists from the consideration of low-level problems to the shaping of defense policy at the highest echelon. Steadily gaining influence in the decade after the war, the so-called defense economists had their heyday in the early 1960s. In this sense RAND had far exceeded its original purpose. In 1967, however, the golden years of systems analysis came to an end. McNamara left as defense secretary in November, becoming president of the World Bank. With his departure his team of economists dispersed: Hitch to the University of California, Enthoven to the private sector in the medical products area, and Rowen back to RAND as president. Only Rowen remained in an area related to defense economics, but his tenure at RAND too was to be cut short by Daniel Ellsberg's leakage of the Pentagon Papers in 1970. By the end of the decade the end of an era had been reached; the bubble had burst.

3. *Conclusion*

The impact of basic economic thought in defense circles had grown without interruption for almost thirty years. Surely this must have reverberated throughout the economics discipline itself, producing a defense economics in the manner that other policy influences have helped develop the existing subdisciplines of education economics, health economics, and public finance? As is now well known, this did not occur.

The consideration of defense issues never attained the status of a significant field among the economics community, and the number of specialized journals and active academics in that area remains very small.
However, during the golden age attempts were certainly made by the
main protagonists to attract some talent into the field. For a few years
sessions on defense at the American Economics Association featured
Enthoven, Enke, and others, all trying to attract academic interest:
"Now that economists have come to occupy positions where they can
make these contributions [to] weapon selection problems, it is to be
hoped that more members of the profession will interest themselves in
this important field of research" (Enke 1965, 426).

Why, despite its burgeoning success in the policy arena, did this
strand of economics not mushroom into something much bigger? One
reason may be the infamy that grew up around such figures as Wohlstetter, Herman Kahn, and McNamara's advisors. Once they entered the
controversial terrain of strategic analysis, they were dealing with issues
which few could approach calmly. All were roundly criticized by advocates of disarmament and attracted a form of public attention that many
academics, however publicly minded, consider unpleasant (see Green
1966; Herzog 1963; Kaplan 1983). Further, some of the central figures,
such as Wohlstetter and Kahn, seemed almost to revel in offending the
sensibilities of those less receptive to the message of economic reason.
Related to this is the fact that strategic thought, however anchored it
may have been in the economic paradigm, was no longer recognizable as
economics per se. It was an extremely sensitive political, moral, and
ethical issue, as much the concern of philosophers and ethicists as
"value neutral" neoclassical economists. But perhaps the most important reason lay in the nature of the economics used, and here Enthoven
is worth quoting at length:

[The] tools of analysis that we use are the simplest, most fundamental concepts of economic theory. . . . The advanced mathematical techniques of econometrics and operations research have not
proved to be particularly useful in dealing with the problems I have
described. Although a good grasp of this kind of mathematics is
very valuable as intellectual formation, we are not applying linear
programming, formal game theory, queuing theory, multiple regres-
sion theory, nonlinear programming under uncertainty, or anything
like it. The economic theory we are using is the theory most of us
learned as sophomores. The reason Ph.D.'s are required is that
many economists do not believe what they have learned until they
have gone through graduate school and acquired a vested interest in
marginal analysis. (1963, 422)

This statement came at a time when the economics discipline in general was, in fact, leaning *towards* the refinement of technique and not away. All the analytical methods above, which Enthoven is quick to disclaim, were by then grist for the academic economist's mill: econometrics was riding high on, inter alia, the apparent success of Keynesian fine-tuning, and game theory, which ironically RAND had been so instrumental in nurturing, was finally finding a place in economic theory. For an economics discipline moving in such a direction, perhaps war as an "economic problem"—to use Kindleberger's term—had become just *too* simple.

The author acknowledges the support of the Pew Charitable Trusts, the helpful comments of Craufurd Goodwin, and the cooperation of many individuals associated with the RAND Corporation, including Armen Alchian, Norman Dalkey, James Digby, Ted Harris, Greg Hildebrandt, David Novick, Jack Stockfisch, Albert Wohlstetter, and Charles Wolf.

References

Baxter, J. Phinney. 1946. *Scientists against Time*. Boston: Little, Brown.

Brewer, Garry, and M. Shubik. 1979. *The War Game*. Cambridge: Harvard University Press.

Brodie, Bernard. 1949. Strategy as a Science. *World Politics* 1 (July): 467–88.

Digby, James. 1989. Operations Research and Systems Analysis at RAND, 1948–1967. *RAND N-2936-RC* (April).

———. 1990. Strategic Thought at RAND, 1948–1963. *RAND N-3096-RC* (June).

Enke, Stephen. 1965. Using Costs to Select Weapons. *American Economic Review,* Papers and Proceedings (May).

Enthoven, A., and K. Wayne Smith. 1971. *How Much Is Enough?* New York: Harper & Row.

Goldstein, J. R. 1961. RAND: The History, Operations and Goals of a Nonprofit Corporation. *RAND P-2236-1* (April).

Great Britain. War Ministry. 1963. *Operational Research in the R.A.F.* London: Her Majesty's Stationery Office.

Green, Philip. 1966. *Deadly Logic: The Theory of Nuclear Deterrence*. Columbus: Ohio State University Press.

Harrod, Roy. 1959. *The Prof: A Personal Memoir of Lord Cherwell*. London: Macmillan.

Haywood, Oliver. 1951. Military Doctrine of Decision and the von Neumann Theory of Games. *RAND RM-528* (February).

Herken, Gregg. 1985. *Counsels of War*. New York: Knopf.

Herzog, Arthur. 1963. *The War-Peace Establishment*. New York: Harper & Row.

Hitch, Charles. 1953. Suboptimization in Operations Problems. *Journal of the Operations Research Society of America* 1.3 (May): 87–89.

———. 1963. Plans, Programs and Budgets in the Department of Defense. *Journal of the Operations Research Society of America* 2:1–17.

Kahn, Herman. 1962. *Thinking about the Unthinkable*. New York: Avon.

Kaplan, Fred. 1983. *The Wizards of Armageddon*. New York: Simon & Schuster.

Katz, Barry. 1989. *Foreign Intelligence*. Cambridge: Harvard University Press.

Kindleberger, Charles. 1978. World War II Strategy. *Encounter* 51:39–42.

———. 1980. The Life of an Economist. *Banca Nazionale de Lavoro* 134 (September): 231–45.

LeMay, Curtis. 1968. *America Is in Danger*. New York: Funk & Wagnalls.

Leonard, Robert. 1990. Creating a Context for Game Theory. John M. Olin, Program in Normative Political Economy, Working Paper 120 (October). Duke University.

Macdougall, G. D. A. 1951. The Prime Minister's Statistical Section. In *Lessons of the British War Economy,* edited by D. N. Chester, 58–68. Cambridge: Cambridge University Press.

Miller, L., et al. 1989. Operations Research and Policy Analysis at RAND, 1968–1988. *RAND N-2937-RC* (April).

Morris, Charles. 1984. *A Time of Passion*. New York: Harper & Row.

Novick, David, ed. 1965. *Program Budgeting*. Cambridge: Harvard University Press.

———. 1988. Beginning of Military Cost Analysis, 1950–1961. *RAND P-7425* (March).

Palmer, Greg. 1978. *The McNamara Strategy and the Vietnam War.* Westport, Conn., and London: Greenwood.

Quade, E. S., ed. 1964. *Analysis for Military Decisions*. Chicago: Rand McNally.

Rostow, W. W. 1981. *Preinvasion Bombing Strategy*. Austin: University of Texas Press.

Shubik, Martin, ed. 1964. *Game Theory and Related Approaches to Social Behavior.* New York: Wiley.

Smith, Bruce. 1964. Strategic Expertise and National Security Policy: A Case Study. *Public Policy* 13:69–106.

———. 1966. *The RAND Corporation*. Cambridge: Harvard University Press.

Stockfisch, Jack. 1987. The Intellectual Foundations of Systems Analysis. *RAND P-7401* (December).

Wallis, Allen. 1980. The Statistical Research Group, 1942–1945. *Journal of the American Statistical Association* 75, no. 370:320–30.

White, Thomas D. 1963. Strategy and the Defense Intellectuals. *Saturday Evening Post,* 4 May, 10–12.

Wohlstetter, A. 1959. The Delicate Balance of Terror. *Foreign Affairs* 2 (January): 211–34.

———. 1964a. Analysis and Design of Conflict Systems. In Quade 1964.

———. 1964b. Sin and Games in America. In Shubik 1964.

Wohlstetter, A., F. S. Hoffman, R. Lutz, and H. S. Rowen. 1952. Selection and Use of Strategic Air Bases. *RAND R-266*. Declassified 1962.

Wohlstetter, A., and H. Rowen. 1951. Economic and Strategic Considerations in Air Base Location: A Preliminary Review. *RAND D-1114*.

Zuckerman, Lord Solly. 1978. *From Apes to Warlords*. New York: Harper & Row.

Rostow, Developing Economies, and National Security Policy

John Lodewijks

> Warfare throws up many economic problems, but the problems do not succeed in holding the interest of economists.
>
> —George J. Stigler (1988)

It has been stated that economic science has devoted relatively little attention to defense and security issues. In this essay I examine the activities of a highly prominent national security advisor, Walt Whitman Rostow, who has been one of the very few in that position with an extensive training in economics. In particular I have used transcripts of two oral interviews with Rostow, on deposit with the Kennedy and Johnson Libraries, the latter of which has only become available since early 1990. I have further restricted my focus to the national security problems of developing countries. For these nations security issues have always been paramount. It is thus not surprising that the neglect of the economic analysis of security issues, as indicated by Stigler's comment, should go hand in hand with the comparative neglect of development economics and its low status in the profession.[1]

Walt Rostow was born in New York in 1916, "one of the three sons of a Russian Jewish immigrant. . . . Walt had always been a prodigy, always the youngest to do something. The youngest to graduate from a school, to be appointed to something. An unusually young graduate of Yale, a young Rhodes scholar. A young man picking bombing targets in World War II. A young assistant to Gunnar Myrdal" (Halberstam 1969, 193–94). During his sophomore year at Yale, he says, "I decided when I was seventeen what I would do in academic life, centered around two large

---

1. See, for example, the editors' foreword and the article by Irma Adelman in the first issue of the *Journal of Development Studies* (June 1974). Or Yotopoulos and Nugent 1976, ch. 1. There are some indications that the status of development economics as an analytical discipline is now improving. Highly respected theorists such as Joseph Stiglitz and Robert E. Lucas have focused their attention on the field, and a recent article by Stern (1989) is a very forcefully written piece describing the promise and opportunities in this subdiscipline.

ideas: one is the application of modern economic theory and statistical analysis to economic history; and the other is the relationship between economic factors and society as a whole" (Rostow 1981, 430). At this early stage he had been convinced of the gross inadequacy of Marxist or any other single cause explanations of history, stating that "Marx's analysis was incomplete in its own day and thoroughly out of date in this century" (Rostow 1964a, 109).[2] Rostow was determined to provide an alternative account of how economic forces interacted with social, political, and cultural forces. Later, when he tried to apply economic theory to concrete historical events and data, he found conventional theory "an incomplete framework for a serious economic historian or analyst of the current scene; and, as I learned more, I judged it increasingly necessary to introduce as systematically as I could political, social, cultural, and other non-economic forces as they bore on economic behavior" (Rostow 1986, 5).

In the summer of 1941 he accepted a post in the Research and Analysis Branch of the Office of Strategic Services in Washington. His book *Pre-Invasion Bombing Strategy* came out of this experience. He next worked in the Department of State as assistant chief of the German-Austrian Economic Division, 1945–46. Galbraith notes that at the end of 1945, when he worked in the Office of Economic Security Policy in the State Department, Walt was on his staff and was regarded as "one of the most effective young officers in the department" (1981, 241).

When Rostow returned to academia, he took up positions as Visiting Professor of American History at both Oxford (1946–47) and Cambridge (1949–50) and then became Professor of Economic History at MIT from 1950 to 1961. At MIT he was heavily involved with the Center for International Studies (CENIS). Under the leadership of Max Millikan, CENIS was set up in 1951 to mobilize the best people and ideas around the question of how to utilize American resources more effectively in the developing world. Research was undertaken on communist countries (funded by the CIA) and the developing world (funded by the Ford and Rockefeller Foundations). Rostow worked extensively on Asian problems in the 1950s, notably from 1953 to 1955. He directed a project for the Center on China which led to *The Prospects for Commu-*

2. Rostow's reaction to Marx and Marxism is important for his later views on national security policy. In his latest book he writes, of Marx: "Out of a childhood and youth without apparent frustration or denial he emerges as a profoundly lonely, self-isolated man driven, in part, by a strand of violence, hatred, and aggression." Marx used classical concepts, but they are "employed in a highly selective and exploitative way for a predetermined purpose," and as a historian he "was notably selective in his use of the facts available to him." However, "the simple, brute fact is that he found it impossible, despite prodigious efforts, to build a scientific foundation consistent with the argument of the Manifesto" and "none [of his] predictions has come about" (1990, 124–25, 137).

nist China (1954) and *An American Policy in Asia* (1955). The main ideas in these works were the need to prevent a power grouping from militarily dominating Asia and the threat of guerrilla warfare in the region. The appeal of communism had to be blunted via political, social, and economic reform and through a greater regional effort in development (Rostow 1972, 283–84). The Center's work also led to a crusade for enlarged development aid, the case for which was expressed in *A Proposal: Key to an Effective Foreign Policy* (1956) (Rostow 1984, 240–45).

As Ben Higgins remembers, mid-1950s

> were years of keen intellectual excitement at CENIS, with virtually non-stop interdisciplinary seminars and discussion groups, in which not only CENIS staff but almost all of MIT's anthropologists,economists, political scientists and sociologists participated in varying degrees . . . [with] a community of scholars arriving at the same broad analytical framework. . . . [Economists such as] Richard Eckhaus, Paul Rosenstein-Rodan, Benjamin Higgins, and Evsey Domar . . . political scientists such as Guy Pauker, Jean Mintz, Hugh McVey, Lucien Pye and Ithiel Poole; sociologist Dan Lerner; economic geographer Karl Pelzer; anthropologists Betty Pelzer and Clifford Geertz. The policy strategy was the Big Push, a development effort on all fronts on a scale large enough to bring increases in productivity that would outrun population growth and promote structural change. (1990a, 54–55, 67–68)

Higgins adds that Rostow was their "shining light," an economic historian with a good grasp of modern economic theory. In 1960 Rostow published *The Stages of Economic Growth: A Non-Communist Manifesto,* a book based on a series of lectures he gave at Cambridge University in 1958. *Stages* has gone through three editions, eighteen reprintings in English, and many translations, and continues to stir up controversy thirty years later. It has been claimed that the book "furnished much of the ideological basis for U.S. foreign policy toward underdeveloped nations of Asia, Africa, and Latin America in the 1960s" (in Rostow 1981, 428).

In 1961, on leave of absence from MIT, Rostow took up a position as deputy special assistant to the president for national security affairs. He then moved to the State Department as counselor and chairman of the Policy Planning Council (1961–66), only to return to the White House again as Johnson's national security adviser.

It is rumored that he was unwelcome on many college campuses after leaving office in 1969. Indeed it is said his former colleagues at MIT would not take him back. He found a position in Texas and states that "there was considerable controversy about my coming to the University of Texas, as there would have been if I had gone to any other American University" (Rostow 1981, 430). But he has put that behind him and continued to be a highly productive scholar since arriving at Texas. He is the sole author of more than thirty books. His latest, *Theorists of Economic Growth from David Hume to the Present,* which came out in mid-1990, is regarded by the author as his "final, substantial work on economic growth." There are many more that he co-authored (or wrote in someone else's name), contributed chapters to, or that were written in his honor; let alone all the journal articles and reviews he has published. Even those who have had grave differences of opinion with him over Vietnam, such as Galbraith, acknowledge that he is "one of the few people in the U.S. who can *think* about foreign policy" (Galbraith 1981).

Rostow and Developing Economies

Rostow developed an approach to economic growth suggesting that developing countries typically proceed through a number of "stages" of development: starting off with a traditional society, building up the preconditions for takeoff, engaging in takeoff, then driving to maturity, and finally proceeding to the age of high mass consumption. In this paper *I restrict the focus to the preconditions period,* as this is the phase most relevant to national security issues.

I have further limited this inquiry to those ideas emphasized by Rostow that were novel or neglected in the development literature of the time. It should be noted that there were many views about the development process which he and other development economists shared. For example, he argued that in the early stages of the preconditions period, developing countries needed to build up the infrastructure of modernization in education, transport, power, and administration, and that often these countries had the natural resources but lacked the capital and technical knowledge to affect the transition to modernization. What was required was a flow of modern industrial, agricultural, and transport technology capable of fending off diminishing returns to land and coping with the Malthusian propensities of the people (Rostow 1971, 29). Development assistance, with modern science and technology, was needed to pave the way for takeoff. Once the country had achieved self-sustained growth, it could acquire the external capital needed from hard loans. These views were fairly typical in the development literature of the times.

What makes Rostow distinctive is his analysis of the forces operating to move a society towards modernization. He argues that "certain generalizations are possible. . . . In all cases, reactions to foreign intrusion, actual or threatened, [are] relevant to the domestic thrust towards modernization. Intrusion appears in many forms, military, political, and economic, as does one kind or another of nationalist, modernizing response" (1971, 95). Also, "the transition is, on this view, initiated by some form of intrusion from abroad . . . nationalist reaction is likely in time to merge with the interests and motives of others who, for reasons of profit, domestic power or status—or whatever—are prepared to act or press for the modernization of the economy" (62). Much then depends, during the preconditions period, on the intrusion of more advanced societies and the character of the reaction to them by the traditional society. There is a need for a positive reaction to external intrusion to avoid the reduction of the society to colonial status. This may require the adoption of modern military technology and the establishment of a centralized government that could effectively promote and focus the strength of the nation (72).

Rostow also makes the observation that soldiers are major actors during this period: "The security dimension of this first phase of modernization has helped determine that soldiers often emerged as the first new men in the transition period" (1971, 61). This has several implications. Given the troubled transition from a traditional society to one capable of sustained industrialization, there is going to be considerable political turbulence. The intrusion by more advanced societies, the raised expectations of citizens, the new demands placed on government, and the shift in the balance of power and influence away from rural areas, all will create political instability (101). This instability does not lend itself easily to stable democratic rule, argues Rostow. Multiple-party factional strife in the preconditions period often leads to soldiers moving in "to clear up the mess." He notes the endemic failure to make democracy work in the developing regions (286–87). The policy implication is the need to create party institutions that force negotiation of a broad consensus, and to discipline within it personal and factional differences (297). Fortunately the takeoff and drive to technological maturity provide an environment more conducive to movement towards democracy than the period of the preconditions for takeoff (181).

A further implication is that during the preconditions period there may be a strong temptation for external adventure. Rostow argues that the politics of the developing nations since 1945 have been marked by a group of autocratic or totalitarian leaders who have chosen to build their domestic politics on "anti-imperialism" and to channel their limited resources into external expansion. These military objectives divert resources away from the domestic tasks of development so that security and welfare objectives conflict. The availability of large external resources permits this postponement of the decision to shift from expansion to growth and welfare (1971, 279–81). He concludes that a good many political crises in the contemporary developing world can be interpreted as resulting from the misallocation of resources between security and growth-welfare objectives (16).

These political and security dimensions of development are often neglected by economists, as is clearly evident in some of the ramifications induced by the imposition of the International Monetary Fund's Conditionality Rules (see Sheahan 1980, 1987; Taylor 1988). From a welfare perspective, leaders in the developing world need to concentrate on development issues rather than external military adventures. However, the benefits of the former strategy are often slow to appear, and since politics comes first, external success may unify a disparate nation.

One of Rostow's strategies to deal with these sort of problems was to promote regional security arrangements, via such institutions as the Asia and Pacific Council, Asian Development Bank, Association of Southeast Asian Nations, and Alliance for Progress in Latin America. He strongly recommended the establishment of regional programs of mutual self-help, such as the Alliance for Progress. He also argued that the United States should be a junior rather than a senior partner in the region. The self-help aspects of economic assistance were always stressed: "Overseas aid can only be helpful to the extent that the government and people of the country organize their own resources. Economic growth is primarily a national enterprise. External assistance is important; but the heart of economic development consists of national measures of self-help" (Rostow 1964a, 85; see also 91). Furthermore, he argued, other industrialized countries had to assume more of the responsibility for the Third World. President Johnson was an enthusiastic supporter of these ideas and "made self-help and regional cooperation the core of his [aid] program" (Kaufman 1987, 98).

Another theme in Rostow's work, consistent with Hollis Chenery's structuralist approach to development policy (see Chenery 1989), is to note that the takeoff is a surge of industrialization focused on a relatively few sectors. Hence there is an enormous gap between the rapidly modernizing major cities and the countryside; this rapid urbanization poses deep social and political problems. Only in the later stage of the drive to technological maturity are spread effects significant. Hence sustained industrialization requires the modernization of the countryside. This involves the diffusion of modern technology in agriculture and a need to widen the market by making manufactured products available in rural areas. This will help to stem the urban drift (Rostow 1964a, 102, 124, 133–35). The key here is that these structural distortions and the unbalanced growth process have political and security implications which must be tackled. To Rostow "[the] central problem of development is not the gap between rich nations and poor nations; it is the gap between the rich and poor parts of the developing nations themselves" (135).

Rostow acknowledges that developing nations need to allocate resources for education, health, and housing. But these expenditures, though necessary, are not sufficient. It is the efforts of the private sector in raising agricultural productivity and industrial momentum for a mass market that is the growth-generating force. The private sector and foreign private enterprise are the main players. President Johnson was initially keen to promote social programs. He authorized a major report on Africa in October 1966 and asked that it be "the most comprehensive study of Africa and our role there ever compiled for a President." The report was kept secret. Its thrust was that in Africa the United States had become enmeshed in an unmanageable range of projects without having competence in any. Johnson concluded from this, in line with Rostow's thinking, that "economic and social development is a slow business, especially among nations in a very early stage of modernization" (Bornet 1983, 182).

We now turn to a case study to illustrate the application of Rostow's ideas on development. The country is South Vietnam, the period 1964–69. Rostow had great sympathy with pacification and village development efforts there. But he did not see these efforts as being crucial so long as the country was open to communist infiltration. Military action against this infiltration was viewed as an essential instrument to permit pacification slowly to be spread and consolidated. More than that, the social and political fragmentation in Vietnam in the early 1960s was typical of countries in that stage of development; it would take time and the emergence of new generations to correct it and yield a solid sense of nationhood. It was this sense of nationhood that might save South Vietnam (Rostow 1972, 286, 457).

By 1966 things had changed fundamentally. The leadership, Rostow claimed, "were just the kind of second-generation figures I had hoped for," young, intensely nationalistic, inexperienced, and energetic people. Most came from the military, because the military in Vietnam "were the best-organized, most competent institution in Vietnamese society." The military "drew to it the best administrative talents," so that "in Vietnam, as elsewhere, the military were the first substantial group to generate a sense of nationhood" (Rostow 1972, 207, 293, 453, 446).

The attacks from the North, as Rostow predicted they would, created a new nationalism in South Vietnam (1972, 435, 466). The nation emerged stronger after the assaults, and the long, slow, hard progress of political development was moving positively in South Vietnam from mid-1965. Public security had been restored, and political, economic, and social development could be initiated, as witnessed by the land reform act of 1970, improvement in communications, roads, schools, and medical facilities, and the introduction of new rice strains.

Rostow describes the period from 1964 to 1969 as a movement from "near-defeat to near-nationhood": his subheading is "South Vietnam: From Preconditions to the Eve of Takeoff" (1972, 470–76). He claims that in 1972 South Vietnam was on the verge of takeoff through a series of agricultural reforms, breaking down the barriers between city and countryside, an education revolution, improvements in public administration, infrastructure developments, and collaboration with foreign firms in industry. Indeed, he states that South Vietnam was, in early 1972, roughly where South Korea had stood in the early 1960s—that in fact the transformation in South Vietnam had been more rapid than that which took place in South Korea.

For another example of Rostow's views, let us turn to a doctoral dissertation completed on President Harry S. Truman's Point Four Program (Taylor 1981). In his inaugural address of 20 January 1949 he emphasized the importance of preventing the spread of communism in developing countries. Point Four of the speech focused on raising the standard of living in the Third World through American capital and technology. A technical assistance program was to be set up to relieve the economic and social distress upon which communism fed. Taylor (143–44) argues that the goal of the Point Four program adumbrated Rostow's "stages," by recognizing that necessary conditions must be met before a developing nation can efficiently utilize large amounts of capital. Indeed, Stanley Andrews, former director of the Technical Cooperation Administration, has stated that in the 1950s Rostow's model was accepted in government (Taylor, 131).

However, the program faced State Department opposition. After the Korean war "the issue of raising living standards in the underdeveloped countries became secondary to armaments for defence against the threat of Communist-inspired revolution from within the country" (Taylor 1981, 7). The emphasis was switched from economic development to military assistance to stabilize government and strengthen the political order. Taylor argues that this aid benefited the ruling elite and gave the government in power the means to resist not only the threat of communism but any other internal reforms as well. It thereby ran counter to the overall development goals, as espoused by Rostow. The existing political structure, in many cases, was not capable of promoting a broadly based growth process and made countries dependent on continued foreign aid.

Rostow and the Communist Threat

> I have for many years been professionally interested
> in the problems of economic development; and there
> are those who may find it odd for an economist to be

also concerned—as I have been—with the problems of countering Communist methods of guerrilla warfare and subversion.

—Rostow (1964a, 85)

Rostow states that he was brought up by parents committed to the pre-1914 democratic socialist tradition (1986, 6). Galbraith mentions that early in Rostow's career he "was thought to be too favorably disposed to trying to work things out with the Soviets" and certainly "not considered a theological anti-Communist in those days" (1981, 469). He had even "been kept out of the State Department at least partly because ancient FBI reports seemed to show a suspicious accommodating taint." Halberstam comments, however, that at MIT during the 1950s Rostow joined a "department which seemed eager to harness the intellectual resources of this country into a global struggle against the Communists." In his speech of June 1961 entitled "Guerrilla Warfare in Underdeveloped Areas," the die was well and truly cast. There Rostow argued that communism could be best understood as a "disease" and that guerrilla warfare was the means by which "scavengers of the modernization process" sought to exploit emergent revolutionary aspirations. Counter-guerrilla action was the shield that would protect the development process from communist disruption until a nation gained the social strength to control the situation itself (Schlesinger 1978, 495). Rostow's *View from the Seventh Floor* (1964a), which includes this paper, is an excellent source for his views on the communist threat.

Rostow believed that the West was "engaged in a fundamental, historical contest . . . [against the] Communist empire and Communist police-state dictatorships." Communism's historical duty had been to impose itself on all societies, even against the will of the majority. Communists intended to persist, with every other means at their disposal, in pressing for the expansion of communist power and influence. The Cold War came down, in his view, to a test of whether the democratic world was fundamentally tougher and more purposeful in the defense of its vital interests than the communists were in the pursuit of their global ambitions (1964a, 35, 43, 48, 78, 105).

Developing countries in the early stages of absorbing and applying the fruits of modern science and technology were undergoing changes that made them "peculiarly vulnerable to Communist tactics of penetration, subversion, and insurrection" (1964a, x). Moscow had "sought to extend its power by orchestrating the instruments of guerrilla warfare, subversion, trade and aid; by appealing to anticolonial and nationalist sentiments; and by projecting an image of communism as the most efficient method of modernization" (7). There was "almost literally no nation in Asia, the Middle East, Africa and Latin America in which the

Communists [were] not investing significant resources in order to organize individuals and groups for the purpose of overthrowing the existing
governments and supplanting them with Communist regimes" (21–22).
In this context Rostow cited guerrilla warfare in Indochina, Burma,
Malaya, Indonesia, and the Philippines, and the invasion of South Korea
and South Vietnam.

The marked acceleration of nationalism and modernization in the
Third World had yielded an environment of endemic turbulence. The
communist strategy was to exploit the inherent vulnerability of the
developing areas (Rostow 1971, 304–6). The communists acted to en-
flame postcolonial ambitions, frictions, and discontents, while associat-
ing "themselves with all manner of forward-looking human and national
aspirations" (1964a, 84). However, the truth was that "communism is
technically inferior as well as an inhuman alternative" (167). Since it was
on the weakest nations that communists concentrated their attention,
communism was best understood as an "infection" or "disease of the
transition to modernization" (85, 114). The Marxists are, then, according to Rostow, "the scavengers of the modernization process. They prey
on every division, weakness, and uncertainty that is likely to beset a
society in the process of its transition to a modern mold" (106).

Communists promoted wars of "national liberation" through systematic subversion building up to urban insurrection or guerrilla warfare.
This, said Rostow, was in full cry in South Vietnam—"a guerrilla war
instigated, supplied and guided from outside the country" (1964a, 22).
Rostow had studied guerrilla warfare problems in the 1950s. There was a
project on this at the MIT Center run by Jim Cross, which he followed
closely. It dovetailed with his interest in the "pathology of the underdeveloped areas—their vulnerability to intrusion, subversion and guerrilla warfare. I learned then that the outcome of a guerrilla war hinged
mightily on the degree of the external margin—on whether the frontier
was open. Malaya was manageable—and the Philippines too—because
there was no substantial external element. In Vietnam there was a big
external margin. There was an open frontier and safe haven and resources for the Viet Cong behind it" (1964b, 82). To deal with this U.S.
national security policy had to accept "the central reality of this type of
controlled, limited politico-military confrontation" (1964a, 42). The
United States had to "destroy this international disease," this "international vandalism" (118).

Rostow stated that in assisting poor nations against guerrilla warfare
the United States had "no interest in political satellites" (1964a, 115). It
would assist nations under military pressure who could not resist by
their own resources. However, an outsider cannot win a guerrilla war; it
can only assist those prepared to fight for their own independence. The

United States had a duty to maintain the integrity and the independence of the modernization process, but it supported the emergence of strong assertive nations which, out of their own traditions and aspirations, create their own forms of modern society (83–84, 90).

One scholar observed in 1968 that for twenty years there had been a "grand consensus" in U.S. foreign policy that the primary threat to national security was Soviet expansion. The Soviets wanted to expand, and growth in their power would bring eventual control over the West. Establishment of additional communist regimes would add to the Soviets' global power and would increase their capacity for expansion. Only U.S. military power could prevent this. No communist could be a genuine nationalist, and any gain for communism was a loss for the United States (Bornet 1983, 189). This captures nicely Rostow's world view in the 1960s.

Rostow as National Security Advisor

> I am by profession an historian and an economist; so my theoretical prism is that of the social scientist. My professional life has been a counterpoint between the world of ideas and the world of public policy: in my case, the emphasis has been on military and foreign policy.
>
> —Rostow (1964a, 45)

> I found a good many references to my alleged views, actions and advice that I rendered when in government. Much of what has been written about me is inaccurate. Some writers have even felt free to put into direct quotation things I never said, reflecting perspectives I never held.
>
> —Rostow (1972, xii)

An occasional consultant to the Eisenhower administration, Rostow was critical of its approach to national security, stating that its "initial stance toward the developing world had been shaped by military and budgetary tactics rather than a theory of history." The focus was on developing countries' relations to communist military power rather than on their domestic political and economic evolution (1972, 87–88).

David Halberstam has described how Rostow then got involved with the Kennedy campaign:

> In the fifties [Rostow] had been something of a star in Cambridge, a man who published and published regularly, whose books were

reviewed in the New York Times. . . . Kennedy, on the make for an intellectual think tank of his own in the late fifties, particularly liked Rostow, liked his openness, his boundless energy, liked the fact that Rostow, unlike most academics, was realistic, seemed to understand something about how Washington really worked, liked the fact that Rostow mixed well, got on with professional politicians . . . always helpful, a demon for work . . . producing papers, memos, ideas, a great idea man. (1969, 193–94)

In Rostow's recollection Fred Holborn was sent up to MIT in November 1957. Holborn was Kennedy's liaison with the academic community and did a lot of work generating contacts and connections between the senator and what could be called the intellectual, bureaucratic elite (Rostow 1964b, 11). There then developed the "Cambridge Group"—the academic "Kennedy gang" at Cambridge—which included, in addition to Rostow, Max Millikan, Paul Samuelson, Dean Clark, Ithiel Poole, and Abe Chayes (20). Towards the end of the 1950s, Kennedy came to be the repository for all of the combined staff work of that decade; the staff work at the universities, particularly in CENIS at MIT, in RAND, and in the Rockefeller Brothers Fund Panels. This work then provided the direction in which he sought to move, whether it be military policy, aid policy, Latin America, Europe, Africa, the Indian subcontinent, arms control, or the various dimensions of domestic policy (113, 149).

In the Kennedy campaign against Nixon, Rostow's formal job was that "starting early in 1960 I built up from my own knowledge, from books, from contacts with Rand and with various military types in and out of the government—a consolidated military position paper. I cleared it in the Kennedy camp almost like a government paper. And it holds up tolerably well as a statement of what the Kennedy administration did in military policy and why" (1964b, 26). His next assignment was to attend the 1960 Pugwash meeting on disarmament in Moscow: "The Russians surfaced a social scientist on their delegation list. He was Head of the Institute of World Economics and Politics named Arzumanyan. Those organizing the U.S. team then wanted a social scientist. They asked me if I would go." At this meeting he was told in no uncertain terms that the Russians "were going to give us hell in the underdeveloped areas" (29–30).

When Kennedy got to the White House, McGeorge Bundy was made special assistant to the president for national security affairs; Rostow was made his deputy. As Rostow tells it, they split up the jobs: "Mac was clearly in charge of the shop but the President would not want me to report through him. We split the crises. I did Vietnam and Laos; he did the Congo and Cuba. We shared Berlin but Mac did most of it. I would do the longer range stuff and did the first planning map for national security affairs. I also generally handled problems from underdeveloped areas, except Latin America, and economic issues. Bundy did AEC, Pentagon problems, and European matters" (1964b, 43).

One of Rostow's jobs was to help the president persuade the Pentagon and the whole town to take guerrilla warfare seriously: "I was one of the few people who had worked seriously on the problem of guerrilla warfare in the 1950s. That's one of the reasons that President Kennedy assigned me to Laos and Vietnam. He knew about it" (1969, 17). "I went down to Ft. Bragg and began to get into how the government was and was not organized to cope with this range of problems. Even with the President leading the way it was like turning the Queen Mary in the Hudson with a tug to overcome the built-in inertia and to get this business taken seriously" (1964b, 45). Schlesinger later commented that the impetus behind counterinsurgency did not come from the military but from Kennedy and social scientists, especially Rostow; he called Rostow "the high priest of counterinsurgency" (1978, 760).

Another key theme in Rostow's work during this period was the "domino theory." For Rostow this was "not a bookish abstraction, but a living network of interconnections decreed by geography, by history, by evident communist activity, and by the balance of forces at work in Southeast Asia" (1972, 496, 428–29). He concluded that "Vietnam really was the hinge to an enormous piece of real estate in the Western Pacific." Everything down to Djakarta, the whole of Southeast Asia, and the Western Pacific, including the Australians, was involved (1964b, 50, 83). He noted that in September 1963 President Kennedy "made the flattest statement of the domino theory that anyone ever made. He believed it, and he was right. There's nobody in Asia who doesn't understand that if we pull out of Vietnam, we'd have to pull out of all of Asia, the place would fall" (1969, 66).

A further aspect of Rostow's role was his willingness to criticize intelligence data and his confidence that he was nearer the mark than most of the "analysts" (1972, 463). It was Bundy's job to handle the intelligence system and community—the institutional side of national security. Rostow notes, however, that Bundy was never "clear as to how an intelligence estimate was made; the nature of the compromises; and how you had to reach deep into it to understand what people knew and didn't know; what they believed, what they said because of previous commitments; what they said to cover their flanks against future investigations; and so on" (40). On the contrary, for Rostow, who had begun governmental life in 1941 in intelligence, "[You] have to find the man down at the bottom who has the files. The real structure of government is an inverse pyramid. You have one man who is knowledgeable; and layer after layer is built on this knowledge, his files" (1964b, 40–41).

Rostow later claimed that he never saw a worse performance by the military than in their advice to a new president in 1961 on Laos: "They were wrong about the situation on the ground. They were wrong in the structure of their planning. They were wrong about Communist logistical capabilities which they grossly overrated." In the meeting on Laos there were seven views: those of the chiefs of the four services (including the Marines), and of the three service secretaries. "No two were the same. The issue was what to do about the creeping Communist offensive towards the Mekong. There was no order, and no consensus. . . . It was chaos. . . . I doubt that Kennedy ever wholly lost his suspicion of the military after his early 1961 experiences" (1964b, 46–47). It was a question of logistics: "I had gotten out the maps of the routes into Laos. I discovered the Chiefs of Staff were feeding the President a quite false view of the relative balance of power in the Mekong Valley. I never saw a President as ill-served as Kennedy was by the military during that period" (80).

In late 1961 Rostow moved to the State Department to help develop some new policy ideas. His role was to expand the alternatives thrown up by the bureaucracy. He was to be the catalyst in generating a new set of initiatives, an ideas man, as chairman of the Planning Council.[3] Work at the Planning Council culminated in a paper entitled "Reflections on National Security Policy as at April 1965." The theme was that the United States was doing too much and the rest of the world was not doing enough, and that other nations could do more for themselves on a regional basis. Other countries needed to take a larger hand in their own destiny, which could only be done by building regional structures. The Planning Council worked on Asian regionalism and political development. In January 1965 an Asian Alliance for Progress and Asian Development Bank were proposed. The Council supported Latin American integration. It persuaded the President to give the Organization of African Unity speech on regionalism; and "we got Ed Korry in and reshaped our African AID programs around that concept" (Rostow 1969, 46–47, 89–91, 93–94).

In 1964 President Johnson asked Rostow to be the U.S. representative on the Inter-American Committee on the Alliance for Progress

---

3. Rostow states that with respect to staff on the National Security Council, "I brought Bill [William J.] Jorden in . . . [Chester] Cooper was going . . . I had to replace Jim [James C.] Thomson, who was going to Harvard, and I got Al [Alfred L.] Jenkins on China. [The staff] was organized somewhat hierarchically. Francis Bator had a little group. He had this brilliant fellow Ed [Edward K.] Hamilton, and I guess he had Larry [Lawrence S.] Eagleberger too . . . I think I elevated Hal [Harold] Saunders [after] [W.] Howard Wriggins left to go to Columbia. When Hamilton left, I got Ed [Edward R.] Fried, who is just superb. Then I got Bob [Robert N.] Ginsburgh over . . . he was my substantive man on military affairs and Vietnam negotiations" (1969, 28–32).

(CIAP). "I launched several initiatives . . . I worked on the concept of the national market and the modernizing of market arrangements. I started a whole line about inflation and the concept of a social contract that was necessary in order to contain the forces making for inflation in Latin America. I could use CIAP as a tool for modest innovation in Latin America" (Rostow 1969, 44).

Taking over from Bundy in February 1966, Rostow became President Johnson's national security adviser. The main issue was Vietnam. Rostow arrived with a definite and decided view on the issue. He had long been convinced that Vietnam would never win in Vietnam with an open frontier; that the frontier could not be closed from within South Vietnam; and that the United States had to make Hanoi pay enough in the North for it to be worth Hanoi's while to close the frontier. In a speech he delivered in June 1961 he gave the first indication that the United States might have to go north. The president called this Rostow's Plan Six: the application of air (and perhaps naval) action against North Vietnam, to get them to stop infiltration (Rostow 1964b, 82–83).

However, Rostow argued that "we [should] fight the war more decisively and fight the climactic phase primarily on the ground, not by bombing them back to the Stone Age. I thought the war could be foreshortened . . . if we went into Laos on the ground and blocked the infiltration trails" (1981, 430).[4] He suggested the invasion of the southern part of North Vietnam in order to block infiltration routes (513). He never held the view that bombing alone could stop infiltration; he just hoped the cost in the North would contribute to a decision to end the war. Bombing was no substitute for progress in the South (Johnson 1971, 367). Military action might provide the time to solve the problem of crystallizing political life around the young, modernizing generation which palpably existed, according to Rostow, in civil as well as military life in Vietnam. What was important was to make the South Vietnamese conscious that their ultimate problem would be to overcome the fragmentation of their political system (Rostow 1964b, 44, 84).

Rostow's role as a national security adviser has come under trenchant criticism. Boulding, for example, says he gave "disastrous advice," with the "inability to relate foreign and domestic events" being "highly characteristic of the whole school of thought which Rostow represents. The assumption that violence can be used cleverly and selectively to obtain narrow and worthy ends without affecting the integrity or morale of the user is the fallacy" (1971, 603). But obviously we cannot decide

---

4. See, in context of bombing, Galbraith 1981, chs. 13–14, on the U.S. Strategic Bombing Survey which questioned the effectiveness of strategic bombing. This survey involved economists such as Galbraith, Burton Klein, Nicholas Kaldor, E. F. Schumacher, Paul Baran, Tibor Scitovsky, and Edward Denison.

these issues here. Vietnam is among the most traumatic events experienced by the United States in this century and will never be free from controversy. Furthermore, "Vietnam decision-making is still buried" in material unavailable to researchers (Bornet 1983, 386).[5] What we can do is to present a range of opinions on security policy during that period. Some observers saw the problem of Vietnam as one of civil war rather than external aggression, or believed that the United States was imposing its will and its values upon peasant nations by force. Another view was that Vietnam was in "the terminal stages of a feudal regime collapsing of its own weight."

One popular perspective is the argument that what was needed was more attention on winning the support of the people of South Vietnam, that the United States erred in seeking a military solution to what was essentially a political problem. Success along these lines might have come if the Johnson administration had concentrated more on developing an effective pacification program to gain control of the countryside. Despite Johnson's personal commitment and the expenditure of lavish funds, the campaign to win the "hearts and minds" of the people failed. A serious commitment to pacification came only after the Vietcong had become deeply entrenched in the countryside. Herring has argued that at least until 1967 such programs were hastily improvised and poorly administered, and pacification and military operations were conducted in isolation from each other (1981, 45). However, it was not simply an issue of providing funds and technical know-how, as cultural differences made it difficult for Americans to understand the local people. The South Vietnamese government also displayed a marked inability to relate to its own citizens.

Some critics have made personal attacks on Rostow. Halberstam, for example, claimed that as Johnson's national security advisor Rostow shielded the president "from criticism and from reality. He deflected others' pessimism and rewarded those that were optimistic. . . . He could always see the bright side of any situation" (1969, 773). He would pounce on any positive news and bring it to the president's attention, and reanalyzed and challenged reports to make them more positive in tone. Halberstam also faults Rostow for his uncritical use of statistical data on Vietnam, particularly the ratio of enemy to Allied casualties and the ratio of enemy to Allied weapons losses. In turn, Baldwin (1973–74)

---

5. The Rostow and Bundy papers are still mostly closed. Rostow has fourteen linear feet of memos to the president, of which only the ones for 1966 and half of 1967 are catalogued. The Johnson Library has 254 boxes of National Security files, most still closed. Meanwhile the controversy over Vietnam continues: see, for example, "Vietnam Revisited" and "Realities and Myths of the Vietnam War," *Wall Street Journal*, 1 April 1982, 26. For a more general treatment see Herring 1981.

has claimed that Halberstam's treatment of Vietnam "fails in both substance and objectivity" and "is a dishonest book." Rostow's support for antiguerrilla warfare has also come under fire from some commentators. Surprisingly, Schlesinger argues that counterinsurgency was never really tried in Vietnam (1978, 763). The military pressed for large units, firepower, and attrition, that is, for a high-technology war.[6]

How has Rostow responded to these criticisms? First, he notes that he was not the architect of U.S. policy on Vietnam. In fact he was in the State Department when the key decisions were made in 1965 and was little involved with Vietnam in 1964 and 1965. But he has a more interesting response on the role of intellectuals and national security policy (1972, 490–92). A significant section of the American intellectual community, he argues, holds a definable ideological vision and applies that vision to public policy. This vision makes it difficult for intellectuals to accept the role of power in domestic and international affairs or to understand the nature of traditional societies. They have approached political development in the Third World in terms of concepts derived from American or European intellectual life. Hence they cannot condone the role of the military in the political life of most developing countries, or the widespread corruption. They do not understand the modernization process or Asian cultures. Though often trained in modern economic theory, intellectuals of the Vietnam era knew little of the economics or politics of development and were ill equipped to deal with Asia and guerrilla warfare. Their knowledge was simply shallow.

We might end the Vietnam issue with excerpts from a conversation between President Johnson and Sam Houston in 1967, which gives an indication of the quandary the president faced:

> Now take this Vietnam mess. How in the hell can anyone know for sure what's right and what's wrong? . . . I got some of the finest brains in this country—people like Dean Rusk, Walt Rostow, and Dean Acheson—making some strong convincing arguments for us to stay in there and not pull out. Then I've got some people like George Ball and Fulbright—also intelligent men whose motives I can't rightly distrust—who keep telling me we've got to de-escalate or run the risk of a total war. . . . I've just got to choose between my opposing experts. . . . [I] wish I could really *know* what's right. (Bornet 1983, 286).[7]

---

6. See Schlesinger 1978, ch. 20 ("The CIA and Counterinsurgency") and ch. 31 ("The Vietnam Legacy"). Schlesinger states that Rostow "came to symbolize, during both the Kennedy and Johnson years, the aggressive, combative liberal nationalism of the era" (54).

7. Herring concludes that "the President was poorly served by his advisers, none of whom displayed exceptional imagination in perceiving, much less coping with, these

Let us turn now to appraisals of policy in other developing countries.[8] LaFeber has argued that in Latin American affairs more importance was placed on preserving stability than on carrying out any significant reforms (1981, 66). United States policy had accomplished its primary goal: containing or eliminating guerrilla groups that threatened Latin American nations. Rostow could rightly state in 1967 that aggressive "romantic revolutionaries" were finally being replaced by "pragmatists" throughout the Third World. On the other hand, the buildup of the Latin American military helped create what Rostow later called "the most profound" of the Alliance for Progress problems: the inability of some nations to maintain constitutional government in the face of military demands and coups. In fact, democratic regimes were often overthrown by military and right-wing dictatorships, Latin American military officers replaced thirteen governments during the decade (LaFeber, 82–83, 85). Yet despite continued military assistance, and heavy aid increases, growth in Latin America was sporadic and uneven.

Rostow and the Economics Profession

> Professor Rostow is usually brief, never dull, always exciting and rarely accurate.
> —N. G. Butlin (1961)

> Economists have for long been divided between what might be called the neo-Newtonians and the biologists. I belong with the biologists.
> —Rostow (1986)

It may not come as any surprise that the economic ideas of this highly influential and prominent national security advisor are very much in the minority position in the profession. Rostow has been subject to vituperative criticism.[9] Yet it is often difficult to discern the actual target of these criticisms—Rostow the man, his views on Vietnam, or his scholarly works. As Boulding says: "It is virtually impossible to discuss

---

admittedly intractable problems. Moreover . . . his critics offered no viable solutions" (1981, 54). The problems were a determined, fanatical foe, willing to sacrifice everything for its cause of Vietnamese nationalism; the threat of Chinese and Russian intervention; South Vietnam's lacking the basic ingredients for nationhood but resenting American domination; and the U.S. people, who wanted success without paying a high price.

8. See Schlesinger 1978, ch. 24 ("Missions to the Third World") and ch. 30 ("The Foreign Policy Breach: Latin America"); also Bornet 1983, ch. 8 ("America: Custodian of the World").

9. See Cairncross 1961; Enke 1964, 201, passim; Habakkuk 1961; Ohlin 1961, 648–55; Hagen 1964, appendix 2 ("The Rostovian Schema"); Kuznets 1965, 213–35; Meier 1984, 90–118.

a work by W. W. Rostow without also discussing the man, for . . . he is a man who has operated extensively in the corridors of power" (1971, 602).

Rostow's "stages" approach has been criticized on several grounds, from the applicability of models to complex historical events to the problems of fit between Rostovian generalizations and particular historical cases. For example, debate continues among historians on whether net investment rates rise markedly during the takeoff, as Rostow indicated they would. Some commentators question his mechanistic view of history and technological determinism. They ask: Do developing countries have to emulate the historical patterns of development? They note that his "stages" represent a historical or chronological description that does not take into account the differences present in *modern* economic development; that is, nineteenth-century experience is of little guidance for the twentieth century.

Others complain that all that Rostow has done is historical taxonomy, that the stages are "empty taxonomic boxes" with quantitative matter introduced by way of illustration, rather than in terms of systematic analysis; or that, at best, stages are only rough heuristic constructs (Boulding 1971, 604–5). Hagen has argued that the division into stages and assignment of some events to one stage and others to another is too far removed from reality to be useful for explanation or prediction (1964, 517). Changes, except political, tend to be gradual. Kuznets comments that the vagueness in defining specific economic factors which are involved in each economic stage precludes any analytic or empirical evaluation (1965, 213–35).

Baran and Hobsbawm (1961) were offended by Rostow's claim to offer "a comprehensive, realistic and soundly based alternative to Marx's theory of how societies evolve" in his *Non-Communist Manifesto*. This is of course not surprising given their sympathies with the Marxist approach. They responded by claiming that Rostovian theory can neither "explain nor predict," for it fails to specify any mechanism of evolution which links the different stages: there is no explanation of why a traditional society should turn into a society breeding the preconditions of the takeoff; Rostow had merely summarized what the preconditions must be; he had not explained but simply had reclassified and relabeled information. The takeoff concept, in their opinion, has no predictive value: things can happen in any of a large number of different ways, as all possible events are covered in the Rostovian schema; the approach is so open-ended that it can never be subject to falsification.

At the 1960 Konstanz conference, organized by the International Economic Association to examine Rostow's views, Robert Solow came to a similar conclusion (see his contribution in Rostow 1963). He questioned the analytical quality of *Stages* and suggested that stage theory may be little more than a literary device. In order to develop rigorous constructs what is needed is the specification of precise behavioral relationships, parameters, and initial conditions—all absent in stage theory.

Perhaps one way to explain the profession's response to Rostow is to acknowledge that his work diverged quite substantially from mainstream work in growth theory, particularly after 1956 with the development of neoclassical growth models. Adopting the Rostovian alternative would have entailed discarding much of conventional economic theory. Rostow's major departures from conventional theory are discussed below, but it should be noted that many of these ideas were current in development literature at the time. Development economics, however, has had an uneasy coexistence with standard economic theory, and Rostow applied his framework not only to developing countries but to world history in general (Rostow 1978).

For Rostow economic growth is not continuous and smooth but rather a discontinuous process which pivots on a sudden takeoff into self-sustained growth. Growth proceeds not by a balanced development of all sectors of the economy but by successive forward leaps of the economy's leading sectors.

> The stages of growth . . . are rooted in a dynamic sectoral analysis of the production process . . . new technology is introduced into an economy via particular sectors which, through linkages to others, provide dynamism to the economy. . . . But these sectors are inherently subject to deceleration and loss of capacity to lead. Regular growth, therefore, requires a succession of leading sectors (or linked sectoral complexes). (Rostow 1971, 19)

Rostow's dissatisfaction with neoclassical utility theory is also clear. In *The Process of Economic Growth* (1952) the focus centered on six different propensities and how they influenced the growth process. While some of these propensities could be directly measured, for others, like the propensity to seek material advance, Rostow looked to history and sociology for assistance in their estimation. While this propensities approach was later dropped, in *Politics and the Stages of Growth* (1971) he talks at considerable length about man as a balancing, not a maximizing, unit. He believes that individuals are caught up in an effort to balance different and often conflicting aspirations—such as security, welfare, and a balance between order and justice—and that man is a social animal (1971, 7, 10). The aggressive instincts of man have important implications:

> A nation's security policy, while partially reflected in the budget, involves fears, and sometimes hopes, so great as to make the

economist's fine calculations at the margin misleading. . . . In certain moments of crisis—for example, Europe in 1914, the Cuban confrontation in October 1962, or the Middle East in 1967—the discontinuities felt by the major actors are such that the elegance of welfare economics or game theory breaks down. One moves from fine calculations at the margin to grosser hopes and fears, and to grosser actions to achieve or to fend them off. (13)

Rostow could never accept the standard *ceteris paribus* assumption. Tastes and behavioral patterns did change, and he hoped that more work by sociologists, political scientists, and historians could help in accounting for these changes and thereby increase our understanding of growth dynamics.

In many ways Rostow's work can be seen as a synthesis of a number of pre-Keynesian approaches. Many of his concepts—propensities, stages of growth, innovation clusters, overinvestment cycles, sectoral analysis, secular stagnation, imperfect foresight by investors—had long been popular in the literature. Indeed one of his critics has noted that in Rostow's work "one sees, gleaming up through the water, a broken image of the school of Schmoller" (Parker 1960, 1058–59), the inference being that Rostow was the historical progeny of the Historicists. Not unexpectedly, Rostow received the same type of criticism that previous stage theorists had received.

My colleague Ken Rivett speculates that there may have been a philosophical influence in the reaction to Rostow's *Stages*. In volume 2 of *The Open Society and Its Enemies* Popper distinguished between science and philosophies of history, such as those of Marx and Toynbee, that hold that history inevitably follows stages. He particularly objected to ambitious predictions about the future, which he argued true scientists could not rightly make. Mention of "stages," even by someone writing a "noncommunist manifesto," would thus be likely to arouse suspicion in at least some readers familiar with Popper, who would insist that worthwhile propositions have to be at least potentially falsifiable.

Rostow's early work, in association with the National Bureau of Economic Research, was on growth and fluctuations in the British economy. W. C. Mitchell was very pleased with the results. The influences of Kuznets and Burns were also acknowledged. This institutionalist perspective can be clearly seen in Rostow's sectoral analysis and his desire to break down aggregates (Lodewijks 1989). The early Keynesians had resisted sectoral disaggregation. Initially Rostow was willing to use some aggregates but leaned towards greater disaggregation. Later he became thoroughly convinced that economics needed to be essentially "restructured" and focus on sectors rather than broad aggregates.

He argued that the methods and concepts developed by economists in the 1950s and 1960s had to be substantially modified to deal with the 1980s and 1990s. There was an obsession with aggregate demand to the exclusion of supply factors, with problems like energy, food supply, pollution control, and research and development all left out of main-stream economics. These issues, he thought, were central and had to be studied on a key sector basis. Mainstream economists, he claimed, always seemed to be using historically outdated concepts and ideas and not coming to grips with new problems (Rostow 1981, 431).

> I am confident that I am essentially correct not because of higher intellect or virtue than my colleagues, but because I am both an economist and an economic historian. I have never been able to accept the conventional wisdom or mainstream economics of the past generation, which has been devoted to macroeconomics: the analysis and manipulation of aggregate demand. As an economic historian, I had to deal also with a world in which the price [of key products] was always changing because of supply factors screened out in macroeconomics. I had to pay attention to new technologies and demographic changes. Therefore I had to be, in my generation, a rather unconventional economist to be a good economic histo-rian. This freed me from the limitations of the reigning macrotheo-ries. (432)

Finally, Rostow has shown a keen interest in cycle theories and the role of technical innovations, again an area that conventional econo-mists have avoided. Rosenberg (1975), for example, has written about problems in the economist's conceptualization of technological innova-tion (see also Lodewijks 1990). Rostow quotes Schumpeter liberally on innovation, and it can be argued that he has been slowly converted into a committed long-cycle theorist. In his *Why the Poor Get Richer and the Rich Slow Down* (1980) he constructs multisector growth models which produce Kondratieff waves.

In summary, Rostow's work clearly diverged from the mainstream and from the alternative Solow-type growth modeling strategy. He said he was concerned about "real economies" with their cycles, with the investment process subject to systematic error leading to overshooting and undershooting optimal sectoral growth paths, with new technology, leading sectors, and increasing returns. He then tried to model this growth process, generating mathematical models which behaved the way he had always asserted the world actually behaved, but using more plausible foundations than the mainstream—that is, *not* assuming full employment, constant returns to scale, neutral inventions, the absence of lags, or a constant income distribution.

The pricetag of Rostow's heterodox approach is the abandonment of much of conventional economics. The approach is non-neoclassical as well as non-Marxist. It involves a great many endogenous variables—saving, technology, population growth, behavioral patterns—all influenced by noneconomic factors and to be handled through a multi-disciplinary approach, a development that disturbs economists. Rostow has also been reluctant to use modern econometric techniques, for he does not think that statistical analysis would reveal additional insights to the already trained observer (see Appendix B to *Stages,* 2d ed.).

We can account for the reaction to Rostow reasonably successfully in terms of his opposition to the basic foundations of contemporary economic theorizing. External factors, however, obviously intrude, particularly opposition to the role he played in Vietnam decision-making. There are also personality issues. He remains a very combative individual who still will vehemently debate the issues. In his interview with me in 1989 he was unwavering in his claim that *The Stages of Growth* model was just as applicable today as it was when he formulated it. He took intense pride in pointing out that Kuznets had recently admitted that his criticisms, made at the 1960 Konstanz conference, were off the mark.

Conclusion

Rostow was one of the very few, along with Francis Bator, Carl Kaysen, and Edward Fried, who during the 1960s combined a training in economics with a high-level government position dealing with national security affairs. Even his critics concede that he was an imaginative and resourceful scholar committed to innovative political and military design. There is also little debate that his policy recommendations were consistent with his economic theories, or that his advice was shaped by the concepts he had developed as a historian and social scientist since the 1930s (Rostow 1972, xvi).

It is also true that his views were more favorably received in government and popular circles than in academia. For example, he reported that in the 1960s "we had all these fellows from the developing countries coming in to see the President and they almost always made reference to the concept of take-off. Kennedy noted that their references had more to do with their interest in aid money than in my virtue as a social scientist—to which I agreed" (1964b, 14). His retort to the economics profession is to say that the views of economists have been far too simplistic, that there are inherent limitations in applying economic methods to security analysis, and that very few problems are purely economic in nature.

There are some broader implications here. For example, the agenda for typical National Security Council meetings during Rostow's tenure, between 1966 and 1969, included topics such as economic development in Indonesia, the world food–population balance, or the Kennedy Round Trade Negotiations, the International Monetary System and monetary crises, and India's food problem (Rostow 1972, 361–62). These are topics on which economists would be expected to contribute usefully. Yet on 7 August 1964, when Walter Heller asked if the Council of Economic Advisors could be an adjunct member of the National Security Council, he was given a curt reply in the negative. Rostow, an outcast from the mainstream, however, had pride of place at the meetings.

On Rostow's contributions in government there will be continued debate. Perhaps we should end with some observations from Halberstam (1969, 56, 197). Rostow, he said, had "a capacity to see patterns where previously none existed, to pull together diverse ideas and acts into patterns and theories." He was "a man of ideas, determined that his ideas should live . . . [a] theoretical man who intended to make all his theories work."

In writing this paper I have benefited from a discussion with Professor Rostow at the Lyndon B. Johnson Library on 28 September 1989. Blaine McCants is responsible for much of the material in the last section of the paper, on the reaction to Rostow's work; his help was greatly appreciated.

References

Adelman, Irma. 1974. On the State of Development Economics. *Journal of Development Studies* 1 (June).

Baldwin, Hanson W. 1973–74. The Best and the Brightest? *The Intercollegiate Review* (Winter), 43–50.

Baran, Paul A., and E. J. Hobsbawm. 1961. *The Stages of Economic Growth:* A Review. *Kyklos* 14:234–42.

Bornet, Vaughn Davis. 1983. *The Presidency of Lyndon B. Johnson.* Lawrence: University Press of Kansas.

Boulding, Kenneth E. 1971. The Intellectual Framework of Bad Political Advice. *Virginia Quarterly Review* 47.4 (Autumn): 602–7.

Cairncross, A. K. 1961. The Stages of Economic Growth. *Economic History Review,* ser. 2, 13:450–58.

Chenery, Hollis. 1989. Growth and Transformation. In *Leading Issues in Economic Development,* edited by G. M. Meier, 5th ed., 97–101. New York: Oxford University Press.

Divine, Robert A., ed. 1981. *Exploring the Johnson Years.* Austin: University of Texas Press.

———. 1987. *The Johnson Years.* Vol. 2, *Vietnam, the Environment and Science.* Lawrence: University Press of Kansas.

Enke, S. 1964. *Economics for Development.* Englewood Cliffs: Prentice-Hall.

Galbraith, John K. 1981. *A Life in Our Times.* Boston: Houghton Mifflin.

Habakkuk, J. H. 1961. Review of *The Stages of Economic Growth. Economic Journal* 71:601–4.

Hagen, E. E. 1964. *On the Theory of Social Change*. Homewood, Ill.: Richard Dorsey.

Halberstam, David. 1969. *The Best and the Brightest*. New York: Fawcett Crest.

Herring, George C. 1981. The War in Vietnam. In Divine 1981, 27–62.

Higgins, Benjamin. 1990a. Anthropology: Social Science, Regional Science, Development Theory—or Literature? Paper presented at a University of New South Wales Department of Economics seminar, 30 March.

————. 1990b. Conversation with the author, University of New South Wales, 30 March.

Johnson, Lyndon B. 1971. *The Vantage Point*. New York: Holt, Rinehart & Winston.

Kaufman, Burton I. 1987. Foreign Aid and the Balance-of-Payments Problem: Vietnam and Johnson's Foreign Economic Policy. In Divine 1987, 79–109.

Kuznets, Simon. 1965. *Economic Growth and Structure*. New York: Norton.

LaFeber, Walter. 1981. Latin American Policy. In Divine 1981, 63–88.

Lodewijks, J. K. 1989. Macroeconometric Models and the Methodology of Macroeconomics. *H.E.S. Bulletin* 11.1 (Spring): 33–58.

————. 1990. Market Structure and Industrial Innovation. *Prometheus* 8.1 (June): 108–28.

Meier, G. M. 1984. *Leading Issues in Economic Development*. 4th. ed. New York: Oxford University Press.

Ohlin, G. 1961. Reflections on the Rostow Doctrine. *Economic Development and Cultural Change* 9:648–55.

Parker, W. N. 1960. Review of *The Stages of Economic Growth*. *American Economic Review* 50 (December): 1058–59.

Rosenberg, N. 1975. Problems in the Economist's Conceptualization of Technological Innovation. *HOPE* 7.4.

Rostow, W. W. 1952. *The Process of Economic Growth*. New York: Norton.

————. 1956. The Take-Off into Self-Sustained Growth. *Economic Journal* 66.261 (March): 25–48.

————. 1960. *The Stages of Economic Growth: A Non-Communist Manifesto*. Cambridge: Cambridge University Press. 2d ed., 1971.

————. 1964a. *View from the Seventh Floor*. New York: Harper & Row.

————. 1964b. Recorded interview by Richard Neustadt, 11 and 25 April. John F. Kennedy Library Oral History Program.

————. 1969. Recorded interview by Paige E. Mulhollan, 21 March. Lyndon B. Johnson Library Oral History Program.

————. 1971. *Politics and the Stages of Growth*. Cambridge: Cambridge University Press.

————. 1972. *The Diffusion of Power: An Essay in Recent History*. New York: Macmillan.

————. 1978. *The World Economy: History and Prospect*. Austin: University of Texas Press.

————. 1980. *Why the Poor Get Richer and the Rich Slow Down: Essays in the Marshallian Long Period*. Austin: University of Texas Press.

————. 1981. Recorded interview by Jean W. Ross, 4 September. In *Contemporary Authors*, New Revision Series, 8:427–32.

————. 1984. Development: The Political Economy of the Marshallian Long Period. In *Pioneers in Development*, edited by G. M. Meier and D. Seers, 229–61. New York: World Bank/Oxford University Press.

————. 1986. My Life Philosophy. *American Economist* 30.2 (Fall): 3–13.

————. 1990. *Theorists of Economic Growth from David Hume to the Present.* New York: Oxford University Press.

————, ed. 1963. *The Economics of Take-Off into Sustained Growth.* Proceedings of a conference held by the International Economic Association. New York: St. Martin's.

Schlesinger, Arthur M., Jr. 1978. *Robert Kennedy and His Times.* New York: Ballantine.

Sheahan, John. 1980. Market-Oriented Economic Policies and Political Repression in Latin America. *Economic Development and Cultural Change* 28.2 (January): 267–91.

————. 1987. *Patterns of Development in Latin America: Poverty, Repression and Economic Strategy.* Princeton: Princeton University Press.

Stern, Nicholas. 1989. The Economics of Development: A Survey. *Economic Journal* 9 (September): 597–685.

Stigler, George. *Memoirs of an Unregulated Economist.* New York: Basic Books.

Taylor, Harry S. 1981. Truman's Point Four Program: Educational Considerations. Ph.D. dissertation. University of Missouri–Columbia.

Taylor, Lance. 1988. *Varieties of Stabilization Experience: Towards Sensible Macroeconomics in the Third World.* Oxford: Clarendon Press.

Yotopoulos, Pan, and Jeffrey Nugent. 1976. *Economics of Development.* New York: Harper & Row